*Critical Essays on*

# CHRISTOPHER OKIGBO

# CRITICAL ESSAYS
## ON
# WORLD LITERATURE

Robert Lecker, General Editor
*McGill University, Montreal*

*Critical Essays on*

# CHRISTOPHER OKIGBO

*edited by*

UZOMA ESONWANNE

*G.K. Hall & Co.*
*New York*

G. K. Hall & Co.
1633 Broadway
New York, NY 10019

Library of Congress Cataloging-in-Publication Data
  Critical essays on Christopher Okigbo / edited by Uzoma Esonwanne.
      p. cm — (Critical essays on world literature)
  Includes bibliographical references and index.
  ISBN 0-7838-0450-4 (alk. paper)
    1. Okigbo, Christopher, 1932–1967—Criticism and interpretation.
  2. Nigeria—In literature. I. Esonwanne, Uzoma. II. Series.

  PR9387.9.O378 Z57 2000
  821'.914—dc21
                                                      00-040989

This paper meets the requirements of ANSI/NISO Z3948-1992 (Permanence of Paper).

10  9  8  7  6  5  4  3  2  1

Printed in the United States of America

*To Dada, Mama, and Phillip*

# Contents

◆

INDIVIDUAL POEM SEQUENCES

GENRE, METHOD, AND MEANING

CRITICAL OVERVIEW

# Publisher's Note

◆

Producing a volume that contains both newly commissioned and reprinted material presents the publisher with the challenge of balancing the desire to achieve stylistic consistency with the need to preserve the integrity of works first published elsewhere. In the Critical Essays series, essays commissioned especially for a particular volume are edited to be consistent with G. K. Hall's house style, reprinted essays appear in the style in which they were first published, with only typographical errors corrected. Consequently, shifts in style from one essay to another are the result of our efforts to be faithful to each text as it was originally published.

# *Acknowledgments*

◆

My gratitude goes to the following, without whose intellectual, practical, and moral support I could not have completed this project: Leonard Achunonu, Sylvana Buttigieg, Nneka and Raymond Edom, Chinyere Esonwanne, Onyinye Esonwanne, Ifesinachi Esonwanne, Amandi Esonwanne, Lemechi Esonwanne, Ifeoma and Ifeanyi Ezeukwu, Amanda Jackson, Obioma Nnaemeka, Ogoma and Eric Nwakuna, Pius Okigbo, Chika and James Orjiekwe, Russell Perkin, Donna Young, editors at Twayne Publishers and Impressions, the Saint Mary's University, Halifax Senate Research Grant Committee, the Harriet Irving Library, the Patrick Power Library, and the Killam Library.

# Chronology

◆

Poems in this chronological history of the poetry of Christopher Okigbo are listed according to initial dates of publication. The titles of individual poems (enclosed in double quotation marks) and poem cycles (in italics) used in initial publications have been retained. The abbreviations *LPT* and *COCP* indicate poems and poem cycles published in *Labyrinths with Path of Thunder* (1971) and *Christopher Okigbo: Collected Poems* (1986), respectively.

| | |
|---|---|
| 1958–1959 | "On the New Year" published in *Horn* and *COCP.* |
| 1959 | "Debtor's Lane (with drums & ogene)," composed at Fiditi in 1959; published in *Horn* 3, no. 2, and *COCP.* |
| 1960 | "Moonglow," composed at Ibadan in 1960; published in *Fresh Buds* 1, no. 2, and *COCP.* |
| 1962 | *Poems: Four Canzones (1957–1961)* published in *Black Orpheus* 11 and *COCP.* This poem cycle contains "Song of the Forest (with ubo)," composed at Lagos in 1957; "Debtor's Lane (with drums & ogene)," composed at Fiditi in 1959; "Lament of the Flutes (with two flutes)," composed at Ojoto in 1960; and "Lament of the Lavender Mist (for three flutes)," composed at Nsukka in 1961. |
| 1962 | "Love Apart," composed in 1960; published in *Reflections* and *COCP.* |
| 1962 | *Heavensgate,* Mbari Publications, Ibadan; published in *LPT* and *COCP. Heavensgate* contains the following poems and sections: |

> "Idoto"
> I "Passage," composed in 1961
> II "Initiation," composed in 1960–1961
> "Bridge"
> III "Watermaid," composed in 1961

IV "Lustra," composed in 1960–1961
V "Newcomer," composed in 1961
"Transition"

*Limits,* Mbari Publications, Ibadan; expanded, revised, and published in *Transition,* vols. 5 and 6–7, *LPT,* and *COCP.* This cycle contains "The Limits I–IV: Siren Limits," composed in 1961, and "The Limits V–XII: Fragments Out of the Deluge," composed in 1961–1962.

1963    "Lament of the Silent Sisters," part of the poem cycle *Silences,* composed at Ibadan in 1962; published in *Transition,* vol. 3.

1964    *Distances I–VI* published in *Transition,* vol. 16.

1965    "Lament of the Drums," part of the poem cycle *Silences,* composed in 1965; published in *Transition,* vol. 18, *LPT, COCP,* and *Black Orpheus,* vol. 17.

"Dance of the Painted Maidens" published in *Verse and Voice* and *COCP.*

"Lament of the Masks" published in *W. B. Yeats, 1865–1965* and *COCP.*

1968    *Path of Thunder* published in *Black Orpheus* 2, no. 1, *LPT,* and *COCP.* This poem cycle contains "Thunder Can Break," composed in May 1966; "Elegy of the Wind"; "Come Thunder," composed in December 1965; "Hurrah for Thunder," composed on 1 January 1966; "Elegy for Slit-Drum," composed in May 1966; and "Elegy for Alto," composed in May 1966.

1971    *Labyrinths with Path of Thunder* published by Heinemann/ Africana Publishing Corporation.

1986    *Christopher Okigbo: Collected Poems* published by Heinemann.

# Introduction

♦

UZOMA ESONWANNE

Christopher Ifeanyichukwu Okigbo, and the criticism that bears his name, are sites on which questions about critical theory and methods appropriate for decoding his poetry in particular and postcolonial African poetry in general are posed, explored, and, in some cases, answered. Given the singularity of Okigbo's poetics, and given that many of his themes—subjectivity and identity formation in postcolonial Africa, the character of poetic inspiration, cultural fragmentation and regeneration, nation building and national consciousness, spiritual faith, and so on—resonate so forcefully with concerns that preoccupy scholars of postcolonial African literature to this day, it is hardly surprising that exponents of diverse critical methodologies and theories are drawn to his work. Thus, with the possible exceptions of Marxist and New Historicist criticisms, other critical methodologies—English Practical Criticism and American New Criticism, Cultural Nationalist *(Bolekaja)* Criticism, Jungian Psychoanalysis, Feminist Criticism, Stylistics, Structuralism, and Deconstruction—are well represented in Okigbo criticism.

So impressive is the body of critical scholarship on Okigbo's poetry that one expects an equally impressive literature on the poet himself. Unfortunately, biographical information about Okigbo is comparatively meager, so meager that one may justly claim that one knows more about Okigbo's poetry than one does about him. Indeed, with the passage of time, Okigbo's biography has been rapidly supplanted by Okigbo mythology. This is because much of what we know today about Okigbo is based largely on anecdotes recounted by acquaintances, friends, and family, and on information culled from a few documentary sources—school magazines, conference interviews,

1

and the like. From these sources has emerged a mythic figure whose reputation as a quirky, controversial, resolute, driven, and passionate sibling, student, teacher, writer, librarian, husband, and soldier precedes (some might say frustrates) any attempt to establish his character. Portraits of his life reflect the passion of the man for his art and the controversy his pronouncements and actions aroused. For some critics, Okigbo was an effete, dreamy idealist and a "frail aesthete." Others consider him a versatile "jock," a man who applied to sports the same creative imagination he manifested in his poetry. Some revere and celebrate him as a seer, *ogbanje* (changeling), reincarnation of his priestly grandfather, and revolutionary nationalist for whom poetry was a votive offering to Mother Idoto, his divine muse, and to his readers. Yet others denounce Okigbo for composing abstruse poetry and soiling his artistry by intervening in the violent and murky politics of Nigeria. Responses to the man and his work are therefore rarely unanimous.[1] Such differences in the reception of Okigbo notwithstanding, we can still distill images of the man and his attitude to his poetry from the recollections of peers such as Wole Soyinka and Chinua Achebe.

"Maren," Soyinka's autobiographical persona in *Ibadan: The Penkelemes Years: A Memoir, 1946–1965* (1994), makes two revealing observations about Okigbo. In one observation, Maren recalls a confrontation he had with European Marxists at a theater festival and conference in postrevolutionary Cuba. Deeply irritated by the Marxists' uncritical celebration of "*utilitarian* art" and advocacy of "state control" of cultural production, Maren wistfully recalls the Okigbo of the 1962 Makerere Conference who, similarly provoked, defiantly declared that he wrote "poetry for poets only!"[2] Not only do such assertions foreclose dialogue, Maren reflects, but in their extremism they also goad the revolutionary interlocutor into violence:

> You are reduced to only one course of action: to abandon all discourse and go all out to make your revolution so you can guillotine Christopher Okigbo, except of course that that mischief-laden leprechaun would still cheat you of triumph by improvising and declaiming an appropriate last-minute eclogue even as the blade fell.[3]

Maren's phrase "mischief-laden leprechaun" captures the playful yet enigmatic element in Okigbo's character to which Chinua Achebe alludes in *Don't Let Him Die: An Anthology of Memorial Poems for Christopher Okigbo, 1932–67*.[4] Furthermore, Maren's comment that Okigbo might yet rob the executioner of his grisly "triumph" bespeaks the passion that the poet invested in his artistic project and that the project, in turn, aroused in his readers.

Maren's second reminiscence, which touches directly on Okigbo's poetry, reveals the intensity of the poet's passion. While being detained for broadcasting a politically subversive message on public radio, Maren received some unusual visits from the poet. On those visits, Maren recalls, Okigbo generally "brought wine and poems, his latest, which they read aloud, Okigbo mostly, since *he loved to listen to what his poems said to him,* to see if they still were as he had *heard* them when written."[5] Maren's anecdote suggests that Okigbo saw poetry as "a socially symbolic act" that, to use Fredric Jameson's characterization of Marxism's fundamental theme, intervenes in "the collective struggle" of Africans to "wrest a realm of Freedom from a realm of Necessity."[6] In the microdrama Maren sketches here, we discern a characteristic dialectical tension one often finds in Okigbo's work, wherein readers encounter poetic utterances that, though seemingly deeply personal, appear nonetheless to strain toward the status of public enactments. Indeed, as the anecdote reveals, it is Okigbo who "mostly" declaims his poetry to Maren, and the latter functions simultaneously as host, witness, coreader, and audience. As primary actor-reader, Okigbo listens to and hears his poetry speak *"to* him." Assuming sentient form, his poetry strives to communicate meaning. However, this meaning appears continuously to be evading the poet's grasp. Thus poetry emerges as an active agent in a drama in which it is also an object of interpretation. Perhaps it is this—Okigbo's facility for producing poetry that, while presenting itself to readers as directed speech, confounds efforts to invest it with a singular meaning—that explains the diverse, and often contradictory, interpretations Okigbo's poetry has inspired, and the tendency among critics to affiliate him with diverse literary movements—symbolism, impressionism, modernism, romanticism, and surrealism.[7] Whatever reasons we may adduce to explain the tendency of Okigbo's poetry to confound readers who seek a stable and univocal meaning, and to account for the poet's own facility at evading the probing eyes of critics who wish to know more of his personal life, it is still possible to construct a minibiographical narrative of his life based on the meager verifiable factual data available.

Most portraits of Okigbo's life emerged after his death, at age 35, in 1967. Before this tragic event, he had achieved both fame for his literary accomplishment—a "slender volume" of verse published posthumously as *Labyrinths with Path of Thunder* (1971)—and personal notoriety for controversial remarks concerning negritude and his putative audience.[8] Christopher was born in 1932 to James and Anna Okigbo. Shortly afterward, Anna died, and James Okigbo raised his children assisted by Eunice, their nurse. The young Okigbo attended a Catholic primary school, where he performed creditably. Upon graduation, he attended Government College, Umuahia, an elite secondary school in Eastern Nigeria, before going on to University College, Ibadan, in Western Nigeria, from which he graduated with a classics degree in 1956. While at Umuahia and Ibadan, Okigbo was active in the social and cultural life of both institutions. From 1956 to 1967, he served in the bureaucracy, taught at Fiditi Grammar School, and worked as a librarian at the newly established University of Nigeria. In addition, he was also a representative of Cambridge University Press and a regional editor for *Transition,* a literary journal then being published in Uganda. Between jobs, he collaborated with Chinua Achebe on a plan to establish a publishing firm and, either in 1963 or 1964, married Safinat Attah, the daughter of the *Attah* of Igbira, with whom he had Ibrahimat, a daughter, in 1966.[9] Finally, in 1967 Okigbo enlisted in the army of the Republic of Biafra, a newly declared secessionist state in Eastern Nigeria created as a response to tensions in the political institutions of the Nigerian federation and massacres of Igbo-speaking peoples in other regions of the nation.

Unfortunately for Okigbo scholars, establishing what poems comprise his canon has proven much more difficult than establishing basic facts about his life. Broadly speaking, we may attribute the canonical problems to three factors. First, as numerous scholars have observed, Okigbo constantly revised his poems. These revised versions were subsequently published in other journals, anthologies, and books such as *Présence Africaine, Modern Poetry from Africa* (1963) and *W. B. Yeats, 1865–1965: Centenary Essays on the Art of W. B. Yeats* (1965) before being issued by Mbari Publications. Second, compounding the problems caused by the revisions is the matter of the chronology of composition and publication. There are differences between the date of composition and the date of publication of some poems. For example, *Limits* was composed between 1961 and 1962 but was not published until 1964. By then, *Silences,* part 1, "Lament of the Silent Sisters," had already appeared (1963), and *Distances* (1964) was under way. Further complicating matters, just before his death, Okigbo compiled his own canon, *Labyrinths,* which in his acknowledgments he declared "somewhat different and . . . final."[10] This volume excluded several poems, among them the cycle *Poems: Four Canzones (1957–1961), Path of Thunder: Poems Prophesying War,* a sequence published posthumously, and occasional verses such as "Lament of the Drums." Evidently he considered these poems unsuitable, as did his friend Sunday O. Anozie.[11] However, others, including Okigbo's publisher Heinemann, considered *Path of Thunder* integral to his poetic oeuvre. Thus in 1971 Heinemann and Africana Publishing Corporation published *Labyrinths with Path of Thunder,* and in 1986 Heinemann went even further by publishing a comprehensive volume entitled *Collected Poems* (1986).[12] Consequently, any ethical twinge critics may feel about having to study poems excluded from *Labyrinths* is complicated by other questions. How, for example, are earlier versions of *Distances* related to Okigbo's "final" version in *Labyrinths*? Should the *Labyrinths* version be considered "final" in the sense of being the culmination of the earlier version, *or* in the sense of being different or distinct from it?[13] And if one were to elect to ignore the poet's declaration, how might one then interpret (the multiple versions of) *Distances*?

Given how difficult these questions are, and given how readily scholars have adopted *Labyrinths with Path of Thunder,* it is hardly surprising that critics have generally evaded them, choosing instead to focus their attention on the problem of Okigbo's canon. Dan Izevbaye is probably the first scholar to construct a chronology of Okigbo's canon. Entitled "Chronological Table of the

Work of Christopher Okigbo," this chronology was first published in "From Reality to Dream: the Poetry of Christopher Okigbo" (1973). Izevbaye based his chronology on *Labyrinths with Path of Thunder.* But because this volume excludes poems such as "On the New Year," it is not comprehensive.[14] The appeal of an inclusive chronology lies in the fact that it comprises the entirety of Okigbo's poetic corpus and therefore provides scholars and casual or curious readers with a handy reference. For this reason, I provide, in the front matter of this book, a chronology of Christopher Okigbo's poetic works.

One obvious area in which the difficulty of specifying Okigbo's canon manifests itself is in the question of the order in which the poems are to be read. Okigbo's admission, in his introduction to *Labyrinths,* that he wrote and published his poems "separately" suggests that critics may consider each as an independent composition. However, since he also insists in the same introduction that all of the poems in *Labyrinths* "are, in fact, 'organically related,' " it follows that they may be read collectively as verse articulating the unified vision of art and life in a postcolonial African state.[15] This, in fact, is precisely the approach much of Okigbo criticism has taken, and the reason is perhaps to be found in the historical conjuncture during which he wrote. Okigbo wrote in the 1960s, a period of political and social instability in Africa and creative ferment among the emergent middle-class intelligentsia located largely in the universities and bureaucracies. As Kofi Awoonor puts it, African writers of the time were "all talking and thinking and talking more . . . trying to find out what writing was, what it was to write."[16] Bursting upon this scene with *Heavensgate* in 1962, Okigbo was promptly received by many of Nigeria's (and Africa's) postindependence cultural elite as Africa's response to the Anglo-American modernists. Nourished on the Anglo-American (European) cultural fare that universities at home and abroad provided, this elite was starving for a literary act that, though homegrown, was nonetheless cosmopolitan. Okigbo's poetry satiated this hunger. In it, they encountered writing that, invoking an indigenous muse, spoke to them in local accents about emergent perceptions of self, personal hopes and dreams of self-fulfillment, and the collective project of nation building. His poetry raised, and prompted critics to address, theoretical questions about literature and culture pertinent to local concerns and contexts.

At the same time, Africa's entry onto the global stage, after almost a century of often violent and repressive colonization that radically altered and reconfigured the cultural landscape of the continent, lent these questions a sense of urgency. Consequently, for these scholars, literary criticism was not just an exercise in textual explication. It was also a socially significant act. After the euphoria of independence had worn off, literary criticism rapidly became enmeshed in questions related to the production, conservation, and reproduction of national literature and culture. Some of the most intractable questions were about language—what is national literature and culture, and in what language should they be composed? Related to this was the question of readers—who were they, and in what literary forms and idioms were they likely to invest their energies as readers? Other questions were even more pertinent to criticism—what is the function of criticism in the postcolonial era, and within what contexts (cultural, historical, and literary) should scholars situate the texts they interpret? How do writers thematize those momentous issues with which everyone was grappling—individual identity, national identity and consciousness, cultural change, and political instability? All these questions impinged on our understanding of, and framed critical dialogue about, *Heavensgate* (1962), the first poem cycle for which Okigbo received public acclaim.

Because few Europhone poets had explored these problems in quite the same poetic idiom as Okigbo did in *Heavensgate,* and given his flair for densely allusive references to classical European, Asian, and African myths, early Okigbo criticism quickly became preoccupied with the search for his poetic "sources." Knowledge of such sources of "poetic influence" would, it was assumed, illuminate his poetics and meaning. In his influential book *The Anxiety of Influence* (1997), Harold Bloom defines poetic influence as "a misreading of the prior poet, an act of creative correction that is actually and necessarily a misinterpretation."[17] In early Okigbo criticism, however, it was the critics, not the poet, who were afflicted. Okigbo was irritated by, if not indifferent to, the debates about his "sources." Obsessed by the poet's sources, critics creatively misread his poems by placing them within supposedly antecedent African and non-African poetic traditions. Furthermore, the combination of practical exegeses with theoretical propositions on Okigbo's poetics, genre, and themes in some of these genetic interpretations gave early Okigbo criticism a dual focus. We will return to exemplars of genetic interpretations of Okigbo's poetry later. For now, let us track the dual focus of early Okigbo criticism through select reviews of *Heavensgate.*

It was with a deep sigh of relief that Anozie welcomed the publication of *Heavensgate.* For him, *Heavensgate* marked the eclipse of "the 'palm-tree'—and—'River Niger' sentimentalism of Chief [Dennis] Osadebay's 'Africa Sings' and its coterie." Thus Anozie's pleasure came as much from the cycle itself as from what it supplanted. This notwithstanding, he was mindful that Okigbo's modernist idiom in *Heavensgate,* bristling as it was with odd syntactic reversals, seemingly unintelligible Latin-sounding phrases, and obscure literary and mythological allusions—"Bird of the sun on tree top sitting / on fig tree top mourns under the lamp: / *etru bo pi alo a she e anando we aquandem*"—seemed "esoteric" and intellectually pretentious to a readership weaned on Osadebay's cultural nationalist panegyrics to "African culture."[18] Anozie's answer to this dilemma was to posit a new readership possessed of attributes—"a positive attitude of the mind, a painstaking disposition, the right type of heartbeat, a good ear"—that, following E. D. Hirsch, we may call the marks of postcolonial "cultural literacy."[19] Denis Williams, another reviewer, was more interested in the literary pedigree of *Heavensgate* than he was in its readership. For him, the poems were testimony of Okigbo's "preoccupation with the word, with 'pure' poetry," which Williams attributes directly to the poet's encounter "with the fathers, with T. S. Eliot and Ezra Pound most patently in this case."[20] "Begat," a biblical copula, might be used to characterize Williams's view of the literary relationship between Pound's *Cantos* and Okigbo's *Heavensgate*. With this biological metaphor, Williams naturalized the relationship between both texts, forcing them into a relationship of "genealogical filiation."[21] Consequently, knowledge of the themes and poetics of Anglo-American modernism became, for Williams, the prerequisite for interpreting *Heavensgate*. In saying this, I do not mean to suggest that Williams considered *Heavensgate* a mere replica of the *Cantos;* indeed, he admitted that Okigbo's tone in parts of "Initiations" may not "ring true." However, Williams felt that Okigbo's failure to echo Pound's tone faithfully confirms, rather than undermines, his genealogy. For evidence, Williams offered Okigbo's preference for the virtues of "honesty and rigour" over "the equivoque, the ambivalence of emotive writing."[22] Finally, Ulli Beier saw *Heavensgate* as a "chant—or rather . . . [an] *incantation*" performed in a "sacred enclosure," and the reader as an intruder held, spellbound, by the "organic fusion" of "Christian and pagan imagery" in the poems.[23] Thus Okigbo becomes priest, the reader a congregant, and interpretation an act of worship. Anozie, Williams, and Beier were, each in his own way, concerned not only with the question of what the poem cycle *Heavensgate* means but also with how it means, and therefore with what critical method the critic might best interpret it.

Beier's application of the term "ritual" to *Heavensgate* (and Okigbo's poetry) inaugurated a line of critical inquiry that runs through Anozie to Annemarie Heywood.[24] But in his review, Anozie confined himself to the "dynamic ritualistic rhythm" of the sequence—to the expressive (language, symbol, imagery, and music) and thematic (priesthood, religious conflict, and syncretism) dimensions of ritual—whereas in "The Ritual and the Plot: The Critic and Okigbo's *Labyrinths*" (1978), Heywood linked the generic conventions of ritual verse to the meaning of Okigbo's poetry.[25] The other line, which I have called genetic interpretation, runs from Williams through Romanus N. Egudu's "Christopher Okigbo and Foreign Influences"—a 1966 doctoral dissertation chapter later published as "Ezra Pound in African Poetry: Christopher Okigbo" (1971)—and M. J. C. Echeruo's "Traditional and Borrowed Elements in Nigerian Poetry" (1966) to Emmanuel N. Obiechina's "Christopher Okigbo: Poet of Destiny" (1980) and Michael G. Cooke's "Christopher Okigbo and Robert Hayden: From Mould to Stars" (1990).

Egudu's "Christopher Okigbo and Foreign Influences" and Echeruo's "Traditional and Borrowed Elements in Nigerian Poetry" are exemplary of genetic interpretations of Okigbo. Like Williams, Egudu believed that Okigbo is indebted to Pound. Egudu traced Okigbo's themes, syntax, and style in *Limits, Heavensgate,* and *Distances* to Pound's *Cantos* 8–10 and described Okigbo's use of Pound as a form of incorporation or "creative deftness."[26] In this sense, Egudu subscribed to Williams's presumption of genealogical literary filiation between Pound and Okigbo. At the same time, however, Egudu did not consider Pound's influence on Okigbo decisive. As "foreign" poets whose influence did not alter the fundamental African character of Okigbo, "a modern West African poet," Pound and Eliot are patriarchs "out of doors."[27] Far more decisive and effective, primarily because it arises from the poet's "own household" and works directly on his imagination, is oral African verse, the ancestral mode of discourse from which Okigbo draws the bulk of his imagery.[28] Okigbo's use of the aesthetic conventions of oral African verse confers upon him the status of an authentic *African* poet.[29] Clearly, Bloom's phrase "the anxiety of influence" does not quite capture Egudu's sense of *Heavensgate*'s relationship with the modernist *Cantos*. But neither, I hasten to add, does its antithesis, the tranquillity of influence. In the end, Egudu's motive for differentiating between decisive oral African "sources" and secondary modernist literary influences appears to be that of establishing the cultural authenticity of Okigbo's poems, especially in *Heavensgate*.

In "Traditional and Borrowed Elements in Nigerian Poetry," Echeruo rendered explicit what Egudu implied: that Okigbo and Pound belong to distinct poetic traditions. Like Egudu, Echeruo attempted to evaluate "influences" that a poetic tradition exerts on another.[30] But in doing so, he made the poet's ability to translate "a local sensibility and an indigenous environment into an alien artefact: the English poem," the measure of his or her success (143). Using this criterion, for example, Echeruo declared that "Lament of the Masks" is a failed project of translation. It failed because in composing his eulogue to W. B. Yeats, Okigbo substituted "formal phrasing" of a literary genre—"That generations unborn might not taste steel"—for the "simple effective lines" of a Yoruba *orìkì* (Yoruba praise poetry): "So that the young generations might no longer / Have to fight any wars." Though minor, Echeruo added, this "variation"

> is wooden. Okigbo's literary-minded imagination is no longer seeking to realize the meaning of the experience in the most telling manner, such a manner that its beauty stands assured; it rather seeks a formal beauty of phrase . . . as if expression were all. (144)

For Echeruo, then, the flaw in "Lament of the Masks" arose from the fact that, in altering the language of the *orìkì*, Okigbo stripped it of the capacity to convey "the meaning of the experience" in a manner most likely to preserve its "beauty." Poetic influence, Echeruo suggested, succeeds if the language that conveys the sense of an experience from one poetic tradition to another does not alter the sense of the original experience. Complimenting Okogbule Nwanodi for his apparently seamless blending of English diction with the conventions of Igbo praise poetry in "Shifting Scenes," Echeruo suggested that originality in a Nigerian English-language poem consists in the success with which it conveys the "beauty of phrase" of the indigenous oral form into the nonindigenous literary form. Conversely, the measure of a successful borrowing from a foreign tradition is to be found in the degree to which a literary poem seamlessly translates "the spirit" of its source into local (Nigerian/African) "sensibility and . . . environment." To do so, the poem must avoid "easy traditionalism" while echoing its precursor (151–52). According to Echeruo, poems in which such transference of "the spirit" of Anglo-American modernist antecedents (Eliot and Pound) into a Nigerian milieu occurs include *Poems: Four Canzones (1957–1961),* "Lament of the Silent Sisters," and *Limits* (152–53). If in the end Echeruo seems unperturbed by the Oedipal scenario that Williams's biological metaphor sets up between Okigbo and Pound and Eliot, it is because Echeruo perceived the former as an *African* whose poetry responds to the "pattern and organization" of his precursors rather than as a literary progeny (153). Okigbo's identities—both as an African who evinces as "a very strong traditional feeling . . . a feeling for the subject of Africa" and as "an 'individual' poet who loves to write, not as an African, but as a 'prodigal' "—thus provide the binary critical framework within which Echeruo explained the poet's "echo" of his precursors.

Today, genetic interpretations of Okigbo have lost their appeal, having come to be seen as "perfunctory" exercises aimed at demonstrating "Okigbo's derivativeness."[31] Although this objection slightly overstates the case, it nonetheless touches on a crucial weakness of such critical enterprise: genetic interpretations place Okigbo's poetry in a causal relationship with its supposed antecedents and imply that knowledge of one suffices for interpreting the other. Stated crudely, such interpretations imply that in explicating Okigbo's poetry, we assume that literary genes determine interpretive destiny. The problem with this suggestion, however, is that verbal performance, rhythmic structures, thematic emphases, and symbolic allusions in Okigbo's poetry are so diffused and subtle as to render genetic analysis virtually impossible. Perhaps, as Roland Barthes charges, genetic criticism is largely designed to satisfy "the myth of filiation."[32] Certainly it appears, in retrospect, like a tedious "industry of source-hunting" and "allusion-counting."[33] But whatever purpose it may have served, the fact that scholars at this specific period felt the need to assign literary progenitors such as the *oríkì,* Pound, Eliot, Mallarmé, and others to Okigbo's poetry requires some explanation.

To explain this necessity, we must turn to Nigerian (and African) political and cultural history. The years from 1957 to 1966, during which Okigbo composed and published his poems, were a period of political decolonization and cultural affirmation in Africa. Indeed, Nigeria acceded to the status of an independent state on October 1, 1960. However, as Neil Lazarus points out, for many Africans, independence did not merely end colonialism. It also ushered in what Kwame Nkrumah, the first president of Ghana, grandly called "the African personality."[34] However, what precisely this postcolonial African "personality" was, was not specified. Indeed, like Yeats's "rough beast" whose "hour [had] come round at last," it lurked in the imagination, at once a promise and a menacing presence.[35] It was left to writers of this period to explore imaginatively an idea that politicians blithely invoked. Thus, for example, Chinua Achebe created in Obi Okonkwo, the protagonist in *No Longer at Ease* (1960), a member of "the nationalist generation of the 1940s and 1950s" who "struggles for a sense of character, . . . a forceful sense of self."[36] Thus, too, Okigbo created the prodigal in *Heavensgate,* a penitent who, after years of wandering, returns home to mother Idoto. In the figure of the prodigal, Okigbo constructed an imaginary postcolonial African subject whose experience of cultural alienation in a rapidly changing world is mitigated by means of an imaginative recuperation of his cultural-genetic ties with ancestral religious ritual, here symbolized by the maternal figure of the goddess. Not only does this recuperation effect a recovery of ancestral ties, but it also legitimates the self produced by the prodigal's wanderings. In other words, Okigbo's early poetry was part of that bold and vast enterprise of "self" formation, nation building, and cultural reconstruction in which writers of the period were engaged. Within this context, we may understand genetic criticism as interpretation that sought to legitimate this project by granting it the literary genealogy it appeared to lack, a genealogy without which the authenticity of the identity of the postcolonial subject, of the nation, and of national culture cannot satisfactorily be established.

Indeed, this makes it clear that in addition to the search for metaphysical origins and the horror of cultural miscegenation, historical forces also drove the anxiety of influence that afflicted early Okigbo criticism. Or stated differently, the anxiety of influence that drove scholars to search for and interpret Okigbo's poetry in terms of an overarching literary tradition was also a manifestation, at the level of interpretation, of the quest for cultural self-definition. In criticism, these forces assumed concrete form in, and were articulated through, the lexicon scholars employed to describe Okigbo's indebtedness to African and non-African precursor poets ("creative deftness," "echoes," "borrowings," and "plagiarism").[37] But it is stated with greater clarity in the following remark by Pol Ndu, one of Okigbo's peers:

> Though *Heavensgate* seems highly intellectualized, Okigbo adequately balances his acquired academicism with Igbo traditional "numinous detail." . . . Authenticity and universality are achieved when the artist has drawn from the deepest layers of his own circumstances.[38]

"Authenticity and universality": these two concepts, inextricably linked, lie at the core of genetic interpretations of Okigbo. Far from denoting critical uncertainty about how to classify Okigbo—as the "strong" poet who makes poetic history by misreading his precursors, or as the "weak" poet who, unable to imagine for himself, idealizes them—they reveal that most critical analyses based on the specification of antecedent poetic texts were actually engaged in a project of cultural and literary legitimization in a field in which, for decades, European aesthetic and formal particulars masqueraded as universal and transhistorical. In this project, words such as "pure" and "African" functioned as a verbal arsenal directed against adversaries who attributed, or were tempted to attribute, alternative literary ancestors to the poet.[39] Commenting on the process by which critics constructed a matrix of orality for African fiction, Ato Quayson observed:

> The general tendency has been to show how the peculiar configuration of orality and literacy in African contexts lends a special quality to African literature. This is joined to the impulse towards defining an ambit of "authenticity" for African literature. . . . At certain key moments, this has led not only to confused categories but also to a pedantic urge to differentiate what can be considered African literature from what cannot.[40]

Quayson's comment is applicable to genetic interpretations of Okigbo's poetry. Indeed, one of these "key moments," the seeds of which were sown in source-hunting interpretations of early Okigbo criticism, occurred shortly after the poet's death.

Within a year, a period when his loss was still being keenly felt, controversy over his literary pedigree flared anew as, postulating the communicative function of oral African verse as the paradigm of "authentic" African literature, Ali A. Mazrui declared in "Abstract Verse and African Tradition" that Okigbo was an abstract poet in whose verse we can observe a radical break with "indigenous modes of poetic expression in Africa."[41] In Mazrui's view, Okigbo's poetry bore a close family resemblance to the paintings of European abstract artists. Like them, it "leaves the reader no room for being *wrong*" and consequently generates multiple interpretations (47). So opaque is the language of some poems in *Heavensgate* that "sophisticated" readers cannot discover their *right* meanings. By contrast, "African poetry in traditional African languages . . . is emphatically an exercise in *meaning*" because in it there "are themes to follow" and "tales to tell," and far from consisting of merely solid parts, "there is a concreteness to the *whole*" (48). Citing Swahili epics, Mazrui admitted that oral African verse may occasionally revel in "sophisticated verbal obscurity." But even when it does, he insisted, such verbal displays do not frustrate efforts by "the sophisticated reader" to determine what their "*right* meaning" is (47). For Mazrui's frustrated hypothetical reader, "Transition," the last poem in the *Heavensgate* cycle, exemplified the failure of communication in Okigbo's verse. Perhaps speaking on behalf of his surrogate reader, Mazrui declared in "Meaning versus Imagery in African Poetry" that the poem sacrifices meaning for "beautiful pictures and patterns of imagery."[42] For Mazrui, nature, which expresses itself in the spoken word, is the paradigm "good" and authentic African poetry should emulate.[43] So by positing nature as his epistemological a priori, Mazrui was able to claim that oral African poetry is a communication device.

As we have seen, "representation," "sophistication," and "meaning" are key conceptual terms in Mazrui's critical lexicon. For example, he held that "meaningful" poetry yields its meaning to "the sophisticated reader," and that the essence of verbal language is located in its "sophisticated capacity for conversational communication," among other places. Similarly, he defined meaning as "a definable significance of what is being asserted."[44] Clearly, Mazrui assumes that these terms are readily interchangeable. But as Hirsch's distinction between "significance" and "meaning" suggests, this assumption is questionable. For Hirsch, meaning denotes the "whole verbal meaning of a text" intended by the author, and "significance" refers to the "textual meaning" of the poem in relation to other minds, eras, and subject matter.[45] Needless to say, Hirsch's distinction has met with considerable skepticism. Yet without getting bogged down in the argument over where meaning inheres, we can still see why some might contend that contrary to Mazrui, whatever Okigbo may have intended to mean in his poetry is to be differentiated from what Mazrui's "sophisticated" reader considers the poet to be asserting. Nor is it clear who may assign "definable significance" to the poetic conversation and controversy oral African verse supposedly makes possible. Furthermore, Mazrui fails to specify the particular qualities that make a specific reading sophisticated and others naive. Finally, in the wake of deconstruction, many students of African literature today would certainly consider the proposition that oral African poetry imitates nature, and that its language is therefore representational, as being dubious at best. By distinguishing between oral African poetry and nature in the first instance, and then construing the former as an imitation of the latter, Mazrui constructed a "mimetic chain" in which nature, the supposed "original," may be shown to be itself an imitation in "a process that is arrested only by positing a divine origin, an absolute original."[46] These objections notwithstanding, however, we must admit that by positing language as a communicative apparatus and making its ability to render its meaning to the reader the focus of his criticism, Mazrui anticipated the "linguistic turn" in Okigbo criticism in which the linguistic mechanism by which poetry imparts meaning becomes the object of inquiry.[47]

Though Anozie does not share Mazrui's instrumentalist notion of poetic language, Anozie shared his concern with language. In his structuralist interpretations, that linguistic turn becomes manifest. We can understand this shift by looking at how Claude Lévi-Strauss conceives of poetry. For Lévi-Strauss, the structuralist anthropologist to whom Anozie is most indebted, poetry is, like myth, "a kind of speech." Translation into other languages cannot alter the "mythical value" of myth. Unlike myth, however, the meaning of a poem is fundamentally altered or distorted by translation.[48] As his comments in various studies of Okigbo's poetry indicate—"Christopher Okigbo: A Creative Itinerary, 1957–1961," "A Structural Approach to

Okigbo's *Distances,*" "Poetry and Empirical Logic: A Correspondence Theory of Truth in Okigbo's *Laments,*" and *Christopher Okigbo: Creative Rhetoric* (1971)—Anozie shared Lévi-Strauss's view of poetry as "speech." Adopting a broadly genealogical approach, Williams, Beier, Egudu, and Mazrui interpreted Okigbo's poetry in terms of its adherence to, or departures from, thematics and poetics elaborated in literary and oral precursors. Adopting a scientistic, structuralist approach, Anozie saw the poems as linguistic phenomena that exhibit all the structural characteristics and conventions of language. Thus he described *Distances* and "Laments" (and, indeed, all of Okigbo's poetry) as "a functional structured universe," systems of communication, and "universes of rhetorical discourse."[49]

In "Christopher Okigbo: A Creative Itinerary, 1957–1961," Anozie described Okigbo as a "Commonwealth" poet who reinvigorated an exhausted English syntax by using it to imagine "new poetic horizons and other structures of experience."[50] These "poetic horizons" and "structures of experience" include the creation of "liturgical rhythms," "variations of images and symbols," the musical affects in *Poems: Four Canzones (1957–1961),* and the identification of alienation as the cause of the disintegration of the "traditional" bonds of filiation. To specify how Okigbo used English syntax to imagine these horizons and experiences, Anozie closely examined the "three essentials" of the rhetorical structure of *Poems: Four Canzones (1957–1961)*—language and rhythm, choice of images and symbols, and form and organization—and postulated "new poetic horizons and . . . structures of experience" to which the poetry refers.[51] For Anozie, the challenge was how to explain the process by which poems perform their referential function. Because he believed that poetry is primarily, if not exclusively, a linguistic phenomenon, he found his answer in its "rules of functioning," which, as Roland Barthes declares in "The Structuralist Activity," he must reconstruct.[52] For Anozie, Okigbo's poetry can be interpreted by following a two-step process: first, the constituent parts, or "universe of codes," of each poem need to be dismantled, before they can be reassembled into their "meaningful patterns of discourse."[53] A brief overview of "A Structural Approach to Okigbo's *Distances*" (1969) and "Poetry and Empirical Logic: A Correspondence Theory of Truth in Okigbo's *Laments,*" both of which are reprinted in this volume, will illuminate his method.[54] Arising from the proposition that Okigbo's poetry is a communication system is the question, By what mechanisms do *Distances* and the "Laments" communicate meaning? We will read both of these essays as attempts to address this crucial question.

In "A Structural Approach to Okigbo's *Distances,*" an essay based on the text of *Distances* (*Transition,* 1964), Anozie tried to answer this question by constituting the rhetorical elements that make up the communicative apparatus of Okigbo's poems as their most persistent structure and the mode by which they transmit meaning. *Silences,* for example, transmits meaning by blending "sounds and symbols" into "a complex system of relationships."[55]

| PROGRESSION | | | | |
|---|---|---|---|---|
| Vertical Dynamics (+) | | | Horizontal (−) Dynamics | |
| pile high, fall, pinned down, split, cut | | | swimmer, roll, suitor, dancers | |
| **ASSOCIATION** | | | | |
| Light | Sound | Colour | Smell | Metaphysical |
| incandescent, fire, lanterns, rays | voice, echo, bells, cry | silver, blood, ash, white reddening | odour, | without flesh or skeleton, without age or memory, dead, freezing, air's marrow |
| **RECEPTION** | | | | |
| Phallic | | | Non-Phallic | |
| island, ambush, tuberose, fruits, interspaces | | | bandages, stretcher | |

Indeed, occurring at "different sensual levels and with varying frequencies," such blending—or forced "ritualistic interaction"—is so pervasive as to constitute a characteristic of Okigbo's poetics (21). In *Distances* as a whole, Anozie identified three rhetorical "structures"—progression, association, and reception (PAR)—which, together with their "substructures" and even subsubstructures, make up the machinery by means of which the poem transmits meaning. The diagram above, for example, illustrates the constituent structures and substructures of "Distances II." Note that whereas in "A Structural Approach to Okigbo's *Distances*" progression, association, and reception are represented along a horizontal axis, here they have been reconfigured along a vertical axis to align the diagram with the rest of the text. Furthermore, unlike Anozie's diagram, which offers readers an inventory of the "structures" in *Distances I–VI* and thus is comprehensive, the diagram extracts the structures of "Distances II" only. These significant differences notwithstanding, we may gain some insights into Anozie's application of structuralist analysis to Okigbo's poetry from our diagram.

On the basis of structures such as those shown in the diagram, Anozie argued that "the poet Okigbo sees the exile's homecoming in *Distances* in terms of a dynamic art experience or movement," which follows two axes: the "linear" (i.e., diachronic or temporal sequence) and the "analogical" (i.e., synchronic or coeval time) (23). In the linear, the exile's movement is represented as a *"Progression* through *Associations* into a form of *Reception."* In the analogical, PAR represents the "triadic structure" or "form of creative communication" of Okigbo's rhetoric in *Distances* and functions as "a recurrent phenomenon" in each movement of the poem (23). So what meaning, one might now ask the structuralist critic, does this decoding of "Distances II" reveal? According to Anozie, it is "that an artist cannot face the ultimate illumination of the symbol (THE WORD) just as mankind cannot in fact bear the ultimate reality (DEATH)" (28). In "Poetry and Empirical Logic," an essay grounded upon the belief that a similar communicative process is at work in the first movement of "Lament of the Drums" (1965), Anozie argued that the drums perform two functions. First, they play the role of "thematic motifs," a function made possible because the poet has conferred upon the drums "certain propositional attitudes" as "anthropomorphic speakers." Second, they facilitate the formulation of "propositions" that also express " 'truth' and 'knowledge' about the speaker's attitude and state" and whose meaning one can "logically" infer from "their syntactical modes of expression."[56] Following an analysis of these functions, Anozie concluded that Okigbo used a "structural mimetic principle of composition" that conceals within "Laments of the Drums" "a system similar to that whereby Drums, when played, as by traditional Yoruba experts, can enter into temporal relationships or musical dialogues with each other, while also communicating, both individually and collectively, a coded *ensemble* of meaningful information and knowledge."[57]

From the foregoing, we can attempt a synopsis of Anozie's probable answer to the question of how Okigbo's poems communicate meaning. Because Okigbo's poems are logically structured communication systems that, individually and collectively, contain laws of "organic composition" by means of which they transmit messages to discerning readers, the task of the reader is to analyze their constituent (phonemic, morphological, and syntactic) rhetorical structures and "inner dialectic" instead of the historical determination of their content.[58] Simply stated, it is that Okigbo's poetry means by either inscribing in the rhetorical structure of the poem the process by which the poet-protagonist experiences a growth in creative consciousness (PAR, in *Distances*) or by conferring on the poem's anthropomorphic speakers "propositional attitudes" that readers can infer from their syntax.[59] If this paraphrase is fair, then we can say that Anozie has remained faithful to structuralist critical theory and has thus secured his reputation as a pioneer of structuralist interpretations of African literature.[60]

But his reputation has come at a price. Over the years, Anozie has been severely criticized for the obscurity of his methodology.[61] More importantly, critics charge that the theses that underpin the structuralist theory of language on which Anozie bases his interpretations of Okigbo's poetry and other African literary texts—signs are arbitrary; linguistic systems possess a relational character; and distinctions between *langue* and *parole,* synchrony and diachrony, are important—are conceptually flawed.[62] Critiques of structuralist linguistics and criticism are now so widely disseminated that we need not rehearse them here. For our purposes, however, perhaps the most telling reservation is to Anozie's habit of bracketing off what he calls "the historical determination" of a poem's content. We see this, for example, in the following statement: "Furthermore, by analysing the inner dialectic of the poem rather than the historical determination of its content, it can be shown that the 'Drums,' the privileged empirical model, serves the poet a dual purpose: as a thematic motif and as a structural praxis."[63] Not only does the phrase "rather than" suggest that the "inner dialectic" and "the historical determination" of the content of "Lament of the Drums" are incompatible, but it also validates the claim that only the analysis of the first could reveal the purposes attributed to the poet. What the historical determination of the content of "Lament of the Drums" is, and why the critic should set it aside, are not made clear. Perhaps it is the sequence of violent political crises that, according to other critics, shook Nigeria and the Congo (formerly Zaire) shortly after independence.[64] But even if we agree that it is, we are still far from understanding why knowledge of these incidents would prevent the reader from recognizing the two purposes that the "Drums" serve. We cannot help but see, in this statement and in others, why many critics remain skeptical of structuralist theory and criticism, particularly of the proposition that poetry is "a system of ordered variants" whose "internal coherence" structuralist theory and criticism are equipped to explicate.[65] By fencing off the historical reference of the contents of "Lament of the Drums," Anozie deprives himself of precisely those "crucial connotations of words" that only a movement "outside the text itself to the cultural and social codes on which it draws" would make possible.[66]

By the early seventies, such debates had generated so many studies of Okigbo that J. M. Purcell was able to compile the first bibliography of Okigbo criticism—"Christopher Okigbo (1932–1967): Preliminary Checklist of His Books."[67] Several factors contributed to this growth. Perhaps the most obvious is the increase in the number of Nigerian and African literary scholars graduating from European and American programs in which they were exposed to unorthodox currents of literary theory and criticism practically unheard of, or only marginally applied, in most African universities of the time. Here the structuralist Anozie and the Pan-Africanists Chinweizu, Onwuchekwa Jemie, and Ihechukwu Madubuike stand as prime examples. Anozie, Chinweizu, and other scholars reignited debates over the meaning of Okigbo's poems and, more importantly, over the use of "foreign" and esoteric critical methods to interpret African literatures. Of considerable importance, too, was the growth of "Commonwealth literature" and black studies, and the proliferation of journals and periodicals, in Africa and beyond. Many of these were devoted solely to African literatures (*Black Orpheus, Transition, Research in African Literatures, Okike: An African Journal of New Writing, African Literature Today,* and *The Conch*). Others (*Journal of Commonwealth Literature, Ufahamu,* and *Présence Africaine*) incorporated African literatures as part of emergent, politically defined subdisciplines of literary criticism. Many dissertation chapters were first published in these journals. Finally, and perhaps most important, was the publication in 1971 of *Labyrinths with Path of Thunder.* For the first time, Okigbo's poetry was available in one volume. To be sure, because he had excluded his last poem cycle, *Path of Thunder,* from the initial volume that he entitled *Labyrinths,* and because he had revised poems published earlier, his declaration in the introduction that the "somewhat different and final" versions contained in the volume were "organically related" applied, strictly speaking, to *Labyrinths.*[68] Still, this did not prevent scholars, many of whom drew inspiration from the (posthumous) exposition of the central themes and motifs Okigbo offered in his introduction, from rapidly conferring upon *Labyrinths with Path of Thunder* the status of an authoritative collection and embarking on summative evaluations of Okigbo's accomplishments.

How controversial this perception of *Labyrinths with Path of Thunder* was can be gleaned from Anozie's strenuous opposition of the publication of *Labyrinths* and *Path of Thunder* in one volume. Conversely, it is possible that Chinweizu, a Nigerian scholar then living in the United States of America and an exponent of Afrocentric cultural nationalist criticism, would have preferred that *Heavensgate,* a volume in whose "tired syntactic jugglery" he discerned evidence of the "anemic modernity" of the poet's earlier efforts, be excluded. For it was in *Path of Thunder,* with its "rhythmic lament," use of stanzas consisting of alternating short and long lines, and recurrence of chorus lines peculiar to African "traditional" verse, that Chinweizu found evidence of Okigbo's homeward journey to "a language of African particulars."[69] In the critical manifesto *Toward the Decolonization of African Literature* (1983), the Bolekaja critics Chinweizu, Jemie, and Madubuike outlined the hypotheses that underpinned this preference. First, in accents reminiscent of Mazrui, they argued that poetry is "an auditory medium" that must possess "a readily available surface meaning" if its "deeper levels of meaning" are to be understood.[70] Second, they redefine "literature" broadly as a multigeneric system of public communication. Finally, they urge critics to recognize oral African discourse as "the incontestable reservoir of the values, sensibilities, esthetics, and achievements of traditional African thought and imagination."[71] To the extent, then, that Okigbo's use of archaic and Latinate diction, alien imagery, "attitudes," "forms, and assorted mannerisms," as well as his addiction to "atrocious punctuation," ambiguity, syntactic inversions, sprung rhythm, alliteration and assonance, and neologisms (all symptoms of the "Hopkin's disease"), impede the reader's effort to comprehend the surface meaning of *Heavensgate,* the Bolekaja critics declared it a mimicry of Anglo-American modernist poetics and thus part of the corpus of modern poetry *in* Africa.[72] Unlike *Path of Thunder,* in which Okigbo incorporates the forms and rhetorical conventions of oral African discourse (musicality and "alternation of long cadenced lines and abrupt declaratives" that, "organized for cumulative impact," reinforce each other and clearly denote "the precise things which Okigbo wishes to convey"), *Heavensgate* is so divorced from the "oral African roots" of Igbo traditional religious poetry that it cannot be included in the canon of modern African poetry.[73]

Given the strident rhetoric in which Bolekaja criticism clothed its theoretical claims and literary interpretations, it is hardly surprising that it aroused equally passionate rebuttals. Understandably, such rebuttals have rightly been directed at the theoretical propositions listed in the foregoing paragraph. Thus, in "Aesthetic Illusions: Prescriptions for the Suicide of Poetry," Wole Soyinka declared the claim that simplicity of expression and transparency of meaning are the cardinal attributes of oral African aesthetics to be outrageous, arguing that traditional African poetry, of which ritual incantatory verse is an example, is "a densely packed matrix of reference."[74] But whereas Soyinka appeared to accept the Bolekaja critics' proposition that oral African discourse constitutes the generative matrix of African poetry, Kwame Anthony Appiah contended that their populist nativism entrapped them in the very "Western cultural conjuncture" they claimed to be resisting:

> The pose of repudiation actually presupposes the cultural institutions of the West and the ideological matrix in which they, in turn, are imbricated. . . . they enact a conflict that is *interior* to the same nationalist ideology that provided the category of "literature" its conditions of emergence: defiance is determined less by "indigenous" notions of resistance than by the dictates of the West's own Herderian legacy—its highly elaborated ideologies of national autonomy, of language and literature as their cultural substrate.[75]

By historicizing Bolekaja criticism and drawing attention to the fact that oral African discourse is a dynamic, rather than inert and unchanging, form of cultural expression and representation, Appiah creates much-needed space within Okigbo criticism wherein it might be possible to rethink, as Eileen Julien and Ato Quayson have so ably done with African and Nigerian fiction respectively, the complex relationship between oral and literary poetics in Okigbo's work.[76]

Also contributing to the growth of Okigbo criticism in the early seventies, though without stirring as much controversy, were exponents of English Practical Criticism and American New Criticism. Some of the assertions they made suggest that they share the genetic emphases found in early Okigbo criticism. Some had written dissertation chapters on Okigbo, and others had published essays on individual poem cycles.[77] Many of them (Egudu, Nyong J. Udoeyop, Omolara Leslie [hereafter referred to as Molara Ogundipe-Leslie], Dan Izevbaye, and Donatus I. Nwoga) were Nigerians. In general, their essays marked a shift toward interpretations that grounded the meaning of Okigbo's poems in the domain of local experiences, be these the renewal of personal faith or the collective anguish caused by the violent political throes in which Africans were caught.[78] Thus, for example, in "Okigbo: A Branch of a Giant Fennel," Udoeyop viewed *Silences* as a sequence inspired by political crises in Nigeria and the Congo, and in "Okigbo's *Distances:* A Retreat from Christ to Idoto" (1973), Egudu casts the protagonist as a repentant prodigal whose journey "home" marks his renunciation of the Christian doctrine of salvation and return to "the indigenous state of purity and bliss attainable in life."[79] Finally, Ogundipe-Leslie's "The Poetry of Christopher Okigbo: Its Evolution and Significance" (1973), in which each poem cycle is represented as a stage in Okigbo's aesthetic and personal evolution from "private anguish to public commitment," identified poetic maturity with the attainment of a distinctively African voice that, though noticeable in earlier poems such as "Lament of the Lavender Mist (for three flutes)" (1961), emerges most clearly in "Lament of the Masks."[80]

In a slightly different mold, and preoccupied with the problem of critical method, were Nwoga's "Okigbo's *Limits:* An Approach to Meaning" (1972) and Izevbaye's "Okigbo's Portrait of the Artist as a Sunbird: A Reading of *Heavensgate* (1962)" (1973). Nwoga's approach to *Limits* is essentially contextual. He saw *Limits* as a sequence whose primary theme is the relationship between the "poet/prophet/messiah figure and his community and its history," which emphasizes "essence and pattern" rather than historical events, and contains Okigbo's statement about the poet's "growth and nature, . . . his position in his community, and . . . the indestructible nature and continuing validity of the creative spirit."[81] To interpret the cycle, the critic needs to become familiar with the multicultural "situations and myths" from which Okigbo drew the "imagery and symbolism" with which he projected "his vision of his state and that of his society," and to understand the aim of Okigbo's "composition and the method" that these images and symbols create.[82] Izevbaye also subscribed to the contextual approach, though he elaborated his methodology fully in "From Reality to Dream" rather than in "Okigbo's Portrait of the Artist as a Sunbird: A Reading of *Heavensgate* (1962)" (1973). However, because the latter work addresses itself to an issue that, at the time, animated Okigbo's readers—namely, the coherence of his work— and because Izevbaye linked his views concerning the poems' unity with his model of contextual interpretation, it is essential to examine his reading of *Heavensgate.*

"Okigbo's Portrait of the Artist as a Sunbird: A Reading of *Heavensgate* (1962)" is possibly the clearest and most persuasive explanation of Okigbo's reasons for revising the 1962 version of *Heavensgate* for *Labyrinths.* Izevbaye proposed that Okigbo was concerned about the "organic unity" of his work. Thus Izevbaye suggested that the poet excised "Transition" from *Labyrinths* because the poem's "triumphant tone" is inconsistent with "the humble and exploratory spirit of *Heavensgate.*" In addition, Izevbaye attributed the problem raised by the perception that "Newcomer," one of the poems in the cycle, consists of fragments composed as separate poems and at different times, to Okigbo's compositional method, which Izevbaye calls "assemblage."[83] Urging readers to accept the loose structure produced by this method, Izevbaye compared the sequences thus produced to "primitive epics" whose "process of composition appears to be the adoption of a conventional, but fairly loose, structure within which individual experiences may establish a logical relationship with one another" (3). After applying this insight to *Heavensgate,* Izevbaye added:

> To the extent that the poem has a biographical—or autobiographical—structure, each of its movements represents the moments of crisis in the hero's life. So it is possible to regard any equivalent structure—like the basic stages of a man's life, Childhood, Adolescence, and Maturity—as the scaffolding around which the poem is constructed. The period of composition notwithstanding, poems about various experiences fit into the various stages whether as crises, or as the cause or the resolution of crises. (3)[84]

Izevbaye amplified his description of Okigbo's poetics in "From Reality to Dream," where he described it as a process of accumulation achieved by the expansion and enlargement of meaning in each "additional poem." Drawing on I. A. Richards's *The Philosophy of Rhetoric* (1964), Izevbaye proposed a contextual model of interpretation. Any critic working with this model acts as a kind of central intelligence who mediates between the poetic text, its intertextual or generic sources, and its extraliterary ("audience, the artist and his society") contexts.[85] In both essays, Izevbaye's understanding of Okigbo's compositional method, coupled with his use of the contextual analysis, produces a reading in which each poem is perceived as a microunit or component piece of a larger, unified edifice of meaning. In other words, for Izevbaye, meaning in Okigbo's poetry accrues cumulatively. Thus, for example, "Siren Limits" (*Limits* I–IV) may be seen as a poem in which Okigbo's poet-protagonist seeks integration with his "second self" after realizing that the reintegration he sought in *Heavensgate* with his ancestral, primordial "self" was impossible.[86]

The linkage of questions of poetic unity and compositional method to critical practice underscores the extent to which, for critics of the period, especially Izevbaye and Nwoga, Okigbo criticism was as much a critical practice as a search for interpretive method. To the extent that they succeeded in this endeavor, we owe them a debt of gratitude. Although they took for granted the conceptual principles that underpinned their theoretical propositions—structural coherence, for example—they were so mindful of the integrity of Okigbo's poetry as poetry that they sought in the poems, and in the poetic traditions to which the critics thought the poems belonged, an understanding of his poetics. Certainly "assemblage," the term with which Izevbaye characterizes the poet's creative method, helps us appreciate how poem cycles and occasional verses that often appear like unrelated fragments might actually fit together. Equally important, Nwoga's suggestion that knowledge of the multicultural sources of the poet's images and symbols is essential for understanding his "vision" acknowledges a fact the Bolekaja critics overlooked: history, in the form of Okigbo's eclectic allusions, spiritual images and symbols, and experiments with form, cannot be stuffed back like the evil genie into the bottle. Still, the contributions of these critics were generally compromised by assumptions in their critical methods. For example, since what Nwoga seeks is a paradigm for creating "a body of *basic* meaning," and since he thinks *basic* meaning must transcend "specific incidents in Africa's or Nigeria's history" to which *Limits* is often associated, he devalues the violent political, social, and military conflicts that convulsed African nations in the postindependence era by designating them as "external" stimuli.[87] This assumption, which we can trace back to Cleanth Brooks's declaration that "[t]he primary concern of criticism is with the problem of unity— the kind of whole which the literary work forms or fails to form, and the relation of the various parts to each other in building up this whole," narrows the scope of Nwoga's and Izevbaye's contextual models of interpretation and, by precluding or limiting analyses of concrete historical experiences inscribed in the poems, effectively impoverishes them.[88]

To some extent, subsequent contributions to Okigbo criticism in the late seventies compensated for such weaknesses in the work of the African exponents of American New Criticism and English Practical Criticism. Two factors—the decline of earlier critical paradigms (especially genetic and cultural nationalist interpretations) and the publication of *Don't Let Him Die* (1978)— facilitated this growth. Edited by Chinua Achebe and Dubem Okafor, this anthology of elegiac verse was designed to mark the 10th anniversary of Okigbo's death and to celebrate his achievements. However, its publication also intensified the tendency, which had only been embryonic in the early seventies, to designate the poet as a "prophet" around whose oracular figure and gnomic pronouncements the meaning of his poetry is believed to coalesce. In other words, *Don't Let Him Die* so intensified the canonization of Okigbo as a "phenomenon" that we are tempted to agree with Joseph Anafulu, who declared that especially in Nsukka, Okigbo seems to have been elevated to the status of "a cult object."[89] Okigbo's canonization coincided with a surge in the number of scholarly dissertations and critical essays in which old themes (the poetics of ritual verse, the construction of identity and the process of self-formation, nation building and cultural politics, and the relationship between oral and written verse) were revisited and new ones (gender) introduced and explored. Many of these studies were comparative (James Murray Wieland, Jonathan Ngaté, and Edward Chukwuemeka Okwu), whereas others, using orthodox but hitherto overlooked methodologies (Annemarie Heywood, Dubem Okafor, and Chukwuma Azuonye), dealt exclusively with Okigbo's poetry. As a younger generation of scholars began grappling with issues broached earlier, or as they began reading Okigbo against his "Commonwealth" and Anglophone and Francophone African peers, they gradually altered our understanding of the meaning of Okigbo's work and our approach to issues raised by his art.

Wieland's "The Ensphering Mind: A Comparative Study of History, Myth, and Fictions in Six Commonwealth Poets" (1978) was one of the comparative studies. For Wieland, Okigbo and his "Commonwealth" peers (A. D. Hope, Allen Curnow, A. M. Klein, Derek Walcott, and Nissim Ezekiel) rely on myth and fiction to deal with the "varying forms of dislocation," the sense of disorder and incoherence, that history has inflicted on them.[90] History, for Okigbo, is a narrative that charts the disruption by slavery and colonialism of ancient "communication" lines linking him with "his tribal [sic] past," and his poetry is a literary vehicle that transports him back into "his spiritual past," where "he experiences another initiation, purification, death and rebirth as he seeks to be reborn into his heritage" (86). Citing Poems: Four Canzones (1957–1961), Wieland argues that Okigbo's attitude to the ancestral past is driven by a pragmatic view of the content of history rather than by nostalgia, as the poet-prodigal's willingness to discard "superfluous" material that might compromise the "integrity" of his poetry in Heavensgate, and his braiding of non-African images and metaphors with the beliefs of "his native religion," indicate (115). Wieland admits that in Path of Thunder, Okigbo no longer perceives "the possibility of renewal or redemption" he imagined in Poems: Four Canzones (1957–1961) and Labyrinths. Wieland insists that Okigbo's poetry is coherent precisely because it is characterized by a pervasive "sense of becoming" and belief in the possibility of change (318–19). There are two weaknesses in Wieland's study. First, his conception of African history is ethnicist. Consequently it construes the Igbo éthnos as the fount of cultural material out of which Okigbo's poet-prodigal produces his self-knowledge, rather than as one in a set of multiple, competing, and radically unstable technologies of self-creation available to postcolonial subjects. Second, Wieland's conception of Okigbo as he sings in Limits as the "embodiment of the African psyche" is essentialist: though Wieland recognizes Africans' impulse to resist cultural degradation, he nonetheless attributes to them a fixed, unchanging, consciousness (332).

Like Wieland, Okwu saw Okigbo's poetry as a project of "self" creation and artistic growth. But rather than stress the artist's dislocation from his natal culture as Wieland does, Okwu argued that that culture is the primary source of the poet's creative energy. Together, Kofi Awoonor, Wole Soyinka, and Okigbo are writers who create "surrogate-poets" or "ideal" artist personae comparable to "major artist-heroes" of classical antiquity.[91] Collectively, they retrieve from the cultural "wellspring" of their societies the "ideal of creative behavior and meaningful participation" that they consider necessary in dealing with contemporary problems (13). Individually, Okigbo's interest in the artist figure in Labyrinths represents a form of "self-examination, a way of gaining a better understanding of his own creative role in the society." Far from representing a point of departure, Okwu argued, Path of Thun-

*der* and all other poems in Okigbo's oeuvre make up "an epic of a poet's growth into a prophetic role" (153).

In *Two African Prodigals: Senghor and Okigbo* (1979), Ngaté staged a rare and illuminating encounter between Leopold Sedar Senghor and Okigbo. By so doing, Ngaté made Okigbo confront Senghor, the poet whose negritude verse Okigbo had once derided as "platform poetry," and through this encounter reveals similarities and differences in their themes, poetics, and politics. For example, both poets use "the theme of the prodigal" to redefine their artistic and social "self." Emerging from this project of redefinition, Ngaté suggested, is the image

> of a person fully capable not only of articulating the needs and desires of his people but also of entering into a fray on behalf of or along with his people. And because he has been forced by circumstances to use the colonizer's language in expressing himself, he tries to give a more African character to his voice by making his own some of the esthetic principles of African oral literary traditions while accepting the influence of those non-African poets who are apt to help him deal effectively with the ambiguity of his predicament as a cultural mulatto.[92]

In *Labyrinths,* according to Ngaté, Okigbo emphasizes "the private side" of the prodigal's self and "the mystical nature of its relationship with Idoto," and in *Path of Thunder* he addresses issues arising from changes in contemporary Africa.[93]

Much of Ngaté's reading was presented in a chapter entitled "Okigbo at the Crossroads: The Language of Myth and Ritual in *Labyrinths*," a slightly revised version of which is reprinted in this volume under the title "Christopher Okigbo, or The Eclectic Poet as Prodigal and Priest in *Labyrinths*." There is a point of consensus between Ngaté and Azuonye, whose essay "Christopher Okigbo and the Psychological Theories of Carl Gustav Jung" (1981) is also reprinted in this volume. Both Ngaté and Azuonye discerned in Okigbo's poetry an exploration of the emergent postcolonial self. For them, the poems are literary projects in the production of an African self. Okigbo's prodigal, Ngaté argued, is a figure capable of traversing "cultural boundaries." The ability to traverse cultural boundaries may be read as the poet's "full and straightforward assertion of his *metissage,* his hybridity." Understood thus, it demonstrates that contrary to those who expect Okigbo's prodigal to return unblemished from his exile, he returns altered by the experience of his literal and metaphorical exile.[94] Thus Ngaté saw the prodigal's hybridity as a "paradoxical situation" in which, being no longer just Westerner or "traditional Igbo," his language assumes a syncretic character. By careful analysis of Okigbo's poetics, Ngaté revealed that the complex syntax, seemingly contradictory fusion of African and non-African cultural elements, nimble shifts from pedantic to colloquial register, and unabashed displays of mastery over

Western myth and literature, testify to the emergence of the prodigal as a hybrid "self." But whereas Ngaté discovered in Okigbo's poetics a hybrid post-colonial African subject, by reading Okigbo's work as the poetic analogy of the Jungian theory of individuation, Azuonye discerned "a fully individuated personality" constituted of "conscious and . . . unconscious components."[95] As with humanist notions of the "individual," Azuonye's Jungian "personality" is an "autonomous and stable" entity who, unfettered by material circumstance, transcends them through poetry.[96] Thus, drawing on Jungian archetypes, Azuonye sketches the postcolonial subject as a self-constituting entity for whom poetry offers the means to personal transcendence.[97]

Like Azuonye's approach, Heywood's interpretive apparatus—genre criticism—is also orthodox. Unlike Azuonye, however, her application of the model in "The Ritual and the Plot: The Critic and Okigbo's *Labyrinths*" (1978) is distinctive. She placed "ritual," a term that critics had applied descriptively to Okigbo's poetry, at the conceptual core of her essay. In her hands, ritual became both the designation for the genre of poetry Okigbo wrote and the source of a critical method for interpreting "difficult poetry" such as Okigbo's. Heywood constructed a three-step, reader-centered paradigm for interpreting ritual verse: reconstructing the effect of the poem on the "reader's imagination"; developing a hypothesis about "the *kind of meaning*" being communicated; and applying "the key appropriate to that *kind of meaning.*"[98] Using these steps, she observed that on reading the poems in *Labyrinths with Path of Thunder* she responded negatively because they lack "discursive continuity" and "operate by establishing stresses, emphases, valences through the patterning" of "firstly, rhythms and sounds, and, secondly, motifs" (48). Some motifs that aroused these negative responses include a sense of topography, generic states/happenings (for example, solitude and sexual encounters), and multivocality. On the basis of this analysis, Heywood defined ritual verse as "poetry which is in itself a ritual instrument," and whose language therefore "enacts, invokes, or conjures." She noted that what strikes Okigbo's readers "is the perception of language as sound rather than sense, and of meaning inhering in the responses of the central nervous system and hypothalamus as much as in those of the cerebral cortex" (52).

Heywood's critical paradigm is interactive: it sees meaning in Okigbo as arising from an encounter between the language of ritual verse and the reader's organs of cognition and sensation. This is the source of her paradigm's originality. Yet the prominence that Heywood's participatory hermeneutics grant the reader in meaning production notwithstanding, her critical paradigm contains a few difficult problems. For example, she based her interpretation on her responses to the motifs in *Labyrinths*. However, it is doubtful that given differences in the central nervous system, hypothalamus, and cerebral cortex of individual readers, her responses can be reproduced. Moreover, even if they could, it is difficult to determine how these readers may ascertain that the lists of motifs they isolated in each poem and their responses to them are not mere products of their imagination. This problem is likely to be even more acute in *Path of Thunder,* a sequence whose designation by Anozie as simple and popular (in implicit contrast to the "private" and priestly *Labyrinths*) she rightly rejected. Heywood suggested that *Path of Thunder* deals "with civil unrest preceding war, but seem again to be articulating not the historic events as such, nor popular feelings about them, but visionary apprehensions of the numinous archetypes of which they are the temporal figures" (60). The evidence she offered for this speculation consists of two thematic streams (Iron Configuration–Cultural History, and White Light–the Initiate) that are united by the haunting concluding lines: "An old star departs, leaves us here on the shore / . . . before a going and coming that goes on forever." But how is one to know that it is not her desire to defend *Path of Thunder* against the charge that it is "political pamphleteering," and thus give the poems free rein to perform their "prophetic, magic function," that so obliges her to construe them as "temporal figures" of transcendent archetypes envisioned by the poet? In the end, it seems that whatever the archetypes critics might be tempted to see in the lines Heywood classified under the theme of Iron Configuration, what remains most compelling about them is precisely their historicity: the crisis of consciousness, explored so brilliantly in *Labyrinths,* of which the violence preceding the civil war may be read as both cause and symptom.

In virtually all the studies of the late seventies, critics either averted their gaze from the most vivid signs of Okigbo's politics, dissociated his poetry from his politics, or pleaded that his political concerns were subordinate to his artistic projects. *Nationalism in Okigbo's Poetry* (1980), Dubem Okafor's first book on Okigbo, reversed this trend. *Nationalism in Okigbo's Poetry* examines national politics in, and the cultural politics of, Okigbo's poetry. For Okafor, Okigbo's poetry is a 70-page synopsis of Nigeria's political history, and the poet himself is a champion of "true nationalism and cultural integrity."[99] Reiterating this thesis in *The Dance of Death: Nigerian History and Christopher Okigbo's Poetry* (1998), Okafor described Okigbo's poetry as "a succinct capsulization of the cultural-political history of Nigeria from the first days of imperialist penetration into the country to the present. . . ."[100] In *The Dance of Death,* Okafor drew upon colonial discourse theory and postcolonial criticism to construct his "'man and his works'" critical method (xiii). This approach allowed him to place his discussion of Okigbo's poetry, developed in four long chapters entitled "Discourse, Blood, and Nation: Nigeria 1914–1996," "The Nigerian/African Writers and their Milieux," "Ethnicity and Cacophony: The Dilemma of Tongues," and "Okigbo: The Man and the Artist," within the milieu of the poet's life and literary career and the events of pre–civil war Nigeria.

"Postcoloniality and the Oracle of Repetition: Christopher Okigbo's Poetry," Okafor's essay in this volume, is a version of a key chapter in *The Dance of Death* entitled "Okigbo's Postcolonial and Cultural Politics." Here Okafor casts Okigbo as a postcolonial poet who, after an initial phase, embarked on the project of cultural rehabilitation (160). In a passage that bears a striking resemblance to Frantz Fanon's three-stage theory of the evolution of "native writers" (Assimilation, Alienation, and Revolutionary Transformation of Self and Nation), Okafor characterized Okigbo's project as a "trinary endeavor" (intellectual preparation; reenactment of the experience of exile and return; and, finally reintegrated into the community, the critique of power and domination).[101] But the similarity is not absolute. If Fanon created a profile of the "native intellectual" as a revolutionary writer with clear secular horizons, Okafor invested Okigbo with mystical powers, and his utterances with sacred value. For him, Okigbo is a "poet of destiny" and an *ogbanje,* a priest and a prophet.[102] Okafor's Okigbo is a *bricoleur* who, in *Limits,* interweaves Mesopotamian, Egyptian, and other myths as a way of "demarcating his field of 'combat,'" by locating in history the source of the cultural, and eventually, political and economic, disaster which have been the lot of Africa and the Third World" (198). And if in *Limits* he makes joint cause with "the wretched of the earth," in *Path of Thunder* he foretells his death and the disintegration of Nigeria's "postcolonial dream": "And in the prophecy of his own exit was contained the sad foreshadowing, not only of the impossibility of attaining the dream and utopia of Nigerian unity and nationhood, but also of the doomed cycle of repetition." For Okafor, Okigbo's poetry serves as an oracular admonition directed at his compatriots. This is particularly true of his reading of *Heavensgate,* whose final poem, "Newcomer," he described as marking the poet's arrival on the threshold of his "cultural and political" mission.

No doubt Okigbo's introduction to *Labyrinths* is the immediate source of the honorifics—"prophet," "seer," "priest," and "poet of destiny"—now frequently applied to him. There, he described his poet-protagonist as a figure bearing a "load of destiny" on his head. However, there is no clear evidence that the phrase refers to Okigbo. The passage of time and the imperatives dictated by the canonization having shrunk the distance between Okigbo and Prodigal/Town-Crier, poet and poet-persona, fond memory has made the extension of these terms to the poet himself commonplace. "The Emergence of the Poet of Destiny," the title of an essay Nwoga contributed to *Critical Perspectives on Christopher Okigbo* (1984), the first anthology of Okigbo criticism, also attests to this development. But it was left to Emmanuel N. Obiechina, whose essay "Christopher Okigbo: Poet of Destiny" we reprint in this volume, to clarify the meaning of this term and make it the scaffolding for a theory of criticism. Obiechina offered two reasons for proposing that we consider Okigbo, Africa's greatest "romantic poet," the continent's "greatest poet of destiny."[103] Like his precursor poets of destiny, Okigbo is, as he demonstrates in his exposition of the poetics of *Labyrinths,* an "author-critic." In addition, Okigbo proclaims himself, and knew that he was, a poet of destiny. As author-critic, he belongs to the category of writers whose "comments and manner of presenting them constitute an extension of the statements contained in their creative texts." As a self-described "poet-prophet" and "poet of destiny," his credentials satisfy the criteria of high seriousness, capacity for understanding the "inner" source of the vocation to prophecy, appreciation of human nature, problems, and predicaments, and a "wholesome assimilation" of self-interest with social destiny. He considered "his poetical career as that of a bearer of special destiny and spokesman of the time and the people."[104] Okigbo's personality, Obiechina argued, is "distinctive and visible" in his work. This personality, which is represented by various poetic conventions (mask or persona) in the early poems and emerged fully as his "true self" in *Path of Thunder* ("I, Okigbo, town-crier" in "Hurrah for Thunder," and "The mythmaker . . . / Okigbo" in "Elegy for Slit-Drum"), is the protagonist manifesting himself as "a speaking voice" and "a physical human presence."[105] In *Heavensgate,* he prepares himself intellectually, psychologically, and culturally for his oracular and prophetic functions; in *Limits* he tests "the level of his achievements in terms of his self-assessment and his handling of public and momentous themes"; in *Distances* he prepares for his "struggle against the forces of chaos" by experiencing death; and in *Path of Thunder* he discards the "oracular exposition" and "lyrical persona" of the earlier sequences for a "social persona" who speaks directly and plainly.[106] Thus Obiechina invested Okigbo with the halo of prophecy.

As we have seen in Okafor's *Dance of Death,* Okigbo's canonization is an ongoing project to which critics such as Okafor and Obiechina contributed in the early eighties. By 1984, the volume of studies had increased so much that Nwoga was able to compile the first anthology of Okigbo criticism, entitled *Critical Perspectives on Christopher Okigbo.* In selecting essays for this collection, Nwoga opted for those that he thought "most expose significant facts and ideas about Okigbo the person, the theme of his poetry, and his significant contributions to the advancement of consciousness of both the private and public aspects of the human condition, and the style of his poetry."[107] *Critical Perspectives* includes a useful though dated map of Nigeria, reviews, interviews, a bio-bibliography, Chinua Achebe's preface to *Don't Let Him Die,* and book excerpts and critical essays. Also reprinted are an English translation of a critical essay in French—Roland Bouyssou's *"Labyrinths,* or the Initiation Quest of Christopher Okigbo" (1972)—and testimonials by friends. Some of the testimonials, especially Kole Omotosho's "Christopher Okigbo: A Personal Portrait" and Peter Thomas's "Ride Me, Memories" are valuable for the portraits they paint of the poet. Other noteworthy essays in this volume include "The Emergence of the Poet of Destiny: A Study of Okigbo's 'Lament of the Silent Sisters' " and "Christopher Okigbo: The Man and the Poet," both of which were original contributions by Nwoga. In this essay, Nwoga created a portrait of Okigbo designed, in part, to establish his personal and literary reputation; and in "The Emergence of the Poet of Destiny," an essay that rescues

"Lament of the Silent Sisters" from critical obscurity, Nwoga argued that the poem is "a universalized shriek of fear and horror at the senseless emptiness of human activity."[108]

Nwoga's contributions and the essays published in *Critical Perspectives* confirmed the global scope of Okigbo criticism. Within a few years, however, more studies appeared. Some opened up new lines of inquiry (gender), and others shed new light on extant themes. Representing the former was Elaine Savory Fido's essay, "Okigbo's *Labyrinths* and the Context of Igbo Attitudes to the Female Principle" (1986). Reading his poems within the context of "Igbo attitudes" to gender, attitudes that she culled from her reading of colonial and postcolonial ethnographic and historiographic studies of the Igbo as well as fiction by a variety of Igbo writers, Fido argued that "a tension between love and fear, desire to submit to intensities of emotional and physical love and desire to remain separate, adoration of the mother and terror of the sexual partner," permeates the "emotional textures" of Okigbo's poetry.[109] Also running through the poetry is a tension between the poet-persona's urge to re-create the maternal images of "traditional religious cults" and his desire to assert a maleness threatened by the feminine "softness and protection" women offer. Calling these tensions the "twists and turns" of desire in Okigbo, Fido declared that they are transcultural traits found in all men. But she believed that Okigbo's ambivalence is also the product of a specific postcolonial male African consciousness that codes Igbo religion and Christianity as "feminine" and "masculine" respectively, and his desire to return to "tradition" marked his alienation from "the male god of patriarchal Christianity" (227). Running through Fido's essay is the assumption that Okigbo's imagination is circumscribed by certain determinate cultural and historical imperatives of the poet's Igbo/African ethnic identity. As a result, she produced a biographical reading of the poetry in which Okigbo is identified with his poet-protagonist and cast as a figure who typifies male Igbo attitudes toward women and femininity. "People who were close to Okigbo," Fido observed, "believe that the poems are all or almost all based on real relations with women" (227). With this methodologically hybrid variant of feminist ethnocriticism, Fido inaugurated the study of femininity and gender dynamics in Okigbo criticism. However, her interpretation is weakened, like others before it, by her identification of Okigbo with his poet-protagonist, and her perception of the poetry as transparent surfaces in which Okigbo's attitudes lie reflected.

These are precisely the sort of problems one does not encounter in "The Achievement of Christopher Okigbo," Robert Fraser's highly illuminating exposition of Okigbo's poetics and themes. Avowedly formalist, this essay is one of the chapters in *West African Poetry: A Critical History* (1986). Freeing the poet from the dungeon of ethnicity, Fraser celebrated the "haunting quality" and transcendence over the "petty historical distinctions" of poetic traditions that Okigbo achieves in *Labyrinths* and eulogized him as a cosmopolitan writer who, though scornful of "literary nationalism," nonetheless remained "deeply indebted to the beliefs and traditional poetic practice of the Igbo people."[110] Evidence of Okigbo's cosmopolitanism abounds in Fraser's reading. Attempting to explain the identity of the female muse in "Watermaid," he suggested that she reminds readers of the mother Idoto mentioned in "Passage," though she is also the "lioness," "watermaid," and "white queen." His identification of the female divinities in African and "exotic" religions, with which readers from diverse backgrounds might associate Okigbo's titles, dramatizes the global scope of the poet's mythic imagination (109–10). But evidence of Okigbo's indebtedness to Igbo religious beliefs and oral poetics is more scarce. Fraser made a few references to these in his discussion of *Heavensgate, Limits, Silences,* and *Distances.* Examples include the poet-prodigal's remorse, as he lies prostrate before the shrine of mother Idoto, over his abandonment of his "traditional gods"; his recovery of the ability to articulate his feelings in an "indigenous note" toward the end of "The Passage"; allusions to Igbo mythological symbols such as the sunbird, Nwanza; and the fusion of the "classic lament" with "traditional Igbo dirge" in "The Limits V–XII: Fragments out of the Deluge" (107–23). Unfortunately, these are not enough to dispel the impression that such references to Igbo beliefs and poetics are largely symbolic, and that Fraser was primarily interested in elements of Okigbo's poetics that exemplify his cosmopolitan imagination. For where he identified such elements of oral African poetics, Fraser did not analyze them with a rigor commensurate with that which he brings to his analysis of allusions to biblical and classical myths. This perception may explain Thomas R. Knipp's observation that Fraser " 'universalizes' Okigbo and de-Africanizes him and his poetry."[111] Still, on the basis of Fraser's close reading of individual sequences, the arguments he advances for considering *Labyrinths* and *Path of Thunder* as mutually related sequences, and his levelheaded and factual exploration of the "political ramifications" of Okigbo's poetry in "The Poet and War, 1966–70," we must count Fraser's study as one of the most readable and enlightening interpretations of Okigbo.[112]

Rounding off Okigbo criticism in the eighties was Catherine Acholonu's "Ogbanje: A Motif and a Theme in the Poetry of Christopher Okigbo" (1988). Acholonu identified *ogbanje* as a Jungian archetypal motif (a recurrent dream or mythic manifestations of the psyche of which humans are ignorant or partly aware). Among Igbo-speaking Nigerians, she pointed out, the term is applied to children when they exhibit "ambiguous" conduct, are fractious, or are perceived to possess dual personality. She advanced Pius Okigbo's testimony that the poet was a "turbulent," "irrepressible," "energetic," "mischievous," intractable, and "talented" child as evidence that he exemplified *ogbanje*—"the repeated reincarnation of a restless spirit, sometimes a water spirit, male or female"—and offered references to water, crossroads, ants, and so forth in *Heavensgate* as proof that the *ogbanje* motif lies at the core of Okigbo's art and life.[113] Acholonu's essay contains several problems. First, the identification of *ogbanje* with Jungian archetypes is misleading, since this translation overlooks the cosmological dimension of the Igbo concept. Second, her catalog of *ogbanje* allusions is so exhaustive that one begins to wonder if *Heavensgate* is not just a poetic celebration of death and rebirth. Third, Acholonu's evidence that Okigbo "saw himself as an *ogbanje* and his poetry as the nebulous utterances of a temporal sojourner"—Achebe's report that Kevin Echeruo, a peer, considered the poet one—is unnecessary.[114] As a metaphysical (not a psychoanalytic) concept, *ogbanje,* like Christ's divinity, does not require proof. No evidence, anecdotal or empirical, can demonstrate the "truth" of either claim. Both are doctrinal articles of faith that require belief, not proof. Finally, even if we accepted the claim that the poet was an *ogbanje,* we would still not be able to demonstrate that the poet-prodigal in *Heavensgate* is Okigbo.

Such identification of Okigbo with his poet-prodigal is a symptom of the declining health of Okigbo criticism that began in the eighties, the publication of several additional studies—Azuonye's " 'I, Okigbo, Town-Crier': The Transition from Mythopoeic Symbolism to a Revolutionary Aesthetic in *Path of Thunder*" (1994) and *The Dance of Death*—notwithstanding. The trend, as we have remarked, has been toward mystification of the poet and canonization of his verse. However, Modupe Olaogun's "Graphology and Meaning in the Poetry of Christopher Okigbo" (1991) suggested that an alternative trend is already under way, one in which efforts will be made to expand and deepen our understanding of the interplay between poetics, politics, and meaning in Okigbo's poetry. Thus, in "Graphology and Meaning in the Poetry of Christopher Okigbo," Olaogun suggested that what and how Okigbo's poetry means depends, at least in part, on graphology; that is, on devices such as "tonality, laconism, ambiguity, symbolism and lyricism," which constitute the visual presence of poetic language.[115] Working in the shadow cast by T. S. Eliot, Ezra Pound, and Dylan Thomas, all of whom were noted for their technical virtuosity, Okigbo uses these graphological devices to sculpt his poems. In "Song of the Forest," for example, he capitalizes "YOU LOAF," the poem's first two words, to impress their typographic and rhetorical significance as "nominative of address" upon his readers' attention. Similarly, he uses ellipsis in "Lament of the Flutes" to indicate that the protagonist's memory is vague and fragmentary, and in *Path of Thunder,* a sequence that relies less on obscure graphological devices than earlier sequences, he uses it to register the protagonist's perception of the inability of words to adequately express meaning. Particularly noteworthy is Olaogun's critique of the tendency among critics to identify Okigbo as his poet-protagonist. In convincing fashion, Olaogun demonstrates that in "Hurrah for Thunder" and "Elegy for Slit-Drum" *(Path of Thunder),* the pronominal "I" is a "mythical construct."[116]

Olaogun's trenchant critique of Acholonu's assumption that "I, Okigbo," the speaking subject of *Path of Thunder,* is Okigbo himself, and Kwame Dawes's interrogation of Okigbo in "Divided in the Brain: Okigbo as Trickster," the last essay in this volume, suggest that Okigbo criticism is gradually being invigorated by a new critical energy. Although as fascinated by Okigbo's poetry as their predecessors were, the contributions of these two critics suggest that in the future, scholars will question conventional "truths" about Okigbo's poetics or probe his pronouncements with more rigor than they have been wont to do since the seventies. Dawes's delicate investigation of Okigbo's "contradictory instincts" exemplifies this trend. In some ways, Dawes's essay rehearses well-known arguments. Thus, he declares that like his peers in the African diaspora, Okigbo grappled "with the tension between tradition and the quest for a new nationalist voice." Convinced, like them, that the cultural experiences of the colonized can be authenticated effectively only if, paradoxically, they are "named" in "the language of the colonizer," Okigbo envisioned himself as one of those who, like Walcott's "New World Adams," is searching for a new voice to fill in "a void of meaning." However, precisely because he saw colonized society as a world characterized by nothingness and disorder, Okigbo sought to create an ordered and stable world in the void. To accomplish this, Dawes concludes, Okigbo used some aesthetic techniques of Anglo-American modernism to compose *Labyrinths*.

More significant, however, is how Dawes makes us see Okigbo anew. Disputing the view of critics such as Kofi Awoonor who depict Okigbo's literary career as a journey from an initial African "innocence" (thesis), through apprenticeships to classicism, Anglo-American modernism, and "European music and religion" (antithesis), to the eventual rediscovery of his "original voice" and priestly function, Dawes suggests that such interpretations need to be reconciled with the poet's "relative silence" about African traditional forms in his introduction to *Labyrinths*. Here Okigbo's use of "similes and metaphors" indicates that he uses Western mythology as a device for translating Igbo "tradition" to a European readership. Consciousness of this readership, therefore, explains why he acknowledges his indebtedness to G. M. Hopkins, Debussy, and a host of non-African writers for "Silent Sisters" but remains mute about his African sources. Dawes suggests that, given the constitution of Okigbo's audience, this "entrapment" in Anglo-American modernist verse is unavoidable. Dawes argues that the explanation masks Okigbo's actual purpose, which is to conceal the fact that "he is torn between these cultural divides." As long as he uses "allusions" to translate his experiences, he remains vulnerable to them. As the poems he wrote over the length of his career show, however, his voice appears "most assured" when he discards these allusions. Okigbo, Dawes concludes, is "the trickster poet," a writer who, in his attempt to communicate with his readers, uses language as a "complex tool" for negotiating "the varied worlds of his literary imagination." Like Mazrui, Dawes explores the problem of communication in Okigbo. Unlike Mazrui, however, Dawes is untroubled by the ability of Okigbo's verse to generate multiple meanings. Olaogun's and Dawes's essays open up new paths to alternative readings of Okigbo, new interpretations in which accepted truths about the poetry and the poet's own explanations of his work are questioned.

The essays in this volume are arranged by genre and chronology in what may be thought of as two sections. The first section consists of two parts covering interviews of Okigbo and reviews of his poetry. We hope that the selections will provide readers the opportunity to "listen" to the poet as he responds to questions about his work, life, and politics, and to examine early reception of his work. The second section consists of critical essays grouped in three parts. Part 3 contains interpretations of individual poem sequences; part 4, essays on genre, interpretive method, and meaning; and part 5, essays that deal with Okigbo's entire oeuvre. Each part should expose readers to the broad variety of Okigbo criticism, taking into account the themes, methodological approaches, and ideological trends that have dominated in the past three decades. *Critical Essays on Christopher Okigbo* ends with a selected annotated bibliography. We hope that the annotations will provide students of Okigbo with handy and helpful synopses of important essays that are either not reprinted or included in this book, discussed in this introduction, or included in earlier bibliographies.

The arrangement of essays in this book is meant to suggest the direction we think Okigbo criticism is likely to follow in the future. Olaogun's probing of the assumptions that underpin interpretations of Okigbo's poetry in the past and Dawes's skeptical scrutiny of the poet's own pronouncements for possible contradictions and underlying motives indicate that in the future, critics will subject the poet and his poetry and prose to far more rigorous interrogation than in the past. As we enter the millennial "brave new world," our longing for interpretations that illuminate Okigbo within the context of post–Cold War realities will grow. Far from diminishing, our anxieties about who we are and how we are (African), about how we live and why, and about what and how we think our material, cultural, and sociopolitical circumstances are, will grow more intense and inevitably drive us toward criticism that, like Dawes's, attempts to demythologize Okigbo and demystify his works. In other words, we anticipate a shift to secular interpretations of Okigbo's poetry that will conceive of them as texts; that is, as "a system of forces institutionalized by the reigning" postcolonial culture in Nigeria (and abroad) with "some human cost to its various components."[117] For example, such criticism might investigate the cost to alternative poetic forms (pidgin verse, for example) of the institutionalization of Okigbo's work. It might examine the mutual invigoration of, and interplay between, poetry, visual art, and music in Nigeria; explore Okigbo's appropriation of formal conventions and poetic idioms from Anglo-American modernism, oral African verse, and various mythologies in terms of the dialectic of repetition; and investigate the "dialectic of self and community" by which the "poet protagonist" and "town-crier" are constituted as postcolonial subjects in *Labyrinth with Path of Thunder*.[118] Only in such criticism will Okigbo, the poet who, in the memorable words of his brother Pius Okigbo, "flashed through the sky . . . and dug a hole in the ground for himself," be celebrated, and a full measure of his art and life begin to be taken, finally.

## Notes

1.   See, for example, the following: Romanus Egudu, "Ezra Pound in African Poetry: Christopher Okigbo," *Comparative Literature Studies* 8 (1971): 153–54; Robert J. Stanton, "Poet as Martyr: West Africa's Christopher Okigbo, and His *Labyrinths, with Path of Thunder,*" *Studies in Black Literature* 7, no. 1 (1976): 11–12; Paul Theroux, "Christopher Okigbo," *Transition* 22 (1965): 20; Ali A. Mazrui, *The Trial of Christopher Okigbo* (London: Heinemann, 1971), 52–53; Chinua Achebe, preface to *Don't Let Him Die: An Anthology of Memorial Poems for Christopher Okigbo, 1932–67,* ed. Chinua Achebe and Dubem Okafor (Enugu: Fourth Dimension, 1978), v; Bernth Lindfors, "Okigbo as Jock," in *When the Drumbeat Changes,* ed. Carolyn A. Parker and Stephen H. Arnold, with A. M. Porter and H. Wylie (Washington, D.C.: Three Continents Press, 1981); Donatus Ibe Nwoga, "Christopher Okigbo: The Man and the Poet," in *Critical Perspectives on Christopher Okigbo,* ed. Donatus Ibe Nwoga (Washington, D.C.: Three Continents Press, 1984); Emmanuel N. Obiechina, "Christopher Okigbo: Poet of Destiny," in *Language and Theme: Essays on African Literature* (Washington, D.C.: Three Continents Press, 1990), 207–9 (This essay was first published as *Christopher Okigbo: Poet of Destiny* [Enugu: Fourth Dimension Publishers, 1980]); and S. Okechukwu Mezu, "Poetry and Revolution in Modern Africa," in *African Writers on African Writing,* ed. G. D. Killam (London: Heinemann, 1973), 106–7.

2.   Wole Soyinka, *Ibadan: The Penkelemes Years: A Memoir, 1946–1965* (Ibadan: Spectrum Books, 1994), 267.

3.   Ibid., 267.

4.   Achebe, preface to *Don't Let Him Die,* v–vi.

5.   Soyinka, *Ibadan,* 368; italics mine.

6.   Fredric Jameson, *The Political Unconscious: Narrative as a Socially Symbolic Act* (Ithaca, N.Y.: Cornell University Press, 1981), 19.

7.   See Obiechina, "Christopher Okigbo," 207–8; and Dan Izevbaye, "From Reality to Dream: The Poetry of Christopher Okigbo," in *The Critical Evaluation of African Literature,* ed. Edgar Wright (London: Heinemann, 1973), 124–25.

8.   Robert Fraser, *West African Poetry: A Critical History* (Cambridge: Cambridge University Press, 1986), 104.

9.   The following sources contain substantial biographical information on Okigbo: Bernth Lindfors, "Okigbo as Jock"; Nwoga, "Christopher Okigbo: The Man and the Poet"; Sunday O. Anozie, *Christopher Okigbo: Creative Rhetoric* (New York: Africana Publishing, 1972); Dubem Okafor, *Nationalism in Okigbo's Poetry* (Enugu: Fourth Dimension Publishers, 1980); and Dubem Okafor, *The Dance of Death: Nigerian History and Christopher Okigbo's Poetry* (Trenton, N.J.: Africa World Press, 1998).

10.   Christopher Okigbo, "Acknowledgements," in *Labyrinths with Path of Thunder* (London: Heinemann; New York: Africana Publishing Corporation, 1971).

11.   Anozie, *Christopher Okigbo,* 171–79.

12.   Okigbo, *Labyrinths with Path of Thunder;* Christopher Okigbo, *Collected Poems,* with a preface by Paul Theroux, introduction by Adewale Maja-Pearce (London: Heinemann, 1986).

13.   For a comparison of the Mbari and Heinemann versions of *Heavensgate,* see Dan Izevbaye, "Okigbo's Portrait of the Artist as a Sunbird: A Reading of *Heavensgate* (1962)," *African Literature Today* 6 (1973): 13.

14.   Izevbaye, "From Reality to Dream," 120.

15. Okigbo, introduction to *Labyrinths with Path of Thunder,* xi.

16. Quoted in Okwu, "The Artist-Figure in Modern West African Poetry: An Approach to the Poetry of Awoonor, Okigbo, and Soyinka" (Ph.D. diss., University of California, Los Angeles, 1978), 9. See also Neil Lazarus, *Resistance in Postcolonial African Fiction* (New Haven and London: Yale University Press, 1990), 1–10.

17. Harold Bloom, *The Anxiety of Influence: A Theory of Poetry* (New York and Oxford: Oxford University Press, 1997), 30.

18. Okigbo, "Passage ii," in *Heavensgate* (Ibadan: Mbari, 1962), 9.

19. S. O. Anozie, "Okigbo's *Heavensgate:* A Study of Art as Ritual," *Ibadan* 15 (March 1963): 11. For the notion of "cultural literacy," see E. San Juan Jr., *Racial Formations/Critical Transformations: Articulations of Power in Ethnic and Racial Studies in the United States* (New Jersey and London: Humanities Press International, 1992), 28. As Anozie's anecdote about his first encounter with the poet suggests, in the years following independence in Nigeria, exposure to an English literature curriculum may have been the prerequisite for achieving cultural literacy. See Anozie, *Christopher Okigbo,* 14–15.

20. Denis Williams, "The Mbari Publications," *Nigeria Magazine* (1962): 71.

21. Edward W. Said, "On Repetition," *The World, the Text, and the Critic* (Cambridge: Harvard University Press, 1983), 118. For additional examples of genetic or "influence" interpretations of Okigbo, see John Pepper Clark, "Poetry in Africa Today," *Transition* 4, no. 18 (1965): 25; and Hezzy Maduakor, "Okigbo and Yeats," paper presented at the Seventh Annual Conference of the Canadian Association of African Studies, Sherbrooke, Quebec, 3–6 May 1977.

22. Williams, "The Mbari Publications," 72.

23. Ulli Beier, "Three Mbari Poets," *Black Orpheus* 12 (1962): 47.

24. See Anozie, "Okigbo's *Heavensgate,*" 11; O. R. Dathorne, "Review of *Limits,*" *Black Orpheus* 15 (1964): 59; Annemarie Heywood, "The Ritual and the Plot: The Critic and Okigbo's *Labyrinths,*" *Research in African Literatures* 9, no. 1 (Spring 1978): 46–64; and Robert Serumaga, "Christopher Okigbo," in *African Writers Talking: A Collection of Interviews,* ed. Dennis Duerden and Cosmo Pieterse (London: Heinemann, 1972), 144. For an account describing the dramatization of this poem as ritualistic experience, see J. A. Adedeji, "A Dramatic Approach to Okigbo's *Limits,*" *Conch* 3, no. 1 (1971): 45–59.

25. Anozie, "Okigbo's *Heavensgate,*" 11–13.

26. Romanus Nnagbo Egudu, "The Matter and Manner of Modern West African Poetry in English: A Study of Okigbo, Clark, Awoonor-Williams, and Peters" (Ph.D. diss., Michigan State University, 1966), 111–12. This chapter was later published as "Ezra Pound in African Poetry: Christopher Okigbo," *Comparative Literature Studies* 8, no. 2 (1971): 143–54. See also A. N. Love, "The Language of Nigerian Poetry" (M.A. thesis, Bristol University, 1969).

27. Bloom, *The Anxiety of Influence,* xv.

28. Ibid.

29. Egudu, "Matter and Manner, 111–12.

30. M. J. C. Echeruo, "Traditional and Borrowed Elements in Nigerian Poetry," *Nigeria Magazine* 89 (June 1966): 142.

31. Modupe Olaogun, "Graphology and Meaning in the Poetry of Christopher Okigbo," *African Literature Today* 17 (1991): 123. See also Okwu, "The Artist-Figure," 2.

32. Barthes, quoted in Olaogun, "Graphology and Meaning in the Poetry of Christopher Okigbo," 123.

33. Bloom, *The Anxiety of Influence,* 31.

34. Lazarus, *Resistance in Postcolonial African Fiction,* 2.

35. W. B. Yeats, "The Second Coming," in *The Norton Introduction to Literature,* 7th ed., ed. Jerome Beaty and J. Paul Hunter (New York and London: W. W. Norton, 1998), 1319.

36.    Simon Gikandi, *Reading Chinua Achebe: Language and Ideology in Fiction* (London: James Currey; Portsmouth N.H., and Nairobi Kenya: Heinemann, 1991), 95.

37.    In addition to Egudu and Echeruo, see the following: Donatus Nwoga, "Plagiarism and Authentic Creativity in West Africa," in *Critical Perspectives on Nigerian Literatures*, ed. Bernth Lindfors (London: Heinemann, 1979); and Jonathan Ngaté, "Two African Prodigals: Senghor and Okigbo" (Ph.D. diss., University of Washington, Seattle, Wash., 1979).

38.    See Pol Ndu, "Mytho-Religious Roots of Modern Nigerian Poetry: Christopher Okigbo—*Heavensgate*," *Greenfield Review* 5, nos. 3–4 (1976–1977): 8.

39.    Bloom, *The Anxiety of Influence*, 5. In Bloom's terms, the critics imagined Okigbo's literary ancestors, be they African or foreign, as "strong poets" and the poet as a figure of "capable imagination" who appropriates their work for himself. Yet in Okigbo's response to the *Transition* conference questionnaire, in which he and other writers were asked to identify "influences and forces" that had affected their writing, he listed the impressionist composers Debussy, Caesar Frank, and Ravel for *Heavensgate* and "everything and everybody" for *Limits*, before asking: "But does it matter?" Whether this was evidence of his "anxiety of indebtedness" or just the expression of pique is open to interpretation.

40.    Ato Quayson, *Strategic Transformations in Nigerian Writing: Rev. Samuel Johnson, Amos Tutuola, Wole Soyinka, and Ben Okri* (Oxford: James Currey; Bloomington and Indianapolis: Indiana University Press, 1997), 2.

41.    Ali A. Mazrui, "Abstract Verse and African Tradition," *Zuka* 1 (1968): 47.

42.    Ali A. Mazrui, "Meaning versus Imagery in African Poetry," *Présence Africaine* 66 (1968): 49.

43.    Ibid.

44.    Mazrui, "Abstract Verse and African Tradition," 49.

45.    Jonathan Culler, *On Deconstruction: Theory and Criticism after Structuralism* (Ithaca, N.Y.: Cornell University Press, 1982), 76.

46.    Ibid., 186–87.

47.    I borrow this term from Richard Rorty, "Introduction: Metaphilosophical Difficulties of Linguistic Philosophy," in *The Linguistic Turn: Recent Essays in Philosophical Method* (Chicago: University of Chicago Press, 1967), 3. Rorty uses "linguistic turn" to denote "the most recent philosophical revolution, that of linguistic philosophy." I use it restrictively here to denote structuralist criticism, which appropriated the axioms of structuralist linguistics for literary analysis and interpretation.

48.    Quoted in Frank Lentricchia, *After the New Criticism* (Chicago: University of Chicago Press, 1980), 125.

49.    Sunday O. Anozie, "A Structural Approach to Okigbo's *Distances*," *Conch* 1, no. 1 (1969): 20–21; and Sunday O. Anozie, "Poetry and Empirical Logic: A Correspondence Theory of Truth in Okigbo's *Laments*," *Conch* 2, no. 1 (March 1970): 54. For a revised version of this essay on *Distances*, see Anozie, *Christopher Okigbo: Creative Rhetoric*, 156–70.

50.    Sunday O. Anozie, "Christopher Okigbo: A Creative Itinerary, 1957–1961," *Présence Africaine* 64 (1967): 158.

51.    Ibid., 160–65.

52.    Roland Barthes, *Critical Essays*, trans. Richard Howard (Evanston, Ill.: Northwestern University Press, 1972), 214.

53.    Anozie, "A Structural Approach to Okigbo's *Distances*," 20.

54.    For a description of his critical objective, see Anozie, *Christopher Okigbo*, 2–3.

55.    Anozie, "A Structural Approach to Okigbo's *Distances*," 21.

56.    Sunday O. Anozie, "Poetry and Empirical Logic," 55.

57.    Ibid., 58.

58.    Anozie, "A Structural Approach to Okigbo's *Distances*," 23; Anozie, "Poetry and Empirical Logic," 54–55.

59.   Anozie, "Poetry and Empirical Logic," 55.

60.   Anthony Appiah, "Strictures on Structures: The Prospects for a Structuralist Poetics of African Fiction," in *Black Literature and Literary Theory,* ed. Henry Louis Gates Jr. (New York and London: Methuen, 1984), 127–28. That Anozie has continued to develop this line of critical inquiry attests to his resilience and conviction. See Sunday O. Anozie, "Negritude, Structuralism, Deconstruction," in *Black Literature and Literary Theory,* ed. Henry Louis Gates Jr. (New York and London: Methuen, 1984), for further developments of this line of African literary theory and criticism.

61.   Chinweizu, Onwuchekwa Jemie, and Ihechukwu Madubuike, *Toward the Decolonization of African Literature,* vol. 1, *African Fiction and Poetry and Their Critics* (Washington, D.C.: Howard University Press, 1983), 289–90.

62.   Appiah, "Strictures on Structures," 128–44.

63.   Anozie, "Poetry and Empirical Logic," 55.

64.   Obiechina, "Christopher Okigbo: Poet of Destiny," 229; Fraser, *West African Poetry,* 124; and Okafor, *The Dance of Death,* 214.

65.   Terry Eagleton, *Literary Theory: An Introduction* (Oxford: Basil Blackwell, 1983), 95–96.

66.   Ibid., 116.

67.   J. M. Purcell, "Christopher Okigbo (1932–1967): Preliminary Checklist of His Books," *Studies in Black Literature* 4, no. 2 (1973): 8–10.

68.   Okigbo, *Labyrinths, with Path of Thunder,* xi.

69.   Chinweizu, "Prodigals, Come Home!" *Okike: An African Journal of New Writing* 4 (1973): 4.

70.   Chinweizu et al., *Toward the Decolonization of African Literature,* 168. Le Roi Jones anticipated the Bolekaja critique of Okigbo. In Jones's review of *Heavensgate,* he observed that "Mr. Okigbo's reading is weakening most of his poems." See Jones, "A Dark Bag," *Poetry* 103, no. 5 (February 1964): 400.

71.   Chinweizu et al., *Toward the Decolonization of African Literature,* 163–74.

72.   Chinweizu, "Prodigals, Come Home!" 1–2; Chinweizu et al., *Toward the Decolonization of African Literature,* 172–79.

73.   Chinweizu et al., *Toward the Decolonization of African Literature,* 189–92, 276–77.

74.   Wole Soyinka, "Aesthetic Illusions: Prescriptions for the Suicide of Poetry," *Third Press Review* 1, no. 1 (September–October 1975): 66. This essay is reprinted in *Reading Black: Essays in the Criticism of African, Caribbean, and Black American Literature,* ed. Houston A. Baker Jr. (Ithaca, N.Y.: Cornell University African Studies and Research Center, 1976).

75.   Kwame Anthony Appiah, "Typologies of Nativism," in *In My Father's House: Africa in the Philosophy of Culture* (New York and Oxford: Oxford University Press, 1992), 59.

76.   See Eileen Julien, *African Novels and the Question of Orality* (Bloomington and Indianapolis: Indiana University Press, 1992); and Ato Quayson, "African Literature and the Question of Orality," in *Strategic Transformations in Nigerian Writing: Rev. Samuel Johnson, Amos Tutuola, Wole Soyinka, and Ben Okri* (Oxford: James Currey; Bloomington and Indianapolis: Indiana University Press, 1997), 1–19.

77.   See, for example, D. Nwoga, "West African Literature in English" (Ph.D. diss., London, 1964).

78.   See, for example, R. N. Egudu, "Okigbo's *Distances:* A Retreat from Christ to Idoto," *Conch* 5, nos. 1–2 (1973): 29–42.

79.   Ibid., 30–41.

80.   Omolara Leslie [Molara Ogundipe-Leslie], "The Poetry of Christopher Okigbo: Its Evolution and Significance," *Ufahamu* 4, no. 1 (Spring 1973): 56.

81.   Donatus I. Nwoga, "Okigbo's *Limits:* An Approach to Meaning," *Journal of Commonwealth Literature* 7, no. 1 (1972): 100.

82.   Ibid., 99.

83. Dan Izevbaye, "Okigbo's Portrait of the Artist as a Sunbird," 2–3.

84. For a similar description of Okigbo's poetics, see O. R. Dathorne, "Okigbo Understood: A Study of Two Poems," *African Literature Today* 1 (1968): 21.

85. Izevbaye, "From Reality to Dream," 131.

86. Ibid.

87. Nwoga, "Okigbo's *Limits,*" 100.

88. Cleanth Brooks, "My Credo: The Formalist Critics," *Kenyon Review* 13 (Winter 1951): 72, quoted in Peter J. Rabinowitz, *Before Reading: Narrative Conventions and the Politics of Interpretation* (Ithaca, N.Y., and London: Cornell University Press, 1987), 141.

89. Achebe and Okafor, *Don't Let Him Die,* viii–ix. Anafulu is quoted in Ngaté, "Two African Prodigals," 132.

90. James Murray Wieland, "The Ensphering Mind: A Comparative Study of History, Myth, and Fictions in Six Commonwealth Poets: A. D. Hope, Allen Curnow, A. M. Klein, Derek Walcott, Christopher Okigbo, and Nissim Ezekiel" (Ph.D. diss., Queen's University, Kingston, Ontario, 1978), ii.

91. Okwu, "The Artist-Figure," ix.

92. Ngaté, "Two African Prodigals," 2. Two years after Ngaté's study, M. Ibrahima Sane completed a French-language comparative study of Senghor and Okigbo entitled "L'Image de l'Africain dans la poésie contemporaine ouest-Africaine: Leopold Senghor et Christopher Okigbo" (Ph.D. diss., Université de Paris III, 1981). Lack of competence in French prevents the editor from discussing this dissertation.

93. Ngaté, "Two African Prodigals," 14–15, 39, 96–101.

94. Ibid., 29.

95. Chukwuma Azuonye, "Okigbo and the Psychological Theories of Carl Gustav Jung," *Journal of African and Comparative Literature* 1, no. 1 (March 1981): 44.

96. Kaja Silverman, *The Subject of Semiotics* (Oxford: Oxford University Press, 1983), 126.

97. Azuonye, "Okigbo and the Psychological Theories of Carl Gustav Jung," 44.

98. Heywood, "The Ritual and the Plot," 47.

99. Okafor, *Nationalism in Okigbo's Poetry,* 10.

100. Okafor, *The Dance of Death,* xiv.

101. Okafor, *The Dance of Death,* 160; Frantz Fanon, *The Wretched of the Earth,* trans. Constance Farrington (New York: Grove Press, 1968), 222–27.

102. Okafor, *The Dance of Death,* 175.

103. Obiechina, "Christopher Okigbo: Poet of Destiny," 208.

104. Ibid., 208–10; and Okigbo, *Labyrinths with Path of Thunder,* xiv.

105. Obiechina, "Christopher Okigbo: Poet of Destiny," 213.

106. Ibid., 214–35.

107. Nwoga, Critical Perspectives on Christopher Okigbo, 4.

108. Nwoga, "The Emergence of the Poet of Destiny: A Study of Okigbo's 'Lament of the Silent Sisters,' " in *Critical Perspectives on Christopher Okigbo,* ed. Donatus Ibe Nwoga (Washington, D.C.: Three Continents Press, 1984), 117.

109. Elaine Savory Fido, "Okigbo's *Labyrinths* and the Context of Igbo Attitudes to the Female Principle," in *Ngambika: Studies of Women in African Literature,* ed. Carole Boyce Davies and Anne Adams Graves (Trenton, N.J.: Africa World Press, 1986), 227.

110. Fraser, *West African Poetry,* 104.

111. Thomas R. Knipp, "Okigbo and *Labyrinths:* The Death of a Poet and the Life of a Poem," *Research in African Literatures* 26, no. 4 (Winter 1995): 199.

112. Fraser, *West African Poetry,* 130–37, 252–55.

113. Catherine Acholonu, "Ogbanje: A Motif and a Theme in the Poetry of Christopher Okigbo," in *Oral and Written Poetry in African Literature Today,* ed. Eldred Durosimi Jones (London: James Currey; Trenton, N.J.: Africa World Press, 1988), 103–5.

114.  Ibid., 105.
115.  Olaogun, "Graphology and Meaning," 111.
116.  Ibid., 125–26.
117.  Said, "The World, the Text, and the Critic," in *The World, the Text, and the Critic* (Cambridge: Harvard University Press, 1983), 53.
118.  Gikandi, *Reading Chinua Achebe,* 95.

# INTERVIEWS

INTERVIEWS

# [Interview, August 1962]

## Lewis Nkosi

NKOSI   Chris, could you just say something about your collection of poems, *Limits*?

OKIGBO   The limit is, I will say, the limit of a dream and the prelude[1] is about one-quarter of it divided into four parts, the first one which is the prelude to the preludes, and the second one which is a response by a chorus, the third one is the first development, and the fourth one is a divagation. Then we go into the heart of the work itself; there are six parts to the main work itself and the last one is almost an epilogue. But I do not think I can say very much about the *Limits*. They happened at the time they happened, and I do not know whether they could have happened at any other time. I wrote the first four parts, in other words, I first wrote the prelude and then there was a long gap of about three months before I did the other parts.

NKOSI   How long did the whole work take you to write?

OKIGBO   Oh, I would say it took—I wasn't working on it all the time but the prelude, the first part of the preludes I did early in August 1961, and I didn't complete the whole work until, I believe, sometime in May 1962.

NKOSI   Is this the first collection of your poems that is going to be published?

OKIGBO   No this is the title poem of the second volume which will be published.

NKOSI   You have had poetry published before in book form?

OKIGBO   Yes, I have *Heavensgate,* which is my first volume published by Mbari Publications.

NKOSI   Who is publishing this latest volume you are working on?

OKIGBO   It is also Mbari Publications. It will be coming off in October with drawings made by Susanne Wenger.

Originally published as "Interviewing Christopher Okigbo, Ibadan, August 1962," in *African Writers Talking: A Collection of Interviews,* ed. Dennis Duerden and Cosmo Pieterse (Oxford: Heinemann Educational Books, 1972). Reprinted by permission of the publisher.

NKOSI    I see. Have you been writing poetry long?
OKIGBO    No, I wouldn't say so.

NKOSI    When did you start?
OKIGBO    I started writing poetry seriously in 1957. I mean everybody wrote poetry at one stage at school and at the university, but I didn't consider that as something very serious. I did some translation from Latin verse to English verse and vice versa but I never really took poetry seriously until 1957, and the first poem I have preserved dates as far back as 1957.

NKOSI    Had you left the university then?
OKIGBO    Yes I had left—I left in 1956.

NKOSI    I see. What inspired you to begin to write? Were you interested in writing before?
OKIGBO    Yes, I was doing a lot of writing before. At school, I was editor of a house magazine. At the university in fact, I had my own newspaper *University Weekly,* which ran into trouble because I didn't have enough money to continue publishing it. But I don't know what inspired me to write poetry other than the fact that—in fact I just started writing poetry at the time, I don't know what inspired me, or what didn't inspire me.

NKOSI    What do you conceive of as your audience? Are there many people in Nigeria who read poetry by the young Nigerian poets?
OKIGBO    In the first place there are not many Nigerians who would read poetry and who would take delight in reading poetry, and there are very few Nigerians who would read poetry that appears difficult. Somehow, I believe I am writing for other poets all over the world to read and see whether they can share in my experience. I believe that the best in poetry has been said, at least for the chamber. Nowadays everything is done for the study and on the few occasions it steals out, I think it is to please, but not a large public. Applause itself is no longer in a necessary personal experience. I think poetry is at the best a mere gesture to stay within a close, closed society or to be liked by the other fellow, one's fellows—so that I don't know how many people would really like to read what I write, but I don't care for applause. I believe that poets anywhere would get hold of my poetry when and if it is published, and it may be possible for them to get something out of the original experience.

NKOSI    Yes, but when you say you don't care for applause, don't you mean that you don't care for the applause from the populace which doesn't really understand the kind of poetry that you write?
OKIGBO    No, because I found that in most cases when my poetry has been applauded, it has been applauded for the wrong reason. I don't think I have

any ambition to become a very popular poet. I think I am just satisfied if a good deal of friends come by my work and get something out of it.

NKOSI   So you really mean that you care for applause from intelligent people like other poets . . .
OKIGBO   Well, if they applaud, I would be delighted that there are some people who think seriously of what I think seriously of. But I don't particularly care . . . I write the thing and it is finished and I particularly would like other poets to get something out of it just as I get something out of the work of other poets, not because I am a poet, but because I think I did take sufficient trouble to go into the thing—to look at the work seriously.

NKOSI   Yes. Chris, there is a circle of very exciting young writers in Nigeria at the moment: could you tell us something about this community; did you use to know each other at the university when most of you were at university, young people like Wole Soyinka, J. P. Clark, and other people who are writing at the moment?
OKIGBO   Yes, I'd say some of us knew ourselves at the university, knew each other, one another, but some of us went before other people. Chinua Achebo, the author of *Things Fall Apart* and *No Longer at Ease,* was with me both at school and at the university. Wole Soyinka was with me at university and we also met at cricket matches when we were at school. Our schools used to play cricket matches against each other. And in fact when Wole made his first public appearance as a singer, I accompanied him at the piano, playing "Amabola," and it was a gorgeous evening. I also accompanied Francisca Pereira, who is now a very well-known singer. I usually accompanied her regularly in musical concerts at U.C.I.[2]

NKOSI   Well, has your interest in music completely vanished since you became a poet?
OKIGBO   Well, I stopped writing music when I started writing poetry seriously, this is in fact what happened, but I just have to have an outlet every time, and I was writing music seriously up to 1956. I started writing poetry when I stopped writing music.

NKOSI   What has happened to this community of writers now that you are all outside the university?
OKIGBO   Well, that is what has given rise to Mbari. We all meet again at the activities organized by Mbari, the Writers' and Artists' Club at Ibadan.

NKOSI   Do you approve of each other's works?
OKIGBO   God forbid! Why should we? How can we approve of each other's work? I mean . . .

NKOSI  Well, I do not know whether the fact that you studied together means that you sort of pat each other on the back on what you are doing. Are there different schools for instance amongst you?

OKIGBO  No, in fact, I think some of us—I think we are all doing different things. J. P. Clark writes poetry, Wole Soyinka writes poetry, and both of them also write well, but they write entirely different things. Wole laughs in his poetry, J. P.'s poetry is more serious, but J. P.'s poetry is quite different from mine and I believe we are doing different things. He has written some very good poems and some very bad poems, and probably I am one of his severe critics, and I think he is one of my greatest adversaries.

NKOSI  I see, that is very interesting. So you do have some kind of literary disagreement?

OKIGBO  Oh yes, we do—a great deal of it.

NKOSI  Are you intending to write only poetry or do you want to write other things besides poetry?

OKIGBO  At the moment I don't know. I was thinking of working on a novel and really did make a start, but I don't know whether I'll ever finish it or even if I finish, whether it will be worth reading. I think that probably I would continue writing poetry until I'm grown up completely, but I do work on other things, you see, when I am not writing poetry. As much as possible, I keep practising—I mean I try to keep informed. If I have nothing to say, I translate from Latin verse into English verse or from Greek verse into English verse and vice versa. I mean if I have nothing to say, I just keep translating—keep playing with work because I have seen that a poet, apart from being a writer, is also a technician. I mean I believe in this. I believe that there is an adage or proverb which says that there is a craft and it isn't just the art alone, there must be the craft. There is real carpentry also apart from the art, and *that* you have to keep practising. This one thing which gives me . . .

NKOSI  So you don't believe in accidental poetry, if I may interrupt?

OKIGBO  A poem can come by accident and a lot of it does come by accident, but it has to be moulded into the form in which you want it preserved and this means a lot of—this embraces the question of craftsmanship. I believe that there is craft apart from the art—if there is craft alone, then you can easily see through the thing and see that there isn't any feeling but art isn't enough, there must be craft also.

NKOSI  Do you have a working knowledge of Greek and Latin?

OKIGBO  Yes: in fact I think that I have a fairly *good* knowledge of Latin, a working knowledge of Greek.

NKOSI  Enough to translate poetry from Greek to English?

OKIGBO    Oh yes. In fact enough Latin to read and understand Latin poetry in the original, and understand before I translate—and in fact enough Greek to translate Greek poetry into English.

NKOSI    What are your main influences in poetry, who influenced you most?
OKIGBO    I think that what has influenced me most is not in fact poets, but the composers, the musical composers are the people who have influenced me more than poets.

NKOSI    Yes. Could you tell us how this influence has worked on your poetry?
OKIGBO    Well, it is very difficult for me to explain, but take "Heavensgate": when I was working on "Heavensgate," I was working under the spell of the impressionist composers Debussy, Caesar Franck, Ravel, and I think that, as in the music of these composers who write of a watery, shadowy, nebulous world, with the semitones of dream and the nuances of the rainbow, there isn't any clearly defined outline in my work: this is what happened in my "Heavensgate." As it stands now, there are parts of it I like very much, some parts of it I don't like but I preserve because—either because friends like it or because they just belong to the work and I really don't want to disrupt the work. I don't want to interfere with the created thing too much once it's done: I will let people pick what they like and leave the rest. Yes, I think that the musicians have influenced me much more than—well, of course, it is the same thing except that the composer is working in abstract form and the poet is working with words.

NKOSI    Chris, at the Kampala conference that we attended, you said some very vile things about negritude poets, about Senghor[3] and other French-speaking African poets. Could you say what you dislike so much about negritude poetry?
OKIGBO    It is not that I dislike it, it is because when you've read a lot of it you just hit through the whole pattern, you begin to have the feeling, or I begin to have the feeling that it is just like working a machine or, if you like, working a *duplicating* machine, you think that it is so easy to do. I don't know how much genuine feelings we have in a lot of negritude poems and the pity of it is that some of the negritude poets could still have been great poets in spite of negritude. I certainly like Senghor a great deal and I like a lot of him: I still believe that he has the loudest voice in Africa.

NKOSI    Just to end this discussion, what do you feel is the greatest lack as far as the literary community in Nigeria is concerned? Amongst the young writers, for instance, what do you think you need most?
OKIGBO    This is a very difficult question for me to answer because I would be able to say what *I* need most, but I would not know what other people need most.

NKOSI    Yes, could you tell us about you?

OKIGBO    What I need most is a more intelligent audience, that's all.


*Notes*

1.    In some versions, the first four sections of *Limits* are entitled "Prelude To The Limits"; in the Mbari publication they are called "Siren Limits" and the last six parts "Fragments out of the Deluge."

2.    University College, Ibadan.

3.    Leopold Sédar Senghor, Senegal—cf. poems in Beier-Moore, Reed-Wake; poems and prose in Reed and Wake's Oxford Univ. Press 3 Crowns edition, and the poems of *Nocturnes,* translated by Reed and Wake (Heinemann, AWS 71).

# [Interview, July 1965]

## ROBERT SERUMAGA

SERUMAGA   Chris, is "Lament of the Drums" a poem you wrote?

OKIGBO   Well, I really don't think I can claim to have written it. All I did was to create the drums, and the drums said what they liked. Personally I don't believe that I am capable of saying what the drums have said in that first part: it's only the long funeral drums that are capable of saying it and they are capable of saying it only at that moment when they talk; then they've said it. They are not capable now or in the future of saying that. So, I don't think that I can claim to have written the poem; all I did was to cover the drums, and to create the situation in which the drums spoke what they spoke.

SERUMAGA   There is a feature in your poetry, specially in the choral poetry—which is the period now you are in, it seems to me—there is a feature of it which it's very difficult perhaps to understand using the intellect only, but when one reads it, one responds to it. How do you explain that?

OKIGBO   Well, because what we call, understanding—talking generally of the relationship between the poetry-reader and the poem itself—passes through a process of analysis, if you like, of the intellectual—there is an intellectual effort which one makes before one arrives at what one calls the meaning. Now I think it is possible to arrive at a response without passing through that process of intellectual analysis, and I think that if a poem can elicit a response, either in physical or emotional terms from an audience, the poem has succeeded. Personally I don't think that I have ever set out to communicate a meaning. It is enough that I try to communicate experience which I consider significant.

SERUMAGA   In other words your approach—what it does really is to make one feel and then understand, rather than make one understand and then feel? Is it?

OKIGBO   Probably that.

Originally published as "Interview with Christopher Okigbo, London, July 1965," in *African Writers Talking: A Collection of Interviews,* ed. Dennis Duerden and Cosmo Pieterse (Oxford: Heinemann Educational Books, 1972). Reprinted by permission of the publisher.

SERUMAGA   Well, before you came to this period of choral poetry, you were writing in a sort of personal vein, for example in your poem, "Heavensgate." What made you change from the personal to the choral?

OKIGBO   I don't think that we can call that a change, because when we talk of my changing from the personal to the choral, it looks as if I made some effort, a conscious effort, as if I had, in fact, designed it. There wasn't any such thing. I found myself as a poet being called upon to show a particular type of responsibility and "Heavensgate" and "Limits," and also "Distances," are in fact the way I have responded to that call. They are, I think, poems that deal with intense, personal experience, and they are, as it were, my own way of responding to an intensely ritualistic experience.

SERUMAGA   There is, on the one hand, what you call ritualistic experience in many of your poems; also there are three themes, death, birth and reincarnation, and when one reads the images that you put in your poetry, one gets the impression (I think this is not a mistake), the impression that you are very close to the traditions of your own society, is this true?

OKIGBO   This is true. In fact, I think that it is a lot of nonsense talk all this we hear nowadays of men of two worlds. I belong, integrally, to my own society just as, I believe, I belong also integrally to some societies other than my own. The truth, of course, is that the modern African is no longer a product of an entirely indigenous culture. The modern sensibility which the modern African poet is trying to express, is by its very nature complex, and it is a complex of values, some of which are indigenous, some of which are exotic, some of which are traditional, some of which are modern. Some of these values we are talking about are Christian, some are non-Christian, and I think that anybody who thinks it is possible to express consistently only one line of values, indigenous or exotic, is probably being artificial.

SERUMAGA   Quite true. And I'd like to explore further your connection with traditional and non-traditional values. Is there anything particular in your life, in the society in which you live which would give you this particular benefit over others (as it seems to me) of being in communication with the traditions more than many people are?

OKIGBO   Well, my maternal grandfather was the head of a particular type of religion which is intimately connected with my village and since I am a reincarnation of my maternal grandfather, I carried this on, and I began to show them my responsibilities in that direction as soon as I grew up; and even when I went to secondary school, I had to take something out of my pocket-money regularly to send home to my grandmother for my maternal uncle who was, as it were, standing in for me until I should grow up to carry on the various periodic rites which were connected with the worship of this particular Deity. And my "Heavensgate," is, in fact, designed to do that sort of thing—it is my own contribution to this.

SERUMAGA   Perhaps this is a pertinent question: does your being a Christian, conflict in any way, in your own mind, with your other duties in this other . . .
OKIGBO   Oh no, I think it is just a way of going to the same place by two different routes. You can now fly from Lagos to London via Rome, on your way back you can fly from London to Lagos via Barcelona. I don't think that there is any conflict. Personally I have never experienced any conflict whatso-ever in this direction. I wear an Italian jacket—I'm not an Italian, I'm an African. I wear a tie and I'm very comfortable. I'm not wearing Nigerian dress—I'm not comfortable in Nigerian dress—it doesn't make me a non-Nigerian. This afternoon I ate lamb chops—tomorrow afternoon I may eat pounded yam at Nigeria House, and I would still enjoy it. It doesn't make me non-Nigerian, or more Nigerian!

SERUMAGA   Talking about your influences in the other direction, or from the other direction there is the non-African influence. From where did you draw these influences—of course granted that they have now been completely inte-grated into one personality—where did they come from?
OKIGBO   I think that I've been influenced by various literatures and cultures, right from Classical times to the present day, in English, Latin, Greek and a little French, a little Spanish, but I think that in fact the question of influence is a very complicated thing. One reads something and says, this might have been influenced by one person. It's often difficult to pin down an influence to a particular source. If those sources have become assimilated into the subject and have come together to form an integral whole it is very difficult to sort them out—to know where the Babylonian influence ends and the classical influence starts, and where the classical influence ends, and where, if you like, the modern influence starts. I have been influenced, generally, by Greek and Roman poets and writers and also by modern English, French, Spanish poets.

SERUMAGA   You read classics at the University?
OKIGBO   Yes.

SERUMAGA   It is quite evident from your poetry that there is this influence. But you consider it now to be completely integrated into a whole?
OKIGBO   It is in fact completely integrated. You know yourself that in my "Lament of the Drums" there is a treatment of the theme of Palinurus. In one section they are identifying the feet of the personage for whom the drums are lamenting with the feet of Palinurus. In another section of "Lament of the Drums" there is a variation on the theme of Ishtar's Lament for Tammuz. This is taken from a Babylonian myth. So that in "Lament of the Drums" alone, we have both: the first part is influenced by the oral tradition in African poetry, because the first part is the drums' invocation—the drums invoking the various elements from which they are made; in the second part they enter their theme song and talk of "Babylonian capture," they talk of

martyrdom, and we remember Christ and Judas and the betrayal; and in the third part they go into the story of Palinurus; they come back in the fourth section, tired and exhausted from their long journey to Rome, and in the fifth section they end with a variation on Ishtar's Lament for Tammuz. So now we have the sort of thing I'm talking about. We have traditional elements, we have classical elements, we have Babylonian elements.

SERUMAGA   But these, when you bring them together in a poem like this one, this is not a conscious attempt to bring them in by natural reaction to the environment.

OKIGBO   In fact, the third part, dealing with Palinurus was written before the other parts, and there is a three months' gap separating that third part from the other parts. I wrote the third part and subtitled it "Lament of the Mariner" and later the theme grew in me, after I had completed it, and I found that that mariner, for whom the flutes and the drums lamented in the third part, which was Palinurus, had grown also into a vegetation God— Tammuz.

SERUMAGA   When we come back to the problem of communication: there is a question often raised about your poetry—that a poet should be able to give society a definite message. Do you agree with this?

OKIGBO   It is difficult for me to answer "yes" or "no" because I can only answer in terms of my own work, because my own work should bear witness to what I believe. "Heavensgate" and "Limits" do not attempt to carry any message whatsoever. If anybody reads a message into them, all well and good. The poems have nothing to do with me, the poems live their own separate lives and when you've created a poem, written a poem it is just like creating something, I'm giving it life. It goes to one audience and speaks one language, goes to another person and speaks a different language—it may go to another person and remain mute and no message is delivered, so that when we talk in terms of communication, it is something that is a little complicated. "Heavensgate" and "Limits"—I didn't have any particular message in mind when I created the two of them. But since then I've started writing through other persons. When I created the drums all I did was to create the drums and the message they deliver has nothing to do with me at all. It just happens that there might be some political tinge in the message of the drums and also the message of the silent sisters[1]—there might also be some political tinge there—but the message has nothing to do with me, nor has it anything to do with my intention.

SERUMAGA   Well talking about your intention, perhaps this is not really an intention, but how long do you feel you are going to go on with this choral poetry?

OKIGBO    I don't know, I wish I could go on for ever, but as you see I don't write very often. In 1962 I wrote only one poem—the whole of 1962, only one poem—"Lament of the Silent Sisters." In 1963 I believe I wrote none. I probably wrote one or two things. But that doesn't mean that I don't keep working. Eventually I decide to present one or two. Last year I wrote "Lament of the Drums" and "Distances," but that was all. This year I wrote "Painted Maidens" and "Lament of the Masks,"[2] and if tomorrow night for instance, I happen to write a poem, I write a poem; if I don't happen to write a poem, I don't bother. I do other things. Poetry is not an alternative to living. It is only one way of supplementing life and if I can live life in its fullness without writing at all, I don't care to write. I haven't got that type of ambition, which some people may have, of becoming a great writer or something like that. Because that is not an alternative to life itself.

*Notes*

This interview with Robert Serumaga was made in Dover Street during the Commonwealth Arts Festival in July 1965. One of the Festival's poetry readings featured, among others, Okigbo's "Lament of the Drums."

1.    "Lament of the Silent Sisters," published first in *Transition;* now included in *Labyrinths,* Okigbo's collected poetry published by Heinemann (AWS 62).

2.    Untraced.

# Interview with Christopher Okigbo, 1965

## Marjory Whitelaw

*Christopher Okigbo, who was born in 1932 and killed in the Nigerian civil war in 1967, was one of the most talented of the West African poets. He was educated at University College, Ibadan, where he read Classics. When I met him he was the Nigerian representative of Cambridge University Press, and living in Ibadan. I recorded this interview with him one warm afternoon in March 1965, in Ibadan. I had met him at the house of a mutual friend who was on the faculty of the University of Ibadan; I thus came to the interview with good credentials, and Christopher accepted me as someone with a serious interest in African life, and talked to me very freely about his poetry.*

*His house was large and well-furnished, with possibly an Italian air about it; the windows were wide open, and, as always in Africa, sounds of the abundant life outside floated into the room—roosters crowed, children laughed, many birds called, and all were recorded on the tape.*

*We began talking about questions being discussed at the time: a writer's commitment to his society, and whether African poets should concern themselves with their African-ness, or, in the phrase of the French African poet Senghor, their négritude:*

*M.W.:* Christopher, do you think of yourself as an *African* poet?
*Okigbo:* I think I am just a poet. A poet writes poetry and once the work is published it becomes public property. It's left to whoever reads it to decide whether it's African poetry or English. There isn't any such thing as a poet trying to express African-ness. Such a thing doesn't exist. A poet expresses himself.

*M.W.:* What about poets who express négritude?
*Okigbo:* Yes, but that is different because it is a particular type of poetry. It is platform poetry. It is platform writing. It is just like being invited to deliver a lecture on a particular subject. But it is valid as poetry when it is good, because we do in fact have this sort of thing in our own poetry in the oral tradition. The poetry of praise, for instance. Platform poetry. You go to a king's

Originally published in *Journal of Commonwealth Literature* 9 (July 1970): 28–37. Reproduced with permission from Bowker-Saur, a division of Reed Business Information Limited, and Marjory Whitelaw.

palace to praise him, and you build up images in praise of him. That sort of poetry is valid provided it is good.

In other forms of poetry . . . the most regular form that is written by young African poets, writing in the English language, is in fact written to express, to bring out a sense of an inner disturbance. We are trying to cast about for words; whether the words are in Ibo or English or in French is in fact immaterial . . . We are looking for words to give verbal concreteness, to give verbal life to auditory and visual images . . . I think this is a separate form of poetry from platform poetry. It just happens that one form is written more here, among English-speaking poets, and one more among French. But the two forms are valid, and I don't quarrel with négritude.

*M.W.:* When you meet the French African poets, do you find that you approach the subject of writing poetry with any kind of agreement?
*Okigbo:* There isn't any kind of agreement. And this doesn't happen only when I come across African poets writing in French. There isn't any agreement at all, even in Nigeria. Some of my contemporaries have different techniques—but this is because they are different persons altogether, and each of us reacts to situations differently from other persons . . . And one person's sensibility is also different from another person's sensibility, and I think that this sort of difference doesn't exist only among Nigerians; it exists all over the world. This is in fact what makes one poem different from another. I have written poems on the same sort of themes as some of my contemporaries—and the poems were entirely different.

*M.W.:* I'm really thinking about the effect of the two very different systems of education (in what were the former colonies of British and French Africa) and the way in which they have produced rather different kinds of people.
*Okigbo:* I think that one major difference in the system of education (if you like, the difference in the colonial system we were subjected to) is the fact that the French African poet finds himself uprooted and casting about for his lost roots. I do not find that sense of alienation because I have always belonged to my own society, and I've never felt uprooted from it. I still go back home for village festivals, and for the more important religious ceremonies.

But the African poet writing in French may not in fact be experiencing this sense of integration, and so he feels uprooted. I believe this is probably what gave birth to the feeling of négritude, and naturally this became translated into political terms, and has now also become an intellectual slogan.

*M.W.:* You say you go back to village festivals—I know you write a great deal about these.

*Okigbo:*   Yes, I do. And I do not feel that in fact as a Christian I have ever been uprooted from my own village gods. We have a goddess and a god in our family, our ancestral gods. And although I do not worship these actively, in the sense of offering them periodic sacrifices, I still feel that they are the people protecting me.

But the way in which I think Christianity can be reconciled with this aspect of paganism is that I believe in fact all these gods are the same as the Christian God—that they are different aspects of the same power, the same force.

*M.W.:*   What shape do these gods take in your family?
*Okigbo:*   Well, we have a carved idol representing a man, and another carved idol representing a woman, and the man we call Ikenga, and the woman we call Udo. And the man is the father of the entire family, for several generations back; the woman is the mother of the whole family, several generations back. And in a large extended family we have just these two gods, Ikenga and Udo.

We offer sacrifices to them periodically. I am here at Ibadan; I don't live at home at Ojoto. So my parents or my uncles will offer sacrifices to them periodically. And the women of the family will from time to time scrub the walls of the shrine where these gods are housed, with fresh mud (the walls of the shrine would be of a mud mixture, a very satisfactory and inexpensive building substance), and the men of the family will repair the thatched roof to prevent it leaking. And once in a while they offer a white hen, or eggs laid by white hens, or kola nuts, or pods of alligator pepper. And I feel, you know, that we still belong to these things. We cannot get away from them.

*M.W.:*   This is purely a family shrine, is it?
*Okigbo:*   This is a family shrine. We have the ones worshipped by the whole town. The whole town, for example, worships the python and the tortoise. The python, I imagine, represents the male deity, and the tortoise represents the female deity. And the whole town worships these two idols, and they (the creatures) are sacred to the whole town. I mean they are sacred to their particular shrines, and we cannot kill them. If in fact you find a python that is dead, you give it a ceremonial burial. Oh, yes. This still happens, even now. And Christianity cannot wipe this out.

*M.W.:*   What does the python symbolize, then?
*Okigbo:*   The python represents the penis. And the tortoise represents the clitoris. One for the male organ and the other for the female.

*M.W.:*   Do you also go to the Christian church?
*Okigbo:*   I haven't gone to church for a long time.

*M.W.:* (*Laughing*) Neither have I. This is a rather theoretical question . . . But you think of yourself as a sort of nominal Christian, do you?

*Okigbo:* I think that over the years I have tried to evolve my own personal religion. The way that I worship my gods is in fact through poetry. And I think that each poem I write is a ceremony of innocence, if you like. The creative process is a process of cleansing. And since I began actively to write poetry, I have never gone to church. So I don't think it would be right for me to say I am a Christian or I am a pagan. I think my own religion combines elements from both.

*M.W.:* When you are away from home, away from the family shrine, is there no need for you to make any religious gestures?

*Okigbo:* No, because these things are done on behalf of the whole family by the people who look after the shrine, members of the family who are at home. There isn't any Ibo family which doesn't have people living at home to carry out these religious observances. And I've never felt the need to go back home to do that because I have people doing it for me. I mean the whole family is one. Just as all the fingers belong to the same hand, the whole family is one. My house belongs to the whole family. Members of the family can come here at any time they like. This is in fact one aspect of the extended family system.

*M.W.:* It's very hard for a lot of Europeans (white people) to understand some of this, because we always tend to think of educated Africans as being faced with a terrible conflict of two cultures, a conflict between the old culture and the new . . .

*Okigbo:* Well, I think the conflict is at times imagined. And where it does exist, it means that the individuals have never really been fully integrated in either of the two cultures, either the traditional one or the European culture.

*M.W.:* You don't feel any conflict?

*Okigbo:* No, I have never felt that conflict. I go out to sophisticated parties in European suits, I come home and they serve me pounded yam in my house, and I eat it with my fingers . . . because this is the only way I have eaten it since I was a child. I have never eaten pounded yam with a knife and fork. This conflict doesn't exist in me.

I have noticed that some of my friends have experienced such conflict—it may be that they have never been fully rooted in the African traditional society or even the European one.

*M.W.:* Do you think that for a lot of Africans today it is difficult to be African?

*Okigbo:* I don't see why it should be difficult. I don't think there is any culture in the world that doesn't have borrowed elements. There is this multivalence in all cultures. Africa happens to be a new society, new in the sense that people are just beginning to know about Africa. So this multivalence is emphasized. It is just like holding something under a microscope—it becomes enlarged. Africa is now under the world's microscope; everybody sees Africa, and nobody bothers to look at any other place.

*M.W.:* I think most Europeans have the idea that if any writer should be "committed" (to use this literary cliché) it should be the African writers. I mean committed to writing about social change, about discovery of identity—that is, he should not be working in isolation, in an ivory tower; he should not have removed himself from the preoccupations of the people of his own time.
*Okigbo:* Yes, but there isn't any society in which people do not write about social change. Social change is not only taking place in Africa; it's taking place everywhere in the world.

*M.W.:* Yes, but in North America particularly there are writers who feel that the writer has a duty to discover himself rather than to discover the world. Thirty years ago writers like Thomas Wolfe were writing about the great panorama of American life, but today they seem, many of them, to be isolated from their contemporaries, to be concerned with self-exploration. They feel no responsibility whatever to their own society. Now the point I want to make is that we in the West might suppose that (because Africa is under such violent pressures of change) it would be difficult for African writers to evade this responsibility.
*Okigbo:* Yes, but I don't think that this sense of responsibility is fulfilled only by writing directly about the change in society, about social change. I believe that any writer who attempts a type of inward exploration will in fact be exploring his own society indirectly. Because the writer isn't *living* in isolation. He is interacting with different groups of people at different times. And any inward exploration involves the interaction of the subject with other people, and I believe that a writer who sets out to discover himself, by so doing will also discover his society.

I don't think that I like writing that is "committed." I think it is very cheap. I think it is the easy way of doing it. Much more difficult than that, of course, is inward exploration. I hope that ultimately people will start doing that sort of thing in Africa. They haven't started doing it yet.

*M.W.:* What would you say, then, is the function of the writer in Africa?
*Okigbo:* Oh, the writer in Africa doesn't have any function. That is, personally I can only say what I conceive as my own function. I have no function as a writer; I think I merely express myself, and the public can use these things for anything they like. I mean . . . you read a poem to a child; a child may

weep. You may read the same poem to other people, and they may burst out into laughter. I don't in fact think that it is necessary for the writer to assume a particular function as The Messiah or anything like that . . . Well, as an individual he could assume this sort of role, but I don't think that the fact that he's a writer should entitle him to assume a particular role as an educator. If he wants to educate people he should write text books. If he wants to preach a gospel he should write religious tracts. If he wants to propound a certain ideology he should write political tracts.

*M.W.:*   I liked Chinua Achebe's idea[1] that the writer was in a sense the teacher also—that is, in Africa.
*Okigbo:*   Indirectly—because everything written in English here is educational. Because people are just learning English, learning it as a second language. So anything written in English becomes educational, whether it is history or poetry or fiction. And indirectly the writer is a teacher. But it isn't only the writer; the newspaper editor is also, indirectly, a teacher. There are lots of people who read nothing except newspapers.

*M.W.:*   Who reads your poems?
*Okigbo:*   I don't know. But I've read my poems to different groups of people. I went to Kano once (in the Northern Region)[2] and I was invited to give a talk at a school, to the whole school. And because I had not prepared a talk, I read one or two poems, and the children burst into tears. I felt that . . . at least they had had experience of the agony I had gone through . . . You know the process of writing the particular poems I read to them had been agonizing. And I thought that they had had a share of the agony of composition. I don't know who reads my poems and I don't think I care. I think that once I've written a poem I've given it a life of its own and the poem should go to anyone it likes. Anybody who is prepared to open his door to it.

*M.W.:*   The poem should go to anybody *it* likes . . . ?
*Okigbo:*   Well, anybody who is willing to let it in. After all, if you go to somebody's house and knock on the door he may open the door or he may not; he may open the door and say, "Good afternoon; I am sorry, I'm resting, I'm busy." Well, I mean the poem should just be treated as a person having its own life, a life of its own. This is the way in which I think of my work.

I think that when a word is committed to print it develops legs, wings even, and goes anywhere it wants to go. It is the same as a talking drum. You may want to speak to someone in a different village; when you play the drum and give him the message, he is not the only one who is listening to it. Anybody who is awake at the time listens to it. And those who wish to take the message will take it. I think the poem has this sort of existence, quite apart from the author.

*M.W.:*   How old were you when you wrote your first poem?

*Okigbo:*   My first published poem . . . Well, my first poem, I believe I was about fourteen. But I haven't preserved it. When I was at school, I contributed poems to our school magazine, but I believe most people did that. We were just learning to speak English at the time. But my first published poem was written when I was twenty-five. My first published poem—it was very short. It is in a back number of *Black Orpheus.*

*M.W.:*   Was there a stage in your life when you decided that you definitely wished to be a poet?

*Okigbo:*   There wasn't a stage when I decided that I definitely wished to be a poet; there was a stage when I found that I couldn't be anything else. And I think that the turning point came in December 1958, when I knew that I couldn't be anything else than a poet. It's just like somebody who receives a call in the middle of the night to religious service, in order to go and become a priest of a particular cult, and I didn't have any choice in the matter. I just had to obey.

*M.W.:*   From where did the call come?

*Okigbo:*   *(Laughing)* I don't know. I wish I knew. I wish I knew. I can't say whether the call came from evil spirits or good spirits. But I know that the turning point came in 1958, when I found myself wanting to know myself better, and I had to turn around and look at myself from inside.

*M.W.:*   And when you say "self," does this mean not only self but also the ancestors, the background?

*Okigbo:*   *(Emphatically)* No. I mean myself, just myself, not the background . . . But you know that everything has added up to building up the self. So when I talk of the self, I mean my various selves, because the self itself is made up of various elements which do not always combine happily. And when I talk of looking inward to myself, I mean turning inward to examine myselves. This of course takes account of ancestors . . . Because I do not exist apart from my ancestors.

In fact I am generally believed, at home, to be a reincarnation of my maternal grandfather, my mother's father . . . although I don't know if this is true, because I didn't meet him in this world. But I know that people return to the world after they are dead, in different forms.

But when I talk of myself, I mean the whole—everything that has gone to make me what I am, and different from somebody else. And this takes account of the ancestry. One cannot escape from that fact. And I don't think this is an entirely African idea.

*M.W.:*   No, no. I am much involved with my own ancestors.

*Okigbo:*   It is unimportant that I don't go to the family shrine to sacrifice the fruits of the soil. My creative activity is in fact one way of performing those functions in a different manner. Every time I write a poem, I am in fact offering a sacrifice. My *Heavensgate* is in fact a huge sacrifice.

As I said, I am believed to be a reincarnation of my maternal grandfather, who used to be the priest of the shrine called Ajani, where Idoto, the river goddess, is worshipped. This goddess is the earth mother, and also the mother of the whole family. My grandfather was the priest of this shrine, and when I was born I was believed to be his reincarnation, that is, I should carry on his duties. And although someone else had to perform his functions, this other person was only, as it were, a regent. And in 1958, when I started taking poetry very seriously, it was as though I had felt a sudden call to begin performing my full functions as the priest of Idoto. That is how it happened.

The opening passage of *Heavensgate,* my first volume of poems published in 1963, is as follows:

> Before you, mother Idoto,
> naked I stand,
> before your watery presence,
> a prodigal,
>
> leaning on an oilbean,
> lost in your legend . . .
>
> Under your power wait I
>     on barefoot,
> watchman for the watchword
>     at heavensgate;
>
> out of the depths my cry
> give ear and hearken.

And there is another part of *Heavensgate.* This is entitled "Lustra," in other words, the rites I perform periodically. And I wrote this when I moved from one house to another. This was the first one I wrote in the new place. And I had to start once more, performing these functions. I will read a part of it and then explain it so that you will understand my own idea of the creative process. There wasn't any question of my taking a decision, you see. It is that I found myself some time ago ready to assume the full responsibilities of a religious priest—a religious priest in the very serious sense of the word:

> So would I to the hills again
> so would I
> to where springs the fountain
> there to draw from

and to hilltop clamber
body and soul
whitewashed in the moondew
there to see from

So would I from my eye the mist
so would I
through moonmist to hilltop
there for the cleansing

Here is a new-laid egg
here a white hen at midterm . . .

*(Here Christopher stopped reading and began once more to talk.)* And the new-laid egg of course is the poem. And the white hen at midterm is the poem . . . And this poem in fact appears in the middle of *Heavensgate*. A white hen at midterm—I mean midterm in the sense of this poem being written in the middle of a longer work. *(Long pause.)*

I take my work seriously because it is the only reason I am alive. I believe that . . . I believe that writing poetry is a necessary part of my being alive, which is why I've written nothing else. I hardly write prose. I've not written a novel. I've not written a play. Because I think that somehow the medium itself is sufficiently elastic to say what I want to say, I haven't felt the need to look for some other medium.

*Here we stopped, for we were both exhausted; the interview had demanded a good deal of both of us, and even now, in re-typing the transcript, I can recollect my feeling of having participated in Christopher's own creative processes. His death in 1967, in the war in Nigeria, makes me all the more grateful that I was able to obtain this record of his attitude to poetry, and to his own work.*

*Notes*

1.   Chinua Achebe, the Nigerian novelist, had recently written an article for the *New Statesman* in which he expressed this point of view. Christopher's reply to this question is based on the fact that all but primary education in Nigeria is in English, but this is a second language, of course, and all Nigerians must work very hard to acquire real fluency.

2.   Of Nigeria.

# REVIEWS

REVIEWS

# The Mbari Publications
# [Review of *Heavensgate,*
# by Christopher Okigbo]

### Denis Williams

*Heavensgate*, poems by Christopher Okigbo, is another matter entirely. Here is measure, control, *craft,* and a refinement of utterance that at times verges on the precious. (Stretch, stretch O antennae / to clutch at this hour). But these poems stand alone in their prodigious ambitiousness. Mr. Okigbo's is the classic vision in which the artist is himself refined out of existence and stands behind the work "paring his fingernails." It is obvious that his preoccupation with the word, with "pure" poetry, should lead a young poet face to face with the fathers, with T. S. Eliot and Ezra Pound most patently in this case. Disconcerting though the result may sometimes be, one feels that the poet is himself sufficiently objective, sufficiently aware of craft as an obsessive concern, to be in no great danger. A passage in *Initiation* for instance, reminds us of lines in one of the Pound CANTOS (I quote from memory):

> And then Elpenor came, our friend Elpenor,
> Unburied, cast on the wide earth . . . etc.

Mr. Okigbo sings:

> So comes John the Baptist
> with bowl of salt water
> preaching the gambit:
> life without sin, without
> life; which accepted,
> way leads downwards
> down orthocenter
> avoiding decisions.

Here, as unfortunately elsewhere, the tone released by the words just doesn't ring true. But the *Initiation* sequence ends:

Originally published in *Nigeria Magazine* 75 (1962): 69–74. Reprinted by permission.

> And there are here
> the errors of the rendering.

It is the occupational pitfall of the artist who attempts that most austere of all disciplines—the articulation of form through the barest, purest relationships he can fashion. His means and processes being so few, he is continually exposed. In the nature of his craft he refuses the equivoque, the ambivalence of emotive writing; the bare stuff left to him is not the stuff for exaltation. It can be put to the sublimest use only by honesty and rigour. Mr. Okigbo obviously possesses both virtues. In the *Watermaid* sequence the voice is authentic and moving:

> So I who am here abandoned,
> count the sand
> by wavelash abandoned,
> count her blessing,
> my white queen.
>
> And the spent sea reflects
> from his mirrored visage
> not my queen,
> a broken shadow.
>
> So I who count in my island
> the moments,
> count the hour which will bring
> my lost queen
> with angel's ash in the wind.

But it is disconcerting in the *Newcomer* to return to:

> of kindred spirits
> anagnorisis and
> ditto of self the prodigal . . .

Here the error is truly in the rendering. We can rest assured however, that Mr. Okigbo is very well aware of the fact.

# *Limits,*
# by Christopher Okigbo

## O. R. Dathorne

Christopher Okigbo's poetry is all one poem; it is the evolution of a personal religion. The poet is a messiah, suppliant, apostle and worshipper. In *Heavensgate* the protagonist moves through various states of spiritual experience which begin with the surrender of the body and the material, to the mortification of crucifixion and the pain of self-knowledge:

> And I said:
> except by rooting,
> who could pluck yam tubers
> from their base?

The endeavour reveals guilt ("whose secret I have planted into beachsand"), cosmic alienation ("The stars have departed and I—where am I?") and finally culminates in the preparation for the betrayal "at the cock's third siren," which anticipates conversion which is itself the annihilation of self.

*Silences* which appeared in *Transition* 8 is the liturgy of the intending initiates who "camp in a convent in the open" and *Limits,* exploring the penetralia of the unconscious state of non-being, narrates the progress towards *nirvana.* The opening images of the first part, *Siren Limits,* describe the reunification of flesh and soul. This can happen because "I have had my cleansing" and we are told:

> Into the soul
> The selves extended their branches. . . .

> And out of the solitude
> Voice and soul with selves unite. . . .

Originally published as *"Limits, by Christopher Okigbo," Black Orpheus* 15 (1964): 59–60. Reprinted by permission of O. R. Dathorne and the Association of Caribbean Studies.

This is a harmonisation with the natural world, one that can wound, but the masochism from "the cruelty of the rose" is aesthetically purifying:

> When you have finished
> And done up my stitches
> Wake me near the altar. . . .

In the second part of *Limits, Fragments Out of the Deluge,* we get first a description of the ruin that is a *sine qua non* of the revolution of the spirit and out of this ruin comes about the regeneration of novelty:

> UPON an empty sarcophagus
>   out of solid alabaster
> A branch of giant fennel,
>   on an empty sarcophagus. . . .

The renewal of life clarifies the mystery of living. Christ, Buddha, anyone who has been re-born out of the dead, knows the truth about self and matter, a truth that eludes others:

> HE STOOD in the midst of them all
>   and appeared in true form
> He found them drunken, he found none
>   thirsty among them.

HE of course knew they were thirsty. The inevitable process of martyrdom followed and too late people asked the "KEY-WORD from stone."

The poet re-assumes the role of personal quest in IX. The Sunbird has been killed, the twin-gods are killed:

> And the gods lie in state
> And the gods lie in state
> Without the long-drum
>
> And the gods lie unsung
> And the gods lie
> Veiled only with mould. . . .

The protagonist who began in *Heavensgate* as a suppliant is deified. This is the last glory of flesh i.e. to be a living god and the final triumph over death and re-incarnation i.e. to be a dead god. It is this that re-vitalises the protagonist, making him symbiotic with non-being: & the cancelling out is complete.

# Shadows of Prophecy
# [Review of *Labyrinths,* by Christopher Okigbo]

PETER THOMAS

This paperback collection of Christopher Okigbo's poems, published under the general title of *Labyrinths,* brings together in final form sequences previously published by Mbari Publications, Ibadan, as *Heavensgate* (1962), *Limits* (1964), and *Silences* (1965), with the addition of *Distances* and *Path of Thunder,* which the poet saw as "organically related" to the rest of his work. I would judge this to be true of any poet's work, and in the light of what I knew of the man this posthumous volume presents to my hindsight not only a voice from beyond the grave, but a conjuring of shadows prophetic of his sudden, violent, and untimely end.

In addition to *Labyrinths,* I have on my shelves an autographed copy of the Mbari edition of *Heavensgate,* addressed "From one poet to another"—and in my files is an early typescript of *The Limits and Other Poems,* bearing on its title page the inscription: "I could never have written this if I did not meet you." I have also a handful of lined sheets torn from a loose-leaved notebook on which Christopher had typed for me some of his earliest attempts at poetry, together with a trial version of what now appears as "Newcomer" at the end of the revised *Heavensgate* sequence. Originally entitled "A Bridge," it is dated 31 December 1960, with the pencilled greeting, "Wishing you whatever you wish me at the turning of the year." These, and a passing reference to my "yet unpublished" work in the Introduction to *Labyrinths,* are my only tangible record of a five-year friendship that grew into something like brotherhood between a now famous West African poet and a still obscure British expatriate devoted to the same exacting craft.

The original *Heavensgate* paid tribute to that friendship in a poem celebrating our recognition of each other's gifts and commitment:

> I am mad with the same madness as the
> moon and my neighbour,
> I am kindled from the moon and the
> hearth of my neighbour.

Originally published in *Journal of Modern African Studies* 11, no. 2 (1973): 339–45. ©1973 by Cambridge University Press. Reprinted with the permission of Cambridge University Press.

The image here is of kinship in our service to the moon, the White Goddess, our common Muse; this also figured in *Heavensgate* disguised as the lioness image of the Watermaid.

*Heavensgate* itself takes its title from a poem of mine about a vantage point overlooking Longleat House, the property of the Marquis of Bath and Wells in Somerset, where Bishop Ken (1637–1711) once repaired to meditate his Anglican hymns and poems. Christopher must have read my "Heaven's Gate" shortly after our first meeting in October 1960, when he told me he had been working on an Easter sequence but had run into a block, could not find a title and did not know how to proceed.

At that time I was holding seminars on Milton and the early English Romantic poets in my bachelor's bungalow on the Nsukka campus of the University of Nigeria, which was still very raw and largely unfinished. Every afternoon I met two successive groups of nine or ten students. Somewhere about dusk at the second or third such meeting, a slim, trim, round-faced young Igbo, with close-cropped hair and a quizzical, slightly brooding look, appeared at the door and asked if he might "sit in" on the class, although he was not a student. When the session was over and the others had gone, my silent auditor stayed on for a beer and a chat. He was, he said, the Acting Librarian, a Classics graduate (1956) from Ibadan University and, he hoped, a poet.

So began my friendship with Christopher Okigbo, an association of kindred spirits interrupted in space and time only by his removal first to the Enugu campus library, some 40 miles away, and then to Cambridge House, Ibadan, where he became C.U.P. representative in Nigeria, as well as editor of Mbari Publications and the West African editor of the influential bimonthly journal *Transition*. Following that second move, my bungalow became his regular habitation when his official travels brought him back to the East; when I could visit Ibadan, his home was at my disposal, whether he was there or not. And always, when we did meet, there was a sharing of views, of music, or of silences, and an exchange reading of our new poems—though he preferred to have me read his for him, because I made them sound better, he said.

Once, in Enugu, I met Christopher with his father and all his brothers, and remarked to him afterwards on the great warmth of affection that seemed to unite them all. They had good cause, he said. The old man (formerly a schoolmaster in Ekwulobia, near the Igbo river town of Onitsha) had seen to it that all his sons received as good an education as possible, and then left it to their inclinations to find suitable vocations for themselves without any pressure on his part. From government work and school teaching Christopher had moved to librarianship, and then become a poet and a publisher. Bede was an agriculturalist, also at Nsukka. Pius, in those days, was Economic Adviser to the Eastern Region Government, married to a lovely French-speaking West African, Georgette, for the birth of whose third child (and first son) the poem "Comes the Newcomer" was added to *Heavensgate*.

By nature generous and hospitable, like his family and most of his people, Christopher wore a public mask of volatile good humour. In private, that mask was sometimes dropped—though seldom for very long—and then I could see why it was that so many of his poems made such profoundly sad, often nostalgic, music. For one thing there was his wife, Safinat, "bonded" to a school in the North, up near Lake Chad. "Every time I meet her," he told me once, "I fall in love all over again." And I shall never forget his radiant face and contagious joy when he announced the birth of his daughter, Ibrahimat—*Labyrinths* is dedicated to them both: "mother and child."

Then there was the matter of his professional work that kept him from his writing—and the worse problem of wanting to write but feeling unready or unable. That was what brought us together over the making of *Heavensgate,* and perhaps lies behind the inscription on the *Limits* typescript: talking with me, or having me read to him, would somehow set him to work again, or temporarily exorcise the paralysis that beset him.

One such conference, quite early in our association, led Christopher to produce one of his most flawless lyrics, and one of the finest modern statements about poetic inspiration I have ever encountered. This is the second "Watermaid" poem in Part III of *Heavensgate:*

> BRIGHT
> with the armpit-dazzle of a lioness,
> she answers,
>
> wearing white light about her;
>
> and the waves escort her,
> my lioness,
> crowned with moonlight.
>
> So brief her presence—
> match-flare in wind's breath—
> so brief with mirrors around me.
>
> Downward . . .
> the waves distil her;
> gold crop
> sinking ungathered.
>
> Watermaid of the salt-emptiness,
> grown are the ears of the secret.

When that was written, I had been talking about the Lady of the Lake and other Muse-like figures who were occupying my own verses just then; I also gave Christopher copies of several of the poems in which they were celebrated. Together with some of my readier students, he was quick to see a connection with the "Water Maid" or "Mammy-Wota" legends in Igbo folk-lore—and so the poem was born.

She was to return in *Limits,* as the image that "insists from the flagpole of the heart" in Section IV. The "armpit-dazzle" of the first poem, "armpit-fragrance" of the second, take on added significance if one recalls Laurens van der Post's comments on Kalahari Bushman mythology in *The Heart of the Hunter:*

> The armpit was a source of special being . . . the place where the quintessence of living things issued. The sun, the source of light and warmth, the great image of the power and glory of reason, was once the armpit of a man of the early race.

As for the moonlight and the mirrors, they are known to every follower of the "goddess" who deals, like the poet's mind, in images; so is the brevity of her epiphanies ("match-flare in wind's breath")—and so are the golden ears of the secret crop not one of us can ever finally harvest. Which is why the poem to be finished at the end of *Limits* IV is nothing less than the poet's own life; for Christopher agreed with me that this must be a poem, too, though I cannot think he then foresaw how soon and how suddenly the poem that was his life would be finished.

The *Limits* typescript was handed to me in April 1962, the revised copy for *Labyrinths* (excluding *Path of Thunder*) being prepared by Christopher in Ibadan in October 1965—by which time, perhaps, he could sense, if not his own death, some shape at least of the troubles that were to come upon the rapidly disintegrating Federation of Nigeria. Images of blood sacrifice, for example, which become explicit in *Path of Thunder* (subtitled "Poems Proph-esying War"), are already hinted at in *Distances;* while the "politicians in the tall wood" of *Distances* III return with the eagles and the robbers in an "iron dance of mortars" in the "Elegy for Alto" that concludes the *Path.*

This, alas, has been the pattern of development in more than one newly independent West African nation in recent years: hard on the heels of the ini-tial euphoria of liberation from the white man's rule has come, first, disillu-sionment with new black masters acting like white men in disguise (or worse), and then bloody massacres or a series of coups that leave the country more rav-aged, weary, and sick at heart than it was before. As one former student wrote to me recently, echoing the Ghanaian novelist Ayi Kwei Armah, not only are *The Beautyful Ones Not Yet Born* but now it seems they may never be.

Among the gifted young writers who, in little more than a decade, have added West African literature to the international map, this disillusionment has produced both scathing satire on the corruptions of society, and a search-ing of traditional values and mythologies for some illumination of the spirit by which to direct their own lives and those of their fellow Africans. The poems and plays of Wole Soyinka are the record of such a quest undertaken, as it were, in public, on behalf of the Yoruba people of Western Nigeria. The collected poems of Christopher Okigbo are a more personal, inward or private account of a similar spiritual journey, undertaken by an Igbo of Eastern Nigeria, equally steeped in the folklore of his own people, and equally conversant with the religion and the culture of the white men whose schools and missions, politics and language, are still forces in the land.

The story told in *Labyrinths*, then, at least to the end of *Distances*, is similar to that by Robert Graves (a favourite with both of us) in his poem for his son, "To Juan at the Winter Solstice": the one to which "all lines or lesser gauds belong / That startle with their shining / Such common stories as they stray into." The pattern traced by that story is the circle followed by Joseph Campbell's hero with a thousand faces, crossing the threshold between outward appearances and inward reality on a night-sea journey to a sacred marriage with a mother goddess (the Watermaid), and thence to a kind of homecoming, transfigured and restored, where in the common light of day once more the poet-hero offers his gift of insight and inspiration (the "Elixir of Life") to all who are willing and able to receive it.

To unfold that journey as it happened to himself, Christopher draws upon Christian imagery, classical and Sumerian mythology, Igbo folklore and ritual, and personal reminiscence elevated to the plane of myth. *Limits* V–XII, for example, carry several references to the *Epic of Gilgamesh* (including Irkalla, Sumerian Queen of the Underworld), to Picasso's *Guernica* (based on the myth of Theseus and the Minotaur), and to Christopher's childhood nurse, Eunice, "known for her lyricism." *Lament of the Drums* III (from *Silences*) names "Celaeno and her harpy crew" and Aeneas' drowned pilot, Palinurus, while both *Distances* and *Heavensgate* combine Christian and Igbo sacrifices— and *Heavensgate* includes such Ekwulobia notables as Kepkanly the teacher (a nickname derived from his march-past chant, *"Akaekpe-Akanni,"* the Igbo equivalent of "Left-Right, Left-Right"), Jadum the half-mad minstrel, and Upandru the linguist, or explainer. Another well-known local figure, Father Flannagan, first principal of Christ the King College, Onitsha, appears in *Limits* VII as one who "preached the Pope's message" in the village orchard— and in a poem now dropped from *Heavensgate* (much to my regret), Christopher also recalled his learning by rote of Greek and Latin tags; and of the English nursery rhyme, "Little Bo-Peep," which came out as *"etru bo pi"* in his Igbo attempt to master the alien words.

That he did eventually master the alien words (and with them the modes of thought) not only of English, but also of Latin and Greek, becomes very clear from a study of the verse techniques employed in any of the poems in *Labyrinths*. As our mutual friend, and fellow Nsukkan poet, Michael Echeruo, said of Christopher in a paper published in *Nigeria Magazine* in 1966, "the poetry of Okigbo is almost the poetry of echoes." With his Classical training and his reading in modern English, French, and American poets, Christopher was from the beginning strongly allusive, if not derivative, in his writing, which, Echeruo claimed, was the product of a "literary imagination . . . a poetry of responses to pattern and organization" (what Christopher himself called "logistics"). At its best, however, when the voices of Virgil, T. S. Eliot, Carl Sandburg, Ezra Pound, or Stephane Mallarmé have been subdued to his own, it is also "the poetry of an African, a native." Only an African, however cosmopolitan, could have written the "Watermaid" poem quoted above; only an African who had mastered much other knowledge could have produced the complex image of poetic growth that is *Limits* II:

> FOR HE WAS a shrub among the poplars,
> Needing more roots
> More sap to grow to sunlight,
> Thirsting for sunlight,
>
> A low growth among the forest.
>
> Into the soul
> The selves extended their branches,
> Into the moments of each living hour,
> Feeling for audience
>
> Straining this among the echoes;
>
> And out of the solitude
> Voice and soul with selves unite,
> Riding the echoes,
>
> Horsemen of the apocalypse;
>
> And crowned with one self
> The name displays its foliage,
> Hanging low
>
> A green cloud above the forest.

The tree imagery here, wrote Echeruo, is reminiscent of Pound's in "A Girl." In its symbolic identification with the poet's need and aspiration, however, it is closer to the chestnut tree in Hervey Allen's novel, *Anthony Adverse,* or the great oak in John Steinbeck's *To a God Unknown.* As for the "Horsemen of the apocalypse" who ride the echoes of all the other poets in the forest of the mind, they have become for Christopher voices of revelation, pointing the way home to his own voice, his true poetic self, until its name can display its foliage, no longer "a shrub among the poplars" but "A green cloud above the forest."

   This is precisely the explanation of the Minotaur myth offered by Joseph Campbell at the conclusion of his first chapter, on "Myth and Dream," in *The Hero with a Thousand Faces.* In his view, the apparently solitary quest is not so lonely, or so terrifying, after all:

for the heroes of all time have gone before us; the labyrinth is thoroughly known . . . And where we had thought to find an abomination, we shall find a god; where we had thought to slay another, we shall slay ourselves; where we had thought to travel outward, we shall come to the center of our own existence; where we had thought to be alone, we shall be with all the world.

How close this comes to Christopher's final comments in his beautifully lucid (and elucidating) Introduction to *Labyrinths*! The book is, he says, "a fable of man's perennial quest for fulfilment," owing as much to Igbo as to Cretan mythology, and directing the reader to the palace of the White Goddess through "the complex of rooms and ante-rooms, of halls and corridors . . . in which a country visitor might easily lose his way." It assumes throughout "a poet-protagonist" whose affinities reach beyond Orpheus to Gilgamesh and Aeneas, Captain Ahab and the Fisher King: "one with a load of destiny on his head." Necessarily, therefore, the work is "a cry of anguish—of the root extending its branches of coral, of corals extending their roots into each living hour." "The present dream," he concludes, "clamoured to be born a cadenced cry: silence to appease the fever of flight beyond the iron gate."

The nature of that flight is preserved in a poem entitled "Transition" at the end of the older, Mbari, version of *Heavensgate*.

> under the lamp into stream of
>     song, streamsong,
> in flight into the infinite—
>     a blinded heron
> thrown against the infinite—
>     where solitude
> weaves her interminable mystery
>     under the lamp.

That this mystery is not only interminable but also cyclical he seems to have realised by the end of *Path of Thunder*, whose concluding image is as nobly resigned to the patterns of change as that of the gathering swallows in Keats's *Ode to Autumn:*

> AN OLD STAR departs, leaves us here on the shore
> Gazing heavenward for a new star approaching;
> The new star appears, foreshadows its going
> Before a going and coming that goes on forever . . .

Here and elsewhere in *Labyrinths* Christopher speaks "as one having authority": an authority he worked for and achieved in just seven years before he was killed defending Nsukka campus, where we had first met, at the age of thirty-five. As Adrian Roscoe puts it in *Mother is Gold:* "The civil war brought Okigbo's career to a tragic and untimely close. But his influence lives on and his achievements stand acknowledged."

# INDIVIDUAL POEM SEQUENCES

◆

# A Structural Approach
# to Okigbo's "Distances"

## Sunday O. Anozie

AN OLD STAR departs, leaves us here on the shore
Gazing heavenward for a new star approaching;
The new star appears, foreshadows its going
Before a going and coming that goes on forever . . .

Christopher Okigbo, "Elegy for Alto"

Lo que parte me deja en la ribera
mirando, al mar, la estrella presentida,
lo que llega me ànnuncia despedida,
ante un vaiven que eterno persevera.

Alberto Quintero Alvarez, "Ante el Mar"

## 1. Structuralism: Its Function and Its Limits

For a poem to be susceptible of a structural approach—and also compensate critical endeavour—it ought to possess first of all an exotic sophistication and even evince by its very nature a certain defiant infrastructure of *signs*. The word "ought" has been deliberately used here because not every poem that may pass for a good work of art can fulfill this requirement. For example, all the poems of Chief Dennis Osadebay in his collection *AFRICA SINGS* (1952) and a great majority of Leopold Sedar Senghor's in *ETHIOPIQUES* (1956) and *NOCTURNES* (1961) possess, on the contrary, an easy and transparent naivety of texture. These are poems that simply say their say, and, sometimes, quite beautifully too. If Senghor's poems bemuse with the languid rhetoric

Originally published in *The Conch* 1, no. 1 (1969): 19–29. Reprinted by permission of the publisher. Sunday O. Anozie is on an extended sabbatical from the University of Port Harcourt, Nigeria, where he is a professor of English. He resides with his family of four in Baltimore, Maryland. His books include *Sociologie du Roman Africain, Christopher Okigbo: Creative Rhetoric,* and *Structural Models and African Poetics.*

and the tired nostalgia that marked the French Decadent poetry, Osadebay's gàmbol around all covered with the dead embers of the English Georgian poetry which, as G. S. Fraser has well pointed out in *THE MODERN WRITER AND HIS WORLD,* contains "a certain intimate plainness of tone" and "sometimes a conscious slight prosiness." On the other hand, poems such as Aime Cesaire's *CAHIER D'UN RETOUR AU PAYS NATAL,* Leon G. Damas's *PIGMENTS,* J. P. Clark's *IVBIE* or Wole Soyinka's *IDUMARE*—not to mention Okigbo's poem-cycles—are all impressively informed by a certain recondite compositeness, a fusion of sound, sense and structure realized in such a way that, to risk repetition, they check rather than attract familiarity.

It would be certainly presumptuous to attempt to define here the term "structuralism." One can only say—and without meaning to sound too respectably ambiguous about it—that the structuralist approach is simply a way of "feeling" (a true structuralist would, by the way, frown at that emotive word) one's way through any given dense system of codes or symbolic relationships. This approach has been found to be both possible and useful in dealing with the problems of human relationships and roles within a given social system (for instance, in their myths, rites of initiation and marriage institutions); in sciences like mathematics and telecommunications, as well as in art and literature (e.g., poetry, music, drama). The dynamic resonance which in recent times the French Claude Lévi-Strauss has given to this approach to analytical thought particularly in the field of anthropology and ethnology,[1] shows how much Natural Sciences are getting to be impressed by the scientific methods of such structural linguists as Ferdinand de Saussure and Roman Jacobson, and that leader also of the Russian Formalist Movement[2]—B. Tomachevski.

According to Professor Claude Lévi-Strauss, the chief exponent of modern structuralism, one would certainly be involved in one form or another of structuralist analysis or approach if one observed at least three things. The first is to consider the work or case under analysis strictly objectively as a functional structured universe. The second is to find out its real nature or the underlying message by deciphering this universe of codes, that is reducing it to its minimum of significant units in much the same way as a structural linguist breaks down language from its syntactical to its phonemic level. The third and final stage would consist—if we understand the Professor well—in reconstituting these residues communicatively into meaningful patterns of discourse. Professor Lévi-Strauss likens this procedure to the art of a potterer ("bricoleur") and in his formidably positivist and rationalistic College-de-France way of thinking, this favourite image of "bricolage" embodies the Professor's belief in a kind of structural determinism ("infrastructure inconsciente") which governs and also penetrates every mode of human and social affairs especially at primitive levels of interplay. For him such transactions are not simply analogous but they are ultimately reducible to a phenomenon of conscious linguistic communication. Hence the Professor is convinced, for instance, that the human kinship system can be elaborated by the spirit at the level of conscious operation into phonological data.[3] Similarly, he has demonstrated that the prohibition of incest and the conduct of exogamy (marriage institution which in a "primitive" society involves a vast exchange system of women among diverse social groups) are functionally conceivable—this was the theme of his doctoral thesis as vast systems of communication.[4] In fact in a book published in 1964, *Le cru et le cuit* (of which an extract of notes, "Le Triangle Culinaire," was printed in *L'ARC*, Special No. 26 of 1965), the Professor holds that, examined under a diachronic and a synchronic schema, the method of cooking of any given society is a language into which that society unconsciously translates its structure, if not also its contradictions. Although Claude Lévi-Strauss may be accused of being whimsically fastidious about considering social facts not as things or ideas but as structures, and society itself as a structure of structures, yet the place given to him here clearly shows how much sympathy we accord to an analytical evolution in social sciences which has or is bound to have decisive implications in the field of modern literary criticism. Here as anywhere else however the dangers and the advantages of structuralism as a critical tool in the assessment of works of imagination are very apparent. Since in considering a poem such for instance as *DISTANCES* objectivity is strictly relative, if not impossible—its rhetorical system composed of so many variable elements.

## 2. THE TRIADIC STRUCTURE OF RHETORIC IN "DISTANCES"

It is possible to conceive of DISTANCES as a vast system of communication. In fact one finds this structural persistence in all Okigbo's poetry. *SILENCES,* for example, illustrates how richly in this poetry sounds and symbols fuse into a complex system of relationships. It is through this that the poem largely communicates its meaning. Thus one important characteristic of Okigbo's poetry in general is that in it different patterns of sound-symbolism and metaphors are always [being] forced into a ritualistic interaction at different sensual levels and with varying frequencies. Examples of this kind of combination are found in: "spread . . . your silences," "your silences suffused in . . . fragrance," "long-fingered winds," "salt face of glass," "silences fade in my stomach," "painted harmonies," and "Silence distils in yellow melodies." In each of these cases it is not sufficient alone to notice the musical interplay of sibilants and fricatives—an operation predominantly phonemic; it is good also to recognize the poet's deliberate and almost ritualistic dislocations of syntax and semantics somewhat after the manner of Eliot's "the river's tent is broken." That was in *SILENCES.*

| | PROGRESSION | | ASSOCIATION | | | | | RECEPTION | |
|---|---|---|---|---|---|---|---|---|---|
| | Vertical Dynamics + | Horizontal Dynamics − | Light | Sound | Colour | Smell | Metaphysical | Phallic | Non-Phallic |
| D.I | | homecoming, descanted, Paddling home, thro'..., miner into..... | serene, bristling, redolent | voice, chanted, laughter | White, dark, | incense | divine, birthday, dream, solitude, phantom. | bowl, nest, inflorescence, white chamber, labyrinth, ant-hole | |
| D.II | pile high, fall, pinned down, split, cut. | swimmer, roll, suitor, dancers | incandescent, fire, lanterns, rays | voice, echo, bells, cry | silver, blood, ash, white reddening | odour, | without flesh or skeleton, without age or memory, dead, freezing, air's marrow | island, ambush, tuberose, fruits, interspaces. | bandages, stretcher |
| D.III | from Dan to Beersheba | | | | | camphor, iodine chloroform ether | prophets, martyrs, lunatics, dantini negritude | white chamber garden, wood | stone steps balcony, clearing |
| D.IV | | The only way to go through... to, | evanescent, resplendent, phosphorescent | catatonic ping-pong | marble | | celestial, halo, pentecostal, void, forms, crucifix | alabaster, triangular, square, circle, hollow-centre, orbs, enclosed. | archway, lintel. |
| D.V | Ascending | | | effervescent, laughter, sighs, music | rose | rose | silence, religion time's stillness, knot of time, wandering rocks, molten stone | sanctuary, bowell, inkwell, abyss, tabernacle, oblong. | archway |
| D.VI | intertwined | darkening towards, homeward, perforated, seeking, entered, come into... | evanescent, aglow | cry of wold, sings, Lo! O maid | variegated, orangery | putrescent, orange | halo, intimacy, cloud, invisible, chaste, instant, solitary, sentient being, naked, interspaces, pure head. | wood, cavern, mouth, labyrinth, oblong, orifices corridors, drum, cymbal, houses, bridal chamber | bandages, cleaning, stone steps |

In *DISTANCES* a not unsimilar practice prevails. The rhetorical system (also synonymous with the form) of this poem can be arbitrarily broken down into three broad structures or dynamic configurations. These can be called *Progression, Association* and *Reception* dynamics respectively (Fig 1). Both *P* and *R* (to use now the first-letter symbols) have, again arbitrarily, been split up each into sub-structures; *A* into several, including the delicate sub-structure which can summarily be called "metaphysical" *(m)*. There is even a possibility of further splitting up each sub-structure again into a 3rd, 4th or 5th sub-sub-structure. The practice would then be identical to the breaking down in linguistic of the morphological into the morphemic and then into the phonemic levels of constituents and so on. This possibility, in the case of *A*, even reaches an infinity degree—hence the additional symbols b, c, d, . . . n, with the symbol m always serving in this group as a highly charged emotive-coefficient.

Now the argument here is this: the poet Okigbo sees the exile's home-coming in *DISTANCES* in terms of a dynamic art experience or movement. In a linear (i.e., diachronic) sense, this movement is treated as a kind of *Progression* through *Associations* into a form of *Reception;* in an analogical (i.e., synchronic) sense, this defines the triadic structure of the poet's rhetoric in *DISTANCES*—that is, its form of creative communication—besides being also a recurrent phenomenon in each of the Movements of the poem.

If the symbol *rs* is taken to stand for the *rhetorical structure* of the poem, +,− respectively for the *vertical* and the *horizontal* dynamics of *P,* and *f, nf* respectively for the *phallic* and the *non-phallic* attributes of R, then quite simply the observation made above (on the internal structure of the communication in DISTANCES) can be expressed schematically as follows:

$$rs \overset{\leftarrow}{\to} p\pm \Big[ A(b,c,d \ldots n)^m \Big] R^{nf}_{\overline{\phantom{n}}f}$$

No more has been done in the above schema than try to define the rhetorical structure of Okigbo's *DISTANCES,* and without any pretension whatsoever to mathematical objectivity, as a reversible process consisting simultaneously in the linear relationship between its three major groups as well as in the internal modification of the roles within each group. This same principle of interaction informs the division of linguistic into the three highly inclusive categories of morphology, syntax and semantic, not to mention the supra-segmentals.

There is a little problem to straighten out with the group which has been called "metaphysical." This name is given to those associational elements and symbols which, whether also in magical or ritual incantations or in certain forms of ordinary human linguistic usage, may not be easily rationally accounted for. In the poem *DISTANCES* these serve not so much as mere sense perceptions as notes to kindle specific emotive atmosphere; it is these in mythical forms of speech which generally create a halo and so serve as coefficients to . . . Two examples may illustrate this generalisation.

First, the sensation or the experience which in *DISTANCES* (henceforth the symbol D stands for DISTANCES) Okigbo denotes with the words "freezing" and "cold" would certainly be a physical impossibility, logically considered, if at the same time and in the same context and situation the other structures of experience which the poet denotes with the words "incandescent rays" and "everlasting fire," were to be considered as logically possible. To argue the contrary would be equal to saying that "red" and "blue" as different colour structures could be seen simultaneously as distinct in space and coexistent in time. That would surely be a perceptual paradox, wouldn't it? But it is precisely on such a system of paradoxes that the whole rhetorical suggestiveness of the poem depends. Hence it does not require any logical effort to establish that "freezing," "cold," "rays," "fire" are structures of poetic experience generally referring or serving as coefficient to things beyond immediate sensual perception.

Perhaps a second example clarifies this. Consider the poet's sentence: "the everlasting fire . . . forgot the taste of ash in the air's marrow." This is a pure "nonsensical" sentence. It is like a magician's incantatory rhetoric. Nonetheless the sentence itself is, like "Quadruplicity drinks procrastination" (cited by the famous English philosopher Bertrand Russell in *An Inquiry Into the Meaning of Truth*), quite syntactically valid. But like all "nonesensical" sentences the poet's statement is "not true," but also "not false." It would certainly require as much effort of logic to prove the falsity of a so-called "nonesensical" sentence as it would to demonstrate logically that, to cite another instance, outside a geometrical plane what Okigbo means to convey in D/4, lines 1–10 is "true" or "false." What is relevant to the argument however is that each of the mentioned perceptual paradoxes, forming part of the rhetorical system of the poem, is the result of the poet's attempt, purely on a subconscious level, to structuralize (that is, give a definite form to) specific experiences either of immediate or of remote past.

## 3. "THE WORD" AS SYMBOL IN D/4

It has already been seen that in the poem, D, the poet Okigbo visualizes the experience of art and creativity as a dynamic three-dimensional movement-towards . . . And it has just been observed that like the language of ritual and magical incantations the linguistic symbols which the poet employs, arbitrary and paradoxical though they may be, do not in fact engage the question of "true" or "false": instead they refer to specific experiences of the poet's, which are thus given certain forms. If these admittedly obvious abstractions are to be useful at all, then they should be able to help (i) to define the place of D

taken in its totality as a communicative universe within the present conceptual context, (ii) to break through certain specific structures, no matter the
obscurantism of Okigbo's linguistic phraseology for recognisable keys to the
underlying message, and (iii) to test the technical unity of the poem by applying the same conceptual formula to each of the component parts or Movements of D.

The first task is easily dismissed. Like the hero in D, everyman faced
with the problem of communication usually starts from an unknown point or
percept, P, then moves through a clustered milieu of associational linguistic
symbols, A (which of course includes both sensual and metaphysical figures as
well), in order finally to arrive—that is, be received into successful communication, R. The predominance in D of the symbols variously classified under
"horizontal dynamics," "metaphysical" and "phallic" shows how considerably
D conforms to this triadic structural principle. If thus one says, for instance,
that

$$P = D1 + D2$$
$$A = D3 + D4 + D5$$
$$R = D6$$

then any $\Delta PAR$ will also be equal to any $\Delta D6(D1 + D2)(D3 + D4 + D5)$.
But this can never be taken for a rigid structure since with the poem D one is
dealing with symbols and dynamic variables, and since also what the poem
communicates at last is in fact neither P, A, nor R, but a whole series of other
relationships and internal modifications of these resulting in the complex
which is rs. In other words, the aim of communication whether in creative or
ordinary life is the ultimate fusion of form and content. By this alone is
rhetoric defined.

This leads naturally to the second problem posed above for, if the conclusion is validated by the argument so far, then one should be in a position to
see why in D/4 Okigbo should express, using geometrical and architectural
images, a strong formalist obsession:

> after we had formed
> then only the forms were formed
> and all the forms were formed
> after our forming . . .

In these words the poet has furnished a hieroglyphical resumé of the argument raised hitherto in this essay, and also provided a vital clue to the question: What is the meaning of the symbol in the "White Chamber"?

The paradoxical ingenuity of Okigbo's art in D/4 lies in the fact, that
the symbol inside the White Chamber is not itself a Crucifix but indeed ordinary words caligraphically structured to resemble one. Besides, they are spe-

cially illuminated with "phosphorescence mantles." They are therefore words to which the poet has given a certain intensely visible form of existence—here a Crucifix. Thus he "formed" them after they "were formed" and they are meant to express nothing but that "form." For a Christian pilgrim salvation is often represented in the form of a Crucifix to which he is expected to bestow his whole spiritual devotion. Using this analogy, Okigbo seems to suggest that creative salvation and illumination for a poet must take the form of a word. The poet also seems to contend that if for a Christian the Crucifix is neither the wood nor the metal of which it may be made, but a symbol of something still higher than these, for a poet a word is more than its external form, the letters that spell it out. Granted that language is given man to hide his thought in, not to reveal it, then the poet's final claim is that a word does not become The Word unless it has become a transcendent symbol, a voice— the only right form in which that which is most creative in man and also most beyond human argument can exist, coextensive with eternity ("after we had formed . . . after our forming . . ."). Thus the exile's "burden of the pawn" is this quest of The Word which is also creative voice.

It is not a coincidence that in D/4 the innermost structure on the sign that guards the entrance through the "archway" should be a "triangular lintel." This triadic image not only informs the internal structure of the Movements of D but also ensures their technical unity and consistency, and this leads to the last point raised above. This formal unity is already evident in D/1. Earlier in *LIMITS III* Okigbo has revealed that the quest of a creative symbol involves a routinal entering through an arched gate. If however in *LIM III* the quest ended in failure and frustration (c.f. "the big white elephant" symbol), in D/6 it is shown as ending in a successful initiation-communion with the true maidenhead of the goddess. In a similar way, the "hurry-on-down" chorus in *LIM III* prefigures the horizontal dynamics of movement on which D now begins:

> From flesh into phantom, on the horizontal stone.

Possible of being represented in a linear or a triangular form

$$\text{Flesh} \rightarrow \text{Phantom} \rightarrow \text{Stone,}$$

this postulate sums up under three categories all possible states of existence in nature. Once established the triadic process is further emphasized by the repetition three times of the incantatory phrase: "I was the sole witness to my homecoming." One may now rather quickly see this process in operation at different levels still within the Movements.

D/1 (a): "Serene lights . . . A nest of fireflies." In this area the poet creates a strong atmosphere particularly through appeals to the senses of sight and smell. The dominant vowels are e, i, o which help to create a mood of surprised but smooth enchantment; the overall symbol is phallic. The exile's three reflective questions—questions which betray his obvious incapacity to decode the message—are expressed and also arranged in significant recipient symbols—the *f* attributes of *R*. He therefore starts from an unknown point or quantity, P.

> D/1 (b): "And in the inflorescence of the White
> Chamber, . . . from laughter to the dream."

This second stage of the same movement is a variation on the first. The dominant appeal here is to the sense of hearing. A "voice" is suddenly identified by the poet-exile and its organicity is stressed in Okigbo's adroit counter-pointing of the same vowels e, i, o with consonants (mainly fricatives) and diphthongs (th) to yield a rhythmical harmony:

> "a voice, from very far away, chanted, and the chamber descanted the birthday
> of earth, paddling me home through some dark labyrinth, from laughter to the
> dream."

The "inflorescence" image confirms this idea of organic symmetry (Nature) while "descanted" stresses the musical relatedness, the harmony within it (Art). If the unknown P were now to shade into Art within Nature, might not the poet's suggestion be that there exists between these two a kind of primordial nativity relationship (also implied in "the birthday of earth")? However, the second stage ends on a point of horizontal progression and the emphasis is persistently on a phallic level ("home," "labyrinth," "chamber").

D/1 (c): Now fully emerged, the "voice" is identified by the exile variously as "incarnate" and "miner into my solitude." With the hero's final petition, "you will go with me . . . again into the ant-hole," the triadic progression is complete. Every effective initiation is a descent (a "regressus ad uterum"), that is, going back to the very original source and the domain of Kepkanly and Idoto in *HEAVENSGATE*.

The three-dimensional quest is equally evident in D/2 where it is treated with greater sophistication of technique. The analysis will continue to be synoptic.

D/2 (a): *Lines I–XIV.* These sketch a premise by developing a central symbol—the "evening." Not an ordinary evening but one that is stone dead and in a desert island:

> "And it was an evening without flesh or skeleton,
> an evening with no silver bells to its tale;
> without lanterns; without buntings;
> and it was an evening without age or memory—"

This is a perfect romantic setting for a piece of horror or science fiction. Even the leaves on the island are dead and flying in the harmattan wind. But if in

D/2 "dead leaves" reach beyond themselves, like the "evening," to become significant symbols, the poet's juxtaposition of "bandages" (attribute of the "leaves") with "finest swimmer" (attribute of the "wind") is also cynically aglow with hints of fatal determinism. Does the exile see his homeward career as pregnant and helpless as the fate of dead leaves in the wind? Does the poet-prophet foresee his own end?

D/2 (b): *Lines XV–XXII.* These lines suggest a stage of strong visual suffering and pains. The incident related here by Okigbo may as well be referring to a true physical experience since the human eyes, if subjected to a zone of intense luminosity (say, for example, the sun in tropical full blaze or even an unduly charged television camera) are bound to recoil in pain. It may, however, be ignored that such a physical confrontation with light is what the poet means. In that case, this second will stand as a transitory stage to one of final illumination; it is a stage, that is, marked by very harsh judgments, trial and accusation through which the exile is bound to pass. It is moreover significant that the whole incident takes place "in the freezing tuberoses of the white chamber." Is the exile now imaginatively anticipating his journey's end and the final encounter with the goddess-muse?

D/2(c): *Lines XXIII–XXXXIV.* In this third stage Okigbo deploys a strong gothic vignette as he attempts to personify Death and also present it as an inclusive symbol. Artistically, Death is here conceived in terms of the Joycean dialectic ("paring her fingernails . . ."), mythically, as being governed in her relationship with her lieutenants by a ritual principle the very reverse of that between Dionysius and his Maenads. In her attitude of masochism towards her devotees, Death is comparable to the Watermaid in *HEAVENS-GATE* whose attributes she also shares—immaculate brightness ("in smock of white cotton") and transience ("in a cloud of incense"). Victims of their own enthusiasm and faithful devotion ("the dancers lost among their own snares," captives in "the interspaces"), the lieutenants are equally accommodated to pain and suffering and the experience of death by savage dismemberment.

If the coded message in D/2 seems to be that an artist cannot face the ultimate illumination of the symbol (THE WORD) just as mankind cannot in fact bear the ultimate reality (DEATH), what is given in D/3 is a new, mainly because a hierarchical, projection of the same banal platitude. This means that it is indeed the hierarchical structure of the poet's vision of art and not the originality of his point of view, that attracts attention. For even in this essentially vertical progression the triadic formula is imminent. At the very bottom—"the tall wood"—level of art-experience one finds justly imprisoned and confused "vendors," "princes," "negritude" and "politicians." In the middle there is "the garden" of dilettantism through which one emerges at "the clearing," graduands from which the poet calls "Dantini." Finally at the very top—the "stone steps," and the marble "balcony" of creative happiness—there is, according to the poets, room enough only for a select few: the "prophets," "martyrs" and "lunatics." Judging from his vantage point of observation and also by reason of his "crucifix" the exile-pilgrim evidently seems to see himself in this cultured but suffering minority. At this stage of his homecoming he seems also ready for the final encounter and illumination. In fact in four words Okigbo succinctly reveals the span and meaning of this spiritual-cum-artistic quest: "from Dan to Beersheba." Or, from *Death* to *Birth*?

## Notes

From a chapter in CREATIVE RHETORIC to be published later in 1969 by Evans Brothers Ltd., London. This essay is based on the text of Okigbo's *DISTANCES* published in *Transition* No. 16, 1964.

1. Professor S. F. Nadel in THE THEORY OF SOCIAL STRUCTURE, 1957, has similarly carried this rigorous procedure even to high level abstractions.

2. cf. "THEORIE DE LA LITTERATURE." Collection "TEL QUEL" (Seuil, 1965). The possibilities of "structuralism" as a method of critical analysis are now being successfully explored by several French critics among whom; Roland Barthes, author of ESSAIS CRI-TIQUES and SYSTEME DE LA MODE, Gerard Genette, author of FIGURES and other members of TEL QUEL and COMMUNICATIONS, the two leading French literary journals

3. ANTHROPOLOGIE STRUCTURALE, 1958.

4. LES STRUCTURES ELEMENTAIRES DE LA PARENTE, 1949.

# Poetry and Empirical Logic: A Correspondence Theory of Truth in Okigbo's *Laments*

Sunday O. Anozie

> And I said:
> The prophet only the poet.
> And he said Logistic
> (which is what poetry is).
>                    Okigbo, *Heavensgate*

## 1. Poetry as Logistics: The Search for "Models"

The aim of this article is to propose one definition of the term *structure* and then relate it to the technique of composition in one of Okigbo's poems. By limiting effort to the first movement of *The Lament of the Drums*[1] it is possible to demonstrate logically that Okigbo's poetry contains its own logistics, its own law of organic composition.

Outside this law Okigbo risks to be misunderstood by critics. For he was not a poet much gifted with words: they did not come to him easily or ready-made. In other terms, the meteor-like impacts of emotions and impressions to which his sensibility was constantly exposed in his particular socio-historical environment, did not register in his poetry equal seismographic verbal signs. Okigbo was therefore compelled to practice a most stringent type of word economy, to seek refuge in obscurantism. This came through working very hard and fastidiously at his poems, in an attempt to impose on them a system of syntactical logic and connexions. Sometimes too he incorporated elements from other poets and writers, cultural frontiers[2] notwithstanding, wherever these appeared relevant to his particular theme.

As a result of this conscious art, Okigbo's poems can be considered as "logical constructions." They are universes of rhetorical discourse within

Originally published in *The Conch* 2, no. 1 (1970): 54–65. Reprinted by permission of the author.

which is articulated a series of syntactical and semantic tensions both on a diachronic as well as on a synchronic level.

The terms "diachrony" and "synchrony" can be defined respectively as: "the changing of a system into another state, or history such as can be analyzed according to the rules of transformation or change": and "an abstraction which states that a signifying system can be studied independently of time."[3] These two terms, now frequently used in structural linguistics, are very important to the understanding of the meaning and definition of *structure.* They form also part of the new set of binary (or dichotomic) oppositions first introduced by Ferdinand de Saussure[4] into the study of the linguistic element. Linguistics is said to be "structural" therefore when it is based upon a system on which several of such, even if aleatory, oppositions are simultaneously articulated.

The term "logical construction" as used above in connection with Okigbo's poetry, does not have exactly the same sense as it would generally acquire in Logical Positivism. This is the doctrine which consists in the claim that "all knowledge, or in the linguistic formulation, all meaningful discourse, consists of two kinds; first, reports of experiential fact, whose claim to truth resides exclusively in that the facts bear them out; and, secondly, logic, interpreted as consequences of calculations within systems whose rules are conventionally established."[5] Implicit in this claim is the fact also that the structure of language is strictly different from the structure of the world and that no metaphysical inference is possible from one to the other. If this is so, then Logical Positivism does not hold any attraction for us here and "logical construction" is considered only as synonymous with "model" or with "structure."

This said, it is possible to define *structure* non-inductively as a system of relationships or as a totality of elements between which exist certain relations such that any modification of an element or of a relation directly affects the rest of the elements or relations. This definition adheres to the first of the four epistemological conditions which in order to merit the name of *structure,* every model should, according to Claude Lévi-Strauss,[6] satisfy. We would be restating the perspective of this article correctly if we say that it is to apply this definition of *structure* to Okigbo's poetry mainly by showing that the composition of *Lament of the Drums* is based upon an empirical model.[7] Furthermore, by analysing the inner dialectic of the poem rather than the historical determination of its content, it can be shown that the "Drums," the privileged empirical model, serves the poet a dual purpose: as a thematic motif and as a structural praxis. Thematically, the poet's method consists in conferring upon these anthropomorphic speakers in the poem, certain propositional attitudes. Structurally, the meaning of these propositions—also "truth" and "knowledge" about the speakers' attitude and state—is logically inferable from their syntactical modes of expression.

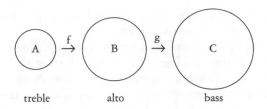

Fig. I: The Syntax of the Drums

This conclusion, if true, is important. First, it argues the relation $R$ in Okigbo's poetry, between form and content or between theme T and structure S; or, again between poetic percepts and factual premisses. Second, and more important, it asserts that language being an ideal model which by uniting with non-linguistic events and experiences can express empirical truth or falsehood, meaning is a matter not only of semantic but of syntactic structure. In what follows, these two arguments will be treated *as if* they were one. The poet's hypothesis, also the basic assumption here, is that the drums, whether they are considered as traditional musical instruments or as speakers in this particular poem, do effectively communicate: they combine both the aesthetic and the cognitive functions of language.[8]

## 2. POETRY AND EMPIRICAL KNOWLEDGE

Movement I of the version[9] of *Lament of the Drums* on which the analysis will be based runs as follows:

> "THEY say
> They will come and take away
> Our drumheads
> They say
> They will take our drumheads
> Into exile
>
> And mangle our tendons
>
> Puncture our membranes
>
> They say
> They will come and strip us
> Of our thunder . . .
>
> If they should come today
> And ask for a praise-song
>
> Tell them
> We have tuned our raw hides

> For a waking
> Tell them
> For the stew-of-seven-souls
> At the waking. . . ."

Now let *A* be any statement of the type *They say/They will.* . . . let *B* be *If they should.* . . , and let *C* be any statement of the type *Tell them* . . . , then the compound statements *A,B,C,* and their substatements or variables constitute *propositions.* In the poem above these three propositions form a coherent universe of discourse *U* and can be represented diachronically as follows:

$$U = A(a,\acute{a}) \rightarrow B \rightarrow C(c)$$

This then is the basic structure, the elementary system of relationships, which has to be grasped and interpreted in the poem. It corresponds also to the syntactic order (see *figure 1*) in which the drums' propositions are arranged.

The *A* statement can be classified under a "memory proposition." By a "memory proposition" we simply refer to a sentence which states a fact relating to a particular occurrence either in the remote or immediate past, such that if this particular occurrence in the past logically precedes and is the cause of another particular occurrence in the future which may be also either remote or immediate, then a "memory proposition" can be presumed to be a factual premiss. This situation is indispensable to all empirical knowledge. The proposition *A(a,á* . . .) contains three variables expressed as different threats directed in the past against the speakers, "Drums," and also coming from things or persons which the threatened speakers themselves *know* because they can only identify as "they." But the impersonal pronoun "they" might just as well signify nothing or everything, and, in consequence of this, the threats might be either factually non-existent or all-existent. This is so essentially because first, memory is fallible or, rather, not indubitable; and second, a "memory proposition" is not strictly verifiable: it does not command at least the same degree of certainty as does, for instance, a judgement of perception (such as, "He's got a dark coat on today"; or "Tomorrow will be Sunday").

The point then is that the speakers called "Drums" have adduced to us a series of "memory propositions" as factual premises on which is based, in a syntactically logical way, the statement *B* to which we will give the name of a "perceptual proposition." By a "perceptual proposition" we mean that the statement *B,* although by its syntax a conditional clause, states a judgement of perception which relates to the condition of a *known* particular event taking place in the future. Since strictly speaking a perception can be neither general nor vague although the words that express it may be so, the judgement contained in the statement *B* may be deemed to be a conditional factual premiss for still another occurrence to come, taking into consideration if we can, all

the circumstances of the speakers themselves, their present propositional attitudes. If for example we replaced the words "they" and "praise song" with
such less vague data as "John" and "a red ball," and if we also modified the
time-indication "today" by prefixing "2 o'clock pm," then it would be seen
that no conditional factual premiss could be more precise or absolute than in
the statement: "If John should come at 2 o'clock pm today and ask for a red
ball . . ." Even this statement which, given our conventional linguistic habits
we may consider as good, is "non-sensical" because of what we *do* know, being
the speaker, about the speaker's present propositional attitude—but then
that is a different matter.

If the compound statement *A* is a "memory proposition" and statement
*B* a "perceptual proposition," we have observed that each pretends to act as a
factual premiss with both of them now leading to statement *C* which can
then be called a "basic proposition." The late English philosopher Lord Russell, who believed that empirical knowledge is impossible without them, has
defined "basic propositions" as "those propositions about particular occur-
rences which, after a critical scrutiny, we still believe independently of any
extraneous evidence in their favour."[10] This means that, in logic at least, a
"basic proposition" can exist or be expressed in the form either of a "memory
proposition" or a "perceptual proposition," symbolically: AvB → C. What the
poet proposes to us, however, is, according to the argument above, a reversal
of this order such that it can be stated thus: the truth-value, T, of a basic
proposition is logically inferable from the sum of the truth-values of its variables, symbolically:

$$T (A \wedge B) \rightarrow T(C)$$

The two symbolic relations just described show that the logician and the
poet (roles which Okigbo himself unites in this context) may be saying nearly
the same thing in two nearly different ways; whereas the one adheres to the
semantics of object-words used in the propositions, the other tends to be
more concerned with the syntactic order of the propositions. The reason, as
already indicated, lies in the nature of the poem itself. The poet is constructing his work on an empirical model; he is attempting to reproduce both the
syntax and the semantics of the Yoruba drums.

The structural mimetic[11] principle of composition favoured here by
Okigbo consists thus in the attempt to describe, or conceal within the poem,
*Laments of the Drums,* a system similar to that whereby Drums, when played,
as by traditional Yoruba experts, can enter, linearly, into temporal relationships or musical dialogues with each other, while also communicating, both
individually and collectively, a coded *ensemble* of meaningful information and
knowledge.

If this analogical interpretation is valid, then the relation T (A∧B) →
T(C) can now be reframed in more than one sense. First, the literal sense:

although structurally different from either the treble $A$ or the alto $B$ drums, the "mother" or bass drum, $C$, can take up and also appropriate the sum of the propositions already initiated by the others, thereby [lending] their "voice," and message, a more resonant and coherent amplification. This effect is achieved among expert drum-players, partly through constant readjustment of drum wave-lengths and vibrations (this is the role of the left hand of the player), and partly by the careful selection each time of a different area of impact between the drum-stick (normally held in the right hand unless the player is left-handed) and the surface of the drums. The over-all impression, to a tutored ear, is analogous to a dramatic monologue or soliloquy enacted by a solo drum in terms of a basic proposition.

Secondly, the same relation can be expressed mathematically in terms of *functions* and *sets*. Let us take a closer look at figure 1, following the arrows. Suppose that to each element (image or variable) of the set $A$ is assigned a unique element of the set $B$. Then by *function*, denoted $f: A \rightarrow B$ or $A \xrightarrow{f} B$, we simply mean a collection of such assignments. Given that $f(a)$ denotes the unique element in $B$ assigned to $a \in A$, then this defines the *image* of $a$ under $f$ or the value of $f$ at $a$. Similarly, if $A, B$ are considered as the domain and co-domain respectively of $f$, then the range of $f$, denoted by $f(A)$, can be expressed in terms of a set of images. This means, too, that given $a \in A$, then its image $f(a)$ is in $B$, the domain of $g$. Hence we can find the image of $f(a)$ under the function $g$, that is $g[f(a)]$. The product of $f$ and $g$ defines that function from $A$ into $C$ which assigns to each $a \in A$ the element or image $g[f(a)] \in C$.

## 3. The Correspondence Theory of Truth in Poetry

Mathematically, the equation stated in above paragraph will satisfy the conditions for the existence of the logical relation $T(A \wedge B) \rightarrow T(C)$. If this remark is valid, then it ought to be valid also to say: to each function can be assigned a corresponding relation just as to each basic proposition there exists a corresponding truth-value. A Correspondence Theory of Truth states that "the truth of basic propositions depends upon their relation to some occurrence, and the truth of other propositions depends upon their syntactical relations to basic propositions."[12] How can one apply this definition to the Okigbo's poem examined here?

First, it has already been shown that each of the Drums' three propositions asserts a factual relationship with some non-linguistic event; secondly, that each of these propositions, as basic propositions, is also forced into a syntactical relationship with each other so that the first two now logically act as factual premises to the third. Granted therefore as immanent this empirical structure of the poem, the essential problem then is how to determine the truth-value of the basic proposition $C$ in relation to the rest of the propositions; in other terms, how to decode the product of $f$ and $g$ which also can define the function from $A$ to $C$. This is equivalent to asking: Is it possible to deduce the meaning of the Drums' propositions uniquely from its specific empirical structure, and, if so, by what decoding manual or system?

From the definition of *structure* proposed at the beginning of this essay, as from the argument so far, it can be deduced that the decoding manual or system is concealed within the poem itself: in fact it is that basic unit, or structure of relationships which the poem expresses.

First we proceed then by conveniently summing up under a table, the argument of the preceding section:

| Propositions | Empirical logical forms | Truth-Value (T) |
|---|---|---|
| $A$ | Memory | F (= false) |
| $B$ | Perceptual | T (= true) |
| $C$ | Basic | $c$ |

Fig. II: The Empirical Structure of Drums' Propositions

Next we try to determine the value of $c$ deductively from the semantic and syntactical structures of the propositions. This operation, in order to be valid, must recognize the earlier logical assumption which states that, where language (by implication Drums) is treated as an ideal model capable of expressing, under certain conditions, both empirical truth and falsehood, meaning is dependent partly on the semantic and partly also on the syntactical order of words or propositions. Here we are concerned only with propositions.

Method I:      By Syntactic Order of Propositions: ($\wedge$ = "and")

$$A \wedge B \longrightarrow C$$

Given:    $A$    $= F$
           $B$    $= T$
Then $T(A \wedge B)$    $= F$
Therefore $C$    $= F$

Method II:      By Semantic Order of Propositions: ($\vee$ = "or")

$$A \vee B \longrightarrow C$$

Given:    $A$    $= F$
           $B$    $= T$
Then $T(A \vee B)$    $= T$
Therefore $C$    $= T$

The result is clearly isomorphic. It is only a verbal disjunction, in this case of the speakers' mental structures, that can assign to the basic proposition, to $g[f(a)] \in C$ or to $c$ that is, both a negative and a positive value. Granted as valid[13] the logical processes by which this result is obtained, then it can be said that Okigbo's aim in the poem above is to describe a "propositional attitude" informed by conflicting impulses, by uncertainty and indecision. But more important, this can only be intended as a logical comment upon the speakers' world at the moment of utterance, since, according to our argument, any given linguistic utterance is circumscribed in time within an empirical referential context.

Against this structuralist view of poetic language as not merely connotative but cognitive, as capable that is of asserting a logically verifiable empirical relationship with the world of facts and experiences, it may perhaps be argued that all major statements in conventional poetry are "basic propositions." They do not require extraneous evidences or factual premises such as are given to us in *A* and *B,* to lead logically up to them. Poetry works with concrete images and arbitrary linguistic symbols which usually obey their own different system of aesthetic and semantic logic, logic that is more intuitive than intellectual. It follows by this principle that poetic propositions are essentially non-inferential: they posit no belief that can in any way be empirically certain or indubitable. Hence propositions in conventionally good poetry, unlike what Okigbo gives us in Movement I of the *Lament of the Drums,* are never as a rule of such a nature that they require factual premises, nor do they ever lead us to any empirical knowledge of Truth. Such, for example, is the famous Keatsian proposition: "Beauty is truth, truth beauty," the truth of which is not empirical truth but an aesthetic absolute.

This is a good but weak argument. Its weakness lies in its unstated premiss, its implied diachronic sense of time. Fortunately, it is neither invariably true to say that events in history or language succeed each other in a horizontal or linear-time, nor invariably false to assert its contrary. Thus structuralism which is based upon a firm recognition of the dialectic of oppositions—the fact that meaning impinges simultaneously upon diachrony and synchrony—tends also to inculcate disenchantment with any epistemological system, particularly in linguistic[14] and in historical[15] philosophies, that accords priority to one dimension of time over the other.

Another weakness in the same argument may also derive from its implied traditional view of poetic language or poetic image as an entity that can be isolated and examined in terms of its historical development in time. In this connection both the earlier distinction[16] made by Claude Lévi-Strauss between poetry and myth and his later attempt to establish a rapport[17] between them, is most instructive. The interpretation of a myth can be placed only on a semantic level where also may be constituted its system of variants. On the other hand, the meaning of a poetic work can reveal itself on a series of superimposed levels, including the syntactical and the semantic. If we suppose with Professor Lévi Strauss that "myths consist not only in conceptual interplays: they are also works of art capable of arousing in those who listen to them . . . profound aesthetic emotions,"[18] then we can hardly resist seeing an analogy between variants of a myth on one hand, and, on the other, those discernible linguistic structures[19] in a poem, by which we denote poetic images, capable

in themselves of generating specific feelings in the right type of reader, of acting as emotive-coefficients. To clench the point made here—on the myth-like
complexity of what is called a poetic image—this passage taken from Noel
Mouloud's recent work, *Langage et Structures,* may be useful:

> Indeed, whether one speaks of an image as the essential theme of poetry or of
> its language as the expressive form, one arrives at the same point: the descrip-
> tion of identical existences. The distance between the thinking subject and the
> object thought, which is rendered possible by the conventional symbolic lan-
> guage, is to a large measure abolished, by the more direct participation of the
> *Self* in the world. An "image" occurs when the *Self* is plunged back into per-
> spective, linked to the world corporally by its situation, and spiritually by its
> aura of projections, reminiscences and hopes. Thus Mallarmé, in the poem *La
> vierge, le vivace et le bel aujourd'hui,* leads us on to identify ourselves with the bird
> caught up in winter snows, and thence to feel the immutability of the past or
> the charge of the negating purity of life. But the *Self* should, in order to accede
> to the world of imagination, be doted with a *"fictive body,"* a *"corporal simu-
> lacrum"* which can resonate with the image. This living body of the poem is its
> very expressive morphic form . . .[20]

## 4. CONCLUSION

Starting with (i) a definition of the term *structure* as a system of relationships,
we have tried to (ii) apply this systematically to the opening movement of
Okigbo's *Lament of the Drums.* By considering the *drums* functionally as a
hypothetical model for the poem and limiting ourselves to the nature of the
more tractable aggregates described as propositions, and also by resorting to
notions derived from logic and mathematics, we have then (iii) briefly hinted
at the possibility of discovering an empirical correspondence, on the basis of
knowledge and truth, between the syntax of the poet's propositions and the
structure of his world. Further anticipating an objection to this view, we
finally tried to clarify some of the basic assumptions implicit in the method of
approach adopted here.

Okigbo may be considered as one of those African creative writers and
artists with an acute sense of form within formlessness. Their intuitions of
language and medium as revealed in their works, are generally linked not so
much with the separable properties of words, images or sound, as with the
ability to discern in these discordant elements a unifying dialectic. Of such
works then it can be said that they present an aspect of a constant striving of
the Self for a "fictive body," an apprehension of a central image or structure.
In fact, approached by way of semiology[21] or structural determinism, rather
than with the metaphysical agnosticism associated with certain schools of linguistic philosophy, the works of these African writers are capable of rewarding close investigation with a knowledge of an original creative system or

epistemological "truth" in which both the writers' tradition and their education may have equally played a part.

## Notes

1.    Written at fitful intervals between October 1963 and December 1964 at Ibadan, and first published in *Transition* No. 18 of April 1965, this poem is a sequel to *The Lament of the Silent Sisters* which had appeared two years earlier in the same Journal. These two "Lament" poems now form the sequence which Okigbo himself entitled *SILENCES*.

2.    Okigbo's range of interest and influences include the classical Greek, the Oriental and Igbo mythologies, the Indian, European and even Latin American cultures. This transforms his poetry often into a formidably erudite and cosmopolitan work. He conceived of art idealistically as a means of achieving a cathartic synthesis of different cultures and civilisations.

3.    J.-B. Fages, *Comprendre le structuralisme*. Paris: Payot, 1967, pp. 120 and 123.

4.    Ferdinand de Saussure, *Cours de linguistique générale*. Lausanne, 1916. For a detailed comment on the innovation introduced by de Saussure, see Oswald Ducrot, "Le Structuralisme en linguistique," in Oswald Ducrot, Tzvetan Todorov *et al.*, eds., *Qu'est-ce que le structuralisme?* Paris: Seuil, 1968, pp. 15–95.

5.    Ernest Gellner, *Words and Things* (Penguin, 1959), p. 87.

6.    Claude Lévi-Strauss, *Anthropologie Structurale*, Paris: Plon, 1958, p. 306.

7.    Every *model* is, at least by inductive definition, empirical. The apparent tautology in speaking of an "empirical model" may therefore serve to lend extra emphasis to the point made.

8.    Okigbo's predilection for traditional musical instruments is seen both in *Four Canzones,* his first published poem as well as in *Path of Thunder,* his last work published posthumously in 1968. See S. O. Anozie, "Christopher Okigbo: A Creative Itinerary, 1957–1961," *Présence Africaine* No. 64, 1967, pp. 158–166. Here, however, *drums* is considered not as a musical accompaniment for the poem but as its hypothetical linguistic model: not as a *supra* but as an *infra*-structure.

9.    In 1965 Okigbo wrote two new additional versions of this movement, each slightly different from the other and both, very different, in terms of *structure,* from the first version. The second appeared in *Black Orpheus* No. 17 of June, 1965; the third and final version is included in *LABYRINTHS* selected in October 1965 and to be published this year by Heinemann. The reasons for these changes have been suggested in S. O. Anozie, *Creative Rhetoric.* London: Evans & Co., 1970.

10.    Bertrand Russell, *An inquiry into meaning and truth* (Pelican Edition), 1962, p. 142.

11.    An attempt has been made to interpret Okigbo's poetry, particularly *SIREN LIMITS,* from the perspective of Neo-platonism. See S. O. Anozie, *op. cit.* 1970.

12.    Bertrand Russell, *op. cit.* p. 272.

13.    Our two methods derive from the logic of connectives and disjunctives in propositions. In logic, the truth values of compound statements $p \wedge q$, and $p \vee q$ satisfy the following properties respectively: (i) if $p$ is true and $q$ is true, then $p \wedge q$ is true; otherwise $p \wedge q$ is false; and (ii) if $p$ is true or $q$ is true or both $p$ and $q$ are true, then $p \vee q$ is true; otherwise $p \vee q$ is false. Reduced to tables these two properties become:

(i)

| $p$ | $q$ | $p \wedge q$ |
|---|---|---|
| T | T | T |
| T | F | F |
| F | T | F |
| F | F | F |

(ii)

| $p$ | $q$ | $p \vee q$ |
|---|---|---|
| T | T | T |
| T | F | T |
| F | T | T |
| F | F | F |

14. The 18th century classical epistemology was based upon the notion of a Universal Discourse as Universal Language. Since language was construed as a system of representation of thought and especially of the linear order in which the various elements of thought succeed one another, linguistic science consisted, for the 18th century philosophers, in the attempt to establish a taxonomy of every language, the possibility latent in each language to sustain a continuous line of discourse. By further emphasizing the study of *Rhetoric*—the disposition in space of the verbal signs that make up each language, and of *Grammar*—the articulation in time of this spatial order, the Classical Period therefore took for granted the rhetorical nature of languages, and so considered Grammar as an exclusive means of reflecting upon knowledge or language in general. But what the Classical Age called a Universal Discourse was in fact no more than a logical euphemism for a common denominator—the belief that all knowledge should manifest itself in linear discourse—which inevitably is epitomised in *Ideology*. (For a detailed treatment of this subject, see Michel Foucault, *Les Mots et Les Choses*. Paris: Gallimard, 1966, pp. 95–107). The birth of symbolic logic associated with Boole's algebra is seen, by Foucault (*op. cit.* p. 310) as contradicting the idea of a universal language on the foundation laid down by the Classical Period. Deeper forms and movements of thought can only be grasped by means of a more symbolic or meta-language: in other terms, through a dissociation of the "general grammar."

15. Marxism can be considered as a typical ideology with the pretension of a Universal language or Universal Discourse based upon the sense of diachrony as a common denominator. In recent years Althusser has sought to apply structural rationalism, through philosophical reflections, to the scientific work of Marx mainly by stressing the fact that all the phenomena present in a given region are determined by the structure of that region and *vice versa*. (Cf. Althusser, *Lire Le Capital*, Paris: François Maspero, 1966; and Althusser, *Pour Marx*, Paris: François Maspero, 1966.) Thus a systematic approach through structuralism can only serve to reveal some of the basic contradictions in the heart of the Marxist ideology (cf. Maurice Godelier, "Systeme, structure et contradiction dans *Le Capital*" in *Les Temps Modernes* No. 246, Nov. 1966, pp. 828–864), just as with the capitalist ideology the break, introduced by the concept of *structure*, may be considered as decidedly total.

16. Claude Lévi-Strauss, *op. cit.* p. 232.

17. Claude Lévi-Strauss & Roman Jacobson, Liminal note to "*Les Chats* de Charles Baudelaire," in *L'Homme*, Jan./April 1962, pp. 5–21.

18. *Ibid.*, p. 5.

19. Elsewhere we identified these with a metaphysical quality: cf. S. O. Anozie, "A Structural Approach to Okigbo's *Distances*," *The Conch* Vol. 1 No. 1, 1969, p. 23.

20. Noel Mouloud, *Langage et Structures*, Paris: Petite Bibliotheque Payot, 1969, pp. 72–73. Translation and italics are mine.

21. "Semiology" can be defined either as a "system of signs" (cf. Ferdinand de Saussure *op. cit.*, 1916: Roland Barthes, "Eléments de Sémiologie" in R. Barthes, *Le Degré Zéro de L'Ecriture*, Paris: Gonthier, 1964, pp. 79–174, also in *Communications* No. 4, 1965, pp. 91–135); or as a science of the "production of models" (cf. Julia Kristeva, "La Sémiologie: Science critique ou critique de la Science" in *The Conch* Vol. 1. No. 2, pp. 23–34).

# Okigbo's Portrait of the Artist as a Sunbird: A Reading of *Heavensgate* (1962)

## D. S. IZEVBAYE

### 1 HEAVENSGATE AND LABYRINTHS

The year 1971 saw the publication by Heinemann Educational Books of *Labyrinths with Path of Thunder,* a collection which is in one respect the final edition of Okigbo's work although, because of the omission of the Canzones and at least two of the later poems, its finality consists not in completeness but in saving editors of Okigbo's poems the trouble of having to decide what the poet actually wrote or intended to write. An additional value of this collection is the poet's introductory interpretation or, as interpretations are never known to be final, a description of the design of the poems which should become the basis of future interpretations. By thus providing the reader with an outline map of *Labyrinths,* Okigbo has cleared some of the paths to his poetic experience and has probably helped to arrest the growing tendency to regard the experience as something that is not available to the reader. This view of the poems as an impenetrable territory has been encouraged by reports of Okigbo's early view of poetry as a type of cult from which the uninitiated is excluded and by the cautious critical explications—often necessarily cautious, admittedly—in which the critic and the reader are unmasked as intruders. This impression of a closed world has been a potential inhibition to response, and the poet has thrown down this psychological barrier by offering the elucidations in *Labyrinths.*

The poetry remains a genuinely difficult one by itself, of course. To be able to find their way through the labyrinths of allusions to personal myths and forgotten cultures many readers will have to rely on the thread of meaning provided in the introduction and the notes. However, this change in respect of the poet's attitude to the reader reflects the difference between *Labyrinths* and the discrete earlier versions of Okigbo's poetry. In the earlier versions the uninitiated reader is understandably excluded from the poetic

Originally published in *African Literature Today* 6 (1973): 1–13. Reprinted by permission of James Currey Publishers and the author.

experience because the poet is himself still being initiated. *Labyrinths* follows the path of exploration or inquiry leading to discovery or revelation. With the poet's discovery of the true pattern of his initiation the reader can now be taken through the different stages until he too is finally admitted into the sanctuary. Each of the earlier sequences is incomplete by itself because it is only an investigation of the poet's partial glimpse of an experience, and only the complete group of sequences can provide a reliable blueprint from which a reader might reconstruct the poetic experience. The earlier poems are not then the true gateways; or if they are gateways they often lead to blind alleys, though they are useful as reflections of the poet's own wanderings and losses of direction before the surer path of his pilgrimage is revealed in the continuity of *Labyrinths*.

The revisions which result in *Labyrinths* are, like most revisions, necessary for a clearer and more accurate statement of the poet's experience. Nevertheless the earlier poems are of value because they tell a fairly accurate story of the process of composition. An interpretation of the revisions shows that in addition to the need for an efficient performance the final version required the tailoring of the old poems in order to fit the new need. One of the most important changes in *Labyrinths* is the cutting out of "Transition" from *Heavensgate*. Without necessarily committing oneself to a fallacy by describing as the poet's intention what is really an effect of the final revision, one may justify the excision of "Transition" by arguing that its triumphant tone is not quite consistent with the humble and exploratory spirit of *Heavensgate,* and that this tone is contradicted, in "Siren Limits," by the poet's use of the image of the shrub or the low growth which confesses a striving towards maturity rather than claim a full maturing of poetic powers. However if there is something inconsistent about the claims of "Transition" in the light of the actual performance of *Heavensgate* this section of the poem is itself less out of place in the original sequence than it would have been in *Labyrinths* within which the *Heavensgate* sequence itself is mainly an introduction or a prelude. In other words it was necessary to eliminate an end which has turned out to be a true end no longer.

If the 1962 version of the sequence would not fit into *Labyrinths* without modification it nevertheless has its own completeness, and the different sections have their justification for being in the poem, although the question that has most frequently been raised is that of the relevance of the parts. The organic unity of Okigbo's poems should seem a fairly commonplace idea by now, since it was emphasized in the earliest as well as in the most recent comments on the poetry—in Anozie's review[1] as well as in Okigbo's introduction. But although this underlying principle of composition has long been recognized it has not always been accepted as generally applicable to all the poems. For example, "Newcomer," the fifth movement of *Heavensgate,* is sometimes seen as separate from the rest of the poem because its sections were originally composed as separate poems and at different times.[2]

The ground for such a doubt is of course Okigbo's method of composition which creates the impression that each poem is an assemblage that may be dismantled and re-assigned to the various sources, like Tutuola's Complete Gentleman. For example, it seems as if some of the units in an Okigbo sequence can comfortably be moved to other positions especially when, because of the omission of existing parts or the addition of others, a new relationship is created between the parts which makes it necessary to re-examine the meaning conveyed. Such a reassignment is evident in both *Modern Poetry from Africa* (1963) and *Labyrinths* where "Bridge" is moved from its place in the middle of *Heavensgate* to the end in order to link the sequence with *Limits*. A discussion of Okigbo's poems therefore should assume the reader's acceptance of the essential looseness of structure arising from this method of composition. In this respect the sequences have a kinship with primitive epics because the poems appear to be a series of predetermined *forms* which attract independent poetic compositions to themselves. An important factor in the composition of extended traditional poems, especially primitive epics, is the fact that poems originally created as separate compositions cease to be considered independent units after they have been organized into larger units. The process of composition appears to be the adoption of a conventional, but fairly loose, structure within which individual experiences may establish a logical relationship with one another. The most favoured structures are usually those connected with social institutions or with religious or ritual performance. The relevance of this to a discussion of *Heavensgate* is obvious. The poem deals with the personal experiences of the hero. Its theme is the growth of a poet's mind. To the extent that the poem has a biographical— or autobiographical—structure, each of its movements represents the moments of crisis in the hero's life. So it is possible to regard any equivalent structure—like the basic stages of a man's life, Childhood, Adolescence, and Maturity—as the scaffolding around which the poem is constructed. The period of composition notwithstanding, poems about various experiences fit into the various stages whether as crises, or as the cause or the resolution of crises. The act of creation may thus be seen to consist mainly in a structural arrangement which makes each unit of the poem subordinate to, and a functional part of, the overall organization.

This emphasis on organization also makes it necessary to adopt a more flexible view of originality with regard to the problem of the literary influences or borrowings in the poems. For the purpose of this essay it is useful to make a distinction between literary echoes and literary borrowings. Literary echoes are resonances of an original, and to get a full experience of the poem the reader requires some knowledge of the original. And although such a poem might have an independent existence, like *The Waste Land,* the poems which it echoes are often part of the aesthetic experience of the poem, since the echoes are adaptations of an accepted context the knowledge of which, while not being essential, is invariably enriching.

In literary borrowing, on the other hand, knowledge of the original context contributes little or nothing to the experience of the new poem. It might in fact be a hindrance to proper critical response. The borrowed phrase or sentence is often used with little regard for its source, as in some of Okigbo's poems where not much is gained from a knowledge of the original poem. For usually Okigbo's interest in his borrowings seems limited to the beauty and the utility of the phrase itself, and the "meaning" or "experience" of the poem is often controlled by its immediate context.[3] This is mostly true even when, as in the title *Heavensgate,* the borrowed word affects the reader's response in the right direction before the context has had a chance to do its work. The discussion which follows is based on the text of 1962. The chart at the end of the essay indicates what sections of *Heavensgate* are available in revised form in *Labyrinths.*

## 2 HYMNS AT HEAVENSGATE

The title *Heavensgate* appears to be a word abstracted from a context, and the context that readily suggests itself is Shakespeare's twenty-ninth sonnet where the bard is lifted from a mood of depression to sing "hymns at heaven's gate" by the thought of love.[4] There is the same movement from despair to elation in the two poems. In both cases the central symbol is a singing bird. Even the image of the importunate outcast at the ears of deaf heaven in the sonnet seems reflected in the prodigal's apparent return to a starting point after an abortive attempt at entry. But it is not essential to see the title as a literary echo in order to notice that the sunbird is the central image of the poem, or that the whole poem is conceived as a musical form in which much value is attached to the interplay of sounds.

The conception of the poem as musical form is apparent in the opening invocation which is used as a prelude to introduce the main motif of the piece. This function is more apparent in the anthology by Moore and Beier where the adopted title "Overture" provides an apt musical analogy by emphasizing the introductory function of the invocation as well as describing the relationship between the suppliant and the goddess. Since the first movement, "Passage," deals with the period of passage from boyhood to manhood, the prelude is appropriately a physical dramatization of an attempted entry into a spiritual or aesthetic state. The central movements of the poem are concerned with such attempts in the present time. The events of the present are explained in the past, which is the period dealt with by the first two movements, "Passage" and "Initiation." "Transition," which is the coda to the whole sequence, anticipates the hero's passage into a future state, a state which is never really achieved in Okigbo's poetry except in *Distances.*

Although "Transition" foretells a state which *Distances* enacts, the vision which it presents—the uninhibited release of unlimited song—is not achieved in the poem itself, as is made clear in the structure of *Heavensgate*. In fact the effective mood of Okigbo's first two sequences is not fulfilment but anticipation. So that even by the end of "Siren Limits" the resolution of the crisis is deferred to future time:

> When you have finished
> & done up my stitches,
> Wake me near the altar,
> & this poem will be finished . . .

## When We Were Great Boys

"Passage" as a whole deals with the hero's early childhood responses to experience. But although there is an attempt, in "Passage (ii)," to recapture childhood experience by reproducing sounds mimicked by the boys, both "Passage" and "Initiation" deal with experience in retrospect. Although "the young bird at the passage" is the observer of the spectacle in "Passage (i)" (probably the onset of a thunderstorm), it is the mind of the mature artist which now interprets this scenery as a reproduction of the creation scene, and takes us back to that period "when we were great boys" and "sang words after the birds."

This second section is central to the first two movements of the poem because the way it uses the symbols of bird and light establishes their significance for the rest of the poem. After the associations built up by this section, light and bird would together herald the lyric impulse in both *Heavensgate* and *Limits*.

Meanwhile "Passage (iii)" picks up the image of the bird with which the preceding section closes, and with it defines and enlarges the theme of creation with which the first section opens. It does this by presenting the two major forms which the boys' introduction into the act of creation has taken. These are represented as at play at the blacksmiths' forge, and at work with the teacher at school. Since these introductions to experience take the form of response, there is possibly a third situation in which it occurs—that of worship in church. But this is not introduced until later.

The emphasis on response as the main factor in the boys' formative period shows that in "Passage (ii)" the boys are passing through a period of pupilage. Those gifts which are to survive into their adult life are already in evidence here—the fascination which song holds for them is evident in their imitation of bird sounds—"kratosbiate." There is also the identification of these sounds with other fascinating sounds the children are made to imitate at school, as in their dutiful response to the sing-song recitation of their teacher, "*Etru bo pi a lo a she* . . ."[5] The metonymy, "white buck and helmet," shows the teacher himself as seen through childhood eyes. As if to show that both experiences are really part of the same experience in spite of their separate locations at school and at play, the flames of the forge become metaphor for the shaping influence of school where boys are pulled through innocence, and the smith's workshop becomes a new setting for learning. The boys show a preference for the latter setting, since the symbols of school influence are consigned to the flames. That is why "burn" is possibly ambiguous in the following extract:

> And we would respond,
> great boys of child-innocence,
> and in the flames burn
>     white buck and helmet
> that had pulled us through innocence. . . .

The lines would normally be read to mean, "we would burn white buck and helmet in the flames"; but it could also imply, "we would burn [be shaped] in the flames."

If religion does not feature as an important influence in those two sections it sounds the dominant note in the rest of "Passage" and "Initiation," and helps to define the unpleasant experiences which force the prodigal to accept the necessity for homecoming. In "Passage (ii)" the real centre of the Christian procession is the overwhelming bewilderment which the poet feels on arriving at a crossroads or a turning point in his development. This mood is achieved through an emphasis on the solemnity and on the mourning colour which marks the procession and which identifies the poet's mood with the traditional feeling of loss and alienation associated with mournings. The fragments of melody, the appeal to a personal saint, "Anna of the panel oblongs," and the refuge in the cornfields among the wild music of the winds complete the mourner's feeling of a broken emotional anchor. Thus begins the prodigal's progress from separation through bewilderment and alienation which are the preludes to his renunciation of the Christian religion.

"Passage (iii)" outlines the hero's initial objections to Christianity; its foreign origin is emphasized in the drama of the seven-league boots striding over distant seas and deserts; its oppressiveness is implied in the designation of Leidan as "archtyrant of the holy sea" (an obvious pun); and the aversion which he feels for Christian ritual and its reward is present in the report on the fate of people like Paul, who, after conversion, become subjected to the:

> smell of rank olive oil
> on foreheads,

> vision of the hot bath of heaven
> among reedy spaces.

## Of Poetry, Religion, and Sin

Having had a foretaste of various forms of experience in "Passage" (play, education, religion), the poet recalls, in "Initiation," his formal introduction into the adult world of religion, poetry, and sex. His introduction to the first takes the form of a ritual initiation, but his introduction to the other two areas of experience occurs as a form of discovery. As might have been anticipated in the previous section, the prodigal's first significant experience of religion takes the form of a painful initiation which he sees rather resentfully as a branding that has the claims of a legal agreement:

> Scar of the crucifix
> over the breast
> by red blade inflicted
> by red-hot blade on right breast
> witnesseth

The pain itself is not the cause but the consequence of his resentment The cause stems from his conception that ideally, the initiated should be

> Elemental, united in vision
> of present and future,
> the pure line, whose innocence
> denies inhibitions.

Instead of this promised transformation the initiated ones turn out to be worthless or corrupt adherents whom the poet has arranged in categories which include lifeless morons, fanatics, and self-seekers. This perversion of good intentions is imputed to cultural differences. Maybe that is why the hero seeks refuge in the memory of a childhood experience in the third section.

The second and central theme of the poem is presented in "Initiation (iii) and (iv)." "Initiation (iii)" returns us the poet's childhood. The theme is music making, with Jadum the minstrel singing cautionary songs from the fairyland of youth till late into the night. The opening lines are a suggestion that Jadum got his name from the sound of his music, "JAM JAM DUM DUM." The emphasis is not so much on his madness as on the music he makes. The power of his minstrelsy over the childish listener is the theme of the section. And yet the fact of his madness is important too, for the identification of poetry with madness is also the theme of "Newcomer (ii)" where the hero is "mad with the same madness as the / moon and my neighbour."

*For Poets Only*

"Initiation (iv)" focuses attention directly on the art of poetry by formulating a poetic. The formulation takes the form of a dialogue with "upandru." The first item defines Okigbo's technique, his delight in mystifying the reader with recondite references. Obscurity is a technique for hiding the poet's thoughts: "Screen your bedchamber thoughts / with sunglasses." The second item, the view that only poets may penetrate beyond this mask, might explain why, as was once reported, Okigbo claimed, "I don't read my poetry to non-poets":[6]

> who could jump your eye
> your mind-window?

> And I said:
> The prophet only,
> The poet.

The bedchamber is introduced in the fifth section where the poet screens his thoughts with a riddle. In this introduction of the third theme, the sexual, the poet rejects the Christian call of "Initiation (i)" for a "life without sin." In his conviction that freedom from lust can come only through indulgence the prodigal has found a philosophy to live by. By this rejection of an alien religion and the adoption of poetry and of a personal code of existence, the prodigal-poet considers his initiation into a new personal world complete, and feels ready for union with Watermaid. "Bridge" represents this stage of the antici-pation of her influence.

*The Homecoming*

The desired union with Watermaid is however not consummated in the third movement. There is a stage missing in the ritual of the prodigal's return, and that is, an identification of the source to which he is returning, and a perfor-mance of the requirements for readmission. "Initiation" has turned out a mis-leading experience. What he describes in the first section is merely an abortive initiation; and although he achieves something in the first two sec-tions by completing the renunciation of his prostituted allegiance, he does not go further than an examination and a discovery of his own purposes in the last two sections. In fact no adequate preparation for the meeting with Watermaid has taken place. That is why, as the poet discovers, "Bridge" has been a premature stage in his homecoming. So although the goddess responds to the prodigal's cry, the revelation is too evanescent to be of perma-nent value to the poet who now watches the loss of the harvest:

So brief her presence—
match-flare in wind's breath—
so brief with mirrors around me.

Downward . . .
the waves distil her:
gold crop
sinking ungathered.

The lament in "Watermaid (iii)" involves not merely alienation but also a loss of the expected harvest. In "Watermaid (iv)," for example, the departure of the stars is used not only as a backdrop to the isolation of the poet; it is also a reference to "Watermaid (i)" in which poetic blessing is expected when the eyes of the prodigal "upward to heaven shoot / where stars will fall from." That is why the prodigal-poet strives to recapture the fleeting strains of poetic inspiration in a passage that anticipates the second movement of *Limits:*

Stretch, stretch, O antennae,
to clutch at this hour,

fulfilling each moment in a
broken monody.

The reason for the failure to achieve full union with Watermaid has been revealed earlier where the suppliant hid the secret in beach sand. The goddess has discovered that the candidate for initiation is ritually unclean and therefore unfit for her presence. All he has done is to go through an adapted form of Christian confession without using a priest—an unsuitable ritual, for Watermaid is unambiguously presented as "native"—in a renunciation of the Christian experience. That is why, in spite of being from the sea, she is "Watermaid of the salt emptiness." Salt water has become distasteful because of its supposed association with the baptismal rites of primitive Christianity:

so comes John the Baptist
with bowl of salt water

Since Watermaid is not a Christian goddess we may assume that she belongs mainly to a non-Christian, even pre-Christian, religion or community.

It follows, then, that the particular defilement we are concerned with is non-Christian and even non-ethical, and that the state of impurity should not be linked with the prodigal's rejection of Christian insistence on continence in the "Initiation" movement. In fact the recurrence of the he-goat-on-heat motif in *Limits* reinforces this view that the uncleanliness which drove Watermaid away from contact with pollution, and makes the "Lustra" movement of *Heavensgate* necessary, is a ceremonial rather than an ethical or moral purification. Ritual offering is necessary only because the poet-hero has been a prodigal and is therefore technically a stranger requiring ritual cleansing before being readmitted into communion with his goddess.

It is this purification feast that is variously celebrated in the three parts of "Lustra": first the traditionally prescribed objects of purification in the first part; then the spirit's hopeful ascent towards acceptance to an accompaniment of ceremonial drums and cannons in the second part; finally, the vegetable and chalk that are offered in the third part as an act of penitence to complete the requirement partially fulfilled by the performances in the earlier sections. Although the offerings are all traditional ones, they possess the attributes of moistness and whiteness which have been associated with the goddess. Also like the goddess, the attitude is "native." It will be noticed that in the line, "whitewashed in the moondew," a common Christian moral attitude has been purged from the word, "whitewash," which is now reinvested with a non-Western, traditional ritual meaning. We may assume that his renunciation is final at this stage.

In the third section the poet adopts the underlying faith of the religion from which he is a refugee; the rejection of the source of the faith is explicit in the attitude of "After the argument in heaven." The doctrine has relevance for the prodigal because it provides reassurance in the analogy drawn with the Christian belief in the Second Coming—the reappearance of his Watermaid, after the fulfilment of the lustral requirements.

It is this expected second coming of Watermaid which makes the fifth movement, "Newcomer," a necessary conclusion for *Heavensgate*. Having lost his first opportunity to achieve communion with Mother Idoto, it is only in "Newcomer" that the poet gets another opportunity to hold himself open to poetic inspiration from his native muse, after his blunder in the "Watermaid" movement. Although "Newcomer" suffers from repetition in the context of the poem since the first two sections take the reader over some old ground, on the whole it moves us a step further towards the close of the hero's development. For example, in the opening lines the peals of the angelus recall the prodigal's state of exile, and the involuntary sign of the cross which accompanies these bells becomes transformed into a gesture of defiance against the usual response. It also serves him as a protective mask to insulate his new individuality from being swamped by communal values:

> Mask over my face—
>
> my own mask
> not ancestral—

Thus, the internalized allegiance which makes it irresistible for the Christian to respond spontaneously at the sight or sound of Christian symbols is tested against the hero's new-found identity. The appeal to the personal "Saint,"

Anna, for succour is a desperate step which he takes because he is threatened by the danger of succumbing to the Christian call to worship.

"Newcomer (ii)," by no means the happiest section, repeats the theme of identity just presented in the first section. It is dedicated to a kindred spirit. Both "spirits" are isolated from the generality of men by their madness—for what is madness but a deviation from commonly-accepted norms of behaviour. It is this common "insanity" of creative spirits which unites the hero and Peter Thomas with Jadum, the mad minstrel of "Initiation (iii)."

The final section of "Newcomer" is also a dedicatory piece: "For Georgette," written as a kind of nativity poem. Although, like the section dedicated to Peter Thomas, this piece was originally occasional, it finds a logical context in *Heavensgate*. Its burden is the final arrival of the much-longed-for inspiration which gave the whole of the *Heavensgate* sequence its exploratory structure and the strongly expectant tone first dictated by the "Watchman for the watchword" in the overture. But this section is not a description of the composition of *Heavensgate*, as Anozie pointed out in the review. It only heralds the arrival of poetic inspiration, for *Heavensgate* is an account of its own uncompleted quest only, and the reader is left at that point of elated expectancy just as inspiration descends—a point just one stage ahead of "Watermaid (i)," and one behind "Watermaid (ii)." A suitable setting to have the muse delivered has been created in "May," "green," and "garden." The "synthetic welcome" suits the experimentation with words and form which gets the poet ready to welcome inspiration when it arrives.

We are now ready for the actual manifestation of the poetic impulse. The blinded heron of "Transition" proclaims the birth of song, and anticipates the fulfilment of the goal towards which *Heavensgate* has been developing. The poem closes by the use of images with which the poet initially dramatized the problems of creation. The heron is of course the "sunbird" of "Passage" now developed into a mature bird, and it is to become the talkative weaver-bird of *Siren Limits*. We are also to meet him in *Fragments out of the Deluge* as the martyred songster who arose, like the phoenix from its ashes, to hymn new songs of its own immortality.

The song of *Heavensgate* ends as darkness descends over the setting, a contrast with the sunrise scene of the opening movement. This is achieved by a tempering of the dominant colours of the poem—transparency replaces the brilliant white of "Watermaid," and soft leaf green replaces the bright, violent colours of the creation scene—i.e., the red, violet and orange of "Passage (i)." Natural phenomena, too, undergo this change: the moon goes under the sea—and it will be remembered that in "Newcomer (ii)" the moon is the source of madness and inspiration, and that the sea is the home of Watermaid, goddess of inspiration. When the song is over, the inspirer goes home to rest, leaving the poet spent but sane; leaving only the shade to cloud the play of colour and sound.

And we have to wait until *Limits* when the poet is seized in a new poetic frenzy, his tongue having been liberated after appropriate purification.

*Notes*

1. S. O. Anozie, "Okigbo's *Heavensgate*, a study of Art as Ritual," *Ibadan*, No. 15 (March 1963), p. 11.

2. O. R. Dathorne, "Ritual and ceremony in Okigbo's Poetry," *Journal of Commonwealth Literature*, No. 5 (July 1968), p. 84.

3. Some would deny that there is any such contextual control of meaning. E.g., Ali Mazrui argues that Okigbo's poetry "leaves the reader no room for being *wrong* in his interpretation." "Abstract Art and African Tradition," *Zuka*, No. 1 (September 1967), p. 47.

4. Note the reference also in *Cymbeline*, Act II, Scene 3: "Hark! Hark! the lark at heaven's gate sings."

5. According to Okigbo himself, this line is a rendering of a child's phonetic variation on the nursery rhyme, "Little Bo Peep." "Death of Christopher Okigbo," *Transition*, No. 33 (October/November 1967), p. 18. The poet eliminates the nostalgia of this lost paradise by leaving the section out of the *Labyrinths* version.

6. Bloke Modisane, "The Literary Scramble for Africa," *West Africa* (30 June 1962), p. 176.

*The Revisions*

| *Heavensgate*, Mbari, 1962 | | *Labyrinths*, Heinemann, 1971 |
|---|---|---|
| Idoto [Overture] | | I The Passage (3 sections) |
| I Passage | (i) | p. 3 |
| | (ii) | p. 4 |
| | (iii) | — |
| | (iv) | p. 5 |
| | | — |
| II Initiation | | II Initiations (3 sections) |
| | (i) } | pp. 6–7 |
| | (ii) } | |
| | (iii) | p. 8 |
| | (iv) } | p. 9 |
| | (v) } | |
| Bridge | | [p. 19 (Newcomer)] |
| III Watermaid | | III Watermaid (4 sections) |
| | (i) | p. 10 |
| | (ii) | p. 11 |
| | (iii) | p. 12 |
| | (iv) | p. 13 |
| IV Lustra | | IV Lustra (3 sections) |
| | (i) | p. 14 |
| | (ii) | p. 16 |
| | (iii) | p. 15 |
| V Newcomer | | V Newcomer (3 sections) |
| | (i) | p. 17 |
| | (ii) | — |
| | (iii) | p. 18 |
| Transition | | -(replaced by what used to be 'Bridge') |

# Okigbo's "Distances":
# A Retreat from Christ to Idoto

## R[OMANUS]. N. EGUDU

If Christopher Okigbo's statement that "Distances" is "a poem of homecoming . . . in its spiritual and psychic aspect"[1] is anything to go by, one has reason to suspect that "spiritual quest" is central to the poem. In spite of the poet's statement however, Okigbo scholars, prominent among whom are Sunday Anozie and Gerald Moore, have tended to emphasize not a spiritual but an artistic quest in "Distances." For though Anozie seems to recognize the presence of what he calls "this spiritual-cum-artistic quest" in the poem, his most recondite discussion of "Distances" is exclusively partial to the artistic quest.[2] And though Gerald Moore sees the poem as a record of a "whole cycle of spiritual and historical exploration," he still considers it a "type of poetic quest for reality,"[3] without, that is, telling us what this "reality" consists in. Another critic, Paul Theroux, holds a view which not only is out of tune with those already indicated, but also tends to be a negation of a meaningful "homecoming"; for he says that " 'Silences' and 'Distances' . . . are concerned with emptiness and disappointment at having arrived," meaning, of course, that "Distances" is concerned with "disappointment at having arrived."[4]

In any event, "Distances" is essentially concerned with a spiritual journey from "foreign" Christ to native Idoto, a journey from the Christian theory of salvation effected after death to the indigenous state of purity and bliss attainable in life. For Okigbo could have reasonably argued using the words of Kofi Awoonor, that salvation is here with us and not somewhere beyond this world:

> Who says there is a resting place elsewhere?
> It is here with us[5]

For Okigbo's protagonist, therefore, the resting place is that "home" which is under the matronship of the Water-Goddess. The process through which he arrived back at this "home" in spite of those "shadows distances labyrinths violences" which are created by Death and the Christian world seen in a

Originally published in *The Conch* 5, nos. 1–2 (1973): 29–42. Reprinted by permission of the author.

vision, which hindered his progress and distracted attention from his quest—this process re-created as a dream vision, seems to me to be the essential burden of "Distances."

Thus starting *in medias res,* and indeed, *in terminos res,* the poet gives us in "Distances I," a resumé of his experiences and the significant sign posts on his road to home. The very first line creates the all embracing atmosphere of a dream vision in which the protagonist undertook his most excruciating journey, not as an ordinary man with flesh and blood, but as a "phantom" or spirit, as one who has conquered time within the frame work of time. And with this setting done, he informs us immediately in the second line that he "was sole witness to [his] home coming"—a line which appears three times in this first part of the poem and which *ab initio* defines for us the end to which the poet and we are moving.

Furthermore, the poet intimates in this early part the main question the answer to which will later constitute the turning point towards the resolution of the dilemma, whereby Idoto will be chosen instead of the Cross or Holy Communion. Thus when he asks:

> But what does my divine rejoicing hold?
> A bowl of incense, a nest of fireflies?

he makes us feel that there is at least some dialectics going on in his mind; for though the rejoicing is "divine," it is not certain whether it points to God like "incense" or to illusion which deceives like the fire of fireflies without heat. This debate or doubt is legitimate since a "voice" which, as will later be shown, is identifiable with the home goddess is already there to rescue the protagonist from the illusion of the beautiful "white chamber" richly decked with flowers, and to lead him "through some dark / labyrinth" to the reality which is in this context the habitat of the home deity. For the white chamber, and the "serene lights on the other balcony" which are "redolent fountains bristling with signs"—all these are in the Christian God's Kingdom of the other world. And it is significant that the "voice" of the home goddess, that "miner into my solitude," that "incarnate voice of the dream" of the ideal state which is the object of the protagonist's quest, should extricate him from that painted paradise! The reason, of course, is that this paradise is mere illusion, and is therefore no paradise for the protagonist. With this exposition effected and the end determined in "Distances I," the spiritual journey begins with "Distances II."

In "Distances II" the protagonist finds himself in the valley of Death—"DEATH LAY in ambush that evening in that Island." This is the same condition of transition "from flesh into phantom" as in "Distances I"; it is an imaginary death, or a temporary loss of conscious life under the influence of anaesthesia, since Okigbo had told us that the poem "was written after [his] first experience of surgery under general anaesthesia";[6] or it may simply be a dream situation in which the protagonist sees himself as dead and in Death's kingdom. The first twenty lines of this part of the poem present a frightful and haunting picture of life or lifelessness in this dark and gloomy valley of the shadow of death: the evening is that "without flesh or skeleton," without "silver bells to its tale," without "lanterns" or "buntings," and above all, "without age or memory." It is therefore a moment outside time, a moment in the eternity of "hell." And if there are no silver bells to the tale, there may be wooden bells such as are used on Maundy Thursday to prepare for the death of Christ on Good Friday. Furthermore, the richly dressed "white chamber" which was referred to in "Distances I," and which happens to be the only illuminated spot in this Erebus, is lit only by the harassing "incandescent rays" of "eyes that had lost their animal / colour"—lifeless eyes that pinned the protagonist—victim "cold, to the marble stretcher." This stretcher is the same thing as the "horizontal stone" on which, as we have seen earlier on, the transformation from "flesh into phantom" took place. This is likely to be the marble platform/or altar on which a corpse is laid as a Requiem Mass is being said for the dead person. This seems to me a more relevant interpretation of this "marble stretcher" or "horizontal stone" than that which equates it with the surgical table on which Okigbo was operated upon;[7] particularly as the remaining lines of "Distances II" and much of the rest of the poem contain significant allusions to and images of the Holy Mass. The futility of the illumination of the chamber of death is further adumbrated by the fact that the "everlasting fire from the oblong window" (which may be the fire of hell?) is not one that produces "ash" from its burning. It is in fact fire that does not burn!

The remaining twenty-one lines of "Distances II" depict "Death" as a priestess-celebrant coming behind her ministrants—"the dancers" who got "lost among their own / snares"—as they file out for the funerary celebration. Dressed "in smock of white cotton," "Death is paring her fingernails," which indicates that there is a non-serious attitude to the celebration; for ironically, she is a minister that thrives on the "blood of [her] attendants" and on the "entrails of her ministrants," just as the Church thrives on the blood of her martyrs. The blood of martyrs is said to be the seed of the Church.

It is significant that the spiritual journey of "Distances" has to start with Death. On one hand, one can view the situation quite literally, seeing death as knocking on the poet's door during his surgical operation. In such a situation, it is likely that the thought of salvation as preached by the Christian religion (which is always present at the background part of his mind) has invaded him. In other words he might have been tempted into reflecting upon the possibility of this salvation, his fear then being that this might ultimately happen to be true. Consequently, he might have been perturbed by the Psalmist's words: "though I walk through the valley of the shadow of death, I will fear no evil: for thou art with me; thy rod and thy staff, they comfort me."[8] But as the last part of "Distances" clearly shows, it is the voice of the home goddess, and not the power of the Psalmist's Lord, that led our protagonist through and gave him the final comfort. On the other hand, the journey in "Distances," being a journey homeward after some wandering, is therefore a kind of "Retreat." And in the Christian "Retreat" situation, it is conventional for the preacher to structure his conference talks around the four last things: Death, Judgment, Hell, and Heaven.[9] The talk on death and Hell is always geared toward making them look so frightful that every sensitive person should dread them and therefore avoid committing sin, particularly as "the wages of sin is death." This structure of the "Retreat" sermons finds a parallel in "Distances," where part II is Death; parts III and IV, Judgment; part V, Hell; and part VI, Heaven. (More will be said about this later in this paper.) It may suffice now to say, as has been earlier indicated, that the Christian images of these four last things, which our protagonist saw in his vision are not quite acceptable to him as necessary stages towards spiritual salvation.

This point is clear in the handling of the themes of pilgrimage and the way to salvation in "Distances" III and IV. "Distances" III places before us a picture of a mock-pilgrimage, of a heterogenous group of "scattered line of pilgrims," among whom are the protagonist himself, who is the chief acolyte, carrying the crucifix, a "torn branch" and a "censer"; prophets, martyrs, lunatics, dantini, dilettanti, vendors, princes, and negritude politicians, people of different professions and vocations, and of possibly irreconcilable spiritual dispositions. This kind of mocking lumping of men of the other world and those of this world had appeared in an earlier poem of Okigbo's:

> square yields the moron,
> fanatics and priests and popes,
> organizing secretaries and
> party managers, better still,
>
> the rhombus—brothers and deacons,
> liberal politicians,
> selfish selfseekers—all who are good
> doing nothing at all.[10]

Here are those who have been initiated, according to the earlier poem. In "Distances" III, we find most of them present again among the pilgrims, who are not bound for the shrine of St. Thomas as in Chaucer's *Prologue,* but rather for "Shibboleth," for a place of Judgment. For they, like the men of Ephraim had escaped from their land and are now returning home, and therefore must be judged by some Gileadites. Thus only those of them who could say "Shibboleth" and not "Sibboleth" could be allowed to return to their home.[11] "Shibboleth" in "Distances" for which the pilgrims are bound, is therefore a watchword for attaining salvation.

One may have reason to ask why our protagonist who is making a homeward journey to his indigenous religion should be carrying the objects which are associated with the religion of his exile. The "crucifix" is a central symbol in the Christian religion. The "torn branch" may be the palm leaves (palm branch) which a Catholic carries to a Palm Sunday Mass. And the censer is used for celebrating the Holy Mass, especially the High Mass. Does it follow that the protagonist who broke away from this religion in "Heavens-gate" has reverted to it now? The answer is, of course, "No." The poet is showing us how the protagonist is being tempted by this vision of part of the Christian world, which contains the elements that contradict its spiritual objective. For it is difficult to see how the pilgrims with their diverse professional or vocational interests could be pursuing the same religious quest. This indeed reminds one of Chaucer's pilgrims whose interests comprehend spiritual and materialistic, serious and frivolous dimensions. This fact, though realistic it may be, makes nonsense of what ought to be a unified purpose of a religious journey. It is possible that the poet of "Distances" wants to show the same kind of futility and meaninglessness of the Christian theory of salvation which accommodates in one group pilgrims whose quests may be contradictory to one another.

In any event, it has already been suggested that there is a pilgrimage (even if it be a sham), and that the end of this pilgrimage is judgment (for after death, follows judgment). The purpose of this judgment is to distinguish those who can find the road to salvation from those who cannot. This road (or way) to salvation, as we gather in "Distances IV," has two signs which every pilgrim must read and interpret accurately, and believe in and adopt in order to attain salvation. These signs not only echo the words of the Bible, but also mock at the ideals they (the signs) are meant to symbolise.

The first sign goes as follows:

> the only way to go
> through the marble archway
> to the catatonic pingpong
> of the evanescent halo.

The frame on which these words are inscribed is quite significant: first, there is the square structure; secondly, there is the "triangular lintel / of solid alabaster" enclosed within the square; thirdly, there is the inscription in a circular form, which leaves the centre hollow. This frame is placed "above the archway" which has no "shutters" and which looks "like a vast countenance." In this background structure, one notices the triangular figure which one sees on the wall of many a Catholic church building, above the altar, which perhaps symbolises the Blessed Trinity. The words of the "sign" can be seen as an elaborate echo of those words of Jesus Christ which have to do directly with salvation: "I am the way, the truth, and the life."[12] In other words, Christ is the way to true salvation, which is eternal life—life of permanence.

However, within the same frame and the words of the sign, we find some elements which strongly negate these Christian echoes and what they stand for. The hollowness of the centre of the structure and the picture of the archway as "shutterless" and "yawning," like "a vast countenance" without a body behind it—all these point to the vacuity and meaninglessness of the sign, that is, from the protagonist's point of view. Thus according to the wording of the sign, the way leads not to a substantial or lasting state of sanctity or blessedness, but to an "evanescent halo" which is characterised by the din of mundane recreation—the noise of "the catatonic pingpong." The protagonist, therefore, seems to be wondering what the great argument is for even taking that way!

The second sign in "Distances IV" is seen some distance beyond the first. Like the first, it is inscribed in a frame which is symbolic in the Christian world, and it contains elements which tend to minimize and even nullify whatever validity that might be associated with it. The words of the second sign are

> after we had formed
> then only the forms were formed
> and all the forms
> were formed after our forming . . .

These words were inscribed on a frame that has the shape of "an immense crucifix." But the crucifix is not made of hard wood or iron or any reasonably durable or substantial material. It is rather made of "phosphorescent mantles" which merely resemble, but are not, "pentecostal orbs." The mantles are therefore fading, non-substantial things, just like the "evanescent halo" of the first sign; for they give off luminosity without combustion or sensible heat. Their light is thus cold, without passion or fervour.

The Cross is the principal means to Christian salvation. Christ had said: "If any man will come after me, let him deny himself, and take his cross, and follow me."[13] It is therefore not surprising that one of the signs that direct men to salvation should assume the shape of a Cross. And the words on the cross are equally significant. We are not told whom the "we" stands for, but we certainly know that they are different from "all the forms"; in fact they are not just forms. Furthermore, we know from the reading of the sign that the "we" stands for an order of beings that were self-created, or self-begotten, and that all forms were fashioned (likely by the self-generated beings) after their forms. If this is so, one suspects that the meaning of the sign, simply put, is "we are the Alpha and Omega"—the beginning and the end—the source of "all the forms," to whom the forms must return. Incidentally, during the blessing of the Paschal Candle in the Easter Vigil, the Celebrant cuts on the lighted candle, a cross, and the first and last letters of the Greek alphabet (A

& Ω) above and below the cross respectively. And as he cuts these letters he says: "Alpha et Omega"—"the Beginning and the End,"[14] implying that God represented by the cross is the beginning and the end of all creations. In this sign and in that in "Distances," there are the cross or crucifix, some lighting apparatus (candle in the former and mantles in the latter), and some form of light. In the Catholic ritual the Paschal Candle symbolises the renewal of Baptism, without which one does not get to Heaven. Similarly in "Distances" the sign, as has been noted earlier is one that leads to salvation.

The use of the plural "we" would naturally refer to the Three Divine Persons of the Blessed Trinity, who are revered and adored each time we make the sign of the Cross on the forehead, the chest and the shoulders. It can be recalled here that in the story of the creation of the world according to the Book of Genesis, the accusative and genitive plural forms of "we" have been used even though reference is made to the singular form "God." Thus in Genesis, 1:26–27, we read: "And God said, Let *us* make man in our own image, after our likeness—so God created man in his own image—." The sign is thus one that points to salvation, but it is ineffective in the circumstance because it is seen as something illusory. In "Distances IV," as in part III, therefore, we are seeing a Christian setting, Christian ideas and beliefs, through the temperament of a poet, who far from embracing (or re-embracing) those ideas and beliefs, has shown them as holding no reward or promise for him, and is therefore bidding them final good bye.

From the thoughts about pilgrimage, about "Shibboleth" the password, in "Distances III," and about the two signs which are the gateway to salvation, in "Distances IV," the protagonist moves on to the issue of actual struggling for spiritual elevation in "Distances V." This part of the poem is set in "the abyss"—which may be the abyss of hell, or the abyss of oneself. In any case, it is a mighty depression from which escape appears impossible, for "each step is the step of the mule in the abyss." Furthermore, this "abyss" is the same as the "anti-hill" (not anthill), which is the opposite of a hill, and therefore symbolises a state of spiritual depression (valley) where thoughts are always negative, hopes non-existing, progress mere "gestures," and sighing palpable and eternal. It is a state of absolute spiritual inertia, a condition which is like that of Vladimir and Estragon, who each time they say "Let us move," simply stand still, motionless.[15] Thus our protagonist's ascending ends up in meaningless "gestures."

The atmosphere is that of the Holy Mass, possibly the Requiem Mass, for we have in "Distances V" the necessary items of such a Mass: the "Sanctuary," the funeral music, the "funerary rose," the water in a small bottle (seen as "water in the tunnel" with its "effervescent laughter"), the wine from grape-vine (Mass wine) with its "open laughter," the tabernacle with the consecrated host inside it, which (consecration) constitutes "the unanswerable question." This probably is a reference to the question of transubstantiation, which is regarded as a mystery. Furthermore, we have the "censers," the "burden of the pawn," which is perhaps the wine in the Chalice which is the blood of Jesus Christ who is the "pawn," the sacrificial lamb, for the salvation of mankind. And this burden or "chaliced vintage"[16] is placed on "the molten stone," which is the altar stone, another important item in the Mass. All these items are "mated and sealed / in a proud oblation"—the Mass itself. This Mass image is clinched with an allusion to the betrayal of Christ by Judas which led to the capture and crucifixion of Christ: "and the scar of the kiss and of the two swords." Before his passion and death, Christ warned his apostles that any one of them who had no sword should "sell his garment and buy one"; and they told him that they had "two swords" there. Shortly after, Judas drew near unto him to kiss him; and Jesus said to him: "Judas, betrayest thou the Son of man with a kiss?" Seeing that Jesus was in the danger of being captured, one of the apostles, using one of the two swords, "smote the servant of the high priest, and cut off his right ear."[17] This biblical reference is significant in "Distances V" for the Holy Mass is a dramatization of the Death of Christ on the Cross; and during the Good Friday celebration, the betrayal scene with the sword episode is rehearsed and dramatized.

If as suggested earlier, "Distances V" is about "hell," an abyss of a kind; it is one from which Christ and Chris (Okigbo) will rise to ascend into heaven shortly after. The rising will not be easy, for there are the "wandering rocks" or the "clashing rocks" between which Odysseus was warned not to pass during his homeward journey, for it had been said that only the *Argo* had ever succeeded in passing between them.[18] Therefore, the "wandering rocks" in "Distances V" symbolize the difficult nature of the passage through the abyss. For the ordinary man, the Holy Mass would be futile once he descends into "hell" and for a superhuman being or for Chris Okigbo who has "transcended" the Christian world, the Mass is not necessary because he will conquer hell after suffering the anguish therein. This is so, particularly since "the question in the inkwell" which perhaps symbolises art, has been answered by means of unified vision, that is, "the monocle." For the artist's heaven is certainly different from the Christian's as is clearly shown in the last part of the poem.

So "Distances VI" deals with these two heavens. In the first half of this last part, there is a voice calling from a cavern:

> Come into my cavern,
> Shake the mildew from your hair;
> Let your ear listen:
> My mouth calls from a cavern . . .

Critics have identified this voice in different ways. Gerald Moore has identified it with the home goddess and the watermaid;[19] Paul Theroux implies this kind of identification in his statement noted earlier;[20] and Sunday Anozie simply states that "a voice . . . beckons him" but goes no further.[21] I do not, however, think that this voice is that of the goddess which we heard in "Distances I" and which we will hear again in the second half of "Distances VI," for, whatever the voice is, it is a distracting one, and it will be contradictory to say that the voice of the goddess which is guiding the protagonist in his quest—journey is at one and the same time distracting him from the same quest! Shortly after the passage quoted above, we learn that the voice calling is one that has created, or is at least associated with "shadows distances labyrinths violences," and that the voice is that of the "Skeletal oblong / of my sentient being."

The word "oblong" here is quite striking, for it had featured in two poems of Okigbo's written before "Distances." In "Time for Worship"[22] there is "Anna of the panel oblongs," who is the organist playing in a Christian church. And it is this Anna whom the protagonist prays to protect him "from them fucking angels." This "Anna of the panel oblongs" therefore belongs with the Christian church, and in fact represents it to the protagonist. Also, in "Siren Limits IV"[23] we see the "oblong-headed lioness" whose "image distracts / with the cruelty of the rose," and against whom "no shield is proof" enough. Since Anna is of the Christian religion and she is distracting the protagonist from his creative quest in "Siren Limits," one may suspect that she is endeavouring to bring the poet back to the Christian religion. That is why the poet, as a reaction to her insistence and harassment, tells her:

> When you have finished
> & done up my stitches,
> Wake me near the altar,
> & this poem will be finished . . .

As Okigbo has told us, "the quest broken off after 'Siren Limits' is resumed, this time in the unconscious"[24] and that is in the poem "Distances"; though, as has been indicated earlier in this study, the quest is no longer artistic as it was in "Siren Limits," but now spiritual. But it is clear that the role of the "oblong-headed lioness" or the "skeletal oblong / of my sentient being" (in "Distances VI") is consistently that of distraction; and that the being associated with "oblong" in these poems belongs with the Christian religion, and in fact symbolises it. For in "Distances VI," the protagonist in a willy-nilly attitude similar to that seen in "Siren Limits," here yields if only temporarily to the distracting voice:

> . . . . I receive you
> in my perforated
> mouth of a stranger, empty of meaning,
> stones without juice—

This is the point at which, according to Paul Theroux, the protagonist feels "disappointed after arriving." But the protagonist has actually not arrived; he has only been momentarily seduced like Odysseus and his men who were temporarily seduced by Circe on their way home. What our protagonist has received is perhaps the Christian Holy Communion, which in his mouth that is a stranger's mouth (for he is now a stranger to that religion) has no meaning at all; it is like eating stones which do not of course yield juice. The protagonist has therefore not accepted what he received, for he, like a goat, still continues in his search for the proper "fodder" while the "leopards"—the forces of the enemy religion—are still "on [his] trail."

In the light of this interpretation, "the same blood that flows" "through the same orifices" from "the same branches / trembling intertwined," this blood may be that of the Crucified Christ whose hands were wedded ("intertwined") with the "branches" of the cross (also known as the tree). And "the same faces / in the interspaces" may be Christ's and those of the criminals crucified along with him. Thus, in spite of this blood and the same "breath" of Christ (which is said to give life) and the same "liquid" (blood again), now unaccompanied by an acolyte (since Christ was deserted), and in spite of the protagonist's own sufferings comparable to those of Christ, he (the protagonist) still pursues his proper quest, his natural fodder. And the accomplishment of this quest is the burden of the second half of "Distances VI."

It is here that the same "voice"—that of the goddess—which we heard in the opening part of the poem, is heard again and with finality:

> And at this chaste instant of delineated anguish,
> the same voice, importunate, aglow with the goddess—
>
> unquenchable, yellow, darkening homeward
> like a cry of wolf above crumbling houses—
>
> strips the dream naked,
> bares the entrails

This is the same voice that earlier in Okigbo's poetry faded "in the damp half-light" which belongs to "the queen," the goddess Idoto.[25] It is the same "incarnate voice of the dream" we heard in "Distances I," which has now in "Distances VI" translated the same "dream" (ideal, object of quest) from the condition of mere dream into that of reality. For after washing his feet in the "pure head" of the "Maid" (Watermaid), and "walking along [her] feverish, solitary shores," and feeding "out of the drum" and drinking "out of the cymbal" (the instruments of her ritual music), the protagonist finally enters into inseparable spiritual union with the goddess, who is now identified with the "watermaid":

> I have entered your bridal
> chamber; and lo,
>
> I am the sole witness to my home coming.

Thus the protagonist—priest and poet—has now arrived back home to the shrine of Idoto, to his home goddess whose legend has been a source of creative material. It is here that we find the unification of the artistic quest of "Siren Limits" with the spiritual quest of "Distances." Both aspects of the quest are symbolised by the goddess, who is Idoto the symbol of indigenous Igbo religion, and who is the "Maid" of the sea, the source of artistic inspiration.

It is significant that the re-union of the poet and the goddess takes place in her "bridal / chamber." With reference to this chamber, Anozie says that it has to do with "the experience of sex and its orgasm" and with the "ecstatic moment of orgasmic illumination."[26] This appears to be too literal an interpretation for a poem whose tone has been that of a serious spiritual quest. The union or "wedding" which takes place in the bridal chamber is far from carnal; it is union at a transcendental or super-sensual level; it is a spiritual wedding analogous to that bridal relationship which exists between Christ and the Church, or that double-sided relationship existing between God and the Blessed Virgin Mary, who is at one and the same time the Mother of God (like Mother Idoto) and the Hand Maid of the Lord (like Okigbo's water-maid); and Virgin Mary and Idoto are water goddesses, the former being called "Stella Maris"—star of the sea.

It should be clear by now that "Distances" is essentially a poem in which the quest for a spiritual home that was some time lost is to be regarded as central. The home which the protagonist has returned to cannot be an artistic home, for he had not lost such a home; rather, the home is that religio-cultural home base from which he was exiled as one gathers from a reading of "Heavensgate." But this home is not devoid of artistic connections, since art grows out of a cultural home. The journey back to this home, like most epic journeys, is naturally punctuated with obstructions, distractions, and wandering into the nooks and crannies of the Christian world which in fact constitutes the labyrinth, the net work, from which the quester must free himself if he must reach home. Because of this obstructionist role of the Christian world, the poet's attitude to it has almost invariably been that of slight or mockery. The images drawn from the Christian world have not been used to promote the cause of Christianity. Thus even if we cannot correctly argue that Okigbo has used religious images irreligiously, we can rightly say that he has used Christian images unchristianly. But this is logical in the context of a poem in which the home sought for is based on a religion (the indigenous Igbo religion), which Christianity had opposed and sought to destroy.

## Notes

1. Christopher Okigbo, *Labyrinths, with "Path of Thunder"* (London: Heinemann, 1971), p. x. The text of "Distances" discussed in this paper is that contained in this collection.

2.   Sunday O. Anozie, *Christopher Okigbo: Creative Rhetoric* (London: Evans Brothers Limited, 1972), pp. 149–170.

3.   Gerald Moore, *The Chosen Tongue: English Writing in the Tropical World* (London: Longmans, 1969), p. 175.

4.   Paul Theroux, "Christopher Okigbo," in *Introduction to Nigerian Literature,* ed. Bruce King (Lagos: Evans Brothers Limited, 1971), p. 140. On another page (p. 145), Theroux also observes that "Distances" traces "the agony of suffering through death's narrow passage"—a remark which does not contribute much to any meaningful study of the poem.

5.   Kofi Awoonor, "In My Sick Bed," in *Night of My Blood (Poems)* (New York: Doubleday & Company, Inc., 1971), p. 26.

6.   *Labyrinths,* p. xii.

7.   Anozie, *op. cit.,* p. 166. Anozie says that "the horizontal stone is, among other things, an operating table." See also *The Chosen Tongue,* p. 173, where Gerald Moore says that the horizontal stone is "at once the operating-table on which the poet passes from waking to dreaming and the altar on which his reunion is consummated."

8.   Psalms, 23:4.

9.   Cf. James Joyce, *A Portrait of the Artist as a Young Man,* Chapter III.

10.   "Initiations," in *Labyrinths,* p. 7.

11.   Judges, 12.

12.   John, 6

13.   Matthew, 16:24.

14.   *The Catholic Daily Missal,* ed. Rev. Rudolph G. Bandas (Minnesota, 1961), pp. 695–696.

15.   See Samuel Beckett, *Waiting for Godot.*

16.   See "Lament of the Drums II," in *Labyrinths,* p. 46.

17.   Luke, 22:36–50.

18.   See Robert Graves, *The Greek Myths: 2* (Penguin Books, 1960), p. 362.

19.   Moore, *op. cit.,* p. 174.

20.   See the first reference in Note 4 above.

21.   Anozie, *op. cit.,* p. 152.

22.   *Labyrinths,* p. 17.

23.   *Ibid.,* p. 27.

24.   *Ibid.,* p. xi.

25.   "Suddenly becoming talkative, etc.," *Labyrinths,* p. 23.

26.   Anozie, *op. cit.,* pp. 151 and 153.

# Silences

## NYONG J. UDOEYOP

### SILENCES

The poems in *Silences* form what Okigbo has called "an interval" between *Limits* and *Distances*. They seem to be the first sequence of Okigbo's poems to derive the greater part of their inspiration from national and international public events. Their author tells us that "Lament of the Silent Sisters" was "inspired by the Western Nigeria Crisis of 1962 and the death of Patrice Lumumba," the first Prime Minister of the Republic of Congo (now the Republic of Zaire); and "Lament of the Drums" by "the imprisonment of Obafemi Awolowo [leader of the Action Group Party of Nigeria, then the ruling party in Western Nigeria] and the tragic death of his eldest son." But like all his other poems from *Heavensgate* to *A Path of Thunder,* this sequence is dominated by the presence of a poet-protagonist who sometimes appears as the "celebrant" or as master of ceremony, the "myth maker," one of the silent sisters or one of the drums.

In the introduction to *Labyrinths* (Heinemann 1971) which brings all his published works under one volume, Okigbo tells the variety of influences which suggested the form of *Silences* to him. These influences together with the occasions or events which inspired the poems establish the sequence as a lament or a dirge, and because of the poet's emotional and intellectual involvement with the events, the poems in a way anticipate *Path of Thunder* which has the added dimension of an actual physical involvement.

"Lament of the Silent Sisters" was first published in *Black Orpheus* (No. 12) and in *Transition* (No. 8) in 1962; "Lament of the Drums" appeared in the same journals (Nos. 17 and 18 respectively) in 1964. There have been numerous alterations in the text of the final version of these poems as they appear in *Labyrinths.* Moreover, some sections have been rearranged for a more dramatic effect and a tighter sequential flow. For example, the first section of "Lament of the Drums" is a revised version of the text as it first appeared in

Originally published in Nyong J. Udoeyop, *Three Nigerian Poets: A Critical Study of the Poetry of Soyinka, Clark, and Okigbo* (Ibadan, Nigeria: Ibadan University Press, 1973). Reprinted by permission of the publisher.

*Black Orpheus* rather than the *Transition* text, while the first section of "Lament of the Silent Sisters" is a revised version of Section 3 (chorus), of the *Transition* text. The section which is called "Introit" in the *Transition* version of "Lament of the Silent Sisters" has been dropped in *Labyrinths*. Writing about *Heavensgate* in his introduction Okigbo says: "The various sections of the poem, therefore, present this celebrant at various stations of his cross," and presumably these alterations and re-arrangement of sections in *Silences* were intended to take care of the logical position of the poet-celebrant at the various stations of his cross. The "Introit" reads thus:

> So one dips one's pen in the ocean,
>     and begins
> to write on the mushroom of the sky . . .
> Thrice they struck him on the eye,
>     three times on the ear,
> and spilt his blood as at a slaughter.
> And then was a continual going to the well,
> until they smashed their calabashes.

Apparently the poet had originally wanted to follow the form of the Mbari version of *Heavensgate* which has an Introit. The purpose of the above lines is obvious; they are intended to announce the presence of a poet-persona and the occasion of inspiration for the poems which follow. But the lines are out of character; they lack the force of drama and ceremonial ritual of the Introit of *Heavensgate,* and the intention is too transparent to have permanently satisfied Okigbo who liked his poetry to wear a mask. It is the transparency of the intention and situation which has led Okigbo to recast the language of these poems, as the need for a more dramatic expression led him to rearrange the sections and their structure. Thus in *Labyrinths* the idea of drama in "Lament of the Silent Sisters" is reinforced with the definite assignation of lines to the two characters, *Crier* and *Chorus,* in each section, and the five sections in the sequence are in the form of exchanges between them, with the apparent exception of, or perhaps even including the theme question: "How does one say no in thunder?", with the answer in section five. In the last two sections where specific lines are not assigned the two sets of characters speak the same lines *"alternatively,"* like a priest-and-congregation reading of the *Psalms* in a church.

I have said something about the transparency of the poet's intention and the unmasked situations as recorded in the poems. The first line of the "Introit" contains an image of poetic creativity:

> So one dips one's pen in the ocean,
>     and begins
> to write on the mushroom of the sky.

Okigbo was much more concerned with poetic creativity than with public affairs in spite of the circumstances of his death. Perhaps the shock of the violence in the new political situation in Nigeria and the Congo in the early '60s was too much for Okigbo to absorb readily in his kind of poetry. Hence the "Introit" flies too abruptly from poetic creativity in one and a half lines to undisguised images of violence the rest of the way. It is probably Okigbo's recognition of this weakness—that his dominant personal preoccupation and the new public reality which also concerns him as a citizen were not properly fused in the original version of these poems—which accounts for the extensive revisions of the *Transition* version. Apart from changes in some pronouns and demonstrative adjectives, section V seems to have undergone the least revision. At least the theme question and its answer was left intact. Its concern is the same as that of the "Introit," but it carries a fitter image for the water journey motif which dominates the sequence. Besides, "One dips one's tongue in the ocean / Camps with the choir of inconstant / Dolphins . . ." is a more powerful, more subtle poetic image than "One dips one's pen in the ocean, / and begins / to write . . ." And yet again, whereas the "Introit" abruptly abandons the development of the theme of the growth of sense and memory, and the problem of poetic articulation in the interest of presenting violence, this part of section V which has been retained fuses the conflict in the public world with the personal struggle of the poet regarding this theme, a fusion which becomes even clearer in *Path of Thunder.*

The discussion of *Silences* in this study follows the text in *Labyrinths.* Okigbo has given some explication of *Silences* in poetic prose in his introduction to *Labyrinths.* The pieces in this sequence constitute an elliptical structure of illusion and reality in their relatedness, and the whole poem is a metaphor for "globules of fresh anguish," public as well as personal and private, such as the poet will go through in *Distances.* We must number the poet-protagonist among the lamentors—Crier and Chorus—for their anguish is his anguish, and the sea of afflictions which is drowning them is a familiar experience to the poet, from the time of "mother Idoto" and the "watermaid" of *Heavensgate.* The image of the storm-tossed ship at mid-sea is not all illusion; it is an apt metaphor for Nigeria and the Congo as they begin to endure the pangs of nationhood, having just emerged from colonial status. Nor is the idea of martyrdom all illusion; although Chief Awolowo did not lose his life at the moment of his trial, he, like Patrice Lumumba had deliberately set his face against all the forces ranged against him, in an unequal match, believing all the while that whatever happened to him, his cause would triumph.

The elliptical opening line of the first section suggests the certainty of an uncertain future which begins in violence and anguish:

*Crier:* Is there . . . Is certainly there . . .
 For as in sea-fever globules of fresh anguish
 immense golden eggs empty of albumen
 sink into our balcony . . .

The myth of salvation and freedom lies beyond the violence and the carrion:

*Crier:*    The cross to us we still call to us,
              In this jubilee-dance above the carrion . . .

But even the myth promises no escape from suffering and the storm; may in fact lead to them. The real consolation is in knowing what course to follow or in having faith in the myth:

> For in breakers in sea-fever compass or cross
> makes a difference: certainly makes
> not an escape ladder . . .

Section II enlarges, as Okigbo says, the illusion of martyrdom. The cry of anguish, however, is real enough in the rhythm of the verse. Besides, the poet restates the historical event, borrowing an image from the myth of Moloch, and tells what his awareness of that image does for him. The horror of the tragedy is almost unreal, hence:

> This shadow of carrion incites
> and in rhythms of silence
> Urges us; gathers up our broken
> hidden feather-of-flight.

In these lines, the potency of the historical situation to inspire the poetic exercise or urge one to physical action is stated. The Congo independence celebration has turned into "this anguished cry of Moloch" with a "thunder of tanks" and "detonators cannoned into splintered flames." The poet is not merely a witness to the event; his roles as agonized witness and victim are fused in the image of one dipping one's tongue in the ocean and crying "to the mushroom of the sky." The suggestion of the double heritage of "our worlds that flourish" and "our worlds that have failed" carried in a "double handful" of "an urn of native earth" in Section III, stands as an eloquent testimony to the anguish experienced. Apparently the failed worlds are those which promised peace and prosperity while the thunderous worlds of tanks and detonators flourish, forcing "This shriek, the music of the firmament . . ." which ultimately will give place to silence. The rainbow, that biblical symbol of God's covenant with man which we met earlier in *Heavensgate* reappears in Section IV of this poem. Its appearance here sets the poet wondering whether he and his fellow travellers on the storm-tossed ship will survive to share in the covenant. It is uncertain whether the poet actually wishes a survival or to become one with the gathering sea: like the drowning sisters who are now human dolphins in the storm-tossed sea:

> The kingfisher gathers his ropes in the distance
> The salt water gathers them inward

> The dipping paddle blades, the inconstant dolphins
> The salt water gathers them inward.
> Will the water gather us in her sibylline chamber?
> And our silences fade into galloping antelopes?

The final section makes clear the poet's wish in the answer to the theme question; clearly he does not wish for survival, not even "To cry to the mushroom of the sky," but rather to be silent and become part of the flux of the sea. Only thus can he share in the music of the dolphins:

> One dips one's tongue in the ocean;
> Camps with the choir of inconstant
> Dolphins, by shallow sand banks
> Sprinkled with memories;
> Extends one's branches of coral,
> The branches extends in the senses'
> Silence; this silence distills
> In yellow melodies.

Not an escape from the stormy sea but a total immersion in it, to grow up in it as part of the sea life—one of the dolphins, part of the coral.

The first section of "Laments of the Drums" suggests that Okigbo viewed the imprisonment of Chief Awolowo—his removal from public life—as the beginning of a national tragedy. It is in that spirit that he invokes the dead ancestors in the image of the long drums and "the elements that make them up," to intervene and prevent the impending calamity:

> Even if you are very far away, we invoke you:
>     . . .
> Hide us; deliver us from our nakedness . . .
>     . . .
> Thunder of tanks of giant iron steps of detonators,
> Fail safe from the clearing, we implore you:

The poet seems to recognize that the tragedy is inevitable, as when the drums lament that "We are tuned for a feast-of-seven-souls," in which case the wish to avoid it is rather like Christ's prayer to his Father to "take away this cup."

Sections II and III indicate the process of the tragic events; for it is a double tragedy at several levels—Chief Awolowo's imprisonment and the death of his son; the Chief's loss to the nation and the deterioration or withering of public life; these and the frustration of the poet whose activities are consequently reduced to "a stifled sneeze." The apocalyptic notion of the nature of the tragedy which the poet laments is reinforced by the use of biblical and classical mythology. In the fifth strophe of section II:

> For we sense
> With dog-nose a Babylonian capture
> The martyrdom
> Blended into that chaliced vintage;

the personage becomes a Christ-like victim whose death, though inevitable, came through an act of betrayal. One recalls that Chief Awolowo's troubles began after a split between him and some of his lieutenants, including his deputy and the treasurer in the ruling Action Group Party of Western Nigeria. The suggested acts of human treachery and human martyrdom constitute the theme song of the drums—or in fact their lament—as they come out of "our soot chamber / From the cinerary tower." The public tragedy is immediately linked with the personal tragedy of the poet-artificer in the image of "a web / Of voices all rent by javelins," in the sixth strophe. So that he becomes one with the rest of the public who will have "To limber our membranes for a dance of elephants."

The other half of the tragedy makes up section III which, dominated as it is by the myth of Aeneas' journey, helps to make even clearer than the previous sections the theme of nation-building and its hazards. Like the individual life, nation-building is a journey of destiny. Okigbo borrows from Virgil's *Aenied* (v. 388 *seq.*) to tell the story of the death of Segun Awolowo just before his father was imprisoned. Palinurus was the son of Jasus, and helmsman of Aeneas. The god of sleep approached him in the disguise of Phorbas, sent him to sleep and then threw him into the sea. In the lower world he saw Aeneas again and related to him that on the fourth day after his fall he was thrown by the waves on the coast of Italy and there murdered, and that his body was left unburied on the strand. The sibyl prophesied to him that by the command of an oracle his death should be atoned for, that a tomb should be erected for him and that a cave should be called after him. In this section of the poem, Okigbo establishes an identity between the dead Segun and his imprisoned father:

> Palinurus, alone in a hot prison, you will keep
> The dead sea awake with nightsong

and again:

> Palinurus, unloved in your empty catacomb,
> You will wear away through age alone

and yet again:

> *It is over, Palinurus, at least for you,*
> *In your tarmac of night and fever-dew:*

The combined personages—father and son—explain the significance of the mariner in the opening couplet of this section. As Okigbo saw it, the Nigerian nation was

> . . . *fishing today in the dark waters*
> *Where the mariner is finishing his rest . . .*

and those left to direct the effort were

> *Some strange Celaeno and her harpy crew,*
> *Laden with night and their belly's excrement,*

who "Profane all things with hooked feet and foul teeth." The poet's despair and that of the public at the turn of events form most of Section IV; for the "bankrupt" leaders of the nation could not reasonably be expected to discharge their obligation to the public no matter the public protest:

> So, like a dead letter unanswered,
> Our rococo
> Choir of insects is null
> Cacophony
> And void as a debt summons served
> On a bankrupt.

But somewhere within this despair lodged a seed of hope. The dead have to be born again; the imprisoned leader must come back to public life if the health of the nation is to be restored and preserved:

> But the antiphony, still clamorous
> In tremolo
> Like an afternoon, for shadows;
> And the winds
> The distant seven cannons invite us
> To a sonorous
>
> Ishthar's lament for Tammuz:[1]

Meanwhile, the poem concludes in section V with laments for the imprisoned leader and his dead son, the sterility which the event has brought about in the national life, for the approaching violence and for the nation as a whole, "the Great River" whose "pot-bellied watchers / Despoil her . . ."

*Note*

1.    Both Gerald Moore and Sunday Anozie regard the white elephant as symbolizing disappointment. I do not think that the context supports this view exclusively. Besides the direction of the infinitives is towards a future action, and together with the refrain which closes this section of the poem, suggests that the rope has not actually been pulled yet. See Gerald Moore, op. cit., and Sunday Anozie, "A Structural Approach to Okigbo's *Distances*," *The Conch*, 1 (March 1969).

# GENRE, METHOD,
# AND MEANING

◆

# Okigbo's *Limits:*
# An Approach to Meaning

## DONATUS I. NWOGA

Interpretations of Okigbo's *Limits*[1] have varied widely from the mystical, through the political, to the personal.[2] All the divergence of opinion unfortunately cannot be attributed to the customary range of reactions which any poem of some complexity normally attracts. The root problem appears to me to have been that of technique: that there has been a tendency to circumvent the complexity by attaching interpretations to those elements of the poems which have fitted into preconceived theories and, therefore, move to conclusions without analysis and elucidation of the images of the poems and the total logic of those images.

What I intend to do in this article, therefore, is to go through *Limits* section by section and suggest interpretations which may give room for discussion towards creating a body of basic meaning. In absolute terms this is not an essential process. Meaning, to Okigbo, was not necessary. As he said in an interview, what each person took out of a poem was independent of the author and that was as it should be:

> I think that when a word is committed to print it develops legs, wings even, and goes anywhere it wants to go. It is in a sense like a talking drum. You might want to speak to someone in a different village, he is not the only one who is listening to it. Anybody who is awake at the time listens to it. And those who wish to take the message will take it. I think the poem has this sort of existence, quite apart from the author.[3]

Moreover, any definition of a poem's images and logic operates at a single level. Great poetry establishes new archetypes. Images become symbols. An idea, situation, emotion significantly expressed creates a new vision and the expression itself becomes transferable to other situations. Each proverb, after all, started off as a satisfying description of an actual event by some individual with a mythopoeic imagination. Definition therefore does not exhaust the meaning of the poem. Significance will differ from individual to individual

Originally published in *Journal of Commonwealth Literature* 7, no. 1 (1972): 92–101. Reproduced with permission from Bowker-Saur, a division of Reed Business Information Limited.

and with time. But it does give a poem an important anchor to try and find out what it actually expresses, especially when its complexity could have pushed it into being abandoned.

Though *Limits* consists of two sections, "Siren Limits" (I–IV) and "Fragments out of the Deluge" (V–XII), I shall analyse each poem independently as it appears in sequence in the collection.

## LIMITS I

At the centre of this poem is sacrifice—"I hang up my egg-shells / To you of palm grove." The rest of the poem describes the poet/protagonist and his state and also the devotional object. We are immediately forced, in trying to see the relevance and logic of the descriptive images, to adopt a non-logical approach. This is a factor both of the non-meaning of the surface logic of the words and also of the juxtaposition of images which are independent of each other. A method is called for which responds to the evocative force of the images rather than their logic. Following this method then, we see *Limits* I as descriptive of sacrifice offered by a protagonist in the phantasmagoric state "Between sleep and waking"—the half-wakeful state in which one is not sure whether one is still in the dream or out of it. It is a sacrifice of cleansing by a protagonist who has returned to his deity from a state of disdainful exile ("Emigrant with air-borne nose"). The erotic state in the imagery of "he-goat-on heat" also appears to apply to the protagonist before his cleansing.

"Queen of the damp half-light" is the deity to whom the sacrifice is offered. It seems appropriate to identify her with Idoto of *Heavensgate,* surrounded here by the atmosphere and activities natural to a village riverside—the raffia palm trees which yield palm wine and the tall bamboos forming a shaded grove. The tiger mask and spear are masquerade cult objects which would normally be kept in the grove rather than in the house.

*Limits* I then constitutes a prefatory sacrifice of submission to a deity, and also creates a pervading atmosphere of time and setting, describing a state of half-dream, half-reality.

## LIMITS II

This sedately moving poem describes the protagonist's progression from weakness and insignificance to prominence. The nature imagery which begins and ends the poem is parallel to, and probably derived from, the traditional saying which describes a prominent man as "the tall tree by which a farmland is known." In the middle of the poem the process of growth is described in metaphysical terms as the union of voice, soul, and selves.

I do not think it is possible to give any specific identity to "The selves." But there is enough in the poem to indicate their equivalence to the essence of experiences, as distinct from the concomitants which would correspond to the "echoes." It is the "thirsting," sensitive person, giving audience to significant experiences, that becomes "crowned with one self." The biblical image "Horsemen of the apocalypse" serves then as a reinforcement of the idea of mystic energy which results to the poet/protagonist when his receptive soul is suffused with the impetus from his experiences. What he achieves is prominence, valid because of its visible, prophetic, and therefore, protective function.

## LIMITS III

A series of vivid visual images is created here and they are difficult to put in meaningful sequence. The total picture of futility does emerge however, from an impressionistic response to the images and is summarized in the last lines of the poem.

Images of a chaotic state open the poem, giving the implications of negligence ("Banks of reed") and destruction and danger ("Mountains of broken bottles"). The refrain "*& the mortar is not yet dry . . . ,*" taken from Ezra Pound, evokes the unready state of the surface on which a work of art was to be reproduced. Already, in the first three lines of the poem, therefore, we are presented with a picture of the unsatisfactory context in which the poet/protagonist has to operate. This context is expanded in the rest of the poem and a conclusion emerges.

The second picture, which appears to have its correlative in the Corpus Christi procession of the Catholic liturgy, enjoins a soft and gingerly movement. With the idea of struggle introduced in "Sun's dust of combat" as a description of "eve-mist," the total impression is one of circumspection, of the careful movement demanded or enforced by the situation of the first picture. Circumspection deepens into futility in the following image of singing, "tongue-tied, / Without name or audience."

At this point, the poem pauses to re-describe the environmental condition of the poet/protagonist's functioning—"the crisis point." The complexity of the poem emerges here in the two possible lines of continued interpretation: one which places the dichotomy between the voice and the protagonist and makes the struggle that of the poet who is not in a state in which the "voice" can have an easy compulsion on him; the other which puts the struggle as that between the poet and the community into which he has to inject his vision—the voice that is reborn. The first line of interpretation, the personal line, would make the "Hurry on down" sequence descriptive of the poet, neglecting the voice, and being in hectic movement for a futile purpose. This line of interpretation tends to agree with Okigbo's statement in the "Introduction" to *Labyrinths,* to the effect that the "Siren Limits" presents a protagonist "in pursuit of the white elephant." Later also he says: "*Limits* was written at the end of a journey of several centuries from Nsukka to Yola in pursuit of what turned out to be an illusion."[4] Such a personal interpretation, however, does not fit in with the earlier parts of the poem, which placed an emphasis on the protagonist in a state of threat or frustration from external sources. Whatever personal element might have been intended, therefore, the poem has expanded beyond it, becoming a statement about the frustration of "the voice," the poet/protagonist within a crisis situation, in the context of the hectic quests for quite illusory objectives which control the attention of his putative audience.

## Limits IV

It is clear that this poem is conceived in the context of another train of ideas in Okigbo and not as a natural progression from the rest of "Siren Limits." And yet it is organically related to "Siren Limits" in that, following upon the frustration in *Limits* III the protagonist has been left open to the diversory compulsion of a love object.

The "lioness" here has changed drastically from the beauty and glory which surrounded her in *Heavensgate.* She is still desired and irresistible ("No shield is proof against her") to the poet but it is with a compulsive ugliness reminiscent of Tutuola's Ugly Ghostess.[5] The description here suggests a zombie type of figure that has emerged from the bottom of the sea with seaweed straggling over the face, in contrast to the golden beauty of the mermaid figure in *Heavensgate.* It is as if the poet is visiting the pain of his frustration on the figure of his love.

And yet the poet is soothed. "Distances of her armpit-fragrance / Turn chloroform enough for my patience" is an example of that type of image that Graham Hough has described in Mallarmé as "no-road sign."[6] "Distances," the functioning noun in the image obviously conflicts structurally with the operating word "fragrance." Chloroform is not a pleasant drug. But just as it relieves the patient of the pains of surgical operation, it would appear that the lioness and her armpit fragrance do lull the poet/protagonist from the frustrations of surrounding insensibility. The operation announced at the end of the poem is both physical (an acknowledgement at the beginning of *Limits* is to a doctor "who nursed him through a most anxious period of illness"), and a spiritual one which will re-fit the poet to complete his poem.

Who is the "lioness," the love object described in such agonized terms here? It is clear that a particular woman participated in the creation of the situation. But the image here goes beyond a particular. It is known that Okigbo read Robert Graves's *The White Goddess* when he wrote *Heavensgate*. This is indirectly acknowledged in the third poem of the "Watermaid" sequence of that poem, where the lioness is referred to as "my white queen." A stage in the relationship between the muse-poet and his goddess/woman is that in which the poet becomes more consciously aware of cruelty. "Being in love does not, and should not, blind the poet to the cruel side of woman's nature—and many muse-poems are written in helpless attestation of this by men whose love is no longer returned."[7] *Limits* IV does, by its imagery and movement, direct one to this state in the poet as being its theme, the lioness being the woman (absorbed into the goddess) implied in Okigbo's statement in the "Introduction": "Limits was written at the end of a journey of several centuries from Nsukka to Yola in pursuit of what turned out to be an illusion."

## Limits V

This poem is the first of the sequence subtitled "Fragments out of the Deluge." It is made up of four disjointed images, further complicated by the notes which Okigbo has added and his amendments to the first-published text which have tried to bring clarity to it. The tendency of the new version and the notes is to postulate the existence of a second self to the protagonist, a result of metamorphosis of the remains (in the first picture of the fennel on the alabaster sarcophagus)[8] after his other self had been destroyed by the lioness ("the beast") now at rest. The Gilgamesh and Enkidu relationship introduced in the rest of the poem recaptures the duality proposed for the hero in the poem.

But all this appears as an after-thought and the poem by itself cannot carry the weight. The attempt to make a consistent meaning has led the poet to re-interpret his poem in a way which makes it inconsistent. He has, through the notes, tried to relate all the images to the hero. "Enkidu" in this version, for example, was "Enki" in the original version, and Enki has nothing to do with the Gilgamesh epic. It would take much more revision to get the words on the page to relate organically to the hero.

The last line "And this is no new thing either . . ." encourages one to retain an impersonal interpretation, which sees the four images as distinct pictures of incomprehensible, ominous, and ephemerally glorious situations, with the last line hinting at the recurring pattern of such situations to as far back as the first human stories. As such, the poem then creates an atmosphere and a premonition of something which, though not definite from anything in the poem, is clearly of not a propitious kind. There is however promise of revival and resurrection of some sort in "the new branch of Enkidu."

## LIMITS VI

A dichotomy is set up here between "He," "they" and "the people." It is sometimes not easy in the poem to distinguish between "they" and the "people" but this is a complexity from life, as the poem shows.

The protagonist is here surrounded with images which evoke the unwanted Messiah—in lines which repeat the words of Christ, recall the story of the Transfiguration ("and appeared in true form") and the feeding of the multitude and the Sermon on the Mount.

The people do not respond to this Messiah figure. The explanation for their insensitivity may be found in the Messiah not being of the type they had expected—"They cast him in mould of iron." Most of the poem presents what appears to be an allegorical story of the rejection, exclusion, and ridiculing of the poet/messiah by the leaders and the rest of the people. If one may attempt an identification in historical time, the Christ story is here telescoped with that of any idealist ("Man out of innocence") and how he would fare with the African political elite ("mongrel breeds" because they are the uncertain products of two cultural and political traditions). Drunk in the euphoria of their new freedom the people would not listen.

## LIMITS VII

This is a most complicated poem with fast shifts of obscure references and images which are non-sequential. But I think we do have a framework for fitting the images together when we realize that the two riddle-like statements which are at the beginning and the end of the poem relate intimately to the biblical Samson legend in *Judges,* Chapters 14–15 (especially 14:8 and 15:4–5). The context is that of Samson's punishment of the Philistines who had tried to cheat him out of a wife.

This evocation makes it easier to see the various images of this poem in some perspective: the picture of kites moving aimlessly around a burning market, the failure of expectations, made more sombre by the simile "Like tombstones from pavements," and the pictures of religious futility and confusion would appear to be the consequences of the rejection of "He" and his re-emergence.

## LIMITS VIII

The sunbird here is a prophetic bird—like the Bird of Truth of various mythologies, like the birds that nested on the walls of Rome to warn the Romans of impending attack. The qualities and attributes of the threatening eagles are those which can justify the interpretations relating the image to colonial missionary and economic exploitation—hard, metallic, and yet fascinating and "resplendent." The fear, and at the same time disregard of the people for the impending disaster concludes the prophecy:

> And small birds sing in shadows
> Wobbling under their bones . . .

## LIMITS IX

New images expand on the characteristics of the protagonist. He is endowed with the power of prophecy of the "blind dog," with the lyricism of a childhood nurse, Eunice, and the brightness of the mythical "dawn's charioteer." It is this protagonist who is rejected—"Give him no chair, they say."

## LIMITS X

This most dramatic of the poems in *Limits* describes the fulfilment of the prophecy of the sunbird. The eagles arrive, kill the sunbird, and ravage the twin-gods of the forest. The curse on the eagles is appropriate and is taken from two lines from a longer poem reprinted in the *English Dialect Dictionary:*

> Malisons, malisons, mair than ten
> That harrie the nest o' the heavenly hen.[9]

The havoc done by the eagles is also presented in the form of the looting and desecration of the twin-gods of Irkalla. The use of Irkalla here links the present circumstances with the Gilgamesh epic to which reference was made in the recurrent patterns in *Limits* V but the twin-gods are identified in the notes as "the tortoise and the python," totems for the worship of Idoto. The two obviously represent the androgynous elements of supreme deities as commonly conceived in West Africa.[10] A desecration of them, therefore, implies a complete rout of what is sacred to the community, both spiritually and economically.

## LIMITS XI

This poem is a lament, in rhythms which create the sounds of long drums, for the gods lying in state. But the implications of the last lines are not clear. Their terseness leaves them open to different syntactic reconstructions, but I think the one that comes nearest to a meaning is one which threatens that just as the gods, desecrated by the eagles, had been abandoned and grown out in the sense of being no longer considered valid, so would the eagles, the colonialists, etc., "grow out" of validity too.

## LIMITS XII

Concluding *Limits* on a note of triumph is this poem, which while darkening and universalizing the image of the havoc that had been done (through the image of Picasso's "Guernica"), announces the revival of the sunbird to sing again. It also posits the existence of an area, physical and spiritual, which is called "the LIMITS of the dream" and is beyond the reach of the destructive forces. The last image, that of "On whose canvas of blood, / The slits of his tongue / cling to glue . . ." is a confusing telescoping of Picasso's work and Okigbo's statement. A meaning is evoked, however, that the sunbird escaped a carnage which could have restrained the voice.

The brutality and desecration inflicted by the beasts on "the forest" is then not complete or final. There is an area of the soul where it could not reach. And the creative visionary spirit survives; "the cancelling out is complete" because the resurrection of the sunbird makes futile the destructive activity of the beasts.

## CONCLUSION

It becomes clear from this analysis that I see the process of achieving meaning from the *Limits,* as from most of Okigbo's poetry, as dependent on two factors: firstly, an acquaintance with the very varied sources of Okigbo's imagery and symbolism: the many situations and myths of many cultures which to him become means with which to project his vision of his state and that of his society; secondly a realization of the aim of his composition and the method it has created. He said himself that he was not trying to convey any intellectually apprehensible meaning:

> Because what we call understanding—talking generally of the relationship between the poetry-reader and the poem itself—passed through a process of

analysis, if you like; there is an intellectual effort which one makes before one arrives at what one calls the meaning. Now, I think it is possible to arrive at a response without passing through that process of intellectual analysis, and I think that if the poem can elicit a response in either physical or emotional terms from an audience, the poem has succeeded. I don't think that I have ever set out to communicate a meaning. It is enough that I try to communicate experiences which I consider significant.[11]

This attitude to "meaning" has dominated the form and created the obscurity which makes the poetry incomprehensible when approached from a logical inquiry into its surface meaning. Technically, it is as if Okigbo, having caught the essence of an experience, casts around for sounds, images and symbols, most of them abstract, which are likely to evoke that experience in the reader.

I have, through a technique dictated by the suggestions above, given what I consider the central experience or significance of each of the sections of *Limits*. From these what emerges as a central theme or common concern of Okigbo at the time is the relationship between the poet/prophet/messiah fig-ure and his community and its history. Parts of the poem may satisfactorily be related to specific incidents in Africa's or Nigeria's history. *Limits* X and XI have been accepted as a description of the colonial and missionary exploita-tion of Africa and the demise of African gods and values. There is also argu-ment whether *Limits* is an allegory of "the great political drama of Nigeria since Independence"[12] or whether "the Congo Crisis of 1960 would be a more relevant analogy."[13] A further argument is possible about whether Okigbo was reacting to the recent historical past of European exploitation of Africa or to the current situation of African exploitation of Africans. Debate or disagreement on these specific issues does not upset the balance of the poem because of the poem's emphasis on essence and pattern rather than on the particular incidents—a pattern is created which produces emotional response transcending the original impetus.

What varies in *Limits* then is the external stimulus and the emphasis rather than the central theme. "Siren Limits" is motivated from individual experience and the emphasis is on the poet's personal growth and frustration both within the community and in the love quest. "Fragments out of the Del-uge" has a more general frame of reference. The consequences of failure to heed the voice of the prophet/messiah are therefore more destructive of the community. In spite of these changes of emphasis, there does come through the underlying theme of the validity and undying nature of the creative ideal and the fate of the group which rejects it. The applications may vary from the national to the international situation, from the physical to the religious level. Okigbo's achievement in *Limits* is that he has created, by taking images and symbols out of other mythologies, a myth with emotive force which is both a record of the African past and a warning and promise for the present and the future. *Limits* then may be taken as Okigbo's statement on the growth and nature of the poet, on his position in his community, and on the indestructible nature and continuing validity of the creative spirit. It is written in terms which evoke the African experience. But within it are elements which direct the reader to its significance in terms of patterns which are archetypal.

## Notes

1.   The first parts of Okigbo's *Limits* appeared in *Transition* in 1962 and in *Modern Poetry from Africa* in 1963. The complete poem came out as a separate Mbari publication in 1964. Its "final version" is contained in *Labyrinths*, Heinemann, A.W.S., 1971. There have been changes in the text of the poem with each publication. The text of *Limits* in *Labyrinths* is used for this paper.

2.   Unrelated interpretations appear in J. A. Adedeji, "A Dramatic Approach to Okigbo's *Limits*," *Conch*, III, 1; S. Anozie, comment on the above in the same issue of *Conch;* R. Dathorne, "Ritual and Ceremony in Okigbo's Poetry," *JCL*, 5; G. Moore, *The Chosen Tongue,* Longman, 1969, pp. 143, 171; D. Nwoga, *West African Literature in English,* unpublished Ph.D. thesis, London, 1964; and R. Egudu, *The Matter and Manner of Modern West African Poetry,* unpublished Ph.D. thesis, Michigan State University, 1966.

3.   M. Whitelaw, "Interview with Christopher Okigbo, 1965," *JCL*, 9, pp. 28–37.

4.   *Labyrinths,* p. xi.

5.   *My Life in the Bush of Ghosts,* Faber, 1954, pp. 86–8.

6.   *Image and Experience,* Duckworth, 1964, pp. 54–5.

7.   *The White Goddess,* Faber, 1959, p. 491.

8.   Okigbo's source must have been the reports of the discovery made by M. Zakaria Goneim of a pyramid close to the Step Pyramid of Zozer at Saqqara in Egypt in 1954. No mummy was found but the more regular interpretation of the fennel found there was that some ceremony had been performed in the burial chamber; see Cottrell, *The Concise Encyclopedia of Archeology,* Hutchinson, 1960, p. 412.

9.   I was directed to this source by Mrs. Jane Imrie of Leeds who typed an earlier version of this paper. The full poem is "The Laverock's Sang" in William Cadenhead, *Flights of Fancy and Lays of Bon-Accord,* Aberdeen, 1853, pp. 114–16.

10.   See Herskovits, *Dahomean Narrative,* Northwestern, 1958, p. 124; Idowu, *Olodumare: God in Yoruba Belief,* Longman, 1964, p. 28; and John S. Mbiti, *African Religions and Philosophy,* Heinemann, 1969, pp. 77–8.

11.   "Christopher Okigbo Interviewed by Robert Serumaga," *Cultural Events in Africa,* 8 (July 1965), Supplement.

12.   J. Adedeji, op. cit.

13.   S. Anozie, op. cit.

# The Ritual and the Plot:
# The Critic and Okigbo's *Labyrinths*

## ANNEMARIE HEYWOOD

Any discussion of Okigbo's poetry leads into questions about "meaning"; most Okigbo criticism ends up as exegesis. The reason for this when examined turns out to be uncertainty or perplexity about *kind of meaning*. The controversies about the formal character of Okigbo's verse relate to the same problem, since they spring from conclusions about *intended meaning*. Perhaps students of Okigbo should be more aware of these processes than they have frequently shown themselves to be, so that the close interdependence between "meaning" and form can be systematically explored and charted. The difficulty is that Okigbo's poetry is, by general consensus, unordinary. It is held to be "prophetic," or "ritual," or "mythic." Yet the implications of these labels (which entail a whole body of inferences about subject matter, form, and "meaning") have rarely been looked at and never coherently examined.[1]

In opening up this critical problem for discussion, I have chosen to start with no more than the most basic requirements—an open mind, humility, and attentiveness to the words on the page—and to pick up critical tools which suggest themselves as helpful as I go along. Thus I hope to avoid the three common snares that threaten Okigbo criticism: stereotyped expectations, faulty critical strategy, and intolerance of the unfamiliar.

Thus far, even the most discerning commentators have, as Nwoga observes, tended to "stay on the level of vague generalisations, or fit elements—not the whole of the poem—into preconstructed molds."[2] Some of these molds are sensitively and attentively constructed. Izevbaye, for instance, provides an illuminating guide to *Heavensgate*.[3] But he does not, in doing so, provide a key that would equally open up *Distances* or *Path of Thunder*. He fails, that is, to tell us by what paths he arrived at his interpretation, and to define Okigbo's poetic strategy. Anozie, who was, as far as I know, the first to call Okigbo's poetry "ritual,"[4] has never examined the consequences. To be sure, he still refers to Okigbo as "*ritually* exploring the process of creative intuition, or as *mythically* projecting the poet's personal experience,"[5] but the

Originally published in *Research in African Literatures* 9, no. 1 (1978): 46–64. © 1978 by Indiana University Press. Reprinted by permission of Indiana University Press and the author.

terms are merely ornamental. The interpretative molds he brings to the verse are the secular, Western ones of personality crisis, "nostalgia," and inner conflict, or even "a genetic [*sic*] struggle between a romantic pursuit of art for its own sake, and a constantly intrusive awareness of the social relevance of art" (p. 175)—something that is simply not borne out by what is there, on the page.

With such a muddled model of the *kind of meaning* under scrutiny, perhaps it cannot be surprising—though it is intensely frustrating—that Anozie's critical tool kit proves grotesquely inappropriate, and his results so arbitrary and unhelpful. Only Nwoga[6] and Etherton[7] have shown awareness of the need for the critic to revise his tools. Since both were writing polemically, taking a defensive stance in the controversy raised by Mazrui's attack on "abstract poetry,"[8] their notes are tantalizingly fragmentary. But although neither analyzes or demonstrates at length, both raise the point that language and form in Okigbo are deployed in a special manner, according to a special strategy that demands special criteria. Etherton speaks of "words of psychic use or magic," Nwoga of "passages . . . constructed with the metaphors as their semantic constituents." These are suggestive hints of the kind of enquiry most likely to serve both the poetry and its reader, but they remain unintegrated.

The final fault besetting Okigbo scholarship may also be illuminated from Anozie's work. In the course of a simplistic reading of *Path of Thunder,* and near the end of his exhausting survey, he remarks: "poetry has (here) ceased to be an *exercise in learned and esoteric snobbery or privacy;* it is henceforth a means of simply describing popular feelings and aspirations in the idiom of the people" (p. 178). Not only is this inaccurate, but it reveals an attitude so profoundly out of sympathy and out of patience with what is being investigated that it must of necessity prevent the critic from understanding and doing justice to it. Modish academicism and ideological cant combine to glue down the sunbird's tongue in newsprint.

One way to approach difficult poetry is to reconstruct its impact on the reader's imagination; then to put forward a hypothetical model of the *kind of meaning* that is being articulated; then to apply the key appropriate to that *kind of meaning* and to see if it opens up the difficulty and promises a coherent grasp of all that may be found on the page. Different keys and models may of course have to be tried; and the full "meaning" or "experience" may elude the reader even when he is rewarded by that indefinable, yet incontrovertible feeling of rightness or fit. In the case of Okigbo, the *kind of meaning,* it is agreed, is "ritual." A number of questions urgently present themselves, namely, *what are we to regard as a ritual strategy?* and *what are the implications regarding the functional elements of such verse* (e.g., the words, images, structuring)? and, finally, *what is the "meaning" or function of such ritual poetic statements?* One implication, at least, should instantly be clear: the most fervently debated problem in Okigbo commentary is a paper tiger. Ritual is neither private, nor abstract, nor obscure in the ordinary sense—even though it may be secret, and closed to uninitiated eyes. Vis-à-vis society, it signifies neither escape, nor withdrawal, nor self-indulgent narcissism—at least not in spiritually alive cultures. Ritual and oracular utterance is as much a part of the living oral heritage of the African poet as are folktales, proverbs, and mocking songs, and is woven into the living texture of experience which he shares with his community. It deserves to be taken into account as a valid source of literary inspiration more seriously than has been the case among academics so far.

Before tackling these questions, I shall briefly recall the steps by which one is led to the conclusion that Okigbo's verse is ritual. How does it act on us? Negatively, one observes that it offers no discursive continuity, that is, it does not tell a story, or trace a train of thought, or articulate the emotional billowings of the psyche. Instead, it seems to be building up a compulsive series of *significances*. It appears to operate by establishing stresses, emphases, valences through the patterning of, firstly, rhythms and sounds, and, secondly, motifs. These motifs—images, symbols, allusions, private references— do not add up to "evocations" (in the sense made familiar by Eliot) of a scene or mood, yet they do add up. To what?

At this point the critic can give up and fit what he has already perceived to the stereotypes in his repertoire. Or he can move in and make himself more closely, more analytically aware of those impressions which his mind retains most vividly after reading through *Labyrinths* and after he has laid down the book. My own list reads as follows:

1. a sense of landscape or setting or, rather, *topography*, for example:
   upward and downward movement
   forest and clearing
   island, shore, sea
   balcony, steps, bridge, church
   These topographical features are not "filled in"; they do not build up to a particular, described landscape (as in J. P. Clark), or to the evocation of a symbolic scene (as in Soyinka). They remain detached, and generic.[9]
2. certain *states*/happenings. These I group as:
   a. solitude
   b. encounter (sexual, sacrificial) between I and Thou
   c. large groups in motion
   Again, these states are generic; they do not picture, or evoke, socially structured events. (Do they symbolize them? This question must be left open.)
3. recurrent *motifs*, such as:
   a. "imagery": e.g.,     birds and beasts
                           musical instruments
                           iron, stone
   What is the function of these "images"? Are they descriptive? evocative? symbolic? "Symbolic" comes nearest, yet it is not immediately clear what is being symbolized, or even whether the symbolism is cultural or private.

b. sensuous properties: colors, smells, sounds

Here we are on surer ground. The colors and smells are used evocatively, to generate emotional response. Yet the emotion seems impersonal. A statement by the poet helps to clarify and focus the function of this evocative sensuousness. *Silences,* he tells us in his Introduction, was written "to explore the possibilities of poetic metaphor in an attempt *to elicit the music to which all imperishable cries must aspire*" (p. xii)—and *"to evoke consonant tunes."* The effect produced is of controlled, generic emotion, emotion harnessed as in music, rather than of lyrical self-expression.[10]

c. allusions, echoes, borrowings

Much fun can be had in spotting these, yet little profit accrues from it. Izevbaye has recognized this: "The borrowed phrase or sentence is often used with little regard for its source . . . not much is gained from a knowledge of the original poem. . . . Okigbo's interest . . . seems limited to the beauty and utility of the phrase itself" (p. 4). But he does not go on to inquire into the functional end implied by his term "utility." That the original matrix is of no consequence is borne out by Okigbo's own reply to a question about influences: "My *Limits* was influenced by everything and everybody. It is surprising how many lines of *Limits* I am not sure are mine and yet do not know whose lines they were originally. But does it matter?"[11]

4. *"themes."* One notes, furthermore, that these motifs are recurrent and tend to coalesce into definite configurations. The eloquence of the verse is bound up with the way in which these configurations are interwoven, varied, and modulated like musical themes; certain motifs reverberate, and certain symbolic figures (e.g., lioness, sunbird) piercingly reappear in new contexts. The obvious next step is to follow through this insight. Motifs might be listed and correlated with their contexts. Such exercises will do much to open up Okigbo's poetry and to clarify the logistics informing it. A brief example may illustrate what I have in mind. "Elegy of the Wind" is one of the most obscure poems in *Path of Thunder.* On analysis it emerges that it fuses within itself three configurations previously established. Let me call them:

a. the White Light configuration (contexts: *Watermaid, Siren Limits IV, Distances*); associated motifs: white light, iodine/chloroform, lioness/goddess, wounding

b. the Iron configuration *(Fragments, Path of Thunder);* associated motifs: eagles/other birds, elephant, thunder, steps, iron, drums, mask

c. the Sapling and Sunbird configurations *(Heavensgate I, Limits II, Fragments XII, Path of Thunder)* share associated motifs of vegetation, silence, rainbow.

The White Light motifs signal ecstatic encounters with the numinous, the Iron motifs visions of cultural history; the Sapling/Sunbird motifs deal with the poet's vocation as man and as prophet. Any exegesis of "Elegy of the

Wind" which fails to take account of this extraordinary fusion of previously disparate themes runs the risk of remaining unresponsive to the implicit suasion of Okigbo's rhetoric.

5. *multivocality*. Although individual motifs tend to cohere in identifiable configurations and thus to trail a thematic significance, they have in themselves no fixed semantic function. They are fluid, multivocal; every context seems to impose on them a modified "meaning": yet they are unvaryingly potent.

Finally we observe that Okigbo's poetic usage is consistent throughout. With the exception of "Hurrah for Thunder" (which strikes one as very much an occasional poem which might not have met Okigbo's own stringent criteria for inclusion among the "final versions" of *Labyrinths,* had the choice been his), the poems of *Path of Thunder* show no sudden change to a popular, demotic mode.

So far, I have simply sketched observations and preliminary inductive generalizations of the kind which, consciously or unconsciously, precede the inference that Okigbo's verse is "prophetic" or "ritual." It now behooves us to pursue the questions suggested earlier.

What do I mean by "ritual verse"? I mean *neither* verse "using elements of myth or ritual to illustrate" something else, some private and aestheticist agony, as Anozie will have us believe, *nor* verse which describes ritual in the somewhat anthropologizing manner common in fiction and exemplified in J. P. Clark's "Abiku," *nor* even verse which dramatically evokes ritual experience, as Soyinka does in *Idanre.* I mean *poetry as ritual,* poetry which is in itself a ritual instrument. The words on the page do not function to body forth a reality beyond them, and to be grasped through them: they *are* the reality and the experience in sensible form.

This inference has implications which the critic ignores at his peril. It implies for one that the formal elements of such verse—such as words, imagery, syntax—do not function in the manner he is used to dealing with. Ritual does not communicate or express; it enacts, invokes, or conjures. Since descriptive models of ritual functioning are not to be found in literary criticism, we must turn to related disciplines, such as anthropology, mythology, and comparative religion, for a key.

Generally speaking, Okigbo uses a language eloquent yet uncommunicative, concrete yet not "natural," private yet impersonal; its texture is richly sensuous, both directly by virtue of its sound and rhythm patterns, and indirectly by virtue of its evocative power. Such is the medium of revelation and ritual, as any account of ritual symbolism will bear out. "Throughout history," Mircea Eliade observes, "sensory activity has been used as a means of participating in the sacred and attaining to the divine."[12] That, to my mind, is the key to Okigbo. Far from being "an exercise in learned and esoteric snobbery," Okigbo's poetry is not even intellectual. In a much quoted, but perhaps insufficiently heeded remark, Okigbo warns of this:

> I think it possible to arrive at a response without passing through that process of intellectual analysis, and I think that if the poem can *elicit a response in either physical or emotional terms* from an audience, the poem has succeeded. I don't think I have ever set out to communicate a meaning. It is enough that I try to communicate experience which I consider significant.[13]

What strikes one is the perception of language as sound rather than sense, and of meaning inhering in the responses of the central nervous system and hypothalamus as much as in those of the cerebral cortex. As a practitioner, Okigbo is much closer, in fact, to Hopkins than to Eliot. One is reminded of Hopkins's "verse as inscape of spoken sound":

> Poetry is speech formed for the contemplation of the mind by the way of hearing or speech framed to be heard for its own sake and interest even over and above its interest of meaning. Some matter and meaning is essential to it but only as an element necessary to support and employ the shape which is contemplated for its own sake. . . . Poetry is in fact speech only employed to carry the inscape of speech for the inscape's sake.[14]

Okigbo did not imitate Hopkins's mannerisms—which belong to the inner life of another language—but used the same "logistical" approach to sound and meaning patterns. For both poets, words sometimes become things with potencies of their own. Hopkins creates such potency by compression of meaning—as witness his Notebook entry, "Every word may be considered as the contraction or coinciding point of its definitions."[15] Okigbo, writing from a life experience in which ritual operations are familiar and commonplace, uses many other techniques as well. (Two Hopkins-style niggles may be mentioned, by the way: does "saying No in thunder" signify, to Okigbo, saying no in the midst of thunder, or saying no in the idiom of thunder? or both? and does "path of thunder" signify the military advance of "iron steps," howitzers and eagles, or lightning? or both?)[16]

In order to illustrate, let us take what is perhaps the most impenetrable poem in the whole book, "Distances IV":

> And at the archway
> a triangular lintel
> of solid alabaster
> enclosed in a square
> inscribed in a circle
> with a hollow centre . . .

The words which make up this statement are not used normally. They do not, that is, collaborate to build up a coherent sentence. For one thing, there is no verb. For another, they do not combine happily in a way that defines what is going on. A structure is built up, to be sure: one may be tempted to image a symbolic gate, but the effort is instantly foiled by what follows, when the "shutterless," "hollow centre" of the inscribed circle is likened to "celestial pincers" and a "vast countenance." These words, taken together, and the images they conjure up *dispel actuality* rather than describe, enrich, or evoke it—a function entirely meet, of course, in a passage that deals with the approach of ritual dissolution and detachment from "all the forms / [which] were formed after our forming." Edmund Leach suggests that this "nonlogicality is itself 'part of the code,' it is an index of what such statements are about," namely, metaphysical rather than physical reality. And "the paradoxical nature of mythological stories is itself a part of their message. What is not natural is supernatural."[17] If this passage has power to move in any way, and I think it has, then it is because the words are significant or potent in themselves. It may be a connotative potency, as in "celestial" and "pentecostal" with their pious associations. Or it may be a potency acquired through previous use in Okigbo's poetic myth, as in "resplendent," "crucifix," and "phosphorescent." Thus, "resplendent" has been associated with the "eagles" of "Fragments VII" (who held "the square under curse of their breath"); "crucifix" brings in the potencies generated in the Kepkanly section of "Heavensgate II" (collocated again with "square" as well as other geometric imagery) and "Distances III"; "phosphorescent" revives the whole White Light configuration (which, in turn, in "Siren Limits IV," has attracted a four-sided figure—"oblong-headed lioness").

Even a brief investigation like this turns up astonishing coherences, unsuspected by more orthodox meaning-hunting. In order to discover more about the significance of these, we might follow through on the geometric motifs which appear to haunt the quoted passage in the form of past associations, as well as in the overt configurations of triangle, square, and circle. Anozie's comment that they "express . . . a strong formalist obsession" is worse than unhelpful; it seems impertinent in every sense of the word. Also irrelevant seems to be the flash of recognition which links this configuration with esoteric and mystic symbolism (e.g., alchemical emblems, the Buddhist stupa),[18] for Okigbo is not writing to an esoteric formula or signaling to those who recognize a recondite symbol. He uses figures of undoubted potency not for their meaning, but for their potency, to lend talismanic power to "significant experiences" of his own. A brief search into all the contexts in which the four-sided figure occurs will bear this out.

The "oblong" as "panel" or "window" recurs in association with "Anna" and the Catholic Church:

> O Anna at the knobs of the panel oblong
> hear us at the crossroads
>
> (p. 5)

> Anna of the panel oblongs
> protect me
>
> (p. 17)

> and the everlasting fire from the oblong window
> forgot the taste of ash
>
> (p. 54)

and in more abstract form in:

> the archway the oval the panel oblong
> (p. 58)

—a curious but consistent spatial distortion of the configuration in our passage. But it is also found in association with The White Light theme:

> Oblong-headed lioness
> No shield is proof against her—
> Wound me, O sea-weed
> Face, blinded like strongroom
> (p. 27)[19]

As "square," the four-sided figure occurs in:

> A fleet of eagles
>     over the oil-bean shadows,
> Holds the square
>     under curse of their breath
> (p. 31)

and

> (way . . .)  forms fourth angle
> duty, obligation:
> square yields the moron,
> fanatics and priests and popes
> (p. 7)

—as well as in our passage from "Distances V." I shall not attempt an explanation. These quotations suffice to demonstrate, I think, not only the building up of potency through repeated usage in powerful contexts of Okigbo's motifs, but also their multivocality.[20] Victor W. Turner is bringing structuralist techniques to bear on puberty, cleansing, and other tribal rituals:

> What is really needed . . . is a typology of culturally recognized and stereotyped situations in which the symbols utilised are classified according to the

goal structure of the specific situation. There is no single hierarchy of classifications that may be regarded as pervading all types of situations. . . .

> If one is looking atomistically at each of these symbols, in isolation from the other symbols in the symbolic field (in terms of indigenous exegesis or symbol context) its multivocality is its most striking feature. If, on the other hand, one is looking at them holistically in terms of the classifications that structure the semantics of the whole rite in which they occur, then each of the senses allocated to them appears as the exemplification of a single principle. In binary opposition on each plane each symbol becomes univocal.[21]

He might be suggesting fruitful approaches to the description of Okigbo's verse.

As with the images, so with the borrowings, the stolen lines, cadences and images from other poets, the allusions to Sumerian myth, the whole mosaic of cross-cultural loot. We have already observed that recognition does not help, but have left the question of "utility" pending. I suggest that these foreign bodies in the poetic tissue are talismans embodying the charisma of Okigbo's original experience of them, as well as the power they carry over from their original context. They are, if you like, words of power, concentrations of inner adventure, which now serve to furnish the poet-hero's ritual. Turner observes a similar phenomenon in connection with millenarian movements:

> . . . in many of these movements much of their mythology and symbolism is borrowed from those of traditional *rites de passage,* either in the cultures in which they originate or in the cultures with which they are in dramatic contact.[22]

Another significant feature of the "obscure" passage we are looking at, and a number of others surrounding it (e.g., *Distances* III, IV, V, VI), is the absence of active verb forms. The poetic statement is an accretion of nominal phrases and lacks those elements of active or causal connection which are provided by verb phrases.[23] Nwoga draws attention to this:

> The emphasis on word and image, the projection of meaning through the cumulation of poignant images rather than through a mental logic of exposition, have affinities with African modes of poetic creation.(p. 36)

He also notes: "Passages are constructed with metaphors as their semantic constituents," a procedure which "demands that the reader escape from the clutches of logical mental sequence" (p. 37). Unfortunately, he leaves the distinction between image and metaphor blurred, and fails to ask himself which of the two—if either—we are dealing with. Okigbo is no imagist; nor does "poignant images" convince as a label for the figurative elements of oral tradition. Even "metaphor" is tricky; we would have to discard critical approaches that look on metaphor as the perception of similarities in dissimilars, and see it functionally, perhaps with Empson, as "a stretching process whereby new areas of reality are constantly enclosed in the language";[24] with Lévi-Strauss as "analogical thought"; or, most aptly, with Cassirer "as genuine presences which actually contain the power, significance and efficacy of the whole." His argument is worth quoting:

> Here one is reminded forcefully of the principle which might be called the basic principle of verbal as well as mythic "metaphor"—the principle of *pars pro toto* ... All mythic thinking is governed and permeated by this principle. Whoever has brought any part of a whole into his power has thereby acquired power, in the magical sense, over the whole itself. What significance the part in question may have in the structure and coherence of the whole, what function if fulfils, is relatively unimportant—the mere fact that it is or has been a part, that it has been connected with the whole, no matter how casually, is enough to lend it the full significance and power of that greater unity.[25]

As for the characteristic syntax, the stringing of nominal motifs, let me quote a single analogy, a description of the idiom used by St. Francis: "His thought was always immediate, personal and concrete. Ideas appeared to him as images. A sequence of thought for him ... consists of leaping from one picture to the next."[26]

Finally, something should perhaps be said in connection with the third question asked above about the "meaning" of this ritual verse. What is, after all this, "the plot which the ritual enacts"? Okigbo's Introduction gives a narrative shape to his *oeuvre* which was imposed on it retrospectively. Nevertheless, it is not an arbitrary editorial grooming—as Izevbaye notes, seeing a similarity, in this respect, with "primitive epics . . . connected with religious or ritual performance":

> poems originally created as separate compositions cease to be considered independent units after they have been organised . . . [by] the adoption of a conventional, but fairly loose structure, within which individual experiences may establish a logical relationship with one another. (p. 3)

The plot enacted is that of the heroic monomyth, the universal pattern of which it may be of interest to sketch:

| | |
|---|---|
| call/dedication | (Before you, mother Idoto, naked I stand . . . out of the depths my cry: give ear and hearken) |
| stripping of outer form supernatural aid | *(Watermaid)* |

quest and ordeals

in a psychological perspective to be seen as self-discovery and self-conquest. It should perhaps be noted that Okigbo's quest is cast in the mold not of Jungian self-integration, nor even of cultic initiation, but of cultural salvation: "a poet-protagonist is assumed throughout; a personage, however, much larger than Orpheus; one with a load of destiny on his head, rather like Gilgamesh, like Aeneas" (Introduction). He therefore revisits in *Heavensgate* and *Limits* not only his personal becoming, but equally that of his people.

dismemberment
union with the goddess

*(Distances)*

*(Distances VI):* a passage from Joseph Campbell's invaluable book shows how closely Okigbo fits into the universal scenario: "The ultimate adventure, when all the barriers and ogres have been overcome, is commonly represented as a mystical marriage with the Queen-Goddess of the world. This is the crisis at the nadir, the zenith, or at the uttermost edge of the world, at the central point of the cosmos, in the tabernacle of the temple, or within the darkness of the deepest chamber of the heart."[27] And Eliade observes: "In all these contexts, the Chthonian Great Mother shows herself pre-eminently as Goddess of Death and Mistress of the Dead, that is, she displays threatening and aggressive aspects."[28]

the boon
return to serve

("a state of aesthetic grace" [Introduction])

*(Path of Thunder):* here the hero functions in a state of power as shamanic mythmaker, oracle, prophet, and sacrifice.

These last poems present themselves as fragments of a communal psychomachia prophetically recorded.

This ritual scenario, the heroic self-initiation of the poet, does not follow any set cultural pattern. Okigbo seems to have created the whole archetypal myth spontaneously out of what his time and place and his individual genius afforded; and his poetry—the struggle with sounds and meanings, patterns and structure—*was* the initiatory ritual by which his destiny materializes. The young man's much lamented death in action gains, in this perspective, complete artistic inevitability.

This may seem an extravagant claim to make for it, but Okigbo's poetry I find yields most if one concedes most to it. *Path of Thunder,* perhaps the most "difficult" cycle in the volume, becomes fully eloquent when allowed prophetic, magic function. To treat it as political pamphleteering is to ignore all but a few lines. There are, to be sure, deceptively simple folkloric passages which appear to be outlining a political fable. But do they actually do so, with even the rudimentary wit and punch of a lampoon, let alone the pregnant good sense of the cautionary tale from which they derive? The political events surrounding the military coup of 1966 are reflected in them in terms both simplistic and incoherent. Moreover, these passages are written in a painfully wooden, jolting, lifeless rhythm and juxtaposed with lines of superb eloquence and subtlety, both of rhythm and implication:

> One tongue full of fire
> One tongue full of stone [?]

This is indeed public poetry. Okigbo is indeed expounding history—but the "meaning" is here even harder to elucidate than before. Apart from the folkloric groundswell, one may isolate two currents of symbol configurations (as already suggested above) and consider firstly their interaction and secondly their drift. I shall sketch what I mean by stringing together merely the lines that introduce and reintroduce each theme, but omitting all those which modulate, vary, and reinforce it. What emerges is something like this:

Theme 1: Iron configuration—Cultural History:

> This day belongs to a miracle of thunder . . .
>      . . . Iron birds
> Held—fruit of flight—tight . . .
> Bring them out we say . . .
> The stories behind the myth, the plot
> Which the ritual enacts . . .
> And the chant, already all wings, follows
> In its ivory circuit behind the thunder clouds,
> The slick route of the feathered serpent . . .
> Remember, O dancers, the thunder . . .
> Remember, O dancers, the lightning . . .
> And a great fearful thing already tugs at the cables of the open air
> A nebula immense and immeasurable, a night of deep waters
> An iron dream unnamed and unprintable, a path of stone . . .
> And the secret thing in its heaving
> Threatens with iron mask
> The last lighted torch of the century . . .
> The mythmaker accompanies us
> The rattles are here with us . . .
> trunk of the iron tree we cry *condolences* when we break
> shells of the open sea we cry *condolences* when we shake . . .

And the horn may now paw the air howling goodbye
For the Eagles are now in sight . . .
The Robbers descend on us to strip us of our laughter, of our
    thunder . . .
The Eagles are suddenly there,
New stars of iron dawn. . . .

Theme 2. White Light—the Initiate:

Earth, bind me fast . . .
White Light, receive me your sojourner, O milky way
Let me clasp you to my waist . . .
Man of iron throat—
I will follow the wind to the clearing
And . . . break
the silence of myth of her gate . . .
O mother mother Earth, unbind me, let this be
my last testament; let this be
the ram's hidden wish to the sword, the sword's
secret prayer to the scabbard . . .
Earth unbind me; let me be the prodigal; let this be
the ram's ultimate prayer to the tether

The lines that close the cycle unite these two streams:

An old star departs, leaves us here on the shore
Gazing heavenward for a new star approaching;
The new star appears, foreshadows its going
before a going and coming that goes on forever. . . .[29]

Within the scope of this article, I can only point at what seems to me significant. But even an exercise like this reveals both the intricacy of the "logistics" and the coherence of the "prophecy" in Okigbo's poetry. A third theme, the configurations around "sapling" and "cotyledon," is interwoven with the two sketched; in "Elegy of the Wind" it burgeons amazingly into a fully developed exposition of fertility ritual and circumcision. The Sunbird motif also requires detailed charting. What emerges, however, even from such a sketchy probe, is a "plot" far larger than the popular singing of a secular, political or military, chain of events. A sense of cataclysm is built up through eloquent passages packed with consonantal collisions, as well as through figures of dread and violence, and through haunting echoes of other apocalyptic visions (e.g., Yeats's "The Second Coming"; the lightning and the eagles of *Matthew 24*. The serpent and the howling horn, as well as the general violence, also occur in the *Poetic Edda*), which surely derives from a mythopoeic rather than a documentary impulse.

There is, in fact, no change of utterance. The poems deal with civil unrest preceding war, but seem again to be articulating not the historic events as such, nor popular feelings about them, but visionary apprehensions of the numinous archetypes of which they are the temporal figures. They are put together according to the laws of Okigbo's visionary imagination, which his Introduction so aptly encapsulates in the metaphor of the coral: "of the root extending its branches of coral, of corals extending their roots into each living hour; the swell of the silent sea the great heaving dream at its highest. . . ."

*Notes*

Italics throughout are my own.

1. Basically, they can be said to imply that the poetry functions metaphorically rather than metonymically. This very useful distinction is elaborated in Edmund Leach, *Culture and Communication* (London: Cambridge Univ. Press, 1976), pp. 12–16.

2. Donatus I. Nwoga, "Obscurity and Commitment in Modern African Poetry," *African Literature Today,* no. 6 (1973), 38.

3. D. S. Izevbaye, "Okigbo's Portrait of the Artist as a Sunbird: A Reading of *Heavensgate,*" *African Literature Today,* no. 6 (1973), 1–13.

4. S. O. Anozie, "Okigbo's *Heavensgate:* A Study of Art as Ritual," *Ibadan,* 15 (1963), 11–13.

5. S. O. Anozie, *Christopher Okigbo: Creative Rhetoric* (London: Evans Brothers, 1972), p. 63. Page references to this work are given in the text.

6. Nwoga, "Obscurity and Commitment."

7. Michael J. Etherton, "Christopher Okigbo, and African Tradition," *Zuka,* 2 (1974), 48–52.

8. Ali A. Mazrui, "Meaning versus Imagery in African Poetry," *Présence Africaine,* no. 66 (1968), 49–59. This is an expanded version of "Abstract Verse and the African Tradition," which appeared in *Zuka,* 1 (1968), 47–49.

9. They repeatedly imply two significant arrangements: (a) the "clear" space surrounded by wilderness (clearing, island), and (b) articulations of ascension or transit. J. E. Cirlot has this to say about spatial symbolism: "In a manner of speaking, space is an intermediate zone between the cosmos and chaos. Taken as the realm of all that is possible, it is chaotic; regarded as the region in which all forms and structures have their existence, it is cosmic. . . . The significance of the vertical or level-symbolism concerns the analogy between the high and good, the low and the inferior" (*A Dictionary of Symbols* [London: Routledge and Kegan Paul, 1971], pp. 300 and 301). And Edmund Leach states: "The material topographical features (both man-made and natural) of the space within which ritual performances take place—i.e., buildings, paths, forests, rivers, bridges, etc.—constitute a set of indices for such metaphysical distinctions as this world/other world, secular/sacred, low status/high status, normal/abnormal, living/dead, impotent/potent" (p. 52).

10. On the symbolism of music, Cirlot remarks as follows: "The symbolism of music may be approached from two basic standpoints: either by regarding it as part of the ordered pattern of the cosmos as understood by the ancient, megalithic and astrobiological cultures, or else by accepting it as a phenomenon of 'correspondence' linked with the business of expression and communication. Another of the fundamental aspects of music-symbolism is its connexion with metre and with number, arising out of Pythagorean theory." His remarks on the symbolic

significance of flute and drum in particular may also intrigue the student of Okigbo: "The cosmic significance of musical instruments . . . was first studied by Curt Sachs in *Geist und Werden der Musikinstrumente* (Berlin, 1929). In this symbolism, the characteristic shape of an instrument must be distinguished from the timbre, and there are some common 'contradictions' between these two aspects, which might possibly be of significance as an expression of the mediating rôle of the musical instrument and of music as a whole (for an instrument is a form of relationship or communication, substantially dynamic, as in the case of the voice or the spoken word). For example, the flute is phallic and masculine in shape and feminine in its shrill pitch and light, silvery (and therefore lunar) tone, while the drum is feminine by virtue of its receptacle-like shape, yet masculine in its deep tones" (pp. 300–01).

11. Quoted in Romanus Egudu, "Defence of Culture in the Poetry of Christopher Okigbo," *African Literature Today,* no. 6 (1973), 21.

12. Mircea Eliade, *Myths, Dreams and Mysteries,* Fontana edition (London: Collins, 1968), p. 73.

13. Quoted by Nwoga, p. 37.

14. Humphry House and Graham Storey, eds., *The Journals and Papers of Gerard Manley Hopkins* (London: Oxford Univ. Press, 1959), p. 289.

15. John Pick, *A Hopkins Reader* (London: Oxford Univ. Press, 1953), p. 82.

16. Okigbo probably read the extract from Melville's letter to Hawthorne in Leslie Fiedler, *No! in Thunder* (Boston: Beacon Press, 1960), p. 6. It is quoted by Anozie in a slightly shortened version: "There is the grand truth about Nathaniel Hawthorne. He says No! in thunder; but the devil himself cannot make him say yes. For all men who say *yes,* lie; and all men who say *no*—why . . . they cross the Frontiers into Eternity with nothing but a carpet-bag—that is to say, the Ego" (p. 171). Ihab Hassan (*Radical Innocence* [Princeton, N.J.: Princeton Univ. Press, 1961]) takes No! to be the sound of the gates of the Self when they burst open "in death-denying denial of quotidian reality" (p. 329). The title appears to have been lifted from Peter Abrahams's novel *The Path of Thunder* and the eponymous work by Countee Cullen. However, the fact that *Come Thunder* wittily incorporates the titles of no less than four well-known works (corridors of power, brush fire, arrows of God, dance of death) would indicate that this "theft" is neither casual nor specially significant. I suspect that such sources are less pertinent to an understanding of Okigbo's purpose than is the thunder in Hopkin's *Wreck of the Deutschland,* and in the Bible, notably the Book of Job—e.g., "Who hath divided a watercourse for the overflowing of waters, or a way for the lightning of thunder" (Job 38:25).

17. Leach, pp. 70 and 74.

18. For a generalized comment on their significance, see Cirlot: "These three figures symbolize the relationship (represented by the triangle) between earth (the square) and heaven (the circle . . .); this explains why these are the essential symbols of so many Cistercian and Gothic facades" (p. 292). And, "According to Heinrich Khunrath, the triangle within the square produces the circle" (p. 202). The exact correspondence to Okigbo's enigma is startling.

19. Anozie asks of these lines: "Can one really escape being hit in this image with a possible allusion to the female genitals?" (p. 84). I think one can.

20. The multivocal (or "plurisignal" or "multivalent") character of ritual and mythic symbolism is generally recognized and well described in the literature. See, e.g., Leach: ". . . the same elements of ritual behaviour keep on recurring. . . . [They] are like the letters of the alphabet; in different combinations they can be made to say different things" (p. 88).

21. Victor W. Turner, *The Ritual Process,* Pelican edition (London: Penguin Books, 1974), pp. 37–38.

22. Ibid., p. 99.

23. George Herbert's *Prayer* is put together in this wise. The first stanza of Blake's *Sunflower* similarly effaces history and self by withholding the main clause.

24. Terence Hawkes, referring to William Empson's *Seven Types of Ambiguity,* in *Metaphor,* The Critical Idiom series (London: Methuen, 1972), p. 63.

25.   Excerpts from Ernst Cassirer's *Language and Myth,* reproduced under the title "The Power of Metaphor," in Pierre Marandra, ed., *Mythology* (London: Penguin Books, 1972), p. 29.

A fertile account of metaphor as used by Okigbo is to be found in Peter Munz, *When the Golden Bough Breaks* (London: Routledge and Kegan Paul, 1973). He sees metaphor as the bridge between "ordinary experience and metaphysical doctrine," and the means whereby "consciousness teases its own definition out of the material world" (p. 97).

26.   M. D. Lambert, *Franciscan Poverty,* quoted by Turner, p. 129.

27.   Joseph Campbell, *The Hero with a Thousand Faces,* Abacus edition (London: Sphere Books, 1975), p. 98.

28.   Mircea Eliade, *Rites and Symbols of Initiation,* Harper Torchbook edition (New York: Harper and Row, 1965), p. 62.

29.   Eliade points out that the universal belief "that Creation cannot take place except from a *living being who is immolated*" (his italics) transcends the mythology of the Earth Mother. "The sacrifice brings about a tremendous transference: the life concentrated in one person overflows that person and manifests itself on the cosmic or telluric scale" (*Myths, Dreams and Mysteries,* pp. 185–86).

# Christopher Okigbo and the Psychological Theories of Carl Gustav Jung[1]

## Chukwuma Azuonye

### I

In two earlier papers (Azuonye 1979 and 1980), I drew attention to a number of insights which might be gained from the psychological theories of Carl Gustav Jung into the nature of reality as experienced in the poetry of Christopher Okigbo.[2] In the first paper (1979), I argued in part that a knowledge of Jung's postulations on the relationship between certain universal geometrical shapes and the forms of images commonly encountered in dreams, visions, myths and fantasies is essential for a proper understanding of Okigbo's use of geometrical symbols in the representation of the memories and initiatory experiences of his poet-protagonist.[3] In the second paper (1980), in which I attempted a diamorphosis of the mythos underlying the "organic unity" of Okigbo's poetry, I demonstrated the feasibility of approaching what Okigbo himself (1965:1) sees as the central theme of his works—"the fable of man's perennial quest for fulfilment"—in terms of the Jungian concept of *individuation,* the process through which an individual attains self-realization through the maximal development and harmonization of the disparate, often conflicting, components of his personality (Jung 1959b). What I intend to do in this paper is to present a more comprehensive and systematic view of the significant points of congruence between Okigbo and Jung both in the light of the earlier discussions and on the basis of additional evidence uncovered in the course of further comparative examination of the writings of the two authors.[4] It is my hope that what I have to say here will go some way in elucidating the meaning and significance of some features of theme and symbolism in Okigbo's poetry which have hitherto been little understood.[5]

Originally published in *Journal of African and Comparative Literature* 1, no. 1 (March 1981): 30–51. Reprinted by permission of Heinemann (Nigeria) and Chukwuma Azuonye.

161

As indicated above, Jungian psychology is primarily concerned with understanding the structure, dynamics and development of the *psyche,* i.e. the totality of the non-physical components of the human personality. Jung saw the psyche as comprising two distinct but interacting systems and levels, namely the *conscious* and the *unconscious* (see Jung, 1959c). The conscious is the only part of the psyche which is wholly known to the individual: it is organized around what Jung terms the *ego,* the complex of perceptions, memories, thoughts and feelings which are bound up with the individual's total awareness of himself as a distinctive being. The unconscious occupies a much deeper stratum of the psyche. It constitutes that part of the psyche of which we are either wholly or partly unaware. Jung makes a distinction between two levels of the unconscious: an outer level which he terms the *personal unconscious* and an inner level which he terms the *collective unconscious.* The contents of the personal unconscious are in the form of repressed or forgotten personal experiences which in given circumstances manifest themselves in the behaviour of the individual as *complexes* (Jung, 1959b). The contents of the *collective unconscious,* on the other hand, are in the form of primordial images of a kind apparently shared in common by humanity as a whole. These manifest themselves in dreams, visions, myths and fantasies in certain regularly recurring shapes and patterns to which Jung has given the name *archetypes* (see Jung 1959a). Jung devoted a great deal of time to the study of the nature and manifestations of the *archetypes,* and much of what we now know as Jungian psycho-dynamics is concerned with the interaction of the archetypes in the course of the development of the personality.

In many of their details, Jung's postulations on the structure, dynamics and development of the psyche are both controversial and controvertible.[6] Nevertheless, they have over the years provided a very useful model for the explication of literary themes and symbols, especially those rooted in folklore and mythology.[7] This is hardly surprising. In the formulation of his theories, Jung made use of evidence not only from psychoanalytic experiments but also from what he saw as a vast reservoir of psychic phenomena faithfully recorded in literature, myth and folklore. He was indeed the first to apply his theories to the study of literature.

The poetry of Christopher Okigbo is pre-eminently amenable to analysis in terms of the Jungian model.[8] It would indeed seem from a careful reading of the poems vis-à-vis the theories of Jung that the poems are conscious attempts to recapture various images from the personal and the collective unconscious experienced by the poet in what appears to be a sustained effort at individuation. In the second part of this paper, I shall attempt to isolate and discuss the forms and manifestations of these components of the structure of the psyche in Okigbo's poetry, and here I shall be looking at the poet-protagonist as a kind of symbolic representation of the psyche in its various aspects. In the third part, I shall deal with the psychodynamics of the poet-hero's journey, paying particular attention to what seems to be the overtly sexual manifestations of his psychic energy *(libido)* and the various ways in which this energy is channelled into creative and spiritual pursuits. In the final section, I shall briefly review the salient features of the most important point of congruence between Okigbo and Jung, namely the process of individuation as manifested in what Okigbo sees as the mythos of his poetry, "the fable of man's perennial quest for fulfilment."

## II

What Okigbo says of *Limits* and *Distances* in his introduction to *Labyrinths* seems indeed to apply to his poetry as a whole, for it is "Man's inner and outer worlds projected, the phenomenal and the imaginative, not in their separateness but in their relationship" (1965:xi). There is here a parallel to the Jungian dichotomy between the conscious and the unconscious components of the psyche, the phenomenal being coterminous with the conscious while the imaginative is coterminous with unconscious both in its personal and collective aspects.

In his conscious orientation towards the world, Okigbo the man seems to differ diametrically from his poet-hero. He was unmistakably the *extroverted, thinking-and-feeling type*[9] whose conscious orientation was towards the external, objective world. Contrarily, his poet-protagonist is essentially an *introverted sensing-and-intuiting type* whose conscious orientation is toward the inner, subjective world. Jung paid some attention to the nature of this kind of relationship between an artist and his work. As summed up in Jacobi (1942:23):

> Often one and the same artist is an extrovert in his life and an introvert in his work, or the other way round. In this they follow the law of psychic complementarity, which seems particularly applicable to those artists who represent in their works what they themselves are not. In order words, their complement.

Prior to *Path of Thunder,* Okigbo seems to have been primarily concerned with representing in his works an area of experience which to the outsider would seem to be totally out of keeping with what, from the attestation of his close personal friends (e.g. Anozie 1972:6–11), was his remarkably extroverted nature. Thus, his poet-hero appears to project not the ego of Okigbo the man but that of an alter-ego, totally different in his functional and attitudinal orientation from the poet himself.

Yet it is possible to isolate in the poems certain conscious perceptions, memories, thoughts and feelings which bear the unmistakable imprint of Okigbo's conscious ego and which, on that count, can properly be regarded as autobiographical (see Azuonye 1980). The picture of the degenerate exile wallowing in shame and degradation in the "Debtors' Lane" *(Four Canzones)* is evidently drawn from life, not from the repressed contents of the personal unconscious but from what Okigbo in full wakefulness remembers of Lagos life in the late 1950's (see Anozie, 1972:26). The same is true of the ghastly picture of the mindless destruction of the shrine of the water-goddess, Idoto, by a section of the Ojoto community in 1926 which Okigbo has deftly woven into section X of his *Limits* (see Azuonye 1980).[10] What we have here is the feeling-and-thinking Okigbo responding, from the perspective of a cultural nationalist, to the destruction of a potent symbol of the traditional religion of his native culture by alienated converts to the Christian faith, who, in fits of anomie, act as agents of the imperialist predator. The same voice of the angry young man responding to the post-independence decadence of Nigerian politics can also be heard in *Silences,* the two sequences written in response to "the events of the day," specifically in response to "the Western Crisis of 1962, and the death of Patrice Lumumba," as well as "the imprisonment of Chief Obafemi Awolowo and the tragic death of his eldest son" (Okigbo 1965:xii). Indeed, *Silences* ends with words ("Lament of the Drums," section V) which seem to presage the platform rhetoric of *Path of Thunder,*[11] the final sequence of poems, in which the poet—completely divested of the introverted orientation towards the inner world—now appears in person as "Okigbo, towncrier" with his "iron-bell" ("Hurrah for Thunder") to forewarn his countrymen of the "thunder among the clouds" ("Come thunder").

Faced with such overwhelming evidence of the active projection of the conscious ego in the poems, it would seem that the Jungian law of psychic complementarity does not apply to Okigbo. His poet-hero is not just an alterego but Okigbo himself, so inseparable from the man that it is difficult to understand him fully without reference to Okigbo's life and personality. The truth of what actually happens inside the poems lies somewhere in Okigbo's own confession that his works represent "man's inner and outer worlds projected . . . not in their separateness but in their relationship" (1965:XI). The introverted sensing-and-intuiting poet-hero who finds strength in "the solitude" of orangeries, woods, groves, seashores and secret chambers as well as in the realms of dreams represents a conscious effort on the part of the extroverted, feeling-and-thinking Okigbo to achieve a unification of opposite tendencies in himself towards the attainment of that psychic balance which Jung refers to as individuation. The law of psychic complementarity thus operates in Okigbo's poetry. By consciously seeking the inner world, "where solitude weaves her interminable mysteries under the lamp" *(Transition)*[12] Okigbo is able, through the poet-hero, to activate what Jung calls "the eternal symbols of mankind which lie dormant in the conscious" (see Jacobi 1942:24). These symbols which are ultimately shaped by the conscious mind and elaborated into the finished work of art are largely of the order of the archetypes of the collective unconscious, but they also include other symbols which are related to the complexes of the personal unconscious—the repressed and half-forgotten feeling-toned memories and ideas tied up with the poet's personal experience of life.

Jung defines *complexes* as "psychic entities that have escaped from the control of consciousness and split from it, to lead a separate existence in the dark sphere of the psyche, whence they may at any time hinder or help the conscious performance" (see Jacobi 1942:37). Each of such psychic entities comprises two elements, a "nuclear element" and its "manifold associations." The nuclear element is essentially an associated group of feelings, thoughts and memories in the unconscious, the origins of which can be traced to certain traumatic events in the past life of the individual. Jung used the word-association test which he had devised for the purpose to identify such associated groups of feelings, thoughts and memories: "Any word that touched upon a complex would cause a delayed response" (see Hall and Nordby 1973:36). Something similar to the effect of the association test appears to occur in certain sections of Okigbo's poetry where the choice of certain words or images has the effect of reawakening certain groups of feelings, thoughts and memories about traumatic past experiences associated with such words or images. A typical illustration of this will be found in *Heavensgate II*.

The memories, thoughts and feelings in *Heavensgate II* are the direct consequence of the poet-hero's encounter with the cross (the Christian church) in the first strophe of *Heavensgate I* so soon after his homecoming and rapprochement with the goddess, Idoto, long forsaken in his exile from his ancestral roots. This encounter with the cross first awakens an impassioned memory of "Anna at the knobs of the panel oblong" (presumably Mrs. Anna Okigbo, Okigbo's own mother), one of the irretrievable victims of the cultural imperialism represented by Christianity. Then comes the trauma of Okigbo's own conversion through Christian education in a primary school, where the "half-serious half-comical . . . school teacher" Kepkanly like his kind elsewhere uses the whip (hyperbolically termed "the blade") to inflict the "cross" like a scar on the minds of defenceless youngsters (see *Heavensgate II*, strophe i, lines 1–13). This emotion-toned remembrance of the cross becomes here the nuclear element of an antichristian complex which subsequently dominates the poet-hero's consciousness. Associated with this are Okigbo's uncompromisingly violent reaction against the materialistic culture introduced in the wake of Christian domination of Africa (*Heavensgate II*, strophe i, lines 26–34) and the rape of African culture, especially its sanctuaries, by agents of Christian iconoclasm (*Limits X*).

Complexes may also manifest themselves in the form of a strong pre-Occupation with something. Thus Hall and Nordby write:

> When we say a person has a complex we mean he is so strongly preoccupied by something that he can hardly think about something else. In modern parlance he has a "hangup." A strong complex is easily noticed by others, although the person himself may not be aware of it. (1973:37)

Jung was also concerned with complexes in this sense. He observed that "A person does not have a complex; the complex has him" (Hall and Nordby 1973:37). In this connection, Jung speaks of the artist's "ruthless passion for creation." The artist, he writes, "is fated to sacrifice happiness and everything that makes life worth living for the ordinary human being." In the early phase of his career, Okigbo projects this kind of strong complex for perfection through his poet-hero. In his passionate pursuit of beauty, represented by various female and feline images, the poet-hero is content to lead a life of "anguish and solitude," to submit himself to "shadows distances labyrinths violences" (Distances, VI), and to suffer a series of deaths. In this early phase of his work, Okigbo the man did not go as far as his hero. But in the strong complex of his hero, there always lurked something of himself which in the end he proved unable to contain. "The complex," as Jung says, "must . . . be a psychic factor, which, in terms of energy possess a value that sometimes exceeds that of our conscious intentions" (Jacobi 1942:37). In Path of Thunder, Okigbo shows an awareness of the danger into which his personal identification with the poet-hero could lead him:

> If I don't learn to shut my mouth I'll soon go to hell,
> I, Okigbo, town-crier, together with my iron-bell
> ("Hurrah for Thunder")

He does indeed "go to hell," when in the wake of the Biafran struggle he becomes so fully identified with his hero that he finds himself attempting to perform in real life feats of heroism of the kind envisaged in the imaginative world of his poetry.

While the complexes of the personal unconscious clearly play an important part in the experience of Okigbo's poet-hero, it is mainly from the deeper stratum of the unconscious—the collective [un]conscious—that much of what we perceive as images and symbols in the poems seem to emanate. The *collective unconscious,* according to Jung, is a reservoir of latent images, usually called *primordial images:*

> *Primordial* means "first" or "original," therefore a primordial image refers to the earliest development in the psyche. Man inherits these images from his ancestral past, a past that includes all his human ancestors as well as his pre-human and animal ancestors. These racial images are not inherited in the sense that a person consciously remembers or has images that his ancestor has. Rather they are predispositions or potentialities for experiencing and responding to the world in the same ways that his ancestors did. Consider, for example, man's fear of snakes or of the dark. He does not have to learn these fears through experience with snakes and the dark, although such experiences may reinforce or reaffirm his predisposition. We inherit predispositions to fear snakes and the dark because our primitive ancestors experienced these fears for countless generations. They became engraved upon the brain. (Hall and Nordby 1973:39–40)

In the last forty years of his life, Jung spent much time studying the nature and manifestations of the primordial images under the new name "archetypes" which he had coined for them. "Among the numerous archetypes that he identified and described are those of birth, death, power, magic, the hero, the child, the tricker, God, the demon, the wise old man, the earth, mother, the giant, many natural objects like trees, the sun, wind, rivers, fire, and animals and many man-made objects such as rings and weapons" (Hall and Nordby 1973:40). Jung wrote, "There are as many archetypes as there are typical situations in life. Endless repetition has engraved these experiences into the psychic constitution, not in the form of images filled with content, but at first, only as *forms without content,* representing merely the possibility of a certain type of perception and action"[13] (Hall and Nordby 1973:41–42).

From among the numerous archetypes studied by him, Jung selected and paid a great deal of attention to five which he considered to be of the greatest importance in shaping human personality and behaviour. These are the *persona,* the *anima* (in men) or the *animus* (in women), the *shadow, the wise old man* (in men) or the *great mother* (in women), and the *self.*

These five archetypes appear rather clearly in Okigbo's poetry marking significant stages in the poet-hero's quest for fulfillment as, in Jungian theory, they mark significant stages of individuation.

The *persona* is the mask through which we seek to carve a favourable image in our social relationships. It is essentially the predisposition to play up to appearances, the urge to behave according to the demands of a particular social role which comes from the depths of the unconscious. Okigbo's poet-hero in his conscious orientation towards the inner world projects an almost monomaniac mask of a contemplative, solitude-seeking and far-seeing man, clearly anxious to be identified as poet, prophet and priest.

The desire to be identified as a poet is particularly strong. Thus the poet-hero's *persona* embodies such traditional symbols of the poet as the sunbird:

> Me, to the orangery
> solitude invites
> a wagtail, to tell,
> the tangled-wood-tale;
> a sunbird, to mourn
> a mother on a spray
> (*Heavensgate* 1, 1:6–11)

or as a bird that must sing, tongue-tied,

> without name or audience,
> making harmony among the branches
> (*Siren Limits* III)

But the *persona* in the long run is only a mask. Beneath it is the *shadow,* our darker side which we generally do not wish to be identified with but which though repressed remains within us, occasionally breaking through the mask to dominate our behaviour often to our embarrassment or frustration. Beneath the poet-prophet *persona* of Okigbo's hero is a degenerate *shadow-archetype,* properly identified throughout the poems as the "prodigal." This *shadow-archetype* is essentially like the figure of the prodigal in the Bible. This darker side of the poet-hero is first revealed in *Four Canzones,*[14] but in *Heavensgate,* there is a sustained attempt to contain its negative effects through the distillation of a proper *persona.* But again and again the *Shadow* keeps breaking through the mask taking more sinister forms. For example, in *Limits I–IV,* soon after the regeneration at the end of *Heavensgate,* the shadow breaks through the mask once again in the guise of Ahab the hero of Melville's *Moby Dick.* Here, the poet-hero's unbridled pursuit of the "white elephant" through "Banks of reed" and "Mountains of broken bottles" turns out to be no less destructive and illusory than that of Ahab's monomaniac pursuit of the "white whale." The Ahab-image is here compounded with that of another famous literary manifestation of the shadow archetype, namely Enkidu, the primitive alter-ego of Gilgamesh in the ancient Babylonian epic. Thus, at the close of *Siren Limits* the poet-hero, bursting as it were with primitive energy, throws himself against the inscrutable "oblong-headed lioness" (section IV) only to become "drowned," like Enkidu his Babylonian counterpart, "in the unconscious."[15]

But, perhaps, of all the five major archetypes, by far the most highly developed in its manifestations in Okigbo's poetry is the *anima.* The anima is the primordial image of woman in man, a counterpart of the animus, the primordial image of man engraved on the mind of woman. The anima appears in dreams, visions and fantasies as in literature and myth in the form of the mother, the loved one, the goddess, the siren, the prostitute and enchantress, the *femme fatale.* The impact of these latent images of woman can be as destructive to the psychic health of the man who projects them as they can be beneficient. They often give rise to an obsessive pursuit of the elusive and the intractable. This is exactly what happens inside Okigbo's poetry where the poet-hero's efforts are pointedly directed toward one goal, union with the *anima* in one of its most ethereal manifestations, a goal which is ultimately realized at the close of *Distances.* Thus Okigbo says in his introduction to *Labyrinths:*

> *Distances* is . . . a poem of homecoming, but of homecoming in its spiritual and psychic aspect. The quest broken off after "Siren Limits" is resumed, this time in the unconscious. The self that suffers, that experiences, ultimately finds fulfilment in a form of psychic union with the supreme spirit that is both destructive and creative. The process is one of sensual anaesthesia, of total liberation from all physical and emotional tension; the end result, a state of aesthetic grace. (1965: xi–xii)

This union with "the supreme spirit that is both destructive and creative" takes place after a long series of gruesome encounters with various forms and manifestations of her image, both negative and positive, in the preceding sequences.

In *Four Canzones* and *Heavensgate,* she appears as Idoto, "the water spirit that nurtures all creation" (Okigbo 1965:xi). In these two sequences, especially in the latter, she is identified as the mother to whom the shadow-dominated hero (the prodigal) must return for psychic regeneration:

> Before you, mother Idoto,
>     naked I stand;
> before your watery presence,
>     a prodigal
> leaning on an oilbean,
> lost in your legend
>                 *(Heavensgate I)*

The anima, according to Jung, is "projected not only on to a pagan goddess" (as here, in the case of Okigbo, on to Idoto), she also represents the totality of man's age-old experience with women; "Every mother and every beloved is forced to become the carrier and embodiment of this omnipresent and ageless image" (see Fordham 1975:53). The image first takes the shape of man's mother and then acquires the qualities of "various women who attract a man in his life time" *(Ibid).* Later, she becomes etherealized, imbued with a "timeless quality" looking rather young and beautiful though "there is always a suggestion of years of experience behind her" *(Ibid:* 54).

There is a hint of the projection of the anima image on to Okigbo's own mother, Mrs. Anna Okigbo, in the two invocations of "Anna . . . of the panel oblong" in *Heavensgate I* and *V.* But the dominant forms in which the anima shows up are essentially ethereal: goddess, watermaid, lioness, and white queen. Okigbo's watermaid is essentially the same as Jung's "mermaid, water spirit, or nymph, who entices a man under the water where she lives so that he must love her forever or be drowned" (see Fordham 1957:54). In *Heavensgate III,* the first vision of the watermaid engulfs Okigbo's hero in a vortex of violence:

> now breaks
> salt-white surf on the stones and me
> and lobsters and shells
> in iodine small.

Later in the same section of *Heavensgate,* the anima appears in another ethereal form:

> Bright
> with the armpit-dazzle of a lioness

> . . . . . . . . . . . . . . . . . . . . . . . . . .
> wearing white light about her

But then she proves as elusive as she is alluring:

> So brief her presence
> match-flare in Wind's breath
> so brief with mirrors around me
>
> Downward . . .
> the waves distil her;
> gold crop
> sinking ungathered.

The end result is a feeling of total frustration and disillusionment:

> And I who am here abandoned,
>
> count the sand by waves abandoned,
> count her blessing, my white queen.
>
> But the spent sea reflects
> from his mirrored visage
> not my queen, a broken shadow,

These tantalizing appearances and disappearances of the anima awaken in the poet-hero a consuming desire to capture her. But when she reappears in *Limits IV,* it is in the destructive form of the "oblong headed lioness" that wounds and destroys the quester's second self.

In certain respects, these images of the distractingly beautiful but elusive female figure that occasionally responds to the hero's consuming passion for her may have been reinforced by Okigbo's encounter in real life with women. It is difficult to assert with certainty; but one gets a hint of a difficult relationship with a particular woman in the poet's life in the confession that "*Limits* was written at the end of a journey of several centuries from Nsukka to Yola in pursuit of what turned out to be an illusion" (1965:xi).[16] Nevertheless, in its vital essence as "gold crop," the anima figure is "the treasure hard to come by," in the search for which the romantic hero must submit to a long series of ordeals and display the patience of the alchemist.[17] Even before the final consummation, (section 11), the anima appears to the hero in one of her most formidable forms, as "Death herself":

> anguish and solitude . . .
> smothered, my scattered
> cry, the dancers,
> lost among their own snares,

the faces, the hands held
captive; the interspaces reddening with blood;

behind them all,
in smoke of white cotton,
Death herself,
the chief celebrant,
in a cloud of incense,
paring her fingernails . . .

At her feet rolled their heads like cut fruits:
about her fell their severed members,
numerous as locusts,

Like split wood left to dry, the dismembered
joints of the ministrants piled high.

She bathed her knees in the blood of attendants;
her sock in entrails of ministrants . . .

This appears to be the last terrifying hurdle, for after this the hero passes
through the great archway on which he sees the largest mandala in the
poems, a magic circle[18] which here, as in Jungian psychoanalysis, anticipates
the "state of aesthetic grace" and "total liberation from all physical and emotional tension" that follows the invitation of the goddess:

come into my cavern
shake the mildew from your hair;
let your ear listen:
my mouth calls from a cavern . . .
*(Distances VI)*

The archetype of the *wise-old-man,* associated with the occasional feeling
of godliness in men, is not so clearly manifest in Okigbo as the other four
Jungian archetypes, but it seems to underline the false sense of "divine rejoicing" with which the hero dares approach the queen in *Limits I.* This kind of
inflationary attitude does not, however, run counter to the hero's more positive identification with great heroes such as Christ *(Heavensgate* and *Distances),*[19] Gilgamesh *(Limits),* Palinurus, Tammuz and Aeneas *(Silences),* etc.,
for these are mythological symbols of self-realization—archetypes of the kind
of fully individualized *self* which the poet-hero seeks to attain.

That Okigbo's poetry is so richly dominated by the archetypes of the
collective unconscious is by no means surprising, especially in the light of the
universality of its mythos, "the fable of man's perennial quest for fulfilment."
As Jung says in his essay "On the Relation of Analytical Psychology to Poetic
Art" (See Jacobi 1942:24),

He who speaks in primordial images speaks with a thousand voices. He enthrals and overpowers, while at the same time he lifts the idea he is trying to express out of the occasional and the transitory into the realm of the ever-enduring. He transmutes our personal destiny into the destiny of mankind, thereby evoking in us all those beneficient forces that have enabled mankind to find refuge from every peril and to outlive the longest night. That is the secret of effective art.

It is also, essentially, the secret of the effectiveness of Okigbo's poetry.

## III

If Okigbo's poet-hero is a large and complex symbol of the psyche in its conscious and unconscious aspects, his progression through *Four Canzones,* through *Labyrinths,* through *Path of Thunder,* and even through the occasional poems, especially *Dance of the Painted Maidens* and *Lament of the Masks,* may be described as symbolizing the dynamics of the psyche, i.e. the character, values and directions of flow of the energy (Libido in Jungian terminology) by means of which the psyche operates.

It would appear from a careful analysis of Okigbo's poetry that the psychic energy which propels the poet-hero is fundamentally sexual in character.[20] The relationship between the hero and the anima is thus often portrayed in sexual images, both of desire and of consummation. Many readers may not be fully aware of the sexual undertones of the opening lines of *Heavensgate:*

> Before you, mother Idoto,
> naked I stand,
> before your watery presence
> a prodigal
>
> leaning on an oil bean
> lost in your legend

The sexual implications of the words "naked" "watery" and "lost" here can only be fully realized if we understand what the "oilbean" on which the hero is leaning really is. In fact, the oilbean here is *Ukpakaoto,* in the mythology of Okigbo's hometown, Ojoto, the consort of the goddess Idoto.[21] There seems to be something magical about the poet-hero's posture here. Leaning on the oilbean seems to be a way of acquiring the conjugal powers of *Ukpakaoto,* i.e. by the law of contact in sympathetic magic (see Frazer 1963:14–15). The consequence of this sexual union with the goddess is unique secret knowledge of the world and human behaviour. It is the *word* or "divine logos" that transforms the "dark waters of the beginning" into the created world.

At the end of the second strophe of *Heavensgate I,* we have another sexual image, that of the young bird

> On one leg standing
> in silence at the passage.

This image may be ambivalent, but one meaning certainly is the idea of the young cockerel standing on heat on one leg as it approaches the hen. In a similar setting—in the "solitude" of the beach in *Heavensgate III*—the hero feels the thrill of sexual consummation as he contemplates a vision of the anima:

> Maid of the salt-emptiness,
> sophisticreamy,
> whose secret I have covered up with beachsand.
> Shadow of rain over sunbeaten beach
> Shadow of rain over man with woman.

The strong sexual energy of the hero is generally channelled positively throughout the poems as a vehicle for the attainment of creative and spiritual goals. Thus, as the hero's quest comes to its end in *Distances,* he experiences the bliss of sexual union with the goddess, in her bridal chamber:

> I wash my feet in your head, o maid . . .
> I have entered your bridal
> chamber; and lo,
> I am the sole witness of my homecoming
> *(Distances VI)*

But this is the final spiritual-creative transformation of an instinctual sexual energy. When overcome by the *shadow,* as in *Limits I,* what we see is the spontaneous outpour of pure animal sexuality:

> Emigrant with airborne nose,
> The he-goat-on-heat.

Another aspect of Jungian psychodynamics which may throw some light on the nature of the experience of Okigbo's poet-hero is the idea that the natural movement of the Libido is both forward and backward, like tidal waves. The forward movement which Jung calls *progression* satisfies the demands of the conscious while the backward movement, *regression,* satisfies the demand of the unconscious. This aspect of Jungian theory has been succinctly summed up as follows in Fordham (1957:18–19):

> Progression is concerned with the active adaptation to one's environment and regression with the adaption to one's inner needs. Regression therefore, (con-

trary to some points of view) is just as normal as a counterpole as sleeping and waking, as long as the Libido is functioning in an unhindered manner, i.e. according to the law of enantiodromia, when it must eventually turn over into a progressive movement. Regression may even mean, among other things, a return to a dreamy state after a period of concentration and directed mental activity or it may mean a return to an earlier stage of development but these are not necessarily "wrong"; rather they can be looked upon as restorative phases—*"reculer pour mieux sauter."*

In Okigbo's poetry switches from *progression* to *regression* are sometimes clearly marked. As we are told in the introduction to *Labyrinths,* "the quest broken off after 'Siren Limits' is resumed (in *Distances*), this time in the unconscious." This transition from active adaptation to the outer world to the inner world is clearly marked at the end of *Siren Limits.* The hero addresses the image, as he submits to her power:

> Distances of her armpit-fragrance
> Turn chloroform enough for my patience—
> When you have finished
> & done up my stitches,
> Wake me near the altar,
> & this poem will be finished . . .

Some of Okigbo's poems are dominated by regressive movements (e.g. *Distances*) while others are dominated by progressive movements (e.g. *Limits V–XII*). But the pattern of progression and regression is discernible in the internal dynamics of particular sequences. *Heavensgate,* for example, begins with a progressive movement, an invocation to the water-goddess, Idoto, in which the returned prodigal attempts to adapt himself to his long-abandoned home, to reidentify himself with his roots. There follows, in the second strophe of the first section, a regressive movement both of introspection and of a kind of return to the very origins of creation, the "dark waters of the beginning." In the third strophe, the poet-hero wakes again as it were from his withdrawal into his inner world and comes face to face with the Christian Church, the external enemy against which he must define his positives.

The second part of *Heavensgate* begins with a regressive movement, this time with what Fordham describes as a "return to an earlier stage of development," in this case to significant childhood experiences stored in the depths of the personal unconscious. These memories assert themselves compulsively on the poet, reinforcing his dedication to the pursuit of excellence through poetry. In *Heavensgate III,* the regressive movement continues, but this time in the deeper stratum of the collective unconscious where the poet-hero encounters some of the most powerful ethereal manifestations of his anima—the watermaid, the lioness, and the white queen.

Finally, in sections IV and V, the hero returns to the progressive active adaptation to his socio-cultural environment, first through the sacrifice for rebirth in "Lustra" (section IV) and subsequently through the celebration of the arrival of a child in the extended family in "New-comer" (section V), an event which he treats here as an objective correlative of his own rebirth.

For Jung, writes Fordham (1957:19),

> Libido is natural energy, and first and foremost serves the purposes of life, but a certain amount in excess of what is needed for instinctive ends can be converted into productive work and used for cultural purposes. This direction of energy becomes initially possible by transferring it to something similar in nature to the objects of instinctive interest. The transfer cannot however be made a simple act of the will, but is achieved in a roundabout way. After a period of gestation in the unconscious a symbol is produced which can attract the Libido, and also serve as a channel diverting its natural flow. The symbol is never thought out consciously, but comes usually as a revelation or intuition, often appearing in a dream.

It seems that the female image in Okigbo's poetry represents such a symbol. It is a symbol which, as we have seen above, has the potential of attracting the strong sexual drives of the poet-hero and converting them into a means for the fulfilment of creative and spiritual yearnings. There is an interesting dramatization of this canalization process in *Heavensgate III* where, as noted above, the sexual image of "shadow of rain over man with woman" appears. Here, the hero is discovered on a seashore burdened with a secret which, after a traumatic encounter with the anima (manifested in the figure of the "watermaid"), he plants "into a dughole." The sexual undertones of the expression "dughole" may not be immediately obvious except to those who are conversant with the Nigerian undergraduate slang ("hole"-female sexual organ). *Heavensgate* was composed at the University of Nigeria, Nsukka, and it is not unlikely that, in the expression "dughole," the sexual implication of the "hole" slang is combined with the traditional Igbo image of the "dog" as a symbol of sexuality.[22] The "dughole" into which the hero's secret is whispered is thus, most probably, a symbol of the female sexual organ, and the secret itself, as I have shown elsewhere, is poetic truth, the seed out of which "the ears" grow in the second strophe like the reeds that grew out of the hole into which King Midas' barber subconsciously whispers the truth of his privileged knowledge that the "king has asses' ears" (see Azuonye 1973, and Graves 1960:11).

This symbolic representation of the canalization of excess sexual energy for cultural purposes is all the more remarkable, in so far as Okigbo's relationship with Jung is concerned, for its congruence with the example of canalization cited by Jung in his essay on "Psychic Energy." Jung cites the spring ceremony of the Watschandis, who dig a hole in the earth, surround it with business in imitation of the female genitals, and dance round it holding their spears in front to simulate an erect penis. As they dance round, they thrust their spears into the hole, shouting *"Pulli nira, pulli nira, wataka."* (Not a pit, not a pit, but a cunt!) During the ceremony none of the participants is allowed to look at a woman. The dance, which takes place in the spring, is charged with extraordinary significance. The dancers, through their movements and shouting, arouse themselves to ecstasy; they are sharing in a magical act, the fertilization of the Earth woman, and other women are kept out of the way so that the libido shall not flow into ordinary sexuality. The hole in the earth is not just a substitute for female genitals, but a symbol representing the idea of the earth woman who is to be fertilized, and is the symbol which transmutes the libido. (Fordham 1957:20)

## IV

When Okigbo describes the central theme of his poetry as "the fable of man's perennial quest for fulfilment" he is stating in the language of a poet-critic something parallel to the central concern of Jungian psychology, the development of personality through the harmonization of the disparate but interacting contents of the psyche. To achieve a fully individuated personality, every individual must strive to activate and understand the contents of the inner state of his psyche, to reach an accommodation both with the complexes of the personal unconscious and the archetypes of the collective unconscious. The contents of the collective unconscious must be made conscious and brought into harmonious coexistence with the conscious.

As we have noted, accommodation with the archetypes of the collective unconscious is particularly important in the individuation process. In fact, the individuation process begins with an encounter with the shadow and the containment of this darker aspect of our inner selves in such a way as to be able to distil a proper persona suited to the total environment in which we find ourselves. This Okigbo does in *Four Canzones* and *Heavensgate.* He contains the prodigal in him, discovers an inner strength in the life of contemplation through poetry and so distils the proper persons suited to this role in his poet-hero. Through the poet-hero, he overcomes the negative and destructive aspects of the anima as well as the tendency toward inflation, the wise-old-man in him. Battling through various obstacles—labyrinths, mazes and distances, and with the aid of traditional magic circles or mandalas, he finally arrives at the state of "aesthetic grace" described in *Distances.* The inner and the outer worlds have been traversed through a long series of progressions and regressions. Now, the unification of the inward and the outward attitudes has become possible. Thus, in *Path of Thunder,* the extroverted "Okigbo, town-crier" is able to take the "forum" and speak with the voice of the conscious "mythmaker" about the events of the day with the subjective strength of the poet-hero who has, in his "journey of several centuries," shouldered his way "through a mass of ancient nights to chlorophyll."

## Notes

1. This paper was originally presented at the Fifth Annual African Literature Conference, University of Ibadan, July 29–August 2, 1980.

2. It is in fact very likely that Okigbo was familiar with the writings of Carl Jung, and there are traces of Jungian terminology in his introduction to *Labyrinths*, notably in his description of *Distances* as "a poem of homecoming in its spiritual and psychic aspect. The quest broken off after 'Siren Limits' is resumed this time in the unconscious." Be that as it may, there is no attempt in this paper to argue that Okigbo's poetry was directly influenced by Jungian psychology. The argument is rather that there are patterns of congruence in the works of both men which illuminate each other and which seem to vindicate the claim of each to a universal vision of reality. In fact, the less evidence there is of any direct influence on Okigbo by Jung the more significant these patterns of congruence will be.

3. This dimension of the congruence between Okigbo and Jung is not discussed further in this paper except in a footnote (17 below).

4. For earlier comparative studies of Okigbo's poetry, see Egudu (1971), Anozie (1972) and Maduakor (1977).

5. Most of the earlier published critical works on Okigbo are concerned with the problem of elucidating the meaning and significance of various features of theme and symbolism in his poetry. See especially Anozie (1963, 1967, 1969, 1972), Dathorne (1964, 1968a, 1968b), Egudu (1971, 1973), Heywood (1978), Ikiddeh (1969, 1974), Izevbaye (1973a, 1973b), Leslie (1973), Maduakor (1977), Moore (1969), Nwoga (1972, 1973, 1975), Theroux (1965) and Thumboo (1969). For the most detailed bibliography of Okigbo scholarship published so far, see Anafulu (1978).

6. The fact of the existence of the "archetypes" is perhaps the most widely disputed aspect of Jungian psychology, one at which literary scholars have often scoffed (see, for example, Kirk 1970: 175–280). But it seems rather clear from Jung's constant use of the term "motif" to denote the "archetype" (e.g. in his essay, "The Concept of the Collective Unconscious," 1959) and from Jacobi's comparison of the idea to "the Gestalt" (1971: 53–55) that it is indeed true—to use the words of Kirk himself—that "all human beings possess similar inborn tendencies to form certain symbols, and these manifest themselves through the unconscious mind in myths, dreams, delusions and folklore" (1970:275).

7. See, for example, Robert James Ewald's doctoral dissertation at Bowling Green State University: "The Jungian Archetype of the Fairy Mistress in Medieval Romance," 1977.

8. Anozie (1972:77) appears to be of a different opinion although he recognizes the relationship between Okigbo's concern in his poetry and some aspects of Jungian Psychology.

9. Subsumed here is the Jungian theory of the "psychological types" including four function-types (thinking, feeling, sensing and intuiting) and two attitude-types (extroversion and introversion) which cut across the function-types. But, as Jung insists, no one individual belongs exclusively to only one or the other of these types. This will explain the use in this and subsequent paragraphs of the terms "extroverted, thinking-and-feeling type" and "introverted, sensing-and-intuiting type."

10. That the shrine of Idoto was destroyed is a little known event recently discussed in a newspaper article (Maduekwe, 1980). I have elsewhere (Azuonye, 1980) attempted to show that the scenes of Christian Imperialist destruction evoked in "Fragments out of the Deluge" (*Limits* V–XII) include some allusions to this event.

11. "By its theme and craft," writes Anozie (1972:174), "*Path of Thunder* differs from the poetry written by Christopher Okigbo up to and including the first half of December

1965." It is essentially the type (in this case the committed poetry of the negritude class) which Okigbo describes in one of his interviews as "platform poetry" (Whitelaw, 1965:29). Anozie (1974:174) explains: "This is so because in it Okigbo makes, for the first time ever, a forthright and direct political statement which undisguisedly defines the poet's own revolutionary option."

12.    These lines from the original version of *Heavensgate* are omitted in the final version published in *Labyrinths*.

13.    Cf. Jacobi's discussion of the *archetype* in terms of the *Gestalt* (1971:53–55). See also Isidore Okpewho's discussion (19:161–162) of the *motif* (to which Jung equates the *archetype*) in relation to the *Gestalt*.

14.    The presence of the shadow-archetype of the Prodigal in this early sequence is one of the indications of its organic relatedness to the subsequent sequences in *Labyrinths* (1971).

15.    See Cirlot (1962:190), under the entry, *Lion:* "For Jung, the Lion in its wild state, is broadly speaking an index of latent passions; It may also take the form of a sign indicating *the danger of being devoured by the unconscious*" (Italics added).

16.    This is probably Okigbo's wife, Sefi, before he married her in 1964. As we are told in Anozie (1972:9), Okigbo was passionately in love with Sefi, but "Although they had a daughter, Ibrahimat, they never lived happily together under the same roof for any length of time."

17.    Okigbo's work is indeed both a ritual re-enactment of an intense personal religious experience and an alchemical work in which is described a passionate quest for the great treasure hard to come by, the *opus magnum* of the alchemist. It will be an illuminating line of research to investigate, in the light of the works of Cirlot (1962), Jung (1953, 1956, 1959), de Rola (1973) and others, the significance as symbols of alchemical transformation—of various colours, metals and the geometrical forms in Okigbo's poetry.

18.    The magic circle, better known by its Sanskrit name, *mandala*, "includes all concentrically arranged figures, all radial and spherical arrangements, and all circles and squares with a central point. It is one of the oldest religious symbols (the earliest known being the sun-wheel), and is found throughout the world" (Fordham 1959:57). Discussed at length in my study of geometrical symbolism in Okigbo's poetry, the *mandala* is essentially "the visual plastic expression of the struggle to achieve order—even within diversity and the longing to be reunited with the pristine, non-spatial and non-temporal 'Centre' as it is conceived in all symbolic traditions" (Cirlot 1962:201). Not surprisingly, the spiritual homecoming of Okigbo's poet-hero, in *Distances,* is anticipated by a vision of the following mandala:

> a triangular lintel
> of solid alabaster
> enclosed in a square
> inscribed in a circle
> with a hollow centre
> above the archway
> yawning shutterless
> like celestial pincers
> like a vast countenance

one can indeed see the vast countenance (the face of God, perhaps) in a simple diagram of this mandala.

19.    The poet-hero's self-identification with Christ in the closing lines of *Distances* ("o maid . . . / I have entered your bridal / chamber") is so wrapped up in an allusion to Catholic thought that most readers may not be aware of it. But Jung's comment in his autobiography (1963) is highly revealing: "In the realm of Catholic thought the Mother of God and Bride of Christ has been received into the divine thalamus (bridal chamber) only recently, after centuries

of hesitancy, and thus at least been accorded partial recognition" (1963:227). Jung's secretary Aniela Jaffe explains in a footnote: "This refers to the Papal Bull of Pius XII, *Munificientissimus Deus* (1950), promulgating the Assumption of the Blessed Virgin Mary. This new dogma affirms that Mary as Bride is united with the Son in the heavenly bridal chamber, and as Sophia (Wisdom) she is united with the Godhead. Thus the feminine principle is brought into immediate proximity with the masculine Trinity." See also Jung's *Answer to Job* (in Campbell, 1971:635–6).

20. Here Okigbo is much more comparable to Freud in his earlier writings than to Jung: "In his earlier writings Freud used the term 'libido' to denote sexual energy: but when he revised his theory of motivation, libido was defined as the energy of all the life instincts" (Hall, 1954:59).

21. The oilbean tree in Okigbo's poetry is probably *Ukpaka-òtò* (lit. Oilbean tree of *Otò*) which, in the mythology of the poet's hometown *Ojoòtò* (lit. the Place of *Otò*), is the consort of the water-goddess *Ido-òtò* (lit. the river of *Otò*). I am indebted to Dr. Zed Chukwujama of the University of Nigeria Teaching Hospital, Enugu, for this information.

22. E.g. the idiom *o nà-àra kà nkita,* "he fucks like a dog." The phrase "dug-hole" is thus a pun on the sexual connotations of "dog" and "hole" in the collocation "doghole." Okigbo is fond of puns and *double entredres* of this kind. Thus, for example, the word *iron* in "Thunder Can Break" (*Path of Thunder,* p. 63) refers simultaneously to the "iron chapter" of Nigerian history represented by the military coup of January 1966 as well as to the new military Head of State, General *Ironsi* (nicknamed *Iron*-sides) and to the ironic imprisonment of the heroes of the coup ("Iron birds / Held-fruit-of-flight—tight") by the new incumbent who did not share their revolutionary ideals. See also *Heavensgate III* where the word ear in ears of the secret" refers both to the reed that sprouts from the hole into which King Midas's barber whispers the secret that the king has ass's ears and to the ears of the king himself the secret (poetic truth)—and the consequences of its exfoliation (see Azuonye, 1973, and Graves, 1960:83f).

*References*

Anafulu, Joseph C. 1978. "Christopher Okigbo, 1932–1967: A bibliography." *Research in African Literatures.* (Spring) 1:65.

Anozie, S. O. 1963. "Okigbo's *Heavensgate,* a study of Art as Ritual." *Ibadan* 15 (March): 11.

———. 1967. "Okigbo's Creative Itinerary: Four Canzones—1957–1961." *Presence Africaine.* 64:158.

———. 1969. "A Structural Approach to Okigbo's *Distances.*" *Conch.* 1:8.

———. 1972. *Christopher Okigbo: Creative Rhetoric.* London and Ibadan: Evans Brothers Ltd.

Azuonye, Chukwuma, 1973. "The Secret of the Watermaid: Dramatisation of the Symbolist Process in *Heavensgate III.*" Unpublished paper, Nsukka.

———. 1979. "Memories, Initiations and Geometrical Symbolism in Okigbo's Poetry." English Departmental Seminar Paper, University of Ibadan, May 1979.

———. 1980. "The Organic Unity of Okigbo's Poetry." English Departmental Seminar Paper, University of Ibadan, March, 1980.

Campbell, Joseph (ed.) 1971. *The Portable Jung.* London: Penguin Books 1980 Edition.

Dathorne, O. R. 1964. "Limits by Christopher Okigbo," *Black Orpheus* 15 (1964).

———. 1968. "Ritual and Ceremony in Okigbo's Poetry." *Journal of Commonwealth Literature* 5 (July): 84.

———. 1968. "Okigbo Understood: A Study of Two Poems." *African Literature Today* 1:2.

Egudu, Romanus. 1971. "Ezra Pound in African Poetry: Christopher Okigbo." *Comparative Literature Studies* 8, ii:143.

————. 1973. "Defence of Culture in the Poetry of Christopher Okigbo." *African Literature Today.* 6 (1973):14.

Fordham, Frieda. 1957. *An Introduction to Jung's Psychology.* London: Penguin Books.

Frazer, J. G. 1963. *The Golden Bough: A Study in Magic and Religion.* Abridged edition in one volume. London: Macmillan.

Graves, Robert. 1960. *The Greek Myths.* Volume 1. London: Penguin Books.

Hall, Calvin S. 1954. *A Primer of Freudian Psychology.* New York: New American Library.

Hall, Calvin S., and Nordy, V. J. 1973. *A Primer of Jungian Psychology.* New American Library.

Heywood, Annemarie. 1978. "The Ritual and the Plot: The Critic and Okigbo's *Labyrinths.*" *Research in African Literatures.* Spring 1:46.

Ikiddeh, Ime. 1969. "Dathorne on Okigbo: A Comment." *African Literature Today* 2:55.

————. 1974. "Iron, Thunder and Elephants: A study of Okigbo's *Path of Thunder.*" *New Horn* 1.ii:46.

Izevbaye, D. S. 1973a. "From Reality to Dream: The Poetry of Christopher Okigbo." In *The Critical Evaluation of African Literature* edited by Edgar Wright. London: Heinemann: 120–148.

————. 1973b. "Okigbo's Portrait of the Artist as a Sunbird: A Reading of *Heavensgate* (1962)." *African Literature Today* 6: 1.

Jacobi, Jolande. 1959a. *The Psychology of C. G. Jung.* London: Routledge and Kegan Paul. 1968 reprint.

————. 1959b. *Complex, Archetype and Symbol in the Psychology of C. G. Jung.* Princeton: Princeton University Press (Bollington Series, LVII). Third Printing 1974.

Jung, Carl Gustav. 1953a. *Psychology and Alchemy.* In Read, Fordham and Adler (eds.) Vol. 9.

————. 1953b. *Alchemical Studies. Ibid.* Vol. 13.

————. 1956. *Symbols of Transformation. Ibid.* Vol. 5.

————. 1958. "Answer to Job." *Ibid.* Vol. II.

————. 1959a. "Archetypes of the Collective Unconscious." *Ibid.* Vol. 19.

————. 1959b. "The Concept of the Collective Unconscious." *Ibid.*

————. 1959c. "Consciousness, Unconscious and Individuation." *Ibid.*

————. 1959d. "A Study of the Process of Individuation." *Ibid.*

————. 1963. Mysterium Coniunctionis. *Ibid.* Vol. 14.

————. 1965. *Memories, Dreams, Reflections.* Recorded and edited by Daniela Jaffe, Trans. from the German by Richard and Clara Winston. Glasgow: Collins. Fount Paperbacks. 14th Impression, 1980.

————. 1967. "On the Relation of Analytical Psychology to Poetic Art." In Read, Fordham and Adler (eds.), Vol. 15.

Kirk, G. S. 1970. *Myth: Its Meaning and Functions in Ancient and Other Cultures.* Berkeley and Los Angeles: University of California Press. 1978 Reprint.

Leslie, Omolara. 1973. "The Poetry of Christopher Okigbo: Its Evolution and Significance." *Ufahamu* 4, i:47.

Maduakor, H. 1977. "Okigbo and Yeats: Landscapes of Identity." Unpublished African Studies Association (USA) Conference Paper.

Maduekwe, Joe. 1980. "How Ojoto Sacked its Goddess." *Weekly Star* (Enugu) March 1980:8.

Moore, Gerald. 1969. *The Chosen Tongue.* London: Longman.

Nwoga, Donatus I. 1972. "Okigbo's *Limits:* An Approach to Meaning." *Journal of Commonwealth Literature* 7 i:92.

————. 1973. "Obscurity and Commitment in Modern African Poetry." *African Literature Today* 6:26.

————. 1975. "Plagiarism and Authentic Creativity in West Africa." *Research in African Literatures* 6:32.

Okigbo, Christopher. 1957–61. *Four Canzones. Black Orpheus* II, 1962.

————. 1960–61. *Heavensgate.* In *Labyrinths,* 1965.

————. 1961–62. *Limits. Ibid.*

————. 1962–64. *Silences. Ibid.*

————. 1964. *Distances. Ibid.*

————. 1965a. *Labyrinths.* Published with *Path of Thunder.* Heinemann, 1971.

————. 1965b. "Lament of the Masks." In Bushrui and Maxwell (eds.), *W. B. Yeats: 1865–1965: Centenary Essays.* Ibadan: Ibadan University Press.

————. 1965c. "Dance of the Painted Maidens." In *Verse and Voice: A Festival of Commonwealth Poetry,* ed. Douglas Cleverdon. London: Poetry Book Society.

Okpewho, Isidore. 1979. *The Epic in Africa: Toward a Poetics of the Oral Performance.* New York: Columbia Univ. Press.

Read, Sir Herbert, Dr. Michael Fordham, and Dr. Gerhard Adler. 1953–68. *The Collected Works of C.G. Jung.* 18 Vols. London: Routledge and Kegan Paul.

Theroux, Paul. 1965. "Christopher Okigbo." *Transition* 5:22.

Serumaga, Robert. 1965. "Interview with Christopher Okigbo." *Cultural Events in Africa* (Supplement) I–IV.

Thumboo, Edwin. 1969. "Dathorne's Okigbo: A Dissenting View." *African Literature Today* 3, 27.

Whitelaw, Marjory. 1965. "Interview with Christopher Okigbo." *Journal of Commonwealth Literature* 9: 28.

# CRITICAL OVERVIEW

◆

# The Poetry of Christopher Okigbo: Its Evolution and Significance

MOLARA OGUNDIPE-LESLIE

"The Lament of the Masks," one of Okigbo's last poems, was written in commemoration of the W. B. Yeats centenary (1865–1965) to be included in a volume published by the University of Ibadan English department.[1]

It was appropriate that Okigbo should write a poem to celebrate Yeats and his influence on other poets since contemporary African writers coming up then had been much influenced by the tradition of modern verse represented by Hopkins and Yeats, Eliot and Pound. Interestingly though, Okigbo does not use a modern English style in this poem; rather, he sings Yeats in the style of the traditional Yoruba praise song in which the attributes of a hero, ancestor or aristocrat are hailed in animal imagery and analogy from nature. Some of the lines here are in fact reworkings of actual praises to the Timi of Ede,[2] whose military kingship was created and the town of Ede was settled in the seventeenth century from the need of the Yoruba emperor to provide a defensive military outpost to the old Yoruba empire of Oyo. Section III of the Lament combines the direct address and the naming of the deeds of the hero, typical of the praise song, with the use of special symbolism, "the white elephant." Such use of special symbolism occurs in the Yoruba praise song, where in contrast to Okigbo's use, the meaning of the symbol was known by all members (at least by the elders) in the community.

> They thought you would stop pursuing the white elephant
> They thought you would stop pursuing the white elephant
> But you pursued the white elephant without turning back—
> You who charmed the white elephant with your magic flute
> You who trapped the white elephant like a common rabbit
> You who sent the white elephant tumbling into your net—
> And stripped him of his horns, and made them your own—
> You who fashioned his horns into ivory trumpets . . .

Originally published in *Ufahamu* 4, no. 1 (1973): 47–54. © 1973 by Molara Ogundipe-Leslie. Reprinted by permission of Molara Ogundipe-Leslie.

In Okigbo's "Lament," the white elephant symbol serves a more Western poetic function because individual interpretation is permissible, even necessary. Yeats's white elephant could be many things: his poetic activity; his mystical ends expressed in his later poetry; even the cause of the Irish.

However, "The Lament of the Masks" is not in the style of poetry associated with Okigbo's name. It represents a new direction in his poetic style, for after this poem he was to speak more and more in an African voice. In fact, by the time he writes his last poems, agonized outcries prophesying war, he had dropped all affectations and was using a poetic rendering of his own conversational voice combined with the style of traditional verse. With Okigbo's name comes to mind a very personal poetry written in so recondite an idiom that it has given rise to critical debate as to its value, its effectiveness and even its nonsensical nature,[3] and as to whether a reader is not a profane intruder into such hallowed and subjective verse.[4] [This may be why the publishers of his volume of verse *Labyrinths* (New York: Africana Publishing Corp., 1971) had him comment on his own work to have the secret from the horse's mouth.] Though the poet or artist is not always the best explicator of his own work, Okigbo's introduction, itself a beautiful prose poem, will assuredly be of immense value to Okigbo criticism.

Born in Ojoto in Eastern Nigeria in 1932 of a father who was a trader and who travelled around a great deal in Nigeria, Christopher Okigbo is said to have lived as a boy in the northern part of Nigeria among the Hausa and Fulani. (Shades of days to come.) Okigbo and his siblings eventually entered the professional middle class in Nigeria. He took a classics degree from the University of Ibadan in 1956 which at that time meant that he studied Greek and Latin literature, Roman and Greek history and culture. He worked at various positions after graduation: as a high school teacher in Fiditi, a provincial town in Yorubaland; as librarian at the University of Nigeria, Nsukka where his poetry flowered, probably due to his reading; and as the West African representative for the Cambridge University Press. In appearance he was small, fine and dapper, in fact somewhat of a dandy; in manner quaintly elegant, irrepressible and hilarious in conversation, animated by a divine madness. Some would say it was all a "put-on." Okigbo loved music and the effect of this is everywhere evident in his verse.

Okigbo's earliest poems, dated 1957 (a year after he left Ibadan University) and ranging from 1957–61, are entitled *Four Canzones,* and they show the influence of his classical education. The first canzone, "Song of the Forest," is modelled on the first verse of Virgil's First Eclogue, Tityrus, which in Joseph Warton's translation goes:

> In beechen shades, you Tit'rus stretcht along,
> Tune to the slender reed your sylvan song;
> We leave our country's bounds, our much lov'd plains,
> We from our country fly, unhappy swains!

You, Tit'rus, in the groves at leisure laid,
Teach Amaryllis' name to every shade.[5]

and for Okigbo becomes:

You loaf, child of the forest,
beneath a village umbrella,
plucking from tender string a
    Song of the forest.
Me, away from home, runaway,
must leave the borders of our
land, fruitful fields,
    must leave our homeland
But, you, child of the forest,
loaf beneath an umbrella
teaching the woods to sing a
    song of the forest.
["Song of the Forest" (with ubo)]

Okigbo's rendering has the simplicity, brevity and delicacy which Warton thinks makes the eclogue natural and delightful.[6] In theme, Okigbo juxtaposes town and country, also in true pastoral tradition.

Okigbo's little poem is a pastoral in Dr. Johnson's sense of "an action or passion . . . represented by its effects upon country life."[7] The poet Okigbo is sitting in Lagos gazing mentally back at the country, writing like Virgil for an urban reading public, musing about a modern Nigerian problem of alienation from rural life. Okigbo has the good taste, though, not to affect the pastoral device of the imitation of the action of actual shepherds. Okigbo's short exercise is nothing of the scope of Virgil's Eclogue which is a long interchange between the shepherds, Tityrus and Meliboeus, in which Virgil brings together Rome's imperial destiny, the young Augustus who is to fulfill it, and the misery of rural Italy into a single poetic vision. Okigbo does not develop his eclogue; nor does he expatiate on public themes. He brings into the poem rather the personal subjectivity of the poet in the twentieth century; in this way, imitating Virgil innovatively and achieving a new approach to the pastoral in material and tone. Might not Okigbo's imitativeness, which is to be permanent in his work, owe something to his knowledge that in the Roman tradition of verse, imitation, even plagiarism, was systematized and honorable? As Virgil took from Theocritus, (among others), so did Okigbo from Virgil, making something new of the pastoral.

In fact, Okigbo's second canzone seems to be a variation on the pastoral device. Instead of two shepherds in a dialogue, there are two characters A and B who in solo and unison poetise about the misery of life, deciding to "rest with wrinkled faces / watching the wall clock strike each hour / in a dry cellar" until they choke and die rather "than face the blasts and buffets" of "the mad generation" presumably in the cities. Despite the imitation of Virgilian pastoral poetry and the echoes of Pound and Eliot, these early canzones also show some African traits. Firstly, three of them are written to be read or sung to musical instruments after the style of Senghor and in the tradition of the indigenous presentation of African oral poetry. Secondly, like Achebe in his novels, Okigbo reveals a partiality to the "goose pimpling" ogene. Thirdly, the poems voice neo-African themes, such as the contrast between the old and the new after colonialism; the traditional and rural in Africa contrasted with the urbanized and the Westernised; the alienation of the Westernised African; the Hobson choice he faces between joining "the mad generation" in the filthy Westernised cities or remaining with the alienated and restless poor in the hinterland; the challenge posed by Western intellectual activity to African thought, in particular African religion—the last a very close subject to Okigbo's heart because he was of the priest's family in his native village.[8]

"The Lament of the Masks" indicates a new development in style from the clear Virgilian statement of the first canzone to the subjective imagery of modern verse:

> TIDEWASH . . . Memories
> fold-over-fold free-furrow,
> mingling old tunes with new.
> Tidewash . . . Ride me
> memories as astride on firm
> saddle, wreathed with white
> lilies and roses of blood . . .

and the forcing of meaning out of sense perceptions:

> We follow the wind to the fields
> Bruising grass leafblade and corn . . .

Despite the literary echoes in this canzone such as "white lilies" and "roses of blood" "woodnymphs" and "snow-patch," the poem does show new confidence in the use of language; as for example:

> Comes Dawn
> gasping thro worn lungs
> Day breathes
> panting like torn horse

and a newly-expressed concern with the religion of his village, in particular the female deity, Idoto, his "Watermaid"; his "lioness with the armpit fragrance"; his "white queen and goddess" whose worship provides some of Okigbo's most beautiful lyrics with their symbolism and imagistic pattern as in *Heavensgate*. Most significantly, however, in "The Lament of the Masks" there emerges for the first time a poetic persona who is put to more than thematic use, who will now and subsequently in mythopoetic form explore the delicate labyrinths of the poet's subjectivity. In the tradition of the modern suffering protagonist, Okigbo's persona will tell the beads of experience, "those globules of anguish strung together on memory." This poetic personality will be increasingly dramatised, placed always at the center of Okigbo's envisioned rituals and creative act. So much does Okigbo identify with this poetic self that in the last poems prophesying war, in particular in the poems, "Hurrah for Thunder" and "Elegy for Slit-drum," the artistic self is inadequately subsumed into vision and experience. The face breaks through the mask.

The fourth canzone, "The Lament of the Lavender Mist," carries forward the theme of memory as an important experiential dimension to our poet's imaginative vision. This theme is now more symbolically expressed than previously. In style, the canzone is more broken in rhythm than the earlier pieces. It is evocative of meaning, cumulatively through phrase juxtapositions, repetitions and re-phrasings, free collocating of images from Christianity and African religion.

> Eagles in space and earth and sky,
>
> Shadows of sin in grove of orange,
>
> Of altar-penitence,
> Over me at sundown,
> Of wind on leaves,
> A song of Christmas of—
>
> Echoes in the prison of the mind,
> Shadows of song of love's stillness,
> Shadows of the stillness of the song
>   Over me at sundown
>   In an empty garden
>     Where
> Wounded by the wind lie dead leaves.

It is this lament which ends with lines which have been anthologised in isolation with an arbitrary title, "Love Apart" in *Modern Poetry from Africa* (Beier and Moore: Penguin, 1963),

> The moon has ascended between us—
> Between two pines
> That bow to each other;
> Love with the moon has ascended,
> Has fed on our solitary stems;
> And we are now shadows

> That cling to each other
> But kiss the air only.

and which has been argued over and discussed as if it was a solitary lyric.[9] Such amputations of poems are often unfortunate, if not unnecessary and misleading.

By 1961, with the writing of "The Lament of the Lavender Mist" in Nsukka, Okigbo had attained his distinctive voice and his chosen stance towards the purpose and the doing of his art. From this lament onwards, the act of creation, the writing itself, is a rite transposed in medium, as when "The Lament of the Masks" ends:

> But will a flutist never stop to wipe his nose?
>
> Night breezes drum on the plantain leaf:
> Let the plantain leaf take over the dance . . .

The poet, as in Soyinka's early poems, is in a self-conscious act of creative ritual. The transposed rite is about experience, limned from memory and recast as ritual, while the poetic self is always at the dramatic center of the creative concentricity. On one level, "The Lament of the Lavender Mist" can be read as the history of a love relationship; on another, as an account of the poet's love for his art and his evolution as a poet. It is the mythopoeic form employed in this Lament which is to energise Okigbo in the following long poems: *Silences* (Transition, 1962), *Heavensgate* (Mbari, 1962) and *Limits* (Mbari, 1962).

The first part of *Silences,* subtitled "The Lament of the Silent Sisters," was inspired, according to Okigbo in his introduction to *Labyrinth,* by the events of the day which were the Western Nigeria crisis and the death of Patrice Lumumba. This Lament shows the poet borrowing from all and sundry, taking poetic flight from any image which touched his imagination. He has admitted in an interview in *Transition* to have been influenced in this period by "everything and everybody."[10] Not only does this lament reveal the rewards of predatory and eclectic reading, it indicates yet another new poetic direction, (more evident in the *Black Orpheus* version) towards the conscious and experimental use of the resources of the song form, such as in the use of choruses, refrains, and repetitions; and in the conveyance of meaning through a contrapuntal use of assonance, dissonance and even pure sound itself. The poet corroborates this intention in his introduction to *Labyrinth* where he says that *Silences* is "an attempt to elicit the music to which all imperishable cries must aspire . . . and the motif itself is developed by a series of related airs from sources as diverse as Malcolm Cowley, Raja Ratnam, Stéphane Mallarmé, Tagore and Lorca" among others.

Most striking in the "Lament of the Silent Sisters" is the symbolist influence of transferring the modality of one sense to another:

> We hear painted harmonies
> From the mushroom of the sky—
>
> Silences are melodies
> Heard in retrospect
>
> And how does one say no in thunder?
>
> One dips one's tongue in the ocean;
> Camps with the choir of inconstant
> Dolphins, by shallow and banks
>
> Sprinkled with memories;
>
> Extends one's branches of coral,
> The branches extends in the senses
> Silence; thin silence distils
>
> In yellow melodies.

Subdued in the *Labyrinth* version is Okigbo's despair with the young African elite for their cultural rape; and his sense of their doom and his by inclusion, a sense which so permeates all his poetry, and which is so often concretised in images of the poet as martyr and sacrificial figure, as to be described as self-destructive by one Nigerian critic.[11] From the "Lament of the Silent Sisters" comes also the title of Kofi Awoonor's dedicatory poem to Okigbo entitled "Lament of the Silent Sister," in his book of poems *Night of My Blood* (New York: 1971)[12] where a female persona is made to sing Awoonor's lament of Okigbo's death. A dramatised sensual encounter objectivises the human incomprehension and failure of emotional contact which is the proper subject of Awoonor's poem. The African association of tenderness (physical and aphysical) with the woman, and the African male's liking for the female consciousness make, in my opinion, the use of Awoonor's persona an appropriate one for Okigbo's dirge.

The second part of *Silences,* titled the "Lament of the Drums," is an agitated poem about deprivation and loss; unavoidable pain and mourning expressed through analogues of unanswered praise songs and unconsummated feasts, uncommencable journeys, and unanswered letters; unstemmable tears of wailing populations; and the lament of Ishtar for Tammuz. The emotions of this poem were aroused, according to the poet in *Labyrinth* in the introduction, by the imprisonment of Chief Awolowo and the death of his eldest son, both Yorubas—which should interest expositors of the ethnic nature of the Nigerian civil war. Like *Distances* (*Transition,* 16, 1964)[13] which is to follow, *Silences* foreshadows orgies of violence and carnage on the national landscape. *Distances* is a unified apocalyptic vision of consummation, rendered as a ritual of sacrifice involving the poet, who as victim and votive personage, walks the experiential stations of his cross, beyond "Death, herself . . . paring her fingernails" to his homecoming to which he is "sole witness."

Okigbo's last poems from "The Lament of the Masks" (1965) to "Path of Thunder" (*Black Orpheus* 21, Feb. 1968, pp. 5–11) exploit, more than his earlier writing, the attributes of African traditional poetry. Not only are popular proverbs and sayings, epigram and innuendo used, [but] dramatic and situational African images abound, such as the ritual of circumcision in "Elegy of the Wind"; animal allegory used in the manner of the folktale in "Hurrah for Thunder"—in a mode J. P. Clark later employs in *Casualties* in a more sustained manner.

It is easy to see how Okigbo could move from exploiting music in general to using a specific musically expressive form such as African traditional poetry. The poems in *Path of Thunder* convey the rhythms of African verse in the long line and in the structural penchant for inculcating complete thoughts in single lines, best exemplified by "Come Thunder" and "Elegy for Slit-drum": the latter being perhaps the most African poem of the group in its structure and presentation, and in its dramatic tensions and use of language. The imagination behind the poem is decidedly African. Yet these poems cohere in mythopoeic vision with the earlier ones. The old symbols return with added meaning: the robbers "who will strip us of our tendons" in "Lament of the Drums" now descend, in "Elegy for Alto," to "strip us of our laughter, of our thunder." The recurrent metaphor of iron, thunder, sentient elements and predatory life are compounded in an African mode to describe the violent political upheaval of the period. The favored elephant symbol reappears as the obdurate Nigerian nation, among other meanings, stumbling towards its doom.

In "The Lament of the Silent Sisters," Okigbo expresses in these lines (from the *Black Orpheus* version):

> We are the dumb bells
> We are the dumb bells
> Outside the gates
> In hollow landscapes:
>
> We carry
>
> In our worlds that flourish
> Our worlds that have failed

> This song is our swan song
> This song the stillness of our breath
>
> This song is our swan song
> This song is our senses' silence

his sense of a personal and generational doom which finds final resolution in "Elegy for Alto":

> O mother Earth, unbind me; let this be
>   my last testament; let this be
> The ram's hidden wish to the sword, the sword's
>   secret prayer to the scabbard

The poet prays to be prodigal in a sense different from, yet cumulative to, the composite sense of his prodigality in *Heavensgate.* In this poem, his last, his prodigality reverses the sense of the word. His prodigality is in the ram's ultimate prayer to the tether, in his artist's bond to his vision and his art; his life at once a sacrifice and a giving.

Okigbo's poetry will have to be evaluated in two sets since the published forms of his poems under the title *Labyrinths* are so dissimilar to their earlier published forms and so re-worked as to be completely new poems. His introduction to the volume sheds light on the artists who have influenced him. No mention, however, is made of Senghor, to whom one finds similarities in poetic modes and in formal presentation—situational and verbal—the main difference being the stance of the poet protagonist.

Okigbo is significant because he did what most of the West African writers in English were doing in the 60's—a very personal poetry in a personal idiom—and he brought this mode to a virtuoso point. He represents their initially "art for art's sake" attitude which changed over time. His development therefore traces a West African pattern of artistic evolution from private anguish to public commitment. In addition, Okigbo exemplifies a neo-African wedding of the African to the Western poetic traditions to the rejuvenation of the effeteness and world weariness of the latter. He is, to my mind, one of the finest African poets in English, to be valued for the sheer beauty of his finely honed verse, his most delicate sensibility, and the artistic discipline which informs the structure and the lyrical simplicity of his verse—a simplicity which conveys a false impression of facility. In much the same way that Achebe leads a school of Igbo novelists, Okigbo can be said to lead and to have brought to being, directly or indirectly, a school of good Igbo poets—Okogbule Wonodi, Romanus Egudu, Michael Echeruo among others—who, in their various ways, are much indebted to Okigbo. This role as teacher is another measure of the importance of Christopher Okigbo.

## Notes

1.   D. E. S. Maxwell and S. Bushrui, eds. *W. B. Yeats: 1865–1965: Centenary Essays* (Ibadan: Ibadan University Press, 1965).

2.   O. R. Dathorne, "Ritual and Ceremony in Okigbo's Poetry," *The Journal of Commonwealth Literature* 5 (July, 1968), 79–91.

3.   *Ibid.*

4.   See Ulli Beier, "Three Mbari Poets," *Black Orpheus* 12, p. 46. Wole Soyinka, "And After the Narcissist?" *African Forum* 1, 4 (Spring, 1966).

5.   Joseph Warton, *The Works of Virgil in Latin and English* (London, 1753).

6.   Joseph Warton, "A Dissertation on Pastoral Poetry," *ibid.,* p. 37.

7.   Samuel Johnson, *Rambler* 37.

8.   See Marjory Whitelaw, "Interview with Christopher Okigbo, 1965," *The Journal of Commonwealth Literature* 9 (July, 1970): 28–37.

9.   See Romanus Egudu, "Okigbo Misrepresented: Edwin Thumboo on 'Love Apart,'" *Presence Africaine* 76 (1970): 187–193.

10.   "Transition Conference Questionnaire," *Transition* vol. 2, no. 5 (July–August, 1962), p. 12.

11.   D. Izevbaye, "Politics in Nigerian Poetry," *Presence Africaine,* 78.

12.   The title "Night of My Blood," by the way, is from Senghor's poem "Congo" in *Ethiopiques.* The phrase also appears in the poem "Chaka."

13.   Recommended studies of *Distances* are Sunday Anozie, "A Structural Approach to Okigbo's *Distances,*" *The Conch* vol. 1, no. 1. (March 1969): 19–29; Gerald Moore, *The Chosen Tongue* (London: Longmans, 1969).

P.S. Since this essay was finished in August 1972, an insightful and scholarly book, *Creative Rhetoric* (London: Evans 1972) appeared in November by Sunday O. Anozie, a personal friend of the poet who, as I recall, practically chose Anozie as his critic. The work is highly recommended.

# Christopher Okigbo:
# Poet of Destiny

### EMMANUEL N. OBIECHINA

Hear the voice of the Bard!
Who Present, Past, & Future sees;
Whose ears have heard
The Holy Word
That walk'd among the ancient trees,

Calling the lapsed Soul,
And weeping in the evening dew;
That might controll
The starry pole,
And fallen, fallen light renew![1]

It seems appropriate to open this discussion with "The Bard," a poem by the British poet, William Blake. Blake was a poet of the romantic movement who, in the true tradition of romanticism, made large claims for poetry and appropriated sublime attributes for the poet, the bard, "who Present, Past & Future sees!"[2] The poet, in the romantic conception, is no ordinary mortal but a divinely inspired artist, a possessed performer through whom hidden truths of the spirit are revealed and through whose influence mankind undergoes regeneration and spiritual rebirth. The poet, in the romantic tradition, functions severally as priest, prophet, and legislator for mankind, as a man speaking to other men with a voice of moral authority strengthened by heightened sensibility. He is a man imbued with an understanding and suffering soul, a kind of a god. Wordsworth echoes a similar view when he wrote in "Resolution and Independence," "By our own spirits are we deified."[3]

The idea of the poet as an inspired performer, a composite prophet or seer, priest, and madman, is much older than the romantic movement itself and is quite familiar in different cultures of the world. It has remained strong

Originally published in Emmanuel N. Obiechina, *Language and Theme: Essays on African Literature* (Washington, D.C.: Howard University Press, 1990), 207–40. Reprinted by permission of Howard University Press and the author.

in European literary history and was well explored by Plato in some of his dialogues, especially in *Phaedrus* and *Ion*. The romantic movement represented one of the highest watermarks of this concept, in more recent times.

Christopher Okigbo conceived of his poetic career in these serious and responsible terms. For him poetry is no mere aesthetic pastime, no simple celebration of verbal ingenuity, no indulgence of intellectual gymnastics. It is a sacred vocation espoused by persons who feel specially called and set apart from all other persons to carry the grave responsibility of speaking for their people about those matters of weight and moment of which a benign Providence has granted them the inspiration to speak with the authority of priests, prophets, and moral legislators.

In a sense, if one takes the totality of Okigbo's self-image and the matter and measure of his poetic output, one would be justified in regarding him as one of the last of the romantic poets, and, in our African context, as the greatest African romantic poet.[4] One could, with equal justification, regard him as Africa's greatest poet of destiny because, in the final analysis, what distinguishes the great poets of romanticism from those of other movements and orientations is their belief, to a point of obsessive inevitability, that they carry a certain destiny that binds them inextricably to the fate of those for whom they speak, who may be their specific peoples or humankind in general.

The enticing paradox surrounding poets of destiny is their embodying at once distinctly individual drives and identities and the most essentially communal attributes: they are, in one breath, intensely themselves, as well as being of the people whose aspirations they articulate in their poetry; they are at one and the same time poets' poets, no less than what the French call "les bardes de communauté," almost in the archaic sense in which the poet sings his song for the edification of his community under his community's powerful impulses.

That Christopher Okigbo saw himself as a poet of destiny, and his creative mission as closely linked to the fate of his community, is without any doubt. The evidence is writ large in *Labyrinths*, a collection of his poems selected, reorganized, and edited by himself, with an unmistakable air of finality in the awesome statement that "the versions here . . . are final."[5] In his introduction to *Labyrinths*, after providing a brief commentary on his poem sequences, Okigbo sums up his poetical intentions in what appears to be a very carefully prepared manifesto:

> A poet-protagonist is assumed throughout; a personage, however, much larger than Orpheus; one with a load of destiny on his head, rather like Gilgamesh, like Aeneas, like the hero of Melville's *Moby Dick,* like the Fisher King of Eliot's *Waste Land;* a personage for whom the progression through "Heavensgate," through "Limits" through "Distances" is like telling the beads of a rosary; except that the beads are neither stone nor agate but globules of anguish strung together on memory.

Every work of this kind is necessarily a cry of anguish—of the root extending its branches of coral, of corals extending their roots into each living hour; the swell of the silent sea, the great heaving dream at its highest, the thunder of splitting pods—the tears scatter, take root, the cotyledons broken, burgeon into laughter of leaf; or else rot into vital hidden roles in the nitrogen cycle. The present dream clamoured to be born a cadenced cry: silence to appease the fever of flight beyond the iron gate."[6]

The introduction of which the above passage is a part presents certain procedural problems to the critic. The poet himself has told us what his poetry is about: "a poet-protagonist is assumed throughout; a personage . . . with a load of destiny on his head." We have here an actor who is also a commentator on his own actions, a writer of his own footnotes. The situation does seem bewildering, if not outright anomalous, to the "professional" critic. That little difficulty deserves to be got out of the way if we are to see our way clear to appreciating Okigbo's poetry in the context of his self-appointed role as "a poet of destiny."

Luckily, we do not have to accept with docility everything a creative writer says of himself, his intentions, and his work. In fact, there are many reasons why we should not trust writers when they turn commentators on their own work, and why we should be on our guard and attend to a writer's self-analysis with more than mild skepticism. In the first place, the process of creativity itself is so complicated and defiant of precise formulations and analyses that even the brightest of writers might yet encounter "areas of dark impenetrability" in the attempt to guide his audience with his own light into the sanctuary.

Another and, perhaps, more compelling reason than the first would seem to arise from the creative and the critical processes tending to draw from different faculties and abilities that are rarely combined in the same persons. One might, of course, be confronted with outstanding exceptions, such as Longinus, Horace, Sidney, Dryden, Johnson, Arnold, Eliot, Sartre, Tolstoy, Henry James, and, in our own day and place virtually every prominent writer—Soyinka, Achebe, Ngugi wa Thiong'o, Clark, Awoonor, and so on. They combine the vocation of creative writer with the profession of literary scholarship. But one must be quick to counter that these examples seem only superficially separated from the generality that validates the truth of the observation. If any of these writers is put on a scale and weighed, the balance would tilt inevitably toward the creative writer or the literary scholar. Even where a fair balance is established, it is soon obvious that readers go to the writer at different times for one or another of his offerings, either for his creative work, or his critical opinions, rarely for both.

There are at least three distinguishable types of author-critics or author-commentators. There are those whose critical views are broad enough to transcend their work and creative intentions, and others whose critical views encompass only their own work. The writers in the first group present no great difficulty to the "professional" critic. They may, as a matter of fact, be successful critics in their own right. The problem is with the author-commentators who take their readers by the hand and conduct them through their work. Apart from the attempt itself being somewhat gratuitous, it also smacks too much of an a posteriori apologia and a validation of consciously chosen stances and creative procedures. When this situation arises, the professional critic is inconveniently required to discuss not only the creative work itself but also its author's commentary, which accompanies it.

The third category of author—commentators with whom the critic has to deal—differs from the two categories mentioned above in the particular sense that the writers' comments and manner of presenting them constitute an extension of the statements contained in their creative texts. These writers are, more often than not, seriously committed to certain ideas that then become their creative inspiration. Such writers feel compelled to expose and extend those ideas outside the "creative" contexts proper. In other words, the critic is not just dealing with commitment to artistic validity, strictly speaking, but, more significantly, is touching upon areas of deeper commitments and responses for which art offers only one medium of exploration. The essay form, whether couched in conventional prose or less conventionally in poetic prose, offers yet another level of reaching a statement that should not be lost sight of.

Writers in this third category tend to see themselves as committed to more seriously objectified concerns than the self-validating artists. They espouse the idea that they carry a special destiny and that their visions are animated by concerns which, even though arising subjectively from within themselves and their intimate knowledge of themselves, lead them through this knowledge toward wider, more socially validating concern with the world around them, a situation in which their subjectivity is objectified by this widening of interest to accommodate the condition of things outside the limited self. Such writers invariably ripen through their creativity and visions into prophets and spokesmen of their people and, sometimes, of humanity at large. The Old Testament world and ancient mythologies and religions have a fair number of these poet-prophets. Names like Ezekiel, Jeremiah, Nehemiah, and Habbakuk in the Old Testament readily come to mind. The New Testament has Paul of Tarsus and that uncanny author of the Apocalypse, John the Divine.

It is obvious from the evidence in his introduction to *Labyrinths* that Okigbo saw himself as a poet-prophet and his poetical career as that of a bearer of special destiny and spokesman of the time and the people. In other words, he belongs to the third category of writers, whose artistic integrity comprehends their individualities and creativeness, as well as their special commitments and functions as articulators of the aspirations, hopes, and fears of their people and times. This assumption is so fundamental and serious that

it should be critically tested before we can reasonably give it credence or proceed from it to explore the wider implications of Okigbo's claim to being a
"poet of destiny."

The first task that immediately comes to view is to examine the credentials of the poet-prophet, in much the same way as the Jews of old used to
examine critically the personal credentials of their prophets. In a world
swarming with noisy, self-appointed spokesmen of the people, a world full of
charlatans and confidence tricksters (they also exist among "artists"), the least
that can be expected of the aspiring spokesman of the people and humanity is
a sign that his inspiration inclines him to high seriousness, to understanding
of the inner springs of himself as prophet-aspirant, a sensitive understanding
of the nature of man, of human problems and predicaments, and a wholesome assimilation of the self and its interest to the broad, inclusive destiny of
a people and the world of people. We must demand of our poet-prophet clarity of view and personal integrity as reliable guides to our better understanding of the forces that tyrannize us. In other words, we must seek to be reas-
sured that the poet *is* of us, that he possesses adequate intellectual scope and
breadth of sympathy to understand our problems, that he has the personal
integrity to tell us the truth as he sees it, and that he is sufficiently assimilated
to our destiny to share our sufferings and agonies, our joys and hopes, our
dreams and reveries. We must insist that he should adequately internalize
these things in order to become the sensitive needle that probes and locates
our emotional traumas, our anxieties, elations, and fears, no less than our
hopes and aspirations. We cannot trust him otherwise.

One point requires clarification to avoid the type of error to which a
number of critics of Okigbo's poetry are prone. When I say that the poet of
destiny should be "of us," I do not imply that he should be like everyone of
us, individually or collectively. To become that, he would first of all have to
abdicate his poetical vocation, since most of us are not only non-poets but
devastatingly prosaic in our individual lives and in our perceptions of life.
There is developing currently a certain prescriptive-cum-proscriptive literary
opinion, pushed aggressively, and not very wisely, by African literary scholars
based mainly in the United States of America, who insist that the African
poet, to be genuinely African, must write like everyone of us. In a recent article, the most outspoken of these critics accused all those poets who do not
meet this demand (chief of whom is Okigbo) of suffering from Hopkins's
Disease.[7]

I find this prescription quite unreasonable. We are not all poets and we
value our poets because they are poets. We would not care too much for them
if they were no poets at all or if their poetry merely reflected our own far-
from-poetical levels of expression. We would probably not expect them to
assume the role of spokesmen or to articulate our aspirations with sensitivity,
intelligence, and integrity; for, even though a fair number of people may lay
claim to intelligence and integrity, what they very often lack are poetic sensi-

tivity and the capacity for imaginative reordering of experience for optimum effect.

It ought to be recognized, however, that an aspect of the poet-prophet's identification with the people for whom he functions as spokesman must be aesthetic as well as historical. In his essay "Tradition and the Individual Talent," T. S. Eliot makes the significant statement that "every nation, every race, has not only its own creative, but its own critical turn of mind,"[8] and, referring specifically to the peculiar relationship of the poet's individual creativity to the general pool of his people's tradition, he writes:

> If we approach a poet without . . . prejudice we shall often find that not only the best, but the most individual parts of his work may be those in which the dead poets, his ancestors, assert their immortality most vigorously.
>
> . . . Yet if the only form of tradition, of handing down, consisted in following the ways of the immediate generation before us in a blind or timid adherence to its successes, "tradition" should positively be discouraged. We have seen many such, simple currents soon lost in the sand; and novelty is better than repetition. Tradition is a matter of much wider significance. It cannot be inherited, and if you want it you must obtain it by great labour. It involves in the first place, the historical sense, which we may call nearly indispensable to anyone who would continue to be a poet beyond his twenty-fifth year; and the historical sense involves a perception, not only of the pastness, but of its presence; the historical sense compels a man to write not merely with his generation in his bones, but with a feeling that the whole literature of Europe from Homer and within it the whole of the literature of his own country has a simultaneous existence and composes a simultaneous order. This historical sense, which is a sense of the timeless and of the temporal together, is what makes a writer traditional. And it is at the same time what makes a writer most acutely conscious of his place in time, of his own contemporaneity.[9]

It is convenient to lean on T. S. Eliot here because his very lucid view helps to settle one of the most vexing questions concerning Okigbo's poetry, namely, its individuality and the poet's insistence on the role, essentially historical and communal, of prophet, priest, and spokesman—in other words, as a poet of destiny. The poet of destiny fits most patently Eliot's description above, because, like Eliot himself, P. B. Shelley, and W. B. Yeats, among others, the poet of destiny is constantly aware of temporality and timelessness as major determinants defining the totality of his creative commitments; he is aware of traditional continuities as well as the vibrancy of each passing moment of experience. Both factors contribute ultimately to the full impression of the self, its roles, and the relative significance of things. Okigbo says of himself and his perception of his role as poet of destiny:

> When I knew that I couldn't be anything else than a poet—I can't say whether the call came from evil spirits or good spirits. But I know that the turning point came in 1958, when I found myself wanting to know myself better, and I

had to turn around and look at myself from inside—I mean myself, just myself not the background. But you know that everything has added up to building up the self—and when I talk of looking inward to myself, I mean turning inward to examine myself. This of course takes account of ancestors.

. . . I am believed to be a re-incarnation of my maternal grandfather, who used to be the priest of the shrine called Ajani, where Idoto, the river goddess, is worshipped. The goddess is the earth-mother, and also the mother of the whole family. My grandfather was the priest of this shrine, and when I was born I was believed to be his incarnation, that is, I should carry on his duties. And although someone else had to perform his functions, this other person was only, as it were, a regent. And in 1958, when I started taking poetry very seriously, it was as though I had felt a sudden call to begin performing my full functions as the priest of Idoto. This is how it happened.[10]

If we believe Okigbo's statement, and there is no good reason why we should not believe him, then we should agree that the major ingredients existed from the very beginning of his poetical career—defining him, by his self-appraisal and appointment, as a poet of destiny. The ingredients are, if we should reduce them further into their relevant constituents, the poet's perception of his unique role as spokesman, priest, and prophet, his perception of the destiny of man or of the specific community within which he places this role, and his perception of the creative process itself through which he communicates his visions. These constituents must be taken one by one and examined with attention so that we can determine whether indeed they exist as essential ingredients of Okigbo's poetry and poetic posture and, therefore, whether the poet has succeeded or failed to carry through his self-appointed role as a poet of destiny.

A poet of destiny must have a definite identity. Even though his destiny tends ultimately to merge with the destiny of his community, he cannot afford to be anonymous or to be seen merely as a blurred presence against the powerful backdrop of themes, techniques, and intentions. The significance we attach to the poetry must necessarily take in our perception of the personality of the poet himself. His integrity must be of an overt kind, since explicitness is essential for a proper rapport between the poet and the people. Homer was not mistaken when he announced to the Greeks for whom he composed or collected The Iliad and The Odyssey that if anyone should ask them about the maker of the poems, they should say it was "the blind man who sings in the Chios." The strong communal nature of the epic poem does not exclude the presence of an organizing spirit who must be seen as a living presence investing the poems with aura and distinctiveness of authentic human warmth. In like manner, the poet of destiny must have a certain concreteness of identity to help his audience to identify with the matter of his poetry, especially insofar as his credibility and the impact of his poetry depend on the distinctness of his voice, the clarity of his visions, and the integrity of his sentiments.

In the poetry of Okigbo, the personality of the poet is distinctive and visible. We are aware of the poet-protagonist, not only as a speaking voice but also as a physical human presence embodying a feeling and suffering soul. The poet speaks, it is true, through a mask or persona, as a convenient convention, appearing now as a prodigal son returning in penitence to a neglected patrimony, now as a sunbird, a weaverbird, an oracle, or as a town-crier, as befits each particularized occasion and its dominant mood. But the evocative nature of the poetry keeps alive and very much in the fore the distinctive personality and identity of the poet to the very end when, under the severe pressure of events, he dispenses with the mask and appears as his true self with: "I, Okigbo, town-crier, together with my iron bell."[11] A little later, the following lines occur in "Elegy for Slit-Drum":

> The mythmaker accompanies us (the Egret had come and gone) / Okigbo accompanies us the oracle enkindles us / the Hornbill is there again (*the Hornbill has had a bath*) Okigbo accompanies us the rattles enlighten us—(69)

Inevitably, the establishment of identity begins with initiation rites. Through initiations, the individual is inducted into distinctly defined roles and is given the psychological and emotional resources to meet the demands of those roles. We are made aware through these processes of the human but privileged presence of the poet, of his sensitivity, imaginativeness, and alertness in the probing of the exterior and interior existences and realities both of man and of the world that surrounds him.

In "Heavensgate," the first sequence of poems in *Labyrinths,* the protagonist is delineated from childhood through adolescence to adulthood, his personality explored through quests that develop the consciousness and lead to an understanding of the self, of the world that impinges on it, and the destiny that entangles the self with the world. We see the poet-protagonist initiated into the triple mysteries that prepare him for the unique role of a poet of destiny: he is initiated into the ancestral role of priest, then into the alienating membership of the Christian religion, and finally into the cult of poetry. Each initiation reveals in more than bare outline the personality of the initiate and the determinant attitudes and moods that are reinforced by the particular experience.

As might be expected, the organization of these experiences does not follow this order strictly. The opening unit, called "The Passage," presents the protagonist as a supplicant at the village stream, Idoto, sacred to the earth-mother goddess. He brings with him an attitude of total humility and surrender, becoming to a returning prodigal son. The idea is that the protagonist, having already been initiated into the Christian faith to the neglect of his obligations to Idoto, the tutelary deity of the community, can only return to the traditional obligations in a mood of repentance and humility:

> *Before you, mother Idoto,*
> *naked I stand;*
> *before your watery presence,*
> *a prodigal*
> *leaning on an oilbean*
> *lost in your legend*
>
> *Under your power wait I*
> *on barefoot,*
> *watchman for the watchword*
> *at Heavensgate;*
> *out of the depths my cry*
> *give ear and hearken—*
>
> (3)

The sense of the poet's inadequacy and humility is written all over this sequence. He stands "naked" before the deity and is a returning prodigal son, as lost as a young bird whose mother has been caught on a spray. His inexperience is conveyed through the analogy with a newly arrived chicken which, the Igbo proverb says, always stands on one leg. The attitude of humility and self-effacement is also typical of Igbo traditional priests face to face with the awesome presence of their deities. But, just as commitment to traditional religion and way of life has a certain imperative, so initiation into the Christian religion and, more particularly, into the Roman Catholic sect of it, is a reality that cannot be wished away. There is a character, a scar or mark of this initiation which remains ineffaceable and as a major conditioner of the poetic consciousness, especially through the centrality of the cross and its association with the redemption of humanity. The crucifix is a powerful image that arrests the sensitive imagination and bends it toward a revolutionary intent. A poet of destiny cannot ignore the significance of the cross, since the self-sacrifice of the Christ never fails to stir the soul out of its torpidity to grasp and preserve the emotional anchor that comes from the contemplation of its powerful image. The permanence of the impact of the cross on the initiate is stated most concretely in the opening verse of "Initiations":

> Scar of the crucifix
> over the breast,
> by red blade inflicted
> by red-hot blade,
> on right breast witnesseth.
>
> (6)

The poet of destiny, because the rhythm of his own inner existence embodies some messianic inspiration, finds in the lesson of the cross one of his deepest impulses to action, an impulse driving him towards heroic self-sacrifice.

Okigbo describes this impulse metaphorically when he says of the poem: "The various sections of the poem . . . present this celebrant at various stations of his cross" (xi).

The Christian faith itself, in its barren orthodoxy, especially in its abstract morality ("life without sin"), is the least satisfactory as an influence because to preach "life without sin" is, in the poet's view, to preach "life without life"

> . . . which accepted
> way leads downward
> down orthocenter
> avoiding decisions.
>
> (xi)

It can only lead to moral passivity. But the cross is different. It symbolizes the ultimate triumph of the spirit over human weaknesses; it represents the more durable aspects of the initiation into Christianity:

> —United in vision
> of present and future,
> the pure line, whose innocence
> denies inhibitions.
>
> (x)

The logic is, of course, that experience is essential to cultivate goodness. To act is to experience, and to experience is to be alive and responsive. Even if in action one makes mistakes, it is still better to learn from such mistakes than to stay passive, "avoiding decisions." The cross is a symbol of action, of redemptive action, and therefore central to the initiation of a sensitive person into heroic virtue. Empty husks of dogma and Christian orthodoxy breed all manner of hypocrites and moral deviants whom the poet identifies through geometrical shapes and patterns:

> Square yields the moron
> fanatics and priests and popes,
> organizing secretaries and
> party managers—
> the rhombus—brothers and deacons,
> liberal politicians,
> selfish selfseekers—all who are good
> doing nothing at all;
> the quadrangle, the rest, me and you.
>
> (7)

The poet presents details of this initiation that indicate how deeply embedded in his consciousness the experience has been. He remembers Kepkanly, who

brought him into the church, and also those whimsical, semidemented min-
strels and village wags, Jadum and Upandru, who complement the picture of
those early exciting days. What, one may ask, is the use of bringing up events
long submerged in the memory of more recent, more significant happenings?
What have the random songs and disjointed speeches of demented villagers
got to do with a poet as up-to-date and modern as Okigbo?

The reason is clear. Initiations are stages through which the intellectual,
psychic, and emotional development of an individual are brought about.
Each stage is stored up in the memory and contributes, when activated, to
defining and highlighting ultimately the totality of the individual's experiences and actions. Earlier in this discussion, the point was made that the
poet of destiny should be "of the people," that his experiences, in the nature
of things, should approximate those of the people, although in some particulars he would be expected to transcend those experiences. By drawing from
the memory bank such common currency as the sayings and actions of generally known characters like Kepkanly (and his unfortunate connection with
Harragin), Jadum the half-demented minstrel and his songs "after the
lights," and Upandru with his corny maxims, the poet is exhibiting an aspect
of this identification with the community, especially with its folk outlook
that leads to the recognition of the importance of individuals, be they ever so
demented, grotesque, or waggish. Such references have the effect of locating
the poet close to the center of his people's folk imagination that takes in
everyone and everything that stimulates its responses. In these special inter-
actions, arising from initiation rites, in which the individual is bound more
closely to the group and the group more closely to the individual, no experience is too trivial, no action too inconsequential; each experience, action,
speech, and gesture helps to provide the emotional scaffolding that sustains
the communal world from which the artist draws to enrich his sensibilities
and the texture of his work.

In "Watermaid," the third section of "Heavensgate," which deals with
initiation into poetry, the experience is largely personal. But the representation of the muse as a watermaid has acquired in recent times fairly wide
acceptance, especially within the group among whom Okigbo matured his
poetic visions. Hitherto, and over a wide area of West Africa, the belief that
the watermaid is reputed to bring wealth and other favors to her favorites is
very well known. What Okigbo and the poets of his connection have done is
to appropriate the existing belief to the service of poetry. The encounter with
the watermaid is therefore a private experience with wider evolving implications.

This initiation is full of anguish because the muse cannot be possessed;
the questing protagonist can only obtain occasional glimpses of this source of
inspiration and cannot therefore sustain long periods of poetical output. The
brevity and brittleness of poetic inspiration drives the poet to a state of near
despair:

> So brief her presence—
> match-flare in wind's breath—
> so brief with mirrors around me.
>
> (11)

The muse is described as "maid of the salt-emptiness sophisticreamy." And yet, the experience itself is magnificent and inspires some of the most splendid poetic evocations of the collection. The beach scene is detailed with fine and sensitive discrimination and the Watermaid is described in all her brilliance and other-worldly splendour:

> Bright
> with the armpit-dazzle of a lioness
> . . . . . . . . . . . . . . . . . . . . . . . .
> wearing white light about her,
> and the waves escort her,
> my lioness,
> crowned with moonlight.
>
> (11)

But the brevity of this experience of poetic inspiration, this encounter with the muse, leaves a hollow feeling of isolation in the poet.

Part of the lesson of this initiation is that isolation is the burden all special and inspired people—priests, poets, prophets, and even philosophers—have to bear. The very intangible nature of their concerns brings them face to face with the despair and loneliness of their situation away from the din and bustle of the world of ordinary people. Initiation into the cult of poetry is, in this respect, a retreat into loneliness and isolation, into areas where the best reward may be a fleeting or fragmentary vision which, if not captured opportunely, is soon lost again—like "gold crop / sinking ungathered." But momentary inspirations become the decisive factors in the making of a poetic career, for, in a process of creativity, it is that flashpoint of intensive experience that gives rise to the most successful poetry. As the poet aptly puts it, what matters is being able to capture that moment of heightened sensitivity and intuitive grasp of the core image inspired by the muse:

> Stretch, stretch, O antennae to clutch at this hour,
> fulfilling each moment in a broken monody.
>
> (13)

Thus, the third initiation is the most problematic but, at the same time, the most relevant in determining the nature of the poetic personality. The feeling of abandonment and isolation, of becoming "an island," sharpens the poet's intuition, enabling him to "clutch" at the flashes of inspiration that come like "match-flare in wind's breath," even while providing the essence of poetic direction.

Initiation is often accompanied by ceremonies of purification and ritual sacrifices. The initiate must throw off the old self and put on a new self, refined and rendered sacred by the appropriate ritual cleansing. The fourth movement of "Heavensgate," "Lustra," concerns this ritual cleansing that reinforces the protagonist's preparation for the poetic vocation. In this development, the conjunction of the previous experiences becomes evident, for here nature becomes the medium through which the three kinds of initiation previously undergone are united. The hills become the focus for the reconciliation of traditional religion and Christianity and provide a core motif and whetstone to the evolving poetic genius of the initiate. Or, to put the matter differently, the poet's initiation into nature, with its corresponding mystical suggestions, resolves the apparent contradictions between the traditional religious impulses and the messianic impulse in the development of the poetic sensibility of the initiate. Sacrifice, which is at the center of both religions, becomes a unifying factor in the poet's experience, and his deepest inspiration.

The logical organization of the verse here requires a comment because it illustrates the best example of a skillful manipulation of material referred to by Okigbo earlier on as "logistics." "Logistics" is a word many commentators on Okigbo have tended to uproot from its context and misconstrue as "acrobatics," or "gymnastics," which they, in turn, interpret as verbal trickery. But "logistics" simply suggests a careful and deliberate deployment of existing material to optimum advantage. There is nothing in this to suggest a forcing of such material into inappropriate positions by mere cleverness or leger-demain.

The first three units of verse prepare the scene for the sacrifice and anticipate the salutary effects of that sacrifice by opening the eyes of the poet to the underlying unity of nature, religions, and poetic inspirations:

> So would I to the hills again
> So would I
> to where springs the fountain
> there to draw from
>
> And to hill top clamber
> body and soul
> whitewashed in the moondew
> there to see from
>
> So would I from my eye the mist
> so would I
> thro' moonmist to hilltop
> there for the cleansing
>
> Here is a new laid egg
> here a white hen at midterm.
>
> (14)

The process of purification, of cleansing, is accomplished by a free and easy exposure to nature, followed by its impact on the poetic consciousness. "Body and soul" must be exposed together; the poetic imagination "draws" from the natural inspiration; the poetic "eye" is cleared to see the hidden likenesses between things apparently dissimilar, to see mystery lurking behind exposed realities. With the poetic imagination thus sharpened, the vital associations are formed to further emphasize the links. Thus, dew-covered flowers suggest "weeping" by nature in remembrance of the death of the Christ, "for him who was silenced." This is further reinforced by the three memorable lines:

> *Messiah will come again*
> *After the argument in heaven*
> *Messiah will come again—*
> (15)

The association of ideas is the hallmark of successful poetic organization. For, here, the initiations and purifications are not an end in themselves but a means to the preparation for the ultimate sacrifice to which all sensitive beings are in the end driven by the very logic of their purity. The intimations are fully established and are centered on the traditional religion. The palm grove is the physical representation of this commitment, while the "long-drums and cannons," which ordinarily symbolize death, here signify the awakening of the somnolent spirit. The poet's return is complete after he has partaken of this revitalization of the spirit through nature and sacrifice.

Two events seem deducible from this highly concentrated versification. First, the spirit of the ancestral dead, as represented during traditional drama festivals like those of the Odo and the Omabe of the Nsukka region, "is in ascent," summoned by the "long-drums and cannons." So also the spiritual consciousness of the poet-initiate is awakened by the newly found integration through appreciation of nature and ritual sacrifice. The overall effect is a certain assurance that the prodigal has indeed come home and can now partake of the richness and glory of the ancestral heritage.

The concluding lines of "Lustra" celebrate this newfound strength and confidence:

> I have visited;
> on palm beam imprinted
> my pentagon—
>
> I have visited, the prodigal . . .
>
> In palm grove,
> long-drums and cannons;
> the spirit in the ascent.

Perhaps it is useful to pause at this stage and look at the oft-repeated but erroneous view of some critics of Okigbo that initiation for him means a flight from Christ to Idoto, a rejection of Christianity in favor of traditional religion.[12] That view seems an oversimplification of a patently complex question. There is no flight, but an affirmation; a discrimination, but not a rejection, since total rejection of Christianity would become a repudiation of one of the most active ingredients of Okigbo's poetic inspiration. What are rejected are the empty husks of theoretical Christianity, the dogmas, which all manner of charlatans push and behind which they perpetrate atrocities against their neighbors and humankind. The critics ought to be more careful by following the signposts so well established by the poet. Okigbo does not talk about "Initiation" in "Heavensgate"; he talks of "Initiations." The preference for the plural word in place of the singular is deliberate and therefore significant in our discussion of his intentions. It is clear that as a poet of destiny, Okigbo cannot afford to shut out of his consciousness experiences that vitalize his imagination and prepare him more adequately to fulfill his chosen task.

In "Newcomer," which concludes "Heavensgate," Okigbo gives poignancy to his acceptance of the Christ motif as an important strand in the fabric of his poetic inspiration:

> Time for worship—
> softly sing the bells of exile,
> the angelus,
> softly sings my guardian angel
>
> Mask over my face
>
> my own mask, not ancestral—I sign:
> remembrance of Calvary,
> and of age of innocence—.

(17)

It is true that he recognizes the Christian connection as a kind of exile, but it is also a part of the functional reality of his total experience. It provides him with one of his many masks which, as he is careful to state, is a personal rather than an ancestral one. In this, as in other similar statements, the poet's integrity is disarming. He does not conceal anything behind a facade of sophistry. He acknowledges sources which individually and collectively account for the richness of his poetry. In this regard, it is useful to note that a major source of his inspiration is the poet's exposure to the world culture through his formal, Western education and, consequently, his grounding in the classics, and, through a variegated reading, in the literatures and mythologies of diverse peoples, countries, and ages. Much of this accumulated knowledge is assimilated in the poetry, in one form or another. Okigbo acknowledges these sources in his introduction to *Labyrinths* in a welter that includes Hopkin's "The Wreck of the Deutschland," Debussy's "Nocturne," Melville's *Moby Dick,* Eliot's "The Waste Land," the work of Malcolm Cowley, Raja Ratman, Stéphane Mallarmé, Rabindranath Tagore, García Lorca, and Peter Thomas.

The same point was made by Okigbo in an interview given to *Transition Magazine* when he said: "I think that I've been influenced by various literatures, right from classical times to the present day in English, Latin, Greek and a little French, a little Spanish."[13] What this means is that the poet's initiations must necessarily take account of his formal education and induction into the literatures and cultures of diverse peoples, places, and times that serve to sharpen his intellectual and emotional responses and to prepare him for the special role as a poet of destiny.

This point is important. Knowledge is necessary for the enrichment of experience, and that enrichment is vital to the sharpening of the imagination and promotion of creativity, because a mind suffused with knowledge is more readily drawn upon in situations requiring firm authoritative statements on the human predicament or aspects of that predicament than one circumscribed and confined within a narrow intellectual groove. Matthew Arnold, one of the originators of modern literary criticism, was right to observe that a successful writer must be a knowledgeable and widely educated man. That condition is even more imperative for the poet who perceives his role as spokesman for his time and people since the framework of his poetic exposition comprehends not just the destiny of himself as an individual but the collective destiny of his community, his race, and mankind in general. Indeed, the matter and manner of prophecy in poetry demand this godlike assurance arising from a certain rootedness in the concrete world of solid and miscellaneous learning. It should be understood, of course, that learning by itself, no matter how profound, cannot satisfy poetic expectations unless it passes through the transforming sieve of the poet's imagination and reissues as a new and refined artefact worthy of aesthetic appreciation.

The uniqueness of Okigbo's poetry and the man's poetic career derive from his successful assimilation of numerous formative influences into an organically unified verse. His poetry answers the strenuous demands of both art and social message and is able to contain great depths and layers of meaning within the most consistently lyrical or poetic framework in the African creative scene. While being the most self-consciously personal of African poets, Okigbo is, at the same time, the most profoundly public in the sweep and spread of his social, political, and cultural commitments.[14]

If we regard Okigbo's sequence of poems in "Heavensgate" as the poet's intellectual, psychological, and cultural preparation for the self-appointed task of oracle and prophet, we would be right to assume also that the sequences known as "Limits" afford the poet an opportunity to test the level of his achievements in terms of his self-assessment and his handling of public and momentous themes. The first four sequences, captioned "Siren Limits," the poet devotes to both a celebration of his newly won inspiration and the successful initiation into the mysteries of life and the bardic cult. But here again the poet's integrity asserts itself in a mixture of excited self-assertion and the recognition of the limitations of vision and performance. The opening glee is soon tempered with the knowledge that fullness of creative stature is still a long way off. That is why the first sequence, which opens with

> Suddenly becoming talkative like weaverbird
> Summoned at offside of dream remembered

and ending with

> Queen of the damp half-light,
> I have had my cleansing,
> Emigrant with air-borne nose,
> The he-goat-on-heat

is followed by the second sequence that opens soberly with

> For he was a shrub among the poplars
> Needing more roots
> More sap to grow to sunlight
> Thirsting for sunlight,
>
> A low growth among the forest—.
> (23–24)

This is no case of self-denigration. The poet expresses a reality born of the awareness that poetic maturity is not attained by sudden flight, that the muse is niggardly in dispensing of her bounties, and that there still remain numerous obstacles separating the initiate from full growth. There are, metaphorically, "Banks of reed / Mountains of Broken bottles" (25) to surmount before attaining maturity and developing an authoritative voice of prophecy. For the present, the poet must be contented to remain an acolyte and must not strain for a recognition that has not been adequately prepared for:

> Then we must sing, tongue-tied
> Without name or audience,
> Making harmony among the branches.
> (25)

The images here are blurred—mist, twilight between sleep and waking, damp half-light, shadow, dream, and anaesthetic suspension of active consciousness. But the important fact is that the task of poetic composition must go on; the dream must be told, in spite of its evanescent quality; the exploration of the poetic process and the labor to cultivate an appropriate voice cannot be abandoned. In fact, the poet has soon to put his achievements to the test, by venturing, even if only tentatively, into themes of public concerns, in the second half of "Limits," called "Fragments Out of the Deluge."

In these "Fragments," the apparent lack of secure confidence is visible and pushes the poet into using an elaborate framework based on Eastern mythology. Mesopotamian and Egyptian images sound impressive but do nothing to enhance the development of a personal voice and vision, and hardly help the reader, in spite of the explanatory footnotes by the author, to obtain more than a precarious and flighty sense of the poet's meaning. Those who accuse Okigbo of deliberate mystification and obscurity bordering on pedantry might find the opening part of this sequence supportive of their accusation. But the rest of "Fragments," which deals with the assault on native authenticities and the despoiling of African traditions, is handled with greater assurance and fine discrimination. The symbols and images are appropriate, the cadences easy, the meanings pithy, and the arguments firm and hard to fault.

In a sense, "Fragments out of the Deluge" ought structurally and thematically to belong with "Silences" and to lead on to "Path of Thunder." They constitute, in varying forms and degrees of intensity, the areas of poetic and prophetic statements. The other sequences—"The Passage," "Initiations," "Watermaid," "Lustra," and "Newcomer" that make up "Heavensgate," "Siren Limits," and "Distances"—demonstrate the various stages of the poet's preparation for the prophetic, bardic role, including his initiations, self-explorations, and testings of the possibilities of poetic statements. A little shuffling of the arrangement of the poems from the way they are organized by Okigbo to the affinities outlined above would do greater justice to his full design and intentions, since establishment of the self-identity of the poet and exploration of the poetic process serve the higher interest of fulfilling the task of prophecy.

It may be argued, of course, and with considerable validity, that the moods, attitudes, and tones of the different sequences, as presented in *Labyrinths with Path of Thunder,* constitute more accurate bases for the division of the parts than thematic affinities; in which case, it might be prudent to follow the poet-editor's arrangements of the sections of the organic poem. The slight difficulty that arises from the choice between the approaches in this discussion is, fortunately, not insurmountable, once it is noted that the author's appraisal of his intentions and designs cannot be accepted as the last word. As stated earlier in this discussion, the artist is not always the best judge of his own creations.

It could be observed, for example, that the posture of innocence and naïveté assumed by the poet up to "Limits" is not altogether justified in view of the skill and excellent control of statement and poetic form achieved in the second part of "Fragments." There is no doubt that Okigbo's maturity of view and control of his medium had reached in this section a high point only marginally surpassed by the later sequences. The gift of prophecy is already assured; the training in divination is complete, and the public spokesman has already emerged. The preparation for the role of poet of destiny is almost complete. What is left is the very delicate probing of the inner man abstracted from the obstacles of flesh and bones, which he carries out in "Distances."

By the time Okigbo came to write "Distances," the incipient disorders of the body politic of the independent state of Nigeria had become a roaring inferno and had begun to evince all the symptoms of a totally uncontrolled and perhaps incontrollable state of social disintegration referred to by sociologists as a state of anomie. We have here a society heaving backward toward chaos.

The role of the creative artist infused with a sense of destiny is quite clear at a time such as this. He would direct his creative energies in an opposite direction from a world propelled toward its chaotic beginnings; it is his duty to attempt to create order out of chaos, and a cosmos out of refractory materials driven by human weaknesses and nature's law backward to their primeval sources. The creative process, in other words, becomes a struggle against the encroaching chaos and attendant disasters. To create is to impose order where active agents hurtle toward a lack of order and in obedience to Hobbesian imperatives. The artist, pulling away from the dominant force of a world in disarray and attempting to steady it and steer it away from its course of disintegration, encounters many-faceted terrors and dangers. The task is made doubly dangerous because it involves taking a positive stand against the primitive impulses and passions that govern man, especially the passion to destroy, to stop the process of creation, to restore chaos, and to perpetuate it. The creative artist is thus up against principalities and powers, against the immense and ingenious machine designed by man for the emasculation of the truly beautiful, the pure, the sublime, and the productive.

For the poet of destiny, the choices in this sort of emergency are even more limited. He has to oppose himself actively through his medium to the agents of chaos and the destroyers of a people's dreams for true liberation. He has to espouse antithetical values to those of a society wheeling toward chaos, with full awareness of the risks and dangers involved which, ultimately, must include the reality of death and physical dissolution. To prepare himself therefore, to meet the challenge of chaos, the poet of destiny must steel himself against that eventuality toward which the logic of his avowed commitments will inevitably carry him.

In "Distances," Okigbo allows himself to experience the reality of death, as a means of bracing himself for the dangerous struggle against the forces of chaos. He recognizes that it is only in the full realization of the consequences of death and dissolution can he, as a quest-protagonist, undergo the final ritual preparation without which the task cannot be followed to its logical conclusion. It is only when the poet of destiny has gone through his initiation into the mysteries of death that he is ready to undertake the final and most dangerous task of his vocation without the inhibitive fear that comes from absence of knowledge.

Okigbo explores the reality of death as a sort of homecoming, as the experience takes him back to the very beginning of things. He experiences moments of rare vivid insight and glimpses of the horrors that await the poet-protagonist in his attempt to reverse the world from its rush toward chaos:

> anguish and solitude . . .
> smothered my scattered
> cry, the dancers
>
> lost among their own
> snares; the faces
> the hands held captive;
> the interspaces
> reddening with blood;
>
> and behind them all,
> in smock of white cotton,
> Death herself,
> the chief celebrant
> In a cloud of incense
> paring her fingernails . . .
>
> At her feet rolled their heads like cut fruits;
> about her fell
> their severed members, numerous as locusts.
> Like split wood left to dry, the dismembered
> joints of the ministrants piled high
>
> She bathed her knees in the blood of attendants;
> her smock in entrails of ministrants. . . .

(55)

Okigbo calls "Distances" a poem of homecoming in its spiritual and psychic aspect, a process of sensual anaesthesia and of total liberation from all physical and emotional tension. It is important to observe that this liberation from what a writer has called the tyranny of form and matter is inevitable to give the poet-protagonist the final exposure that qualifies him for the role of prophet and poet of destiny. Until now, exposure and preparation for this role has been sustained in concrete terms, in images and symbols of initiation that chain the mind to the sensitive body. The prodigal at heavensgate is a physical being: naked, standing barefoot, leaning on a sacred oilbean tree. Nature images abound here, and when the ground shifts to initiation into Christianity, the concreteness of the cross is pervasive and even moral states are not abstracted but are given concrete, geometrical patterns. In the "Watermaid" sequences, the sea and the beach and all kinds of marine scenery are presented; so also are the sky and the stars. In "Lustra" and "Newcomer," the hills, the palm groves, flowers, and long-drums and cannons provide appropriate setting for the ritual preparation for the long quest. "Siren Limits," in which the quest itself is already under way, presents the protagonist's self-appraisals largely in concrete images and symbolic terms: he is "a shrub among the poplars," "a low growth among the forest," "little stream to the lake." In "Distances," however, everything is dreamlike, evanescent, intangible—"from flesh to phantom." This is the most difficult level of experience to capture and the most essential to complete the cycle of preparation for the apocalyptic role for which the poet has been building up his resources and initiatives.

Nor should we be surprised that the exploration of this level of poetic consciousness should be reserved for the last stage in the evolution of the actions and the terrible events that challenge the very limits of the poet's resourcefulness and affirmations. The vision imprisoned in solid matter may appear adequate at the beginning when the stakes are relatively low, but with the escalation of the crisis to the threat of total collapse of the state and the dream behind it, new issues come to view, and new questions necessarily arise that radicalize our expectations of the poet of public commitment. We ask: does this spokesman know enough? Is his experience adequate to qualify him as spokesman? Has he felt the terror of the intangible, of the inchoate and fluid state of being from which the process of creation began? Can he speak authoritatively of those deep mysteries that surround humanity, especially in those harsh moments when we are helplessly pushed back toward the sources? Can the poet bear the terror of dissolution and death, or will he lose heart at the first sight of the massive, heaving movement toward the chaos of the beginning? Can he endure the painful immensity of isolation and abandonment, and the final dissolution of his own individual being? In other words, we ask if the poet is equipped to deal with death with integrity, candor, and sensitivity—not as an abstract reality, but as a fate that constitutes part of the common heritage of a people being systematically pushed back into the cave of disaster, into the womb of chaos.

There is very little doubt that Okigbo passes these exacting tests. His poetic sensibilities, refined and sharpened by each stimulus in the vast escalating disaster of the Nigerian national crisis, imaginatively penetrate that intangible void, the abysmal and original chaos, from which creation grew. "Distances" reports this vision:

> . . . Beyond the archway
> like pentecostal orbs

resplendent far distant
in the intangible void
an immense crucifix
of phosphorescent mantles:

*after we had formed*
*then only the forms were formed*
*and all the forms*
*were formed after our forming . . .*

. . . each step is the step of the mule in the abyss—
the archway the oval the panel oblong
to that sanctuary at the earth's molten bowel
for the music woven into the funerary rose
the water in the tunnel its effervescent laughter
the open laughter of the grape or vine
the question in the inkwell the answer on the monocle
the unanswerable question in the tabernacle's silence—
Censers, from the cradle,
of a nameless religion:
each sigh is time's stillness, in the abyss. . . .

(57–58)

This quality of poetic perception, it must be insisted upon, distinguishes the poet of destiny from the ordinary lyricist, the songbird who warbles about the vicissitudes of life without necessarily partaking of their toil, or from the heroic poet who shares, often vicariously, in the glories and surface levels of a people's predicaments. The poet of destiny is not only a sharer of his people's aspirations, a prophet and spokesman for them in time and out of time, but a carrier of their burden in the last resort when they are overwhelmed by calamity and driven backward toward dissolution and chaos. The essential difference here is that the poet of destiny would be in the forefront of his people's celebrations; he would carry the cross in front of them as they tread the weary path to their calvary. He does not bring up the rear in their march to Golgotha, nor does he loiter behind to supply the footnotes after their crucifixion. His kind of poetry is not "an emotion recollected in tranquility" but a red-hot cry, integral and definitive, of the very rhythm of the action that engenders it.

Okigbo's perception of the world around him acquires a critical focus in "Fragments Out of the Deluge." He sees this world as vitiated by insidious forces of oppression. All is destruction here, a solidification into stone and iron, reinforced by tombstone images, by deadness and insensitivity. A deliberate policy of emasculation and destruction of creativity is ushered in by colonialists and Christian missionaries. They are symbolized by "a fleet of eagles."

But the poet, as the keeper of the common seal, whose sensitivity, in spite of the efforts of these twin oppressive forces to destroy him, survives to tell the tale. He describes the disaster and attempts to rouse the people (already reduced to impotence) to fight for their heritage. It is the poet-protagonist versus the spoilers and emasculators of the people. The people, lulled into a false sense of well-being, are lost in their innocence: "And there was none thirsty among them" (29). "The chosen / mongrel breeds / with slogan in hand, of / won divination," the collaborators with the oppressors, join in despoiling the unsuspecting people. But the poet, as sunbird and natural champion of the traditional heritage, carries the battle deep into the enemy camp, and, by painting a most terrifying picture of the desolation that comes with the invasion, attempts to jolt the people out of their complacency into an awareness of the nature of the disaster that has overtaken them. Perhaps, in all African poetry, including that by the most aggressively negritude poets, no writer has created such a picture of the total destruction of the native tradition by the invasion of Europe, as recorded in Okigbo's "Limits XI."

> And the gods lie in State
> And the gods lie in state
> Without the long-drum.
>
> And the gods lie unsung,
> Veiled only with mould,
> Behind the shrine house.
>
> Gods grow out
> Abandoned;
> And so do they. . . .
>
> (34)

It is bad that gods should die at all; it is terrible that they should be denied the basic funeral rites ordinarily accorded to simple mortals. In European myths, the death of gods has evolved into the cyclic phenomenon of the seasons—the gods die with the coming of winter to be resurrected in spring. In other words, they are dead only in the figurative sense of a suspension of active natural life, followed inevitably by revival. In Africa, on the other hand, where people's consciousness is deeply informed by a sacred, metaphysical view of life, the undermining of traditional religion with its symbolic representations amounts to an unhinging of things that give stability and anchorage to life.

There is a warning in all this. When people allow the core of their culture to be destroyed and their sacred beliefs to be desecrated, they lose the cohesive aspects of their society and their psychological anchor and are ready to be enslaved by foreigners and converted to foreign ways. That is also why successful colonialism begins with an attack on its victims' religion, sacred myths, and cultural beliefs. The poet, as the guardian of the common heritage, has the duty to save the people, through his art and craft, from a disaster worse than death, a rout as total as the overthrow of the Titans. His uniqueness lies in his indestructibility; for, though the gods are as vulnerable and as fragile as the people who create them and the ends for which they make them, the poet escapes the net of the enemy's treachery and brutality by his activated imagination and creative intelligence, which thus become the final insurance against permanent enslavement of the people. Out of an encounter as gory as the scene depicted by Picasso in "Guernica," the poet, like the proverbial phoenix, rises to continue the task of leadership and inspiration, by carrying the burden of his people's destiny. His duty is to oppose the enemy's brutality and destructiveness with his constructive and creative humanism. His duty is to sing his admonishments to his people, to renew their fallen light, as Blake puts it in "The Bard."

In Okigbo's *Labyrinths,* this bardic role expands in "Lament of the Silent Sisters" (1962) and "Lament of the Drums" (1964). "Fragments out of the Deluge" (1961/62) treats the reader to a robust cultural nationalism in the wake of the heady celebration of formal independence; but "Laments" follows the eruption of post-independence crises in the former Belgian Congo and Nigeria, the emotional focal points being the assassination of Patrice Lumumba, the first prime minister of the Congo, and the imprisonment of Chief Obafemi Awolowo, the leader of the opposition party in the Nigerian Federal Parliament, followed by the death of his eldest son. What these events did was to sharpen the awareness that political independence brought with it unforeseen dangers more threatening than those predictable atrocities of colonialism. The unleashing of barbaric violence on little-suspecting people, and the cynical strategies of neocolonial imperialism to destroy real independence and replace it with puppetry, sounded the alarm that the great tragic drama that had opened with colonial incursions was about to reach its climax.

The mood deepens in "Lament of the Silent Sisters" and the tone becomes more tragic and somber. The structural organization of the poetry is more complex, while a more widely defined context replaces the lens through which the lyrical persona viewed events until now. The emotional pitch is raised by the use of movements in the verse, structured round the Crier and a chorus of anguished nuns, the point of reference being Gerard Manley Hopkins's "The Wreck of the Deutschland," a poem that recalls the drowning of several Franciscan nuns in a noncombatant ship torpedoed during the First World War.

The poet exercises great ingenuity in the use of two sequences to vary the angle of view and to reinforce one set of events with the help of the other set, harmonizing the feelings of despair that attend the two events. The hopelessness of a ship sinking in the ocean without chance of rescue is used to depict the hopelessness of the African situation when imperialist eagles and "Scavengers" descend with unparalleled ferocity, bent on reestablishing themselves in the so-called independent states. "How does one say NO in thunder?" is a question that echoes through the void. There is no answering action.

The images are saturated with despair and impotence, golden eggs empty of albumen; compass and cross that fail to provide an escape; absence of anchorage, shank, or archways. In place of action, there are rhythms of silence, broken hidden feather-of-flight, hollow seascapes without memory, swan song, sense's stillness, and worlds that have failed. The dominance of sibilants and fricatives tends to underline the feeling of exhaustion and hopelessness. The paralyzing sense of futility and despond cannot be disguised; there is no lulling of the people into a false sense of well-being. All is fear and cowardice typified by "yellow images," "voices in the senses' stillness," "painted harmonies."

In contrast to the helplessness of the victims, the imperialists and their local collaborators ("the choir of inconstant dolphins") appear now as "a fleet of eagles" and now as steely, all-conquering phalanx with "cast-iron steps cascading down the valley all forged into thunder of tanks / and detonators cannoned into splintered flames" (40).

The poet laments the impotence of the people that invites the aggression of their oppressors. At this stage, there is no positive response except to "dip one's tongue in the ocean / (camp) with the choir of inconstant dolphins by shallow sand banks / sprinkled with memories / and to maintain a silence distilled in yellow melodies" (44). In other words, there is hardly anything viable to do to oppose the oppressors' massive violence other than to find outlet, at least temporarily, in "silence."

The mood of this first "Lament" is largely defeatist and an expression of hopelessness by sensitive Nigerians at the sudden and treacherous return of the imperialists with the active collaboration of some local politicians. This mood is reinforced by the involvement of a women's chorus, aptly, because mourning and lamentation are conventionally associated with women in several cultures. In many African societies, dirges and funeral lamentations are associated more with women than with men, and, even in pre-industrial Europe, as in the case of the dying King Arthur of the Round Table, women were charged with the task of lamentation and funeral wailing. The poet is therefore realistic in his use of the silent sisters to give emotional underpinning and reinforcement to the heart-rending destruction of the hopes and prospects of the independent states of Africa overwhelmed by a new, brutal oppression of imperialist Europe.

It is noteworthy that two years separate the first "Lament" from "Lament of the Drums." Those two years were critical in the unfolding chaos that was rapidly swallowing up the Nigerian nation. Violence had become endemic and the governments were proving unequal to the task of leading the people forward in a peaceful, harmonious atmosphere. The workers were growing restive, life was full of insecurities, and the absence of a national sense of direction created a favorable atmosphere for corruption to thrive in. The resources of the country were being stolen by public trustees or being fought over by those eager to get their fingers in the pie. It had become clear that the country had been plunged headlong into the abyss, and that the forces of disorder were propelling it toward its fatal destiny.

The texture of the poetry in the second "Lament" is finer; the voice of prophecy is firmer and more authoritative. Some of the earlier images reappear but in sharper focus. The cadence is slower, more evenly measured, almost leisurely. The worst is now known. We experience the effect of the calm that follows a great catastrophe and, in turn, prepares the way for an even greater catastrophe. Before the poet there stands the "chaliced vintage" that must be drunk.

The key evidence for this radicalization of crises and the willingness to confront it can be seen in the syntactical movement of the second "Lament" sequences. If we compare the opening movement of "Lament of the Silent Sisters" with the opening invocation in "Lament of the Drums," we are struck by the broken syntax of the former and the slow, steady, almost cheerful flow of the verse in the latter. In the first "Lament," the Crier opens with the fear-suffused lines:

> IS THERE . . . Is certainly there—
> For as in sea-fever globules of fresh anguish
> immense golden eggs empty of albumen
> sink into our balcony . . .

How does one say NO in thunder—(39). The element of confusion and uncertainty capped by terror is manifested in the broken syntax of the first line. We have a certain incompleteness in both the sentence structure and the structure of meaning in the lines following. In contrast, "Lament of the Drums" opens with fully rounded syntactical structures:

> LION-HEARTED cedar forest, gonads for our thunder,
>
> Even if you are very far away, we invoke you:
>
> Give us our hollow heads of long-drums . . .
>
> Antelopes for the cedar forest, swifter messengers
> Than flash-of-beacon-flame, we invoke you:
> Hide us; deliver us from our nakedness. . . .
>
> (45)

Here the syntactical control is not only firm, but even complex, with phrasal and clausal elaborations, and the powerful, highly accentuated, end-placed sentence, "we invoke you." The opening epithet, "lion-hearted," is obviously transferred from the poet or his persona to the "cedar forest." It is quite clear that what the earlier crises have achieved is to rouse a deep resolve in the poet to confront the dangerous issues threatening the security of all. There is no more room for illusions but a certain inevitability that the crises have intensi-

fied and that suffering is about to become the common heritage of those
beguiled by the hope of redemption. The voice of prophecy is firm and
unequivocal: there will be unparalleled suffering and death, and many will
suffer martyrdom because "the robbers"—the imperialists and their internal
collaborators—are on the offensive and bent on destroying all who stand in
the way of wholesale spoliation of the so-called independent state. The poet
proclaims the threat unequivocally:

> . . . We sense
> With dog-nose a Babylonian capture,
> The martyrdom
> Blended into that chaliced vintage.
>
> (46)

But the challenge of the robbers will not be adequately answered because
those who should tackle it are themselves too deeply sunk in corruption to
muster the will to resist:

> Nothing remains, only smoke after storm—
> Some strange Celaeno and harpy crew,
> Laden with night and their belly's excrement.
> Profane all things with hooked feet and foul teeth.
>
> (47)

The one man, Palinurus, capable of standing up to the robbers, has already
been put away to rot in detention:

> Like palm oil fostered in an ancient clay bowl,
> A half-forgotten name; like a stifled sneeze. . . .
>
> (48)

But this failure to resist oppression does not bring reprieve; instead, it calls
forth more intensive oppression and more widespread destruction. The
prophecy that concludes this section of the "Laments" is fulfilled to an
uncanny exactitude in a matter of months by the immense escalation of
Nigerian political crises:

> *The wailing is for the fields of crop:*
>
> The drums' lament is:
> They grow not . . .
>
> *The wailing is for the fields of men*
>
> For the barren wedded ones;
> For perishing children . . .

> *The wailing is for the Great River:*
>
> Her pot-bellied watchers
> Despoil her. . . .
>
> (50)

But the crises and destructions of 1964 were to be far surpassed by those of 1965. From May 1965, Okigbo began the sequences of poems he called "Path of Thunder," which record the hallmarks of the tragic events that led up to the Nigerian civil war. Okigbo was greatly troubled by the further escalation of violence, lawlessness, and corruption that made sustaining a stable civil state increasingly difficult. He put his poetic integrity at the service of his battered country and allowed the full benefits of his poetical maturity to shine through in spite of the desperate nature of the situation. His poetical sensibilities, now sharpened to razor-edge, cut through the tangled mass of passionate complexities to grasp at the core of the deadly issues. The stakes had become too high to be dealt with through poetical disguises and farfetched analogies. The very immediacy and magnitude of the dangers called for a certain directness of address and plain speaking somewhat at odds with the stances of his earlier poetry. Moreover, it had become obvious that the stages of oracular exposition had come to an end and the stage was set for plain-speaking, for a directness of address, which constitutes the acme of the apocalyptic tradition. All prophets, oracles, and diviners must, at crisis points of their vocations, lay aside their specialized medium to espouse the simplest and directest modes of address. The essential paradox here is that the profoundest truths are reserved for the simplest and most direct language structure. The masks are laid aside and the man speaks in his own voice:

> I have lived the sapling sprung from the bed of the old vegetation:
> Have shouldered my way through a mass of ancient nights to chlorophyll;
> I have lived the oracle dry on the cradle of a new generation.
>
> (64)

And elsewhere, later:

> If I don't learn to shut my mouth I'll soon go to hell.
> I, Okigbo, town-crier, together with my iron bell.
>
> (67)

Okigbo recognized the dangers of plain speaking at a time of immense passions and irrational violence, but here his poetic responsibility asserted itself: the stakes were just too high to allow for the fine consideration of personal safety. He assumed the full responsibility of a poet of destiny who would not stand aside from the cataclysmal waves threatening the survival of his people. He recognized the revolutionary nature of the events sweeping through the land, as well as the risks that formed part and parcel of such events; for, a revolution, like a boa, might destroy its own children in its fevered movement. A poet as self-conscious as Okigbo could hardly be expected to be ignorant of the deepest implications of the forces sweeping over the land or to ignore the vast opportunity which the situation constituted for the writer whose destiny was coterminous with that of his country and his people.

In "Come Thunder," which was written in December 1965, when the state of anomic violence had reached the peak of disaster, the poet made his final prophecy, which was to be fulfilled to the minutest detail by the events of the next four years. It deserves to be quoted in full because it constitutes the apex of Okigbo's poetry in its prophetic and apocalyptic grandeur:

> Now that the triumphant march has entered the last street corners,
> Remember, O dancers, the thunder among the clouds . . .
> Now that laughter, broken in two, hangs tremulous between the teeth,
> Remember, O dancers, the lightning beyond the earth . . .
> The smell of blood already floats in the lavender-mist of the afternoon
> The death sentence lies in ambush along the corridors of power;
> And a great fearful thing already tugs at the cables of the open air,
> A nebula immense and immeasurable, a night of deep waters
> An iron dream unnamed and unprintable, a path of stone
> The drowsy heads of the pods in barren farmlands witness it,
> The homesteads abandoned in this century's brush fire witness it,
> Magic birds with the miracle of lightning flash on their feathers . . .
> The myriad eyes of deserted corn cobs in burning barns, witness it;
> The arrows of God tremble at the gates of light,
> The drums of curfew pander to a dance of death;
> And the secret thing in its heaving
> Threatens with iron mask
> The last lighted torch of the century. . . .

(66)

The dancers referred to here were the politicians, the effete public servants, and the exploiting classes who made common cause with imperialism to snuff out the bright prospect of independence. These were too far gone in corruption and decadence to heed the urgent import of prophecy. Of course, such people never read any literature as exacting and exalting as poetry. The spiritual dimension informed by social justice was far away from their lives, and with the insensitivity of renowned comedians, they pushed their country over the precipice into abysmal violence and civic disorder.

In January 1966, Nigeria experienced a coup d'état that brought the army into power politics in the country. Okigbo, like most of his contemporaries, reflecting popular disenchantment with the misrule of the civilian politicians, welcomed the change with enthusiasm because that change, even if only for a brief while, called a halt to the anarchy which had immobilized the country. But he was also one of the first people to warn that popular enthusiasm was not enough, it could be, and is, as easily dissipated. The celebration of the coup in "Elegy for Slit-Drum" and written for "rattles accompaniment" is composed in jerky, elliptical syntax, embodying mixed sentiments of hopes and considerable foreboding:

> The cabinet has gone to hell
> the timbers are now on fire
> the cabinet that sold itself
> ministers are now in gaol—
> condolences quivering before the iron throne of a new conqueror:
> the mythmaker accompanies us (the Egret had come and gone)
> Okigbo accompanies us the oracle enkindles us
> the Hornbill is there again (the Hornbill has had a bath)
> Okigbo accompanies us the rattles enlighten us—
> condolences with the miracle of sunlight on our feathers—.
>
> (68–69)

The rattles provide ideal musical punctuation for the jaunty minstrel rhythm that at this stage has become the dominant impulse in Okigbo's verse. Minstrelsy is musically versatile and highly inspired in sentiment, as well as providing many grants for social commentary. Musicality, which has from the very beginning become a major defining principle of Okigbo's verse, attains the highest flights in these last poems, mainly because the events themselves yield the greatest concentration of emotive response, which finds loftiest expression in outgoing musical celebrations. The simplicity and directness of the lyrical sentiments invite, with a certain inevitability, a musical approach that thoroughly utilizes the rhythmic advantages of caesuras, end-stoppages, accentuated lines, and repetitions.

The nature of the situation itself requires a lifting of the masks and the revelation of the true resonance of the natural voice. The lyrical persona whose self-conscious individuality up until now controlled the poetic inspiration is overridden by the social persona who absorbs the deeply felt fears and anxieties of a whole people. The "us," which increasingly supplants the "I" of the earlier sequences, symbolizes this acceptance of the destiny of the individual within the larger, inclusive destiny of the group. The poet's assertion in "Elegy of the Wind" that he had lived the oracle dry on the cradle of a new generation marks a significant, nearly total submergence of his individuality within the wider, collective interests of the entire people. The mythmaker Okigbo, whose outlook is objectified in the unique role of community poet, can no longer stand aside from the "us," the collectivity, now hemmed in by immense possibilities of both salvation and damnation. The poet is lost in the people. Okigbo, the poet, "accompanies" us, the people, and his rattle music unifies the emotional aspirations of the group. The mixture of dread and elation at these new developments is suggested by "the miracle of sunlight on our feathers" and the "quivering before the iron throne of a new conqueror."

The limited euphoria of the military coup was soon over. By May 1966, it had become clear that the forces of reaction had re-emerged and that the hopes for redemption of the nation were not to be realized. In "Elegy for Alto," Okigbo, now fully integrated into the collective consciousness of the people and sensing the imminence of the great terrible times ahead, wrote his final testimony, in which he bemoaned the death of a great dream. The country stood at the brink of war, and the reversion to chaos, only temporarily staved off, continued with accelerated speed. For a man who had stood at the center of the great dream of Nigerian nationhood, the alienation and sense of doom were most distressing and painful:

> For beyond the blare of sirened afternoons, beyond the motorcades;
> The voices and days, the echoing highways;
>    beyond the latescence
> Of our dissonant airs; through our curtained eyeballs,
>    through our shuttered sleep,
> Onto our forgotten selves, onto our broken images;
>    beyond the barricades
> Commandments and edicts, beyond the iron tables,
>    beyond the elephant's
> Legendary patience, beyond the inviolable bronze bust;
>    beyond our crumbling towers—
> Beyond the iron path careering along the same beaten track—
> The Glimpse of a dream lies smouldering in a cave, together with
>    the mortally wounded birds.
> Earth, unbind me; let me be the prodigal; let this be the ram's
>    ultimate prayer to the tether. . . .
>
>                                   (72)

The signs of dissolution were unmistakable:

> —The Eagles are now in sight:
> Shadows in the horizon—
> The robbers are here in black sudden steps of showers, of caterpillars—
> . . . . . . . . . . . . . . . . . . . . . . . . . . . . . . . . . . . . . . . . . . . . . . . . . . . . . . . . . . .
> The eagles descend on us.
> Bayonets and cannons—
> . . . . . . . . . . . . . . . . . . .
> Politicians are here in this iron dance of mortars, of generators—.
>
>                                     (71)

Nothing remained but to leave "the cave" of the wrecked dream and to seek shelter and safety in the open air of his nativity, to discard the large but unrealized dream for another destiny with a new sense of freedom: *So let the horn paw the air howling goodbye.* . . . (71). Herein again, Okigbo, the oracle, the prophet, the town-crier, the sunbird, reaffirms for the last time the integrity of his individuality as a seer. Borrowing the profound words of the Spanish poet Serafén Alvarez Quintero, that in a time of immense upheavals in the lives of peoples and nations the great natural law of change and continuity remains the permanent and inviolable reality, Okigbo wrote:

> An old star departs, leaves us here on the shore
> Gazing heavenward for a new star approaching;
> The new star appears, foreshadows its going
> Before a going and coming that goes on forever. . . .
>                                                    (72)

In this masterly stroke of prophetic insight, he foretells not only his own going but the course of events that were to come and to affect the world whose humanistic values he had so vitally and singlemindedly and beautifully illuminated, and within which he had painstakingly sowed the seed of imperishable love and harmony against the wild, subversive passions of materialistically bound obsessions.

The crumbling of a great edifice is always a painful spectacle; so also is the dissolution of a great dream. But it is in the nature of things that the greatest dreamers are also the greatest despairers; the most refined and sensitive souls are the most tragic sufferers when great hopes dissolve. Thus, Wordsworth could write, in "Resolution and Independence":

> We poets in our youth, begin in gladness;
> But thereof come in the end despondency and madness.[15]

Christopher Okigbo, like most of his contemporaries, believed in the great dream of Nigerian nationhood. This dream, always assumed and implicit in his poetic exertions, formed one of the great impulses of his creativity. In this regard, he was like most of the creative artists of his generation—fine and plastic artists, musicians, novelists, dramatists, creative journalists, and so on, who were deeply animated by the stirring events affecting the evolving and potentially great nation. But, more than his contemporaries, Okigbo's imaginative integration with the hopes and aspirations of his people was so total, so close, that with the sudden collapse of the dream it also meant, of course, that he himself had come to the end of things. The poet of destiny cannot survive independently of the destiny of his people which he had taken up and made his own. Romantic poets, in spite of their dreams and idealism, almost surmounted the failure of their dreams: they managed to dream other dreams, because of their imaginatively detachable abilities. Only poets of destiny among them, because of the integrative nature of their commitment, their inextricable identification of their individual destinies with those of their people, find it hard to create new destinies and new dreams when those of the people have collapsed.

The special nature of the relationship of poets of destiny with their peoples and their people's aspirations makes it almost inevitable that the world can only have very few such poets at any given moment of history, but more so in this modern age. In antiquity, there was a greatly integrated world outlook, and many communities probably had their poets of destiny, their bards, who sounded their heartbeats and reflected their deepest yearnings. But in the modern age, with its consuming passion for egotistic self-definitions and self-fulfilments, the breed of such poets has dwindled to almost none. Christopher Okigbo and, undoubtedly, Pablo Neruda of Chile and Latin America, were perhaps, among the last of that breed. Neruda's commitment to his native Chile and his beloved Latin America was as total as Okigbo's to his people of Nigeria, and both poets, in the nature of things and of their peculiar commitments, were destined to meet a tragic end. The worldwide tributes that have been paid to these two poets offer incontestable testimony that their greatness transcended the narrow limits of poetic creativity.[16] They stood for those values of light and truth and love and freedom and compassion without which nations and peoples perish and generations go to perdition. Neruda summed up such unique commitment in two memorable lines of personal testament that conclude his poem "Do Not Ask Me," when he wrote:

> I have a pact of love with beauty:
> I have a pact of blood with my people.[17]

Such could also be Christopher Okigbo's testament.

## Notes

1.  William Blake, "Song of Experience," *The Norton Anthology of Poetry*, 3d ed. (New York and London: Norton, 1983), 503.

2.  Ibid.

3.  William Wordsworth, "Resolution and Independence," *The Norton Anthology of Poetry*, 3d ed. (New York and London: Norton, 1983), 547.

4.  The present writer does not quite agree with those critics who say that Okigbo's poems suffer from an overromantic concern with the poet as hero. See, for example, Dan Izevbaye, "From Reality to Dream: The Poetry of Christopher Okigbo," in *The Critical Evaluation of African Literature*, ed. Edgar Wright (London: Heinemann, 1973), 148. The view here is that the poetical tasks undertaken by Okigbo and the seriousness of his statements require certain validation, including the unravelling of the processes of poetic maturation and the laying bare of the poet's own credentials. Notwithstanding the Eliot canon enjoining impersonality and a poet's detachment from his work, certain kinds of poetry gain considerably from the poet's personal distinctiveness. The assumption is that the poet's personality is deeply involved in the experience he is exploring; he is both subject and object. The presence of the poet or his

persona(e) in the poetry is inseparable from the total effect of the poem. Accounts of childhood and adolescence often trace an individual's journey to consciousness through the struggle to understand oneself and the world one lives in. As someone has validly asserted, such accounts, in a good proportion of African and Afro-Caribbean writing, generally have the salutary effect of indicating the issues upon which the individual has focused his powerful imagination.

5.    Christopher Okigbo, *Labyrinths with Path of Thunder* (NewYork: Africana Publishing, 1971), 7. As if Okigbo anticipated that he would not survive the storm already gathering in Nigeria, he painstakingly revised and reorganized his poems before his death in July 1967. This volume was published posthumously by Heinemann and Africana Publishing in 1971.

Some commentators on his poetry have noted the nature and extent of these revisions. He not only altered the structure of the poem, but strengthened its poetic voice. See, for example, Theo Vincent, "Okigbo's *Labyrinths*" in *Black Orpheus* 2, 7 (1972): 32. In the revision, Okigbo may have benefited from the more perceptive of his early critics by getting rid of weaknesses such as were noted by M. J. C. Echeruo in "Traditional and Borrowed Elements in Nigerian Poetry," *Nigeria Magazine* 89 (June 1966): 142–55. For the most comprehensive bibliographical study of Okigbo's poems and the critical commentaries on them, see Joseph C. Anafulu, "Christopher Okigbo, 1932–1967: A Bio-Bibliography," *Research in African Literatures* 9 (Spring 1978): 65–78.

6.    Okigbo, *Labyrinths*, 14.

7.    See Chinweizu, Onwuchekwa Jemie, and Ihechukwu Madubuike, *Towards the Decolonization of African Literature* (Washington, D.C.: Howard University Press, 1983), 174–83, 208–9. Chinweizu exempts Okigbo's last poetic sequence, "Path of Thunder," from the censure directed at the rest of his poetry for its "Euro-modernist" tendencies in "Prodigals, Come Home!" *Okike, An Africa Journal of New Writing* 12 (April 1978): 40–46.

8.    T. S. Eliot, *Selected Essays* (London: Faber, 1969), 13.

9.    Ibid., 14.

10.    Interview with Marjory Whitelaw, *Journal of Commonwealth Literature* 9 (July 1970): 34–35.

11.    Christopher Okigbo, *Labyrinths with the Path of Thunder* (New York: Africana Publishing, 1971), 6. Subsequent page references for quoted material are given in the text.

12.    See, for example, R. N. Egudu's "Okigbo's 'Distances': A Retreat from Christ to Idoto," *Conch* 5 (1973): 29–42. Christopher Okigbo's attitudes to Christianity and the traditional religion are clearly stated by him in the interview with Marjory Whitelaw referred to earlier. In his view, ". . . all these gods [of traditional religion] are the same as the Christian God. . . . They are different aspects of the same power, the same force." Whitelaw, "Interview with Christopher Okigbo, 1965," *Journal of Commonwealth Literature*, 30.

13.    Interview by Robert Serumaga published in *Transition* 7, 33 (1965): 18.

14.    The text of *Labyrinths with The Path of Thunder*, shorn of the crudities of the earlier versions, justifies the statements embodied here. The tantalizing allusions and diversionary images regarded by Paul Theroux and some other commentators as the sources of the so-called obscurity of Okigbo's poetry (see, Theroux, "Christopher Okigbo," in *Introduction to Nigerian Literature*, ed. Bruce King [Lagos and London, 1971], 135–51) in this collection have been either eliminated altogether or have been successfully assimilated to a new organic unity. A comparison of earlier and later versions of the poems will indicate the profound transformations Okigbo wrought in intentions, strategies, and meanings. Whereas his earlier poems, individually and, perhaps, collectively, failed to yield a consistently powerful and unified vision, the consciously edited, condensed, and organically structured final work achieves his vision in a way no other African poet has succeeded in doing to this day.

15.    Wordsworth, "Resolution and Independence," *Norton Anthology of Poetry*, 547.

16.    See Chinua Achebe and Dubem Okafor, eds., *Don't Let Him Die: An Anthology of Memorial Poems for Christopher Okigbo, 1932–1967,* with a preface by Chinua Achebe (Enugu: Fourth Dimension Publishers, 1978). Contributors were from Nigeria, Africa, and different

parts of the world. Many of them had never met Okigbo in life, but were inspired by the distinctiveness of his poetry and the vitality of his personality in his poetry. The poet of destiny may be of a nation or nationality, but the very uniqueness of his commitment transcends national boundaries and makes the poet a citizen of the world.

17.    There is also a remarkable similarity between the personal history, creative career, and death of Garcia Lorca, the young Spanish poet who died in the Spanish Civil War on the side of the Republicans, and Okigbo who died in the Nigerian Civil War. Both men were driven by the logic of their peculiar commitments and destinies to pay the final price. Okigbo admired Lorca's poetry exceedingly.

# The Achievement of Christopher Okigbo

## Robert Fraser

When in 1967 the young Igbo poet Christopher Okigbo met his untimely death at the age of thirty-five on the battlefield of Nsukka during the Nigerian Civil War, he left behind him enough poetry to fill one slender volume.[1] Yet this tiny offering, a mere seventy-two pages in length, arguably represents the most revered trophy in the gallery of English-language verse in Africa, and Okigbo himself the most talented of modern African poets. The verse of *Labyrinths,* as his collected works have come to be known, has a strange haunting quality, difficult to account for in orthodox critical language. It also triumphs over petty historical distinctions by refusing to lend itself to any one tradition, making a mockery of our painful efforts to allot it to any definable school or recognizable manner. It is the product of a deeply sophisticated mind, as steeped in the mythologies of Europe, Asia, and the ancient world as in the folklore of the rural Igbo amongst whom Okigbo grew up. Okigbo was a man of wide and voracious reading in the literatures of Greece and Rome which he read while a student of classics at the University College of Ibadan, in the poetry and legends of ancient Babylon, which he encountered in translation, and in the literatures of Europe and America, in which he retained a lively interest throughout his life. For him, to be a writer was to partake in an international community of letters. He disdained any suggestion of literary nationalism, going as far as to turn down a prize at the first festival of black arts held in Dakar, Senegal, on the grounds that he could not consider himself an exclusively African writer.[2] Yet all of his poetry is deeply indebted to the beliefs and traditional poetic practice of the Igbo people with which he never lost touch. In his delicate cadences the music of oral Igbo poetry blends with echoes from the modern English poets and with the strains of American jazz, which he loved to play on the clarinet while still an undergraduate. Thematically too his work may be viewed as an attempt to reconcile these various traditions and, above all, to come to terms with the tension between residual Christian promptings and the claims of indigenous Igbo theology.

Originally published in Robert Fraser, *West African Poetry: A Critical History* (Cambridge: Cambridge University Press, 1986), 104–37. © 1986 by Cambridge University Press. Reprinted with the permission of Cambridge University Press and the author.

One persistent problem in attempting to discuss Okigbo's work meaningfully is that, patient reviser as he was, most of his works have appeared in different versions under different imprints. The better part of the sequence known as *Limits* and *Silences* for instance appeared in the pages of the influential East African journal *Transition,* which, under Rajat Neogy's editorship, did so much to advance the cause of African letters in the early and mid-sixties.[3] Mbari of Ibadan, the Nigerian publishing house responsible for bringing out first volumes by a number of promising poets of the period, also issued the whole of *Heavensgate* (1962), *Limits* (1964) and *Silences* (1965), before, in 1965, Okigbo decided to sit down to revise all of the earlier poetry, which he proposed to reissue, with the new sequence *Distances* (already published in *Transition* Vol. 4 No. 16, 1964) under the joint title *Labyrinths.* He wrote an introduction for this project, which, however, never came to fruition before his death. Meanwhile, under the impact of the Nigerian *coup d'état* of January 1966, he wrote a fresh sequence called *Path of Thunder* which was performed in his lifetime but not published. As a result, a lengthy correspondence ensued between Okigbo's literary executors, Heinemann in London and his lifetime friend Sunday Anozie, who had been close to the poet during the composition of the early work, and who could hence be expected to know something of his intentions.[4] Anozie argued against the joint publication of *Labyrinths* and *Path of Thunder* but eventually the practicalities of publishing won the day, and the printed version of Okigbo's work now most widely available contains both works, in revised versions, dubbed by Okigbo himself as "final" together with the 1965 introduction which, however, only applies to *Labyrinths.* A strong case can be made for reprinting the Mbari booklets in an accessible form, but, meanwhile, it seems best to confine oneself to an analysis of the later, Heinemann version, while bearing in mind that the differences between this and the first editions sometimes vary enormously, the differences in the text of *Silences,* for example, being especially marked.

In his preface Okigbo clearly states that he regards the trilogy of *Limits, Silences* and *Distances* as an interconnected sequence, and *Heavensgate* as an anticipatory sequence which is "organically related" to it. In his monograph Sunday Anozie endorses this arrangement, and also sees *Heavensgate* as apprentice work.[5] It will be instructive, therefore, to deal with *Heavensgate,* the trilogy, and *Path of Thunder* in turn as statements belonging to successive phases of the poet's career, and then to turn to the question of their mutual relatedness.

Okigbo states that *Heavensgate* was "originally conceived as an Easter sequence."[6] There is much evidence in the text of Christian antecedents: references to the Biblical version of Creation, to ecclesiastical processions, to John the Baptist. One has therefore to treat with extreme caution Romanus Egudu's view of Okigbo as an anti-ecclesiastical, anti-clerical poet,[7] since these insignia are not here treated as icons to be destroyed but as facets of the poet's inner experience. The most one can concede is that these Christian images do tend to recede towards the end of the sequence, "Lustra" and "Newcomer" in particular drawing on predominantly pagan sources. Indeed the reference to the initiate as "prodigal" in the very first lyric suggests an at least partial regret at personal infidelity to the traditional gods, one catalyst of which may be seen as Christian conversion. The posture *vis-à-vis* the Christian faith is thus strongly ambivalent. Though, conceived of in Christian terms they almost seem at points to be desiring a reconversion to a state of apostasy, even if the phrases in which this intention is expressed often bear strong Christian overtones, and the orthodox Christian terms of reference also come back in full force in later sequences, albeit suffused with exotic references.

We know from Anozie's account that Okigbo wrote *Heavensgate* shortly after a brief return visit to his home village of Ojoto, where he re-encountered the traditional mysteries and in particular the cult associated with the riverain goddess · Idoto.[8] We learn further from Okigbo's own testimony that as a young boy he was expected to shoulder the burden of the priesthood of this cult when he grew up, but later found it impossible to reconcile this with his professional career as librarian and publisher. The opening section of "The Passage" recounts his feelings of guilt. As he stands before the neglected shrine he is seized with a feeling of regret and reclines symbolically on the totems of "the oilbean, the tortoise and the python" which he would have employed in his capacity as priest. Yet at the very moment of his greatest yearning he gives expression to this feeling in a précis of the opening sentence of Psalm 130, one of the greatest penitential supplications of the ancient church:

> Out of the depths my cry:
> give ear and hearken . . .
> (*Labyrinths*, p. 3)

This leads him straight into an evocation, at the beginning of the next lyric, of the Biblical vision of Genesis, the first act of a God who is Alpha and Omega, whose physical intervention begins with the creation of tiny wavelets of ultra-violet light and culminates with the holocaust of Armageddon, "the fire that is dreamt of." This reference, however, is only one strand in the texture of a lyric that is compounded of many echoes, from the evident allusion to the Eliot of *Burnt Norton* in the third stanza to the side-glance at the mediaeval carol "I sing of a maiden" in the last line. The rainbow in stanza three is elusive, but its occurrence in a context so rich in Biblical echoes seems to justify Paul Theroux's connection of it with the Covenant of the Old Testament,[9] even though his additional interpretation of it as a "snake capable of both leading and devouring the poet" is over complex and confused. Okigbo at this stage is merely embarking on his religious journey, and is concerned typically with false beacons, one of which may well be the all-embracing

Christian view of history as God-directed. Anozie sees the boa-constrictor as a powerful emblem of religious intuition,[10] but we must note that it is "bent to kill" and thus Theroux's suggestion of sinister intent cannot entirely be dismissed. At this point Okigbo almost seems to anticipate the thematic concerns of "Fragments out of the Deluge" from *Limits* where Christianity is viewed simply as a destructive agent. In any case, at this stage, the poet's search for authentic visionary inspiration seems to be captive to Christian trappings to the extent that the mother-goddess Idoto comes to be viewed in the guise of a Madonna ("a mother on the spray"). Only at the very end with "the young bird at the passage" does an indigenous note intrude.

The last segment of "Passage" is among the most beautiful moments of the whole sequence. The "silent faces at crossroads / festivity in black" may, as Anozie suggests, be implicitly satirical,[11] but the satire appears, to the present reader, to be muted beneath a dominant strain of ambivalent reverence. Okigbo would have seen plenty of such processions in the rural Igboland of his youth, and the slight reek of cassocked stuffiness in "the hot garden" cannot overlay the devotional atmosphere of the first three stanzas, the last of which leans heavily on Eliot's *East Coker.* The "Anna at the knobs of the panel oblongo" may indeed be Okigbo's mother, but she is also St. Anne. Furthermore, the "old lovely fragments" practised on the consoles of provincial organs in the Eastern Nigerian countryside are in no sense set up in contrast to the spontaneous music of the wind "leaning over / its loveliest fragment" in the last line, but is on the contrary seen as complementary to it. Hence, at this juncture, which corresponds to the first station of the poet's cross, Christian and African religious intimations are made to fuse, to haunting effect.

It is only with "Initiations" that a divisive note begins to emerge. The plural of the title is meticulous, since the poet is recalling his three-fold initiation into three distinct and potentially conflicting schools of thought: the Christian/individualistic, the professionally artistic and the ancestral and folk-loric. The first of these has obviously been the most insistent, coercive and puzzling, and to it Okigbo devotes forty-three lines. In the first stanza, the sign of the cross inscribed in water on the initiate's forehead is compared horrifyingly to the branding of a slave with "red-hot blade." The comparison seems extreme, but seen from the vantage point of one newly seized with a desire for spiritual emancipation, is naturally and historically fitting. Kepkanly, as we know from the author's footnote, was the village schoolmaster who initiated Okigbo himself into the mysteries of the Catechism, and, therefore, as a locally recruited employee of the colonial educational system, both the instrument of missionary instruction and its victim. The result of the education he offered is induction into the safe port of Christian commitment, where the agonizing complexity of moral responsibility disappears in a reassuring "confluence of planes" corresponding to the "orthocentre" of a triangle. An orthocentre is the point at which the perpendicular from the vertices of a triangle meet. "Ortho-," however, also suggests "orthodoxy," and hence a completely water-tight creed, such as the church supplies for weaker brethren, those who do not share the poet's compulsion to forge a personal spiritual vision. The symbolism of geòmetric figures seems to distil the angularity of attitude characteristic of those with blinkered minds, constricted either by the simplifications of Christian doctrine, by the petty bureaucracy of "fanatics and priests and popes / organizing secretaries and party managers," or, worse still, by the sheer rapacity of the social parasites: "brothers and deacons / liberal politicians / selfish self-seekers" (*Labyrinths,* p. 7).

It may be instructive here to dwell on the note of social criticism present in these lines. Most commentators on Okigbo's work have tended to interpret his development in the light of an evolution from private to public concerns, and yet here, close to the beginning of his first sequence, we have an unmistakable suggestion of disaffection with the status quo of the Federation of Nigeria which was, at the time of Okigbo's writing, little more than two years old. Its starting point is a recognition of the gap between the morality of the new political élite and the controlling moral vision of the old lore, represented in the two ensuing sections by Jadum the village minstrel and Upandru the "explainer" who were jointly responsible for introducing the young Okigbo into the subtleties of Igbo belief and custom. Both of them, we notice, possess characteristics of the poet, Jadum his visionary madness and Upandru his deliberate tactical manipulation of meaning; yet these sources of traditional poetic energy will never be released until the poet learns to tear out his limiting inhibitions by the root, a process violently suggested by a quotation from the incantation recited by the rural Igbo on the occasion of a ram's castration:

> And he said to the ram: Disarm.
> And I said;
> Except by rooting,
> Who could pluck yam tubers from their base?
> (*Labyrinths,* p. 9)

When this process is metaphorically complete, the poet is free to renew his quest unencumbered by alien restraints.

"Watermaid" issues in a new mood. Abhorring false gods, the poet is observed in quest of a presiding lady or muse. The identity of this female figure, who crops up at regular intervals throughout the rest of *Labyrinths,* and who in *Distances* reveals herself as the focal point of the poet's search, takes us into a web of connected mythologies. Though clearly reminiscent of the Mother Idoto of "The Passage" (with whom at the culmination of *Distances* she also seems to fuse), she is at once a "lioness," a "watermaid" and a "white queen." These titles seem to connect her with a whole series of divinities which derive from both African and exotic religious traditions. West African readers will automatically think of the "Mammywata" common in local folklore. More specifically, Yoruba readers are likely to remember Lemanja, goddess of the sea, that ubiquitous figure worshipped throughout the area of the black diaspora, from Oyo to Haiti to Brazil; while European readers are more likely to think of Isis or Diana, Egyptian and Graeco-Roman goddesses who are both identifiable with the White Goddess whom the British poet Robert Graves regards as the chief source of authentic poetic inspiration.[12] Indeed the constant references to white as the colour of her adornment, and a reiterated link with the moon, lead one straight to Graves's theory with which Okigbo was clearly familiar and which will henceforth provide a useful analytical tool in discussing the intellectual scheme of *Labyrinths,* in the Introduction to which the "White Goddess" features as an organizing idea (*Labyrinths,* p. xiv). Graves's theory will be discussed in greater detail at a more appropriate point, but suffice it here to say that the White Goddess is regarded, both by Graves and Okigbo, as at once the guide and tormentor of the dedicated artist, with whom she is intermittently obsessed but whom she is constantly in danger of destroying. She therefore serves as an apt symbol for the beguiling risks of the poetic vocation which offers fugitive glimpses of ultimate truth while constantly harassing the unfortunate victim with threats to his sanity and self-respect.

The essence of the goddess consists in her elusiveness. Thus in the three sections of "Watermaid" we are granted three transient visions of this female persona taken from three different perspectives. "Watermaid" as a whole is in fact largely concerned with various ways of seeing, the open eye of the observer being compared with a number of heavenly bodies. In the first section the eye of the prodigal poet surveys the barren landscape of a sandy beach for evidence of a secret which he has earlier buried. Exactly what this secret is does not emerge until the later section "And I am here abandoned" where we learn that the poet is languishing for loss of his "white queen" without whom he has no access to wisdom or knowledge. Meanwhile he is teased by maddening memories of her longed-for presence, "maid of salt-emptiness, / sophisticreamy." Indeed the second section can be read as a hymn of praise to the goddess, here viewed with the flattering eye of a worshipper. The hymn has much of the intensity of a Catholic paean to the Madonna, a *Salve Regina,* but also recalls instances throughout world literature of mystical encounters with the muse, a fine instance of which occurs at the culmination point of Apuleius' fable *The Golden Ass,* Graves's translation of which Okigbo may also have read.[13] After this moment of possibly illusory enlightenment, a mirage thrown up in the fevered mind's eye, the poet is left with a feeling of anti-climax and abandonment. In the very last section he regards his goddess, here unequivocally identified with the moon, not with the passionate eye of one possessed, but with the bleak objectivity of one who knows that his attentions are rejected, his goal as far off as ever:

THE STARS have departed,
The sky in monocle

> surveys the worldunder
> The stars have departed,
> and I—where am I?
> (*Labyrinths,* p. 13)

One of the most impressive qualities of *Heavensgate* is its versatility of mood, recalling at times the change of tempo associated with the structures of classical music. Here, at the end of "Watermaid" with its listless adagio, we bound straight into the opening lines of "Lustra" with their bucolic recollections of Housman and early Yeats. The return to the countryside, which in "The Passage" was a matter of solemn dedication, here achieves all the lightheartedness of a vacation spree. Likewise, the search for the moon goddess, which in "Watermaid" was conducted in an atmosphere of nervous exhaustion and strain, is rendered here in language which recalls a holiday expedition. Whether the "mid-term" of the last line of the first section is a literal reference to the academic or legal recess matters little; the fundamental fact is that the poet has taken a momentary break from high seriousness before plunging into the deliberate self-impalement of "The flower weeps, unbruised." It is a lull before the storm, since the *Lacrimae Christi* mood of the next poem represents the low point of the poet's quest, a dark night of the soul relieved only by a faint hope of a Second Coming: "Messiah will come again." If, as Okigbo suggests in his Preface, the various sections of *Heavensgate* represent the stations of the poet-celebrant's cross, this section is the last obstacle before enlightenment can be reached. The return to a Christian language here and in the sections immediately following reflects a sense of remoteness from a homogenous, authentically traditional truth. On visiting the village palm-grove, where the spirits of the ancestors reside, however, the poet is released from his burden of doubt by a customary inscription of five parallel lines of chalk, the customary manner of greeting between man and ancestor, man and man, familiar in all Igbo households. With that a fanfare of "drums and cannons" announces the triumphal return to a confident mastery of knowledge. The prodigal has paid his respects and his offering is finally accepted; and with that the quest embarked on in "The Passage" is almost complete.

There remains, however, a coda, "Newcomer," evidently intended as a postscript to the main sequence, but considered by many commentators as unsatisfactory. There are several reasons for this. First, whereas the sequence proper has been dominated by two figures, the poetic persona who recounts his own spiritual adventure in the first person singular, and the mother-mistress-muse to whom he addresses his attentions, "Newcomer" introduces a male personality who is described in the third person. This is clearly the "Newcomer" of the title, but who is he? The reference in the second strophe to the Angelus, the thrice-daily prayer in which Catholics reiterate the angels' greeting at the Nativity, would seem to connect him with Christ. Yet in the last stanza of the same lyric we have a note of ardent rejection aimed at the heavenly host:

> Anna of the panel oblongs
> Protect me
> from them fucking angels;
> (*Labyrinths,* p. 17)

The ambivalent attitude towards Christianity noted in the earlier sections has here reached extremes. The fragmented syntax of the fourth strophe merely reinforces the impression, not merely of ambivalence, but of thematic muddle. It is with relief that we turn to the limpid clarity of "For Georgette," which reads as a wedding anthem or song to the spring, very reminiscent in atmosphere to the *Song of Solomon,* in which a bridegroom is addressed in similar terms. However, this has hardly solved the problem, since, though in mediaeval theology Christ was often seen as the bridegroom of the church, the link with the thematic concerns of the rest of *Heavensgate* still seems slender. The sense of dissatisfaction we feel was clearly shared by Okigbo himself, since this section was subjected to drastic alteration, one whole poem (addressed to the Welsh poet Peter Thomas) having been excised, and the very last lyric (which in some versions is entitled "Bridge"), having moved position from the beginning to the end. The probable truth is that, as the scattered sub-titles suggest, these are occasional pieces which the young poet attempted to bring within the frame of a culminating movement, but which failed ultimately to cohere.

There is just one element in "Newcomer" which proves of importance, as it enables us to make sense of an insistent strand that runs through the whole of *Labyrinths.* This is the description of the poet in the very first line of "Bridge" as "standing above the noontide." Here the poet clearly envisages himself as the sun, a possible rival to the lunar presence of the muse who right at the end of *Heavensgate* he would seem to have supplanted. A look at the mythological antecedents of *Heavensgate* places this in context. In his Introduction Okigbo refers to the poet-celebrant as "a personage like Orpheus" (*Labyrinths,* p. xi). The fact that he later comes to be associated with the sun refers us straight to a common version of the Orpheus myth, quoted here by Eratosthenes of Alexandria: "Orpheus believed the sun, who he named Apollo, to be the greatest of the gods. Rising up in the night he ascended before dawn to the mountain called Pangaeum that he might see the sun first. At which Dionysus, being enraged, sent against him the Bassarids who tore him in pieces."[14]

The Bassarids were the Maenads whose possession by the god Dionysus caused so much trouble in Euripides' *The Bacchae,* and their fatal rage against Orpheus was caused by the fact that his new-found devotion to the sun was an act of disloyalty to the moon goddess whom he had previously worshipped. Thus here, right at the heart of *Heavensgate,* we have a reference to the supplanting of a moon by a sun cult, a theme which proves to be of fundamental relevance to Okigbo's three following sequences. It is thus not for nothing that Okigbo called this last poem a "bridge," though Theroux's comparison of it to a solo bridge passage in jazz is also germane.[15]

It would be an error to see the opening of *Limits* as in any way continuous with *Heavensgate,* yet there are many factors which connect them. Indeed much of the thematic structure of *Limits,* which has never been satisfactorily construed, concerns preoccupations which run through from *Heavensgate* and, above all, the central trio of poet / protagonist, mistress / muse, and a third masculine figure who is only, however, properly identified in the new sequence. Again, the ascription in the very opening lines to the hero of *Limits* of a prattling loquaciousness, "suddenly become talkative / like weaverbird," would seem to connect him sardonically with Orpheus, drunk with song. The mistress / muse appears in the last strophe of the same lyric, and *Limits* II sees the entrance of a male rival who is once again identified with Christ in a passage which recalls the Messianic prophecy of Isaiah 53:

> For he was a shrub among the poplars,
> Needing more roots
> More sap to grow to sunlight,
> Thirsting for sunlight.
>
> (*Labyrinths,* p. 24)

The consistency of this triple scenario both in *Limits* and in the remaining portions of *Labyrinths* is too remarkable to be merely coincidental, and demands explanation in terms which will satisfy our sense of Okigbo's stability of vision, grounded as it was in a firm grasp of classical and African mythology.

As previously mentioned, there is a clear parity between the triumvirate of *Labyrinths* and the trio of personages which occur in Robert Graves's theory of poetic ancestry articulated in *The White Goddess.* All true poetry, claims Graves, is written in a state of trance induced by the poet's recollection, conscious or unconscious, of an ancient mythological theme, which is to be found in various forms in Celtic, Babylonian, Greek and African folklore:

> The theme, briefly, is the antique story . . . of the birth, life, death and resurrection of the god of the waxing year; the central chapter concerns the god's losing battle with the god of the waning year for love of the capricious and all-powerful Threefold Goddess, their mother, bride and layer-out. The poet identifies himself with the god of the waxing year and his Muse with the Goddess; the rival is his blood-brother, his other self, his weird. All true poetry . . . celebrates some incident or scene in this very ancient story.[16]

The mythological scheme here suggested enables us to make sense of a number of facets of *Limits* that otherwise might perplex the reader: the intrusion of a third party with whom the poet both does and does not identify, the nameless threat under which the poet seems to be languishing, and the ambiguous place of the triple queen in his affections. Taken together with the theme of the obliteration of the moon by a sun cult already proposed, this helps us to tie together many of the loose ends in *Limits*. If the poet-protagonist, who is in love with the moon goddess, is identified with the waxing year, then his destruction at the hands of a rival associated with the rising sun comes to seem a fitting conclusion to a projected tussle between two religious systems. Moreover, if the rival, who is related to Christ, is seen as the agent or accomplice of the sun cult, then we add a significant dimension: the ascendancy of a male-orientated, sun-inspired religion coincides with the usurpation of the ancient shrines by Christianity. This is precisely the theme explicitly spelled out in "Fragments out of the Deluge," the second half of *Limits*.

Armed with this scheme we can begin to make sense of the various sections of the sequence. *Limits* I expresses the gratitude of the poet-protagonist to Idoto, his muse and queen, to whom as "he-goat-on-heat" he is sexually bonded, for her progressive enlightenment of his condition. In *Limits* II his attention is distracted by the appearance of his *alter persona,* a Christ-like figure whose evident isolation and need to communicate attract him. This person is, however, literally his weird or fate. Despite a superficial appearance of weakness (shared incidentally by the missionaries on their first appearance), his sun is potentially in the ascendant, and the lyric which introduces him ends on a note of menace, an acrid smell of Armageddon:

> Horsemen of the apocalypse;
>
> And crowned with one self
> The name displays its foliage,
> Hanging low
>
> A green cloud above the forest.
> (*Labyrinths,* p. 24)

*Limits* III corresponds to a moment of confusion, a mingling of dissonant voices, as the insistent claims of the poet and rival clash:

> And this is the crisis point
> The twilight moment between
> Sleep and waking
> (*Labyrinths,* p. 25)

The stealthy advance of the rival cult is as muted as a cat's paw, and, in the "dust of combat" the poet mistakes the rival's voice for his own, so that their voices appear stifled by a similar constraint:

> Then we must sing, tongue-tied,
> Without name or audience,
> Making harmony among the branches.
> (*Labyrinths,* p. 25)

In a desperate attempt at rededication to the traditional gods, the poet undertakes a pilgrimage to the Sacred Cable Point at Asaba, but "the dream wakes / the voice fades," and the protagonist is finally left with a lucid sense of his own downfall.

Though this scheme may seem over-tidy, there is no doubt that, at the end of "Siren Limits," the sense of personal eclipse is complete. The "image" of the loved Goddess in the first strophe of *Limits* II is evidently a memory, and much of the poignancy of that lyric comes from a strong sense of loss and failure. The closing lines find the poet, like the evening sky of Eliot's *Prufrock,* etherized upon a table, stunned it would appear by a recollection of his mistress's fragrance. As he metaphorically loses consciousness, he brings the lid down on his own creative effort, thus signalling in the reign of the predators in "Fragments Out of the Deluge," whose sacrificial victim he has become:

> When you have finished
> & done up my stitches,
> Wake me near the altar,
> & this poem will be finished . . .
> (*Labyrinths,* p. 27)

The morbidity of the close here is given graphic shape by the use of one stark visual image, a hideous embodiment of the act of self-immolation. Indeed, if the poetry of *Limits* marks an advance on that of *Heavensgate* it is by reason of the superior potency of its visual appeal, and much of it can be absorbed on first reading at the level of a series of vivid tableaux. At the beginning of "Fragments Out of the Deluge," for instance, we are transported to the exotic surroundings of an Egyptian tomb where a "beast" is still licking its chops after making a meal of the poet's corpse. The horror of this image is heightened when we appreciate that the sarcophagus stone was originally selected as a coffin-making material by the Greeks in the belief that it had the power to devour the flesh deposited within it. Okigbo's own footnotes to this section direct our attention to its underlying mythological significance. The poet-hero here is depicted as Gilgamesh "legendary king of Uruk in Mesopotamia" and the beast is promptly identified as "the lioness of *Limits* IV who destroyed the hero's second self" (*Labyrinths,* p. 28). We further learn that this second-self is none other than Enkidu, who in the ancient Babylonian *Epic of Gilgamesh* features as the king-hero's companion and shadow-self who, after his downfall and death at the hands of the revengeful goddess Ishtar, becomes the object of Gilgamesh's frenetic, bereaved search.

There are obviously a whole host of implications to be picked up here. If we are right in connecting the lioness with Ishtar, the goddess's slightly ghoulish carnality represents one aspect of her personality since it was commonly held that Ishtar had two principal characteristics: she was both the compassionate mother goddess and the lustful goddess of sex and war. Identified in the ancient world with Isis, the Egyptian moon-goddess, and, by extension, with the Graeco-Roman figures of Artemis, Aphrodite and Hera, she has already appeared in *Heavensgate* in her alternative rôle as the nurse of the poet's nascent talent. It is on her ruthless destructiveness, however, that the *Epic of Gilgamesh* itself concentrates. Here, for instance, is the complaint of Gilgamesh, as, disturbed by the goddess's attentions, he catalogues the long list of her amorous victims:

> For Tammuz, thy youthful husband,
> Thou has decreed wailing year after year.
> The variegated roller thou didst love
> Yet thou didst smite him and break his wing.
> Now he stands in the graves, crying "Kappi!"
> Thou didst love the lion perfect in strength
> But thou didst dig for him seven and yet seven pits.[17]

The love of Ishtar for her ill-fated young consort Tammuz represents, as we shall see, one major strand running through *Silences,* yet suffice it to note here that, in the context of *Limits,* Ishtar supplies the female component of the human-cum-comic triangle already mentioned as a structural element in the total sequence. The two male protagonists coincide, in this case, with Gilgamesh and Enkidu, the blood brothers depicted in the *Epic of Gilgamesh.* Thus at this point Okigbo would seem to have conflated two myths, the legend of a love triangle surrounding the fickle affections of a goddess who destroys one lover that she may enjoy a second, and the saga of Gilgamesh with its portrayal of two male friends locked in eternal bonds of loyalty. The second of the friends then comes to stand for none other than the rival who re-enters in *Limits* VI and appears in the guise of both Christ and Enkidu. There is a strong flavour once again of Isaiah's prophecy, already echoed in *Limits* II, and the italicized refrain which serves for the second verse paragraph is also redolent of Matthew 6:27 and Luke 4:24. Yet Enkidu is clearly intended in the references to the forced training which the hero undergoes, since the domestication of Enkidu, originally a wild man of the plains, is a dominant theme of the second tablet of *Gilgamesh.* With his acceptance into the royal household of Uruk, Enkidu enjoyed a brief period of ascendancy, evoked in *Limits* VII, where the rising star of a male rival is associated with the spread of alien belief associated in Africa with the arrival of Christian, and, in the case of Igboland, more specifically Catholic, missionaries. The section then ends appropriately with the vision of an Igbo village in flames, introducing a suggestion of violence taken up in the next lyric where colonial intervention is described in terms of a military attack or—prophetically as it happens—of an air raid. To view this episode objectively and dispassionately is clearly impossible and hence it is rendered in the form of a lament delivered by Nwanza the sunbird who is, as Anozie reminds us, among the most powerful of Igbo religious symbols, and hence a likely focus for proselytizing attack. The inevitable terror of her attitude is distanced in *Limits* X, where the same incident is described retrospectively in the past tense. The continuity here, however, is broken by a short interlude at *Limits* IX where the cries of a blind dog, known for its prophetic skill, take us at once forward to a vision of menacing desolation and backward to a dimly recalled memory of Okigbo's childhood nurse who herself seems to merge imaginatively both with the threatened sunbird and with the softer aspects of the goddess's personality. Does this composite female persona here fear the possibility of her own destruction? The penultimate stanza of *Limits* X, where the devastation of the traditional shrines is related to the dwindling of Irkalla, Sumerian goddess of the underworld, would seem to give substance to such an interpretation. Moreover, there is a clear reference throughout these closing sections to the growth of a male-orientated sun cult at odds with the lunar influence of the goddess, who, through Eunice her mouthpiece, gives a clear indication of her personal anxiety at the spreading of solar supremacy:

> Give him no chair, they say,
> The dawn's charioteer,
> Riding with the angry stars
> Toward the great sunshine.
> (*Labyrinths,* p. 32)

By *Limits* XI the sacred shrines lie deserted, bereft both of official praise and the dignity of office, honoured only by the muffled strains of the poet and the chirping memory of the sunbird who, as the sequence draws to a close, calls our attention to the humiliation of another great people, the Spanish insurgents of Guernica who suffered a similar baptism of fire in the Civil War. Here allusion and prognosis fuse, for the reference to Picasso's canvas of 1937 brings us up against the perennial violence of every age at the very moment at which it highlights the plight of the Igbo, poised, as Okigbo wrote, a mere three years away from the first bombing raids on Enugu.

Okigbo clearly regarded the double sequence *Silences* as transitional between *Limits* and *Distances.* There are several clear senses in which this is the case. First, it marks a temporary recession from the first person singular, consisting as it does of a couple of highly ritualized lamentations in choric style. Secondly, whereas the programme of *Limits* delineates a downward curve, ending at a point of bleak self-annihilation, and that of *Distances* an upward curve towards self-restoration, *Silences,* which occupies the lowest point, represents an attempt to come to terms with the tragic condition. It is best considered in the light of two tragic odes, of the kind which the Athenian dramatists employed to comment on the action of their tragedies, and with which Okigbo, as a student of the classics would have been familiar. Each sub-sequence is scored for a distinctive ensemble which plays the part of a choric commentator on a central tragic incident. The "Silent Sisters," as Okigbo reminds us, recall both the Sirènes, of Debussy's third Nocturne and the drowning Franciscan nuns in Hopkins's *Wreck of the Deutschland.* They also function, however, as a chorus of village women whose rôle as observers and sufferers recall the choruses of Attic tragedy. The drums endorse their incantation with reverberations which resound with the accents of the long dead: they are the ancestors commenting on the world of the living. In both cases, however, the archetypal tragic event is classical and the same: the decease of Tammuz, lover of the goddess Ishtar, god of the waxing and of the waning year. Like Adonis, Tammuz was said to die each winter and to be reborn with the spring: he thus represents both rivals portrayed in the *Limits* sequence, both the discarded lover and the one who will supplant him. It is thus in a very direct sense that *Silences* comments on the aftermath of *Limits* to which, in one sense, it may be regarded as an epilogue. The climax of the sequence, to which both phases of it ascend, occurs in the closing section of "Lament of the Drums," where the quotations in italics consist, in slightly reworded form, of extracts from the "Lament of the Flutes of Tammuz" quoted by Sir James Frazer near the beginning of his volume on *Adonis, Attis and Osiris* from *The Golden Bough.*[18] Frazer's commentary provides us with a vivid account of the original context:

> His death appears to have been annually mourned, to the shrill music of flutes, by men and women about midsummer in the month named after him, the month of Tammuz. The dirges were seemingly chanted over an effigy of the dead god, which they washed with pure water, anointed with oil, and clad in a red robe, while the fumes of incense rose into the air, as if to stir the dormant senses by their pungent fragrance and wake him from the sleep of death.[19]

Extending the argument, it is possible to infer that, since Tammuz's death is associated with the transition between the phases of the waning and waxing year central to the mythology of *Limits* where it is associated with the supplanting of a sun for a moon cult, and hence with the usurpation by militant Catholic Christianity of the sanctity of the old shrines, then the pivotal calamity of *Silences* can be identified with the historical hiatus featured in "Fragments Out of the Deluge." This, however, is to take its political dimensions as all embracing. In fact, the true theme of *Silences* runs far deeper than any such précis might suggest.

The real theme of *Silences,* succinctly stated, is the triumph of the authentic tragic consciousness over the demeaning facts of decay and death.

"Tragic" here must be taken to mean "congruent with the spirit of Greek tragedy," yet, in order to explain to himself the mode of its operation, Okigbo has drawn wider in his understanding of the tragic condition. His main source, apart from the Greeks, is a set of remarks on tragic awareness contained in a letter from Herman Melville to Nathaniel Hawthorne (written when they were close neighbours in New England), a line of which Okigbo quotes as two strategically important points. Melville's letter, a fulsome and rather ingratiating one, written in acknowledgement of a gift to him of Hawthorne's *House of the Seven Gables,* ends by ascribing to the elder author a special kind of authorial courage, the sort which, refusing the blandishments and easy comforts of political or religious ideology, manages to stare the tragic facts of human existence straight in the face and to exult in the very teeth of their negativism. It is this ability to transcend superficial and assertive palliatives for human suffering by the power of the undiluted creative will which Okigbo sees as the mainstay of the tragic sense, and which simultaneously appealed to that side of his nature which, at least in 1964, was so deeply suspicious of the ideological stances associated with cultural nationalism, *négritude,* and opportunistic Marxism. The last paragraph of Melville's letter is worth quoting in full:

> There is the grand truth about Nathaniel Hawthorne. He says NO! in thunder; but the Devil himself cannot make him say *yes.* For all men who say *yes,* lie; and all men who say *no*—why, they are in the happy condition of judicious, unencumbered travellers in Europe; they cross the frontiers into Eternity with nothing but a carpet-bag—that is to say, the Ego. Whereas those *yes*-gentry, they travel with heaps of baggage, and, damn them! they will never get through the Custom House. What's the reason, Mr Hawthorne, that in the last stages of metaphysics a fellow always falls to *swearing* so? I could rip an hour. You see, I began with a little criticism extracted for your benefit from the *Pittsfield Secret Review,* and here I have landed in Africa.[20]

Melville's distrust of yes-saying ideologues, and his preference for those who are able to thrive on the bleakness of the philosophical "no" is central to Okigbo's vision in *Silences.* In his Introduction he states that the "Lament of the Silent Sisters" was partly inspired by the death of Patrice Lumumba, first prime minister of Zaïre, killed by competing ideological interests. Lumumba had been in one sense a victim of Tshombe's Katangese secession of 1960, in another the victim of foreign interests masquerading under the disguise of a political programme. Okigbo prefers to see him as the victim of narrow thinking, of ideological systems promulgated by those who say "yes" too shrilly and wrongheadedly. Thus not only does he feature, like Tammuz, as a tragic protagonist, but also, like the Christ whose fate his recalls, as the prey of unscrupulous and shallow interests:

> They struck him in the ear they struck him in the eye;
> They picked his bones for scavenging:
>
> (*Labyrinths*, p. 40)

The allusions to Christ the pascal lamb may seem odd in the context of a poem partially concerned with bewailing the trampling by his followers over African religious susceptibilities. The texture of *Silences,* however, reveals other Christian elements. In their capacity as drowning Franciscan nuns the Silent Sisters begin by invoking the crucifix:

> The cross to us we still call to us,
> In this jubilee dance above the carrion
>
> (*Labyrinths*, p. 39)

The redemptive processes of Christianity are therefore revealed as one strand in the tragic exultation through which the Sisters affirm the victory of life over death, joy over suffering. In the choral antiphon which constitutes the last section of "Lament of the Silent Sisters," the chorus invokes the contours of Gothic ecclesiastical architecture:

> Pointed arches:
> Pieces in the form of a pear
>
> (*Labyrinths,* p. 43)

*Pointed Arches* was the title of Okigbo's projected work on the aesthetics of poetry on which he was engaged when felled in action. All of these allusions suggest that while, on the simplest polemical level, Christianity is condemned as the violator of traditional African Sanctity, at another, higher level it is seen as one element in an inclusive higher religious consciousness, bordering on the tragic sense, which is continually held at bay by the forces of intellectual and political bigotry. It is in this light that the extracts from Ishtar's lament for Tammuz quoted in Section V of "Lament of the Drums" can be viewed, not so much as a dirge for the passing of traditional Igbo religious certainties as a lament for the dwindling of the totality of man's spirituality in the face of ruthless and prejudiced forces.

Armed with these observations on the overall scheme of *Silences,* we can now turn to examine the individual sections. The fragmented and storm-tossed syntax of the opening strains of "Lament of the Silent Sisters" evokes a state of chaos and panic in which the mind gropes after consoling certainties, such as those offered by the Christian crucifix. These offer a "difference" rather than an escape ladder because, though supplying an explanation for the necessity of suffering, they supply no means of avoidance. Suffering has to be lived through, whether in the berth of a sinking ship or in the perturbations of the religious vocation. The intervention of the chorus in paragraph five reminds us for the first time of the threatening forces of ideological restraint, associated at this stage with the predators of "Fragments Out of the Deluge." Yet the chorus leader is not distracted in his task of leading the intoxicated dance and ode in which the worshippers in a manner reminiscent of the choruses of Attic tragedy, celebrate the triumph of the tragic spirit over the reality of death; "this jubilee dance above the carrion."

In Section II the chorus identifies itself more clearly with a group of village women bound for the communal well, their classic lament merging with the strains of a traditional Igbo dirge. Their opening statement harks back to the previous section, in its concern with the celebratory power of music and dance over the fact of death, and its reiteration of the nightmare of violent oppression. Moloch was the Carthaginian sun god to whom devotees fed their firstborn in an attempt to placate his wrath. His presence reminds us of the persistence of a male sun cult in the midst of the traditional feminine mysteries: the Sister's cry is both to Moloch (to save them from immolation) and on behalf of Moloch (as a gesture of further religious integration). The grammar of the last sentence of Section II and the opening lines of Section III is continuous, as the plaintive sentiments of the latter represent the burden of the Sisters' complaint. Silence here is regarded as the consummation of music. The Sisters are "dumb" because they neither speak nor sing; yet this very silence is more eloquent of memory, regret and determination than the "shriek" torn from them by the menacing "shadows" of circumstance. The shadows are compared to the "long-fingered winds" which, in the following section, also continuous with the foregoing, reappear as the "wild winds" which "cry out against us." The Sisters' only defence, once again, lies in their silence, which, like the rainbow and the sea's froth, offers an infinity of chromatic shading.

Much attention is paid to form in these sections. Section III is for full chorus with an occasional interpolation by the leader in the form of a refrain. Sections IV and V are antiphons proper: that is, the leader and his acolytes speak alternately, sharing the burden and privilege of statement. There is also a progression of theme: Section IV contents itself with an analysis of the subtle nuances of "silence" as a weapon against misfortune, while Section V concerns itself more positively with the transcendental power of art, the "Pointed arches: / pieces in the form of a pear" to which all poetry aspires. This power is of a kind to transform and subsume all tragic manifestations: even Judas Iscariot here numbers magnificently amongst the performers of the choric dance. In the true and absolute silence that lies beyond achieved artistic statement all lesser forms and means of expression, the constituent "melodies" which make up the final tranquillity, fall into place and can be observed nostalgically in long-view:

> Silences are melodies
> Heard in retrospect:
> (*Labyrinths*, p. 43)

The effect of this turn of thought is to transform the context of the quotation from Melville's letter, so that when the question appears for the second time it seems to have accumulated its own answer: the finest way to assert the power that lies beyond negativity, to "say NO in thunder," is to keep one's peace. Frenetic assertion of an attitude is of no use here. What is required of the artist, as of the truly tragic spirit, is to keep counsel with his own inspiration, to dig deep down into the resources of the personality so as to tap the inner serenity into which all effort and all expression ultimately reaches. In the closing lines of Section V the miracle of the tragic exultation which conquers despair is explained as an achievement of the complete human personality at ease with itself.

"Lament of the Drums" also celebrates the tragic event, but from a different angle, and largely in prospect. Lyric V finds the drummers limbering up for their performance, invoking the various materials that go towards the construction of their instruments in a manner characteristic of a number of West African drum literatures, Igbo, Yoruba and Akan. They also aim to keep at a distance the tragic facts of dissolution which underlie the impending catastrophe ("Thunder of tanks of giant iron steps of detonators") but the effort is inevitably frustrated, and Section II finds them in full spate proclaiming the sacrifice which will be necessary to lend full savour to the threatening disaster. Okigbo says somewhat tantalizingly in his Introduction of 1965 that "Babylonian capture," "martyrdom" and "chaliced vintage" suggest that someone may have been betrayed by his disciples. Certainly the Christian liturgical element is there, underpinning the wealth of traditional Igbo references. Yet an earlier paragraph suggests that he had something much more specific in mind, namely the incarceration of Obafemi Awolowo, the first premier of Nigeria's Western Region, in September 1963 on charges of attempting to undermine the Federal leadership, and his desertion in his hour of distress by such as Chief Akintola, the deputy whom he had left in charge of regional politics while he fought his campaign at the national level. Thus Awolowo joins Patrice Lumumba, Tammuz and Christ to form a pantheon of tragic figures whose demise the drums, as the Sisters before them, lament. They are joined, at the beginning of Lyric III by Palinurus, Aeneas' homesick helmsman in his voyage across the Mediterranean back from Troy, who, washed ashore near Velia after three days' exposure at sea, was cruelly murdered by the local inhabitants and left unburied on the foreshore. He hence wanders for ever in a limbo of non-entity, far from the comforts of interment and the safe port of entry into Hades. The whole of Lyric III is a lament for his fate, half-elegy and half-recreation of that hideous state of non-being endured only by those disowned by all of their fellows, journeying endlessly. As such, in his unredeemed condition, Palinurus is prey to the full force of divine vengeance, operated on by the infernal agency of the harpies, weird ravenous creatures with women's faces who hound him down under the eye of the vengeful Calaeno, daughter of Neptune and Terra. He is thus a perfect subject for the "Lament of the Drums" in their sacrificial plea for mercy and divine forgiveness. The possibility of release from the prison of endless torment, wished upon Palinurus by his master Aeneas during a visit to him in the underworld in *Aeneid* VI, leads us on to the limpid beauty of lines 19 and 20 of this matchless lyric:

> Tears of grace, not of sorrow, broken
> In two, protest your inviolable image.
> (*Labyrinths,* p. 47)

The tears are of grace because the drums, in their sacrificial, cleansing function, have worked the miracle of ultimate release from divine displeasure. Their music is thus an act of grace. The tears are hence broken in two, and each half bears etched on its trembling surface a permanent picture of Palinurus in his lasting significance as redeemed victim. These lines give an extra poignancy to the previous paragraph's "It is over, Palinurus, at least for you": for Palinurus, life is over, but so, at last, is Purgatory.

The Palinurus motif, in its insistence on the final power of grace, leads us quite naturally on to the next section in which the drums thunder out once more in an ecstasy of complaint, only to be rebuked by a conciliatory note which informs us that the shrill hysteria of full-throated protest ("our rococo / choir of insects") is powerless beside the still, sad music of antiphonal understatement. This takes us once more back to the calm of the conclusion of the "Lament of the Silent Sisters" to which this verse is evidently an allusion. As *Silences* rises to its culmination, Sisters and drums join their voices in one common hymn of praise which blends with the inherited strains of Ishtar's lament for Tammuz, in which the Babylonian god, victim of his mistress's lust and destructiveness, is coaxed back to life with the seductive, gentle inflections of the flutes. The quotation from the Babylonian hymn, which has an important historical connection with the text of the *Epic of Gilgamesh* so important to *Limits,* constitutes, as Okigbo puts it, a "variation" in rephrased language on the "Lament of the Flutes of Tammuz," translated for the general reader in James Frazer's *The Golden Bough.* Despite its heart-breaking solemnity it is a song of hope: Tammuz will rise from the dead, the shrubs will flower, the fields, the river and the men come back to life. In this rapt moment of tragic invocation, we have a perfect distillation of that power, shared by mystic and artist alike, to triumph over sheer negativity, which Okigbo found so appealing in Melville's comments in his letter to Hawthorne. Only one discordant note intrudes, in the concluding couplet, in which the "pot-bellied watchers," the overfed ministrants of the shrine, are admonished for their cupidity and greed which, going unchecked, will ruin the redemptive process once again. In this word of warning, seemingly out of place in the calm of the close, lies one of the few sinister political overtones of *Silences,* a reference back to the wholesale destruction of "Fragments Out of the Deluge" and a foreboding of the holocaust to come in the yet unwritten "Path of Thunder."

Okigbo left us two distinct clues to the interpretation of *Distances.* The first is its integral relationship with the sequence which precedes *Silences,* namely *Limits,* to which it affords an inner, psychological equivalent; the second being its origin in the experience of undergoing surgery. It is quite plain that, on a simple narrative level, the whole piece may be read as a literal description of the mind's turmoil during a course of anaesthesia. Section I finds the poet prostrate on the surgery table, looking up at the immense lamps hanging above him ("serene lights on the other balcony"). As the anaesthetic takes hold he drifts off into a world of phantasy in which he joins a procession of pilgrims from an island where "death lay in ambush," through a lintel over which hangs a magic inscription, and into an inner sanctum where he experiences a complete, and possibly erotic, possession of the goddess whom he had sought throughout *Limits.* It would be wrong, however, to see this as nothing but phantasy: the journey has its symbolic connotations, and, though *Distances* is mythologically less dense than the earlier sequence, opens out on to a world of cosmological cultural reference.

Section I, I would suggest, finds the poet in the same abject position as that described in *Limits* V, though there he was stretched out in the tomb, here on a "horizontal slab" which, while recalling the "empty sarcophagus" of the earlier piece, seems also to hold out the possibility of resurrection. It is interesting that Okigbo interdisperses the lyrics of this sequence with the line "I was the sole witness to my homecoming," thus seeing the whole process in optimistic long-shot. Unlike *Limits, Distances* is to be read as a song of hope and rejoicing. As such it takes its lead from the relative positiveness of the closing lines of *Silences,* in which Tammuz's revival seems imminent; it can even, like *Heavensgate* before it, be regarded as an Easter sequence. On the symbolic level the "lights on the other balcony" are clearly those of Heaven, but before he reaches them the poet must experience entry into the underworld of fear and death, the "dark labyrinth" that leads eventually out into the clear light of day. In this journey the poet is both pilgrim and onlooker, simultaneously involved, and, in a manner very typical of dream experience, completely detached from the process. It is in the latter capacity that, in the closing lines of Section I, he addresses his own voice as it sings the liturgy of self-immolation and renewal:

> Miner into my solitude,
> incarnate voice of the dream,
> you will go,
> with me as your chief acolyte,
> again into the anti-hill . . .

Section II finds us straight away plunged into the nightmare world of a *danse macabre* presided over by "Death herself, the chief celebrant," seen as a murderous woman whose blood-lust reeks of the goddess's less savoury characteristics. It is a black mass, attended by incense, flesh and blood, in which the poet features as the member of a band of travellers, trapped on the island, hounded by fear of "such great events" and talking incessantly to keep their spirits up. He is also one of the allotted sacrificial victims tied to a slab. (The link between this and fears induced by a surgical operation is straightfor-ward.) The splitting of personal identity here is another feature of the dream, but also reflects the symbolic ambivalence of the poet's meaning, since he is concerned to see himself both as forfeit to death and destruction and as capa-ble of rising above these limitations. He will only achieve this, however, if he subjects himself to a long process of initiation, and Section III finds him again as one of the select band of pilgrims bound "from Dan to Beersheba," the for-mula used, in the Books of Judges and Samuel, to describe the outer limits of the Kingdom of Israel.[21] The reference to Shibboleth in the first stanza is also to the Book of Judges, this time to the incident described in the twelfth chap-ter, in which Jephthah, in an attempt to distinguish his own people, the Gil-leadites, from the fleeing Ephraimites, used the pass-word "Shibboleth" whose soft opening syllable the enemy could not pronounce. Both allusions fix the idea of an utter exclusiveness reinforced by the use of special emblems: the crucifix, the censer, the medicaments of camphor and iodine. The poet then is numbered amongst a unique band of postulants whose way lies up stone steps, across a balcony inhabited by the manic and the inspired, to a clearing where, blocking their path, they encounter "dilettanti; / vendors princes negritude," the reincarnations, it would seem of the "brothers and deacons, liberal politicians, selfish self-seekers" who tortured the poet's progress in *Heavensgate*.

At last they reach the inner sanctum, the threshold of which is marked by a sign comprising the three principal geometrical figures: square, circle and triangle. Beyond hang the orbs whose tantalizing presence the poet had observed at the beginning of his quest "on the other balcony." The cryptic phrases of the italicized refrain

> after we had formed
> then only the forms were formed
> and all forms
> were formed after our forming

almost seem to justify Sunday Anozie's account of the sequence as concerned with the number 3, reflected in crucifix, lintel and other recurrent patterns. Anozie, however, builds too elaborate a superstructure on this.[22] The trinitar-ian concept is fundamental to the Christian as to other religions: I can see no more significance in it here than attaches to the Biblical allusions in the previ-ous section, as mystical emblems which enforce the idea of a cult. The poet, it will be remembered, is under an anaesthetic: thus his intimations which in earlier sequences were conveyed by a multiplicity of literary references, here assume a vivid visual shape suggestive of the forms of dream. There is a sense of mystery, and of closed, hermetic codes, culminating in Section V in the posing of "the unanswerable question in the tabernacle's silence." The censers which swing in the sanctuary come "from the cradle / of a nameless religion." The poet is fumbling his way towards a truth which he cannot articulate, and which certainly does not attach itself immediately to any of the great recognizable religious systems. This accounts, I believe, for the surrealistic method of Lyric V with its intriguing references to "sweat over hoof in ascending gestures" and "the question in the inkwell." The general shape of events is clear enough: the poet, possibly mounted, like Christ, on a donkey, is ascending the steps of a shrine, which, when he enters, shimmers with light and water. The refrain "each sign is the stillness of the kiss" takes us back to the language of "Lament of the Silent Sisters." Clearly, just as in that sequence, silence was the consummation of music, so here the intimacies of a kiss, imprinted perhaps on the goddess's at last receptive body, is the culmination of the religious rite. There are other side glances at the possible sexual nature of this final reunion, as in the words "mated and sealed / in a proud oblation," as if, in making love to the goddess, the poet has redeemed himself from the taint of sin and death which earlier encumbered him. Yet the distance set between this and any recognizable theology is emphasized by such lines as "the burden of the pawn" and "the scar of the kiss and of the two swords," where Okigbo seems to be constructing his own myth, not surprisingly in this freely floating world of dream, the irrationality of which reaches its climax at the end of this section.

Section VI, by contrast, discovers the poet coming back to consciousness and reassembling his bearings. "Homecoming" here carries, among other connotations, the simple sense of growing lucidity to one's surroundings. As his external circumstances sort themselves out, so the poet begins to make sense of the wild *pot-pourri* of myth, emblem and phantasy which has accompanied him on his inner voyage. Where the previous section emphasized discrepancy, diversity and imagistic innovation, the stress here is on the reconciling homogeneity of all myth:

> For it is the same blood,
> through the same orifices,
> the same branches
> and the same faces
> trembling, intertwined
> in the interspaces.
> (*Labyrinths*, p. 59)

Thus the "proud oblation" of the previous section blends itself with the redemptive processes of other great religions, including the Hebraic and Christian. The call of the goddess becomes recognizably that of the inscrutable lady in Eliot's early poem "La Figlia Che Piange":

> Stand on the highest pavement of the stair—
> Lean on a garden urn—
> Weave, weave the sunlight in your hair—[23]

Gradually the elements of the dream sort themselves out: the season (which is also the season of Tammuz's uprising), the tall wood in which the politicians lower, the stone steps to the altar, the dark labyrinths of the poet's passage, the oblong inscribed above the lintel to the shrine. It is a kind of resumé, but also an act of recognition. And the culmination of this progressive enlightenment is the poet's delighted identification of his mistress, embraced in the enchanted recesses of the shrine, with the white queen, for whom he had previously felt a chaste dedication. Only when he has recognized both her and rites attending her is he free at last to recognize himself in his new state of spiritual apotheosis:

> I am the sole witness to my homecoming
> (*Labyrinths*, p. 60)

With this line we reach the conclusion of *Labyrinths* as originally evisaged in the revisions of 1965. The Heinemann volume, however, goes on to include a further sequence, written in the aftermath of the first 1966 *coup*, and published posthumously, called *Path of Thunder*. Sunday Anozie, in the monograph published five years after Okigbo's death, devotes much space to a discussion as to whether the eventual decision to publish these two rather different works in one volume was justified. His reasons for deciding against—that Okigbo had clearly come to the end of one phase of his development and was about to start another; that the poetic language of *Path of Thunder* is in a different register and addresses itself to different ends—seem cogent enough. *Path of Thunder* can clearly be viewed in two ways: as an immediate response to the political crisis of 1966 and as a further, and as it happened final, stage in the evolution of Okigbo's *oeuvre*. I have chosen here to postpone a discussion of the poem's political ramifications until chapter 10, preferring to concentrate in the present chapter on the extent to which this last sequence may be interpreted as an outcrop and extension of the earlier work.

First, I think that we have to consider the meaning of Okigbo's concluding statement at the end of *Distances:* to what does this state of homecoming correspond? A nebulous answer could be returned: a state of spiritual perfectedness perhaps, or a state of grace. However, if we consider the statement, not merely in the context of *Distances* alone, but of *Labyrinths* as a whole, I think we may elicit the more positive answer that he has returned precisely to the geographical and vocational circumstances evoked at the very beginning of *Heavensgate:*

> BEFORE YOU, mother Idoto,
> naked I stand;
> before your watery presence.

Idoto, as we have already seen, was the riverside goddess whom Okigbo's grandfather served as priest and whose ministry he himself was expected to inherit. In other words, Okigbo has returned to his ancestral state of priesthood. And this leaves him with the pressing problem of his function. What is the best and most effective way, in the context of modern Nigeria, to serve the ancient gods and hence render an honest account of one's ministry? If we turn to *Path of Thunder* written immediately after the eruption of the ominous events of January 1966, we can find one possible answer: to warn, to preach, to exhort. This is the unpopular rôle for which Okigbo has elected, a rôle rife with misunderstandings, but the only one in which he can adequately fulfil his triple initiation, by Kepkanly, by Upandru, by Jadum:

> If I don't learn to shut my mouth I'll soon go to hell,
> I, Okigbo, town-crier, together with my iron bell.

*Path of Thunder* is strident, explicit, outright art: its reiterated images and ritualistic repetitions speak of a state of rapt possession in which a priest, one gifted with divine knowledge, utters his declamations and judgements. It is poetry of foresight and warning: in the full Old Testament sense, poetry of prophecy. Just as the Hebrew prophet Amos warned the people of God that, unless they changed their ways, their city would be made a desolation, so Okigbo is telling his fellow countrymen that, unless they put their house in order, the newly won state of independent Nigeria will fall about their ears. Okigbo is sometimes accused towards the end of his life of having forsaken the primrose path of the pure art and plunged himself into full-blooded political statement and action, degrading his calling in the process. Indeed one extremely fine philosophical novel, Ali Mazrui's *The Trial of Christopher Okigbo* is constructed around a dialectic generated by this view.[24] The most effective riposte to this criticism is that increasingly, as his art matured and the political environment in which he was working swam into finer focus, Okigbo came to see poetry and priesthood as synonymous, and priesthood as constituting a state of possession which, in modern Africa as in traditional Igboland, carried a strong political prerogative.

We have already noted that the constituent poems of *Labyrinths* carry implications of tempo and mood which suggest a musical framework. *Path of Thunder* takes this principle further by envisaging a score for percussion instruments against which it may be performed. Sometimes, as in the very opening lines, the instructions are included in the text:

> Fanfare of drums, wooden bells, iron chapter.

Otherwise, especially in the last two sections, they appear in the titles as suggestions for scoring. Throughout, however, there is a strong implied background supplied by a flexible musical pulse, lending the rolling lines and repeated cadences dignity and weight.

The opening salvo, for instance, *fortissimo,* envisages a holocaust of cataclysmic proportions, conveyed by clashing metal and deep drums. Then at line seven the volume suddenly drops, and we are left surveying a desolate ruined landscape:

> Barbicans alone tell one tale the winds scatter.
> (*Labyrinths,* p. 63)

Gradually the audience fall into place as "hostages" to an occupying army, which is as yet unidentified. Yet of one fact we are assured, that the monumental events described are part of a pattern older than the present crisis, older than the society involved, older even than the written verse or the individual speaking voice. They belong rather to that larger backdrop of legend and myth upon which Okigbo's earlier sequences, and *Limits* in particular, drew so freely:

> Bring them out we say, bring them out
> Faces and hands and feet,
> The stories behind the myth, the plot
> Which the ritual enacts.
> (*Labyrinths,* p. 63)

Seen thus, the precise political context of the present troubles, soon to identify itself as that attending the first Nigerian *coup d'état* of 1966, falls into place as an instance of that ageless history of oppression and betrayal which concerned Okigbo in "Fragments Out of the Deluge." Viewed thus, the connections between *Path of Thunder* and the poetry of *Labyrinths* become increasingly clear.

Meanwhile Okigbo interpolates an interlude, "Elegy of the Wind," which has less to do with the political events under consideration, or with their mythological backdrop, than with the poet's perspective on history. The kernel of the piece is a reworking of Wordsworth's famous lines in "My Heart Leaps Up":

> So was it when my life began
> So is it now that I am a man;
> So be it when I shall grow old
>     Or let me die!
> The Child is father to the Man;
> And I could wish my days to be
> Bound each to each by natural piety.[25]

In Okigbo's variation this becomes:

> The man embodies the child
> The child embodies the man; the man remembers
> The song of the innocent,
> Of the uncircumcised at the sight of the flaming razor—
> The chief priest of the sanctuary has uttered
>   the enchanted words;
> The bleeding phallus,
> Dripping fresh from the carnage cries out
>   for the medicinal leaf . . .
>
> (*Labyrinths*, p. 64–5)

Seen against the Wordsworth original, "Elegy of the Wind" becomes a meditation on innocence and experience. It is organized around two image clusters: one concerning the hard surfaces and sounds of metal; the other, concerning the gentle unforced processes of organic growth. The latter are throughout connected with intimations of childhood which blend fetchingly with the poet's own adult voice. Thus the poet begins with a determination to break the "iron gate" of experience and suffering against the "twin tremulous cotyledons" of his own tender exploratory yearnings. He is a "man of iron throat," who has had, after all, to come to terms with the abrasive facts of experience; yet it has been his constant endeavour to win through the dull blanket of adult conformity to "chlorophyll," to the healing processes which have been his imaginative mainstay since early childhood. In his capacity as perennial child he can afford to relive his early adolescent fear of the "flaming razor," the heated knife which circumcised him, and, in so doing, in crying out for the "medicinal leaf" which serves as a balm for necessary suffering, to find a way through violence, upheaval and pain to the peace that lies beyond. Inevitably he shrinks from the ordeal, from "the narrow neck of the calabash," but a fully mature attitude for him seems to lie in an acceptance of these facts and a transcendence of them. (Once again, links with the wisdom of "Lament of the Silent Sisters" are manifest.) It will be seen here that Okigbo is concerned with *necessary* suffering, just as circumcision is necessary to adult manhood. The implication of this for what is to follow is important. The sufferings of Nigeria during the *coup* are to be viewed, not as an unwarranted interruption of an orderly progress, but as part of an inevitable process of cleansing and renewal without which Nigeria will never be whole.

Consequently the next section "Come Thunder" begins on a welcoming note:

> NOW THAT the triumphal arch has entered the last street corners,
> Remember, O dancers, the thunder among the clouds.
>
> (*Labyrinths*, p. 66)

The reference to thunder takes us back to "Lament of the Silent Sisters," where "to say NO in thunder" was a sign of the acceptance of the negation underlying all experience. Here Okigbo is torn between his advocacy of cleansing violence, "the Lightning beyond the earth," and an irresistible sense of foreboding. Clearly the *coup* is a welcome act of deliverance, yet, once accepted, the way lies through the escalating violence of unprecedented proportions:

> And a great fearful thing already tugs at the cables of the open air,
> A nebula immense and immeasurable, a night of deep waters—
> An iron dream unnamed and unprintable, a path of stone.

Once again the hard, unyielding surfaces of stone, the "iron mask" worn by history, threatens to throttle the unhurried processes of growth which lead to natural, unforced maturity.

In the lyric which follows, "Hurrah for Thunder," the political context of the current crisis comes more clearly into view. The elephant, "tetrarch of the jungle," felled by the caustic intervention of thunder, can be no other than the Federal prime minister, Sir Abubakar Tafawa Balewa, killed on the night of 15 January 1966 by a group of young army officers, inspired by increasing resentment at his régime, at the Eastern / Northern domination of the Federation, and at irregularities in the Western Regional election of 1965. His death is welcomed as a release from his "obduracy," yet, prophet and priest as Okigbo was, he cannot help but warn that this recourse to blood, once accepted and vindicated, may lead to untold consequences which will fall on the heads of the perpetrators.

> But already the hunters are talking about pumpkins:
> If they share the meat let them remember thunder.
> (*Labyrinths,* p. 67)

The following lyric, "Elegy for Slit-drum" is dominated by a tone of ironic celebration. As the civil constitution is rescinded, and soldiers assume the day, the poet indulges in a moment of mock rejoicing:

> parliament has gone on leave
> the members are now on bail
> parliament is now on sale
> the voters are lying in wait—
> (*Labyrinths,* p. 68)

The action of General Aguiyi-Ironsi of taking over the leadership of the *coup* after its successful enactment by junior officers is likewise fêted in lines which, nevertheless, draw attention to the "iron mask" he wears, the same mask as indicated the cruel face of human history in its path of retribution and mutual destruction (prophetically, as it happens, since Ironsi was himself assassinated in a subsequent *coup* that very July):

The General is near the throne
an iron mask covers his face
the General has carried the day
the mortars are far away—
(*Labyrinths,* p. 69)

In the collage of references which follow Okigbo pauses for a perfect
parody of a tabloid headline announcing the collapse at the hands of the military of Britain's carefully promoted legacy of parliamentary democracy:

Jungle tanks blast Britain's last stand—

As the pitch rises, Okigbo warns of an accelerating pace of destruction in
which animal feeds on animal, violence begets violence, and the cleansing
path of thunder widens into a wilderness of destruction.

Then, with the last lyric, envisaged as a slow plaintive lament for alto
saxophone accompanied by the solemn beat of drums, Okigbo comes to the
heart of his message. The growing holocaust which is about to envelope
Nigeria is here seen, less as a new and unforeseen danger, than as the reestablishing of an ancient pattern, the return of those "eagles and "robbers"
who carved so unmistakable a wake of despoliation in the annals of "Fragments Out of the Deluge":

THE EAGLES have come again,
The eagles rain down on us—
(*Labyrinths,* p. 71)

This is one of the earliest entrances into West African poetry of that theme of
neo-colonialism which later was to become such a mainstay of political
lament. Yet even here Okigbo is concerned less with topicality than with an
effort to view the whole process historically as part of that endless cycle of
destruction, renewal and perpetuated strife which has interested him ever
since the outset of *Labyrinths.* As the sequence draws to a close he brings
together threads and images from previous stages of his development in a culminating vision of the "dream" of wholeness and human integrity beset with
forces which would set upon and devour it. And, as, gazing up at the night
sky, he seizes on the image of a pulsing star as a symbol of man's intermittent,
frustrated fumbling for peace, order and fulfillment, it is hard to resist the
conclusion that here he had achieved a definitive vision, not merely of the historical period on which he was commenting, but also of the themes which
inspired his life's work.

Seen thus, Okigbo's *oeuvre* reveals itself as a prolonged meditation on the
processes of decay and renewal, processes with both personal and societal
dimensions which come to the fore at different times. *Heavensgate* concerns
the initiation of a would-be priest into the mysteries of his vocation. In *Limits,*

this development is carried through to a stage at which contradictions begin to emerge. The poet's dedication to his muse leads him into alienation from himself and rivalry with other dedicatees. In historical terms, explored in "Fragments Out of the Deluge," this may involve the appearance of a rival religion whose influence results in the destruction of the very shrines at which the priest ministers. The havoc thus wrought may not be avoided or explained away by complacent and trite systems of thought, whether political or philosophical. The only true poetic response to misfortune is to "say NO in thunder," that is to accept the negation and to thrive upon it. It is to this task that the dual choric ode known as *Silences* addresses itself.

Once reconciled with the facts of suffering, the priest is free to retrace his steps, and, triumphing over death, to meet his divine mistress in an erotic embrace. As *Distances* draws to its conclusion the poet signals his awareness of his homecoming, thus begging the question of the rôle that he is now fit to play. With the final assumption of his priestly mantle, the poet-priest now realizes that it is incumbent on him to warn and to teach. Yet what message can he convey save the experience which he has lived through in his own person? Thus he meditates on the fluctuation between joy and despair, fulfillment and devastation which operates as an invariable law both within the individual and the society which he creates. In *Path of Thunder* the tribulations of contemporary Nigeria come to be viewed as one phase in the pulsing pattern of human history, a sudden but necessary eclipse in the "going and coming that goes on for ever."

To speak thus is to simplify, but it is worth while reminding oneself that Okigbo's preoccupations constitute grand themes which have obsessed poets through the ages. Of all the poets dealt with in this volume Okigbo has the strongest claim to be considered a writer of permanent standing, since, though firmly grounded in the traditions and realities of the region in which he grew up, his talent was of the sort which reaches out and embraces every time and place. He also possessed to a marked degree that authentic poetic *mania,* the spirit which drives an individual to express himself even at the cost of his sanity, life and self-respect. Okigbo is said to have given his life for a political cause. It might be truer to say that he gave his death to Biafra, his life to the creation of some of the most delicate lyrics written in the English language in Africa.

*Notes*

1.   Christopher Okigbo, *Labyrinths with Path of Thunder* (London: Heinemann, 1971). All subsequent page references are to this edition. For convenience the name *Labyrinths,* though strictly confined to the first four sequences only, has been used throughout to signify the volume as a whole.

2.   *A Reader's Guide to African Literature,* eds. Hans Zell and Helene Silver (London: Heinemann, 1st edition, 1972), p. 168.

3.   For individual sequences, cf. "Lament of the Silent Sisters" in *Transition* 8, 1963; "Distances" in No. 16, 1964.

4.   Sunday O. Anozie, *Christopher Okigbo: Creative Rhetoric* (London: Evans, 1972), cf. especially pp. 171–3.

5.   *Ibid.,* pp. 41–2.

6.   *Labyrinths,* p. xi.

7.   Romanus Egudu, "Defence of Culture in the Poetry of Christopher Okigbo" in *African Literature Today,* Vol. 6: *Poetry in Africa* (London: Heinemann, 1973), pp. 26–46.

8.   Anozie, *Christopher Okigbo,* pp. 42–3.

9.   Paul Theroux, "A Study of Six Poets: Voices out of the Skull," *An Introduction to African Literature,* ed. Ulli Beier (London: Longman, 1972), p. 125.

10.   Anozie, *Christopher Okigbo,* p. 45.

11.   *Ibid.,* p. 48.

12.   Cf. Robert Graves, *The White Goddess* (London: Faber, 1948).

13.   Cf. Lucius Apuleius, *The Transformation of Lucius or The Golden Ass,* trans. Robert Graves (London: Penguin, 1950).

14.   *The White Goddess,* p. 92.

15.   Theroux, "Six Poets," p. 127.

16.   *The White Goddess,* p. 24.

17.   Alexander Heidel, *The Gilgamesh Epic and Old Testament Parallels* (Chicago, Illinois: University of Chicago Press, 1946), p. 51.

18.   Sir James Frazer, *The Golden Bough: A Study in Magic and Religion* (London: Macmillan, 3rd edition, 1935–6) V. *Adonis, Attis and Osiris: Studies in the History of Oriental Religion,* Vol. 1, pp. 9–11.

19.   *Ibid.* I have quoted the extract at length in "Christopher Okigbo and the Flutes of Tammuz" in *A Sense of Place,* ed. Britta Olinder (University of Gothenburg, 1984), pp. 191–2. Another version of the Lament, in some respects closer to Okigbo's may be found in Jessie Weston, *From Ritual to Romance* (Cambridge: Cambridge University Press, 1920), p. 37. Okigbo may well have been familiar with Weston's book as a major source for Eliot's *The Waste Land.*

20.   Merrell R. Davies and William H. Gilman (eds.), *The Letters of Herman Melville* (New Haven: Yale University Press, 1960), Letter 83, 16 April 1851, p. 125.

21.   Cf. Judges 20, 1; 1 Samuel 3, 20; 2 Samuel 3, 10.

22.   Anozie, *Christopher Okigbo,* pp. 158–68.

23.   T. S. Eliot, *Collected Poetry and Plays* (London: Faber, 1969), p. 34.

24.   Ali Mazrui, *The Trial of Christopher Okigbo* (London: Heinemann, 1971).

25.   *The Poetical Works of William Wordsworth,* Vol. 1, ed. Ernest de Selincourt (Oxford University Press, 1940), p. 226.

# Postcoloniality and the Oracle of Repetition: Christopher Okigbo's Poetry

## Dubem Okafor

Behind any consideration of the "postcolonial" is a basic assumption—that the facts of empire and colony were and are an important determination, in both immediate and mediate instances, for the discourses and cultures of all the people involved on either the colonizing or colonized side of the momentous historical encounter. This dialectical view, which applies whether one is talking about Nigerian and Indian or about "English" and American literatures, runs counter to the usual and complacent traditional disciplinary position that insisted (and often still insists) that English culture was neither affected nor shaped by its foreign and imperial policy. It implies a recognition of the reciprocal, albeit unequal, impingement of the two sides and has been described as a "realistic" position, in that it sees imperialism as a beneficial evil, and in that it also sees the imperialist as not totally devoid of humanity, nor the imperialized as not totally incapable of inhumanity. According to Edward Said, there are

> large groups of people who believe that the bitterness and humiliations of the experience that virtually enslaved them nevertheless delivered the benefits of a national self-consciousness, liberal ideas, and technological goods, benefits over time that seem to have turned colonialism into a much less unpleasant thing. (Said 1993, 18)

Bearing in mind that this "benefit" of especially "a national self-consciousness" is, at best, dubious, it is still fair to observe that the position thus articulated balances the unilateral and unilineal view of the history of imperialism and colonialism that used to see only a drama of giving and receiving, of doing to and suffering, by the colonizer and by the colonized, respectively.

We know that as it started out, imperialism was a system of invasion, warfare, coerced, outrageous, abnormal, and violent imposition, and the exploitation and expropriation of goods and resources—human and material—by European powers. As Said sees it, "here occurred ravages of colonial people

---

This essay has been adapted specifically for this volume and is published for the first time by permission of the author.

who for centuries endured summary justice, unending economic oppression, the total distortion of their societies and their intimate lives, and a recourse-less submission given to them as a function of unchanging European superiority" (22). But it is not as if the presumption and thinking behind that militarism and consequent control have receded into prehistory. The sad fact of contemporary "History" is that the same "philosophical" and cultural anachronism that was used to "justify" imperialism now informs a lot of colonial discourse and colonialist and neocolonialist cultural productions that find it ideologically convenient to continue to propagate, perpetuate, and disseminate the binary myths of superiority/inferiority, benevolence/ingratitude, civilization/backwardness, enlightened/savage, rational/emotional, intellectual/ physical, literate/oral, good/bad, and white/black, as if there cannot exist other possibilities, other gray or indeterminate zones.

It is the superiorist refusal even to consider the possibility that there might reside some sense in the *other*, already castigated as inferior, that accounts for the interpretive outrage flaunted by Dennis Duerden in his "influential" book *The Invisible Present* (1977). After warning that "it is extremely important for an understanding of these societies to get away from the sense of the word 'symbol' used to describe identifiable objects existing in modern European art," and asserting that a typical African society "avoids the use of representations of objects as if they were symbols" (10), Duerden ventures into an area where he claims particular expertise and authority:

> It appears, however, that the artist in nonindustrial African society, be he *poet, painter, or storyteller,* wishes to avoid making his symbols permanent, wishes somehow to prevent them from becoming *universally accepted* Symbols. It follows that when describing the uses of art in African society we should make it plain that it appears as if *generally accepted symbols are being used unintentionally and not state affirmatively that it is the intention of the artist to use such symbols.* (11; italics mine)

The treatment of "symbols" here has resulted in a complete denudation of their meaning. According to *The New Princeton Encyclopedia of Poetry and Poetics* (1993),

> a symbol is a device of the poetic art when it refers to something else in the poem; it is a power of poetic language when it refers to the way words and rhythms can evoke mystery; it is a function of the whole poem when it refers to the kinds of meaning a literary work can stand for; it is a form of therapeutic disguise when it refers to the ways in which a poem stands for the working out of the author's inner disturbance; and it is an index of cultural values when it refers to the ways in which man's products reveal his attitudes. (835)

By this definition, then, African artists, including Okigbo, not only understand symbols and symbolism well but also use them intentionally. As for the question of permanence, that becomes pertinent only with regard to the plastic arts, including architecture, where the artists simply obey the imperatives of ecology as well as their people's ways of life. The artists' "obsession" with impermanence, therefore, simply reflects their cosmological understanding of the universe and of the transitoriness of everything within it. With regard to Okigbo, one of the earlier critical charges against him was not that he does not use symbols in his poetry but that his mastery of the symbolist craft, which enables him to appropriate symbols from both indigenous and exotic doxa, mixing these with his private symbolism, has left his readers often confused. In the early phase of his poetic career when that charge of obscurity can be sustained, Okigbo was simply being a true "internationalist," symbolist poet whose poetry was characterized, like the best of the symbolist school, with "[i]ts overwhelming concern with the non-temporal, non-sectarian, non-geographic, and non-national problem of the human condition: the confrontation between human mortality and the power of survival through the preservation of the human sensitivities in the art forms" (Balakian 1977, 10).

That was when Okigbo's moods were wont to be "impish," as Chinua Achebe would describe them in his preface to *Don't Let Him Die* (Achebe 1978, x), and when, exhibiting an "esoteric attitude" toward art, Okigbo preferred to move, like the symbolist poets, "in closed circles communicating solely with [his] own breed" (Balakian 1977, 10). In an interview with Lewis Nkosi, Okigbo quickly proffered an explanation or rationalization for this "elitism": "[T]here are not many Nigerians who would read poetry and would take delight in reading poetry, and there are very few Nigerians who would read poetry that appears difficult. Somehow, I believe I am writing for other poets all over the world to read and see whether they can share in my experience" (Duerden and Pieterse 1972, 135). That was Okigbo in 1962, master of the poetic symbol, whose "artistic vision, freed from national [even Pan-African] ideals, focused on the relationship between the subjective, purely personal world of the artist, and its objective projection" (Balakian 1977, 10), and who, by grafting the French and European branches of the symbolist practice to the autochthonous poetic stem, contributed, in effect, to bringing symbolism "to its apotheosis as an international literary movement" (10).[1]

Born in 1932, the very year that the negritude movement was inaugurated in Paris by black (African and diasporic) intellectuals, Christopher Okigbo was one of those whose poetry contributed and bore testimony to this internationalization of symbolism. Because the critique of negritude has continued to emphasize its essentialization of blackness, it is important to cite Okigbo's judicious appraisal of that program. When in a 1963 interview Dennis Duerden suggested that negritude "starts with the idea that there's some sort of specific mental attitude that characterizes someone who's black— . . . this is what negritude seems to be saying; that all black people have some specific mental attitude" (Duerden and Pieterse 1972, 139), Okigbo was quick to correct him:

I don't quite agree. I don't think this is what negritude seems to be saying. I think that *negritude seems to be saying that black people who have somehow felt a sense of alienation are now looking for their roots, which I think is a perfectly legitimate thing to do* . . . I think too that on another side the political equivalent of negritude tends to assert an African personality. (139–40)

This point needs to be emphasized not only because it represents a corrective on some misreadings of negritude but, more importantly, because it will be found to constitute a major part of Okigbo's own postcolonial project. For even though the Francophone and Anglophone programs appeared to be taking different routes, their aims were the same: to rehabilitate their societies.

Okigbo's contribution to the cultural rehabilitation of his society can be seen as a trinary endeavor. First he had to equip himself intellectually to confront a system that, first and foremost, was grounded in a formidable epistemology, albeit false and deliberately distorted; second, he needed to retrace the exilic route and assume a base and vantage point at "home"; and third, with the confidence and assurance of a reintegrated prodigal, and the courageous wisdom of a poet of destiny, he could begin his critique.

Ironically, Okigbo's exile was part of his preparation. Even though it was not a path willingly "chosen," his exile enabled him to acquire a Western education and immerse himself in world cultures, and these experiences were to prove indispensable. In the end, he became thoroughly familiar with most civilizations and cultures of the world and could read, speak, write, and translate Latin, Greek, Spanish, French, Italian, Portuguese, Igbo, Yoruba, and English. In his own words:

I translate from Latin verse into English verse or from Greek verse into English verse and vice versa. . . . I think that I have a fairly good knowledge of Latin, a working knowledge of Greek.
. . . In fact enough Latin to read and understand Latin poetry in the original, and understand before I translate—and in fact enough Greek to translate Greek poetry into English. (Duerden and Pieterse 1972, 137)

What we are describing here is not an exercise in mechanical translation. Okigbo's was a serious and devoted commitment to the acquisition of the linguistic and cultural tools that he would need in his lifework. The objects of his study were so thoroughly mastered and so completely assimilated that in his poetry it is useless to chase the elusive shadows of influence. Paradoxical as it may sound, Okigbo's preparation for this task could not have been complete without the alienating experience of Christianity. He was born into the Roman Catholic family of James and Anna Okigbo. His father was an educator and school headmaster, and in those days, a schoolteacher was also a worker in the Lord's vineyard, the mission, and was always next in command to the parish priest, whose duties James Okigbo filled whenever the priest could not, for any reason, make it to Sunday worship. Okigbo was born into this religious environment, a family whose every child must be baptized in the church, according to the strict laws of the church. The powerful papal representative of this church, Leidan, from his "Holy See" in Adazi, promulgated innumerable edicts, pronouncements, and injunctions against everything traditional, including religion and all its paraphernalia (Udechukwu 1984, 81). He was immortalized in Okigbo's remembrance of the coming of "the first missionaries and invaders, scrunching their boots through the sacred places and clamping their alien law upon the land" (Moore 1984, 278):

> Behind the walled gods
> in market
> boots over mandos
> and byelaws thereto appended
> by Leidan,
> archtyrant of the holy sea.
> (Quoted in Moore 1984, 278)

Of baptism itself, which would ordinarily be welcomed with excitement and joy by the baptisand, and marked with rejoicing and flurried preparation of postbaptismal entertainment by the family, it is significant that what the sensibility of Okigbo the poet captures is the

> rank smell of olive oil
> on foreheads,
> vision of the hot bath of heaven
> among reedy spaces.
> (Quoted in Moore 1984, 278)

As if that was not enough, the experience itself is represented in the most excruciatingly painful and terrifying of terms. And who else but the now notorious "alienator," Kepkanly, would wield the branding blade?

> Scar of the crucifix
> over the breast,
> by red blade inflicted
> by red-hot blade
> on the right breast witnesseth
>
> Mystery which I, initiate,
> received newly naked
> upon the waters of the genesis
> from Kepkanly.
> (Okigbo 1986, 22)

The important thing about this baptismal experience is that notwithstanding its terror, it left only a scar, which, though permanent, is only physical and superficial, not psychical. It would, therefore, not hinder in the least the poet's impending mission. As a matter of fact, the baptismal scar marked the completion of the poet's alienation, as well as his readiness to begin the penitential journey home.

But Okigbo's retracing of the exilic route is a complicated and tedious process of "initiations" and purifications beginning with "The Passage," reaching the final acceptance of "Lustra," and climaxing with the celebration of "Newcomer," where he assumes his own mask and is confident of the ancestral protection from Anna, his late mother. Okigbo then appropriately begins his return, his movement of reintegration in all contrition and humility. He had been forced to wander among alien and distracting orthodoxies and isms; his return now as repentant and supplicant must be sincere:

> Before you, mother Idoto,
>     naked I stand;
> before your watery presence
>     a prodigal
> leaning on an oilbean,
> Lost in your legend.
>
> Under your power wait I
>     on barefoot,
> watchman for the watchword
>     at *Heavensgate;*
>
> Out of the depths my cry:
> give ear and hearken . . .
>                    (19)

The nakedness of the returning prodigal implies total surrender and helplessness before the neglected deity to whose absolute power and authority the poet "on barefoot" now submits. Distracted by nothing now, and consumed totally by his devotion—"Lost in your legend"—the poet has confidence that his supplication will be heeded. Indeed, the poet's devotion and single-mindedness are beginning to pay off, and there is every sign and hope that "out of the depths [his] cry" will be heard. This is because, unlike the ultraviolet rays that "foreshadow the fire that is dreamed of," and that is reminiscent of the apocalyptic devastation of the fires of Armageddon, the rainbow here "foreshadows the rain that is dreamed of," which will soothe the weary returning prodigal. As if he had already been given the positive sign, he happily but heavily withdraws in solitude to the "orangery," there to embark on extensive introspection, but also, like a truly contrite prodigal

who had earlier abdicated his filial duties, "to mourn / a mother on a spray."
His acceptance and integration are not yet final, but at least he has not been
rejected and turned back; in fact, he has been allowed entry up to "the passage," where, as the wise hen newly arrived at new surroundings, he stands on
one leg until he gets used to the new place. In Okigbo's case the "new place"
is the old but now estranged and defamiliarized milieu.

Passage iii continues the mood and atmosphere of bereavement and
mourning of Passage ii by introducing

> Silent faces at crossroads:
> festivity in black . . .
> Faces of black like long black
> columns of ants
>
> (5)

whose "festivity in black" is an oxymoronic suggestion of either the passing
on, at a ripe old age, of the deceased (in which case his funeral usually
becomes a festival) or the second funerary rites for one long dead (in which
case the prodigal's fulfillment of a filial duty long abandoned could be instan-
tiated). In any case, the procession leads to the "bell tower" of St. Odilia's
where the "Christian" departed also had their "hot garden," the Catholic
Church cemetery, which truly, not merely symbolically, after all life's journeys
and races, represents the final destination, "where all roads meet." It is here
too that the poet's mother was laid to rest, and in the poet's new mythopoeic
order that transcends Roman Catholic sectarian exclusivism, she has assumed
her place among the sanctified ancestors. In her own right, she can answer
the cry or prayer of her son:

> O Anna at the knobs of the panel oblong
> hear us at crossroads at the great hinges
>
> (5)

It is interesting how Robert Fraser, in a strained and gallant effort to rescue Okigbo from a possible charge of atavism or paganism, tries to underline
the continuing presence of Christianity in, and thus the continuing relevance
of Christian interpretation of, Okigbo's poetry. Thus Fraser says that "The
'Anna of the knobs of the panel oblongs' may indeed be Okigbo's mother, but
she is also St. Anne" (Fraser 1986, 108; italics mine). It is true that naming in
the Roman Catholic tradition has always depended on the finite repertoire of
saints. Indeed, in Igboland, until very recently, not to be called by one of the
saints' names meant that one was not baptized, not Christian, and therefore
pagan! Also, because all such saints' names were as a rule European and English (the Igbo having produced no saints), to be called by a saint's or Christian name was to be called by an English name: in colonized Igboland, Chris-

tianity and Englishness were interchangeable. But they definitely were not interchangeable in the sense Fraser suggests when he says that "at this juncture [of Okigbo's poetry] Christian and African religious initiations are made to fuse, to haunting effect" (108). Okigbo's mother was named after St. Anne, but in this poem, Okigbo was not thinking of St. Anne; Anna Onugwualuobi was already a respected ancestor, capable not only of answering prayers but also of protecting her son from "them fucking angels" and saints and other mythological creations of Roman Catholicism. How can it be otherwise when Okigbo has shed all sartorial and other encumbrances associated with his alienation and exile, and, as before the flaming forest, he stands both naked and unshod on holy ground, the only sad reminder of his exile being the sign of that hot blade?

> Scar of the crucifix
> over the breast,
> by red blade inflicted
> by red-hot blade,
> on right breast witnesseth.
> (Okigbo 1986, 6)

This is how Okigbo begins "Initiations," the second long poem in the *Heavensgate* sequence, about which two comments are in order. First, the poem's position in the sequence has no historico-chronological significance because as *remembering,* the events described took place before the penitential return of the poet-prodigal in *Passages.* However, it does show the importance of memory to this poet, who must recall and reenact the events that colluded to produce his present impasse. Second, it is important to note that here "initiations" is pluralized, for they dramatize a series of junctures in the initiatory continuum: the alienating initiation into Christianity and the consequent abruption of his traditional allegiance; and his initiation into poetry and into prophecy, from Jadum and Upandru respectively, but the two representing, in reality, a certain inseparability. It is therefore incorrect to describe the experience as the "three-fold initiation into *three distinct and potentially conflicting schools of thought:* the Christian/individualistic, the professionally artistic and the ancestral folkloric" (Fraser 1986, 108; italics mine). Igbo traditional individualism has always been predicated on the overarching superordinacy of the collectivity, and the artistic has always been in the service of the group. Moreover, there should be no reason to bring in the notion of ideologically fractious and "conflicting schools of thought" here, since in his definition of poetry as "logistics," Okigbo conflates the notions of prophecy and poetry.

After the horrifying sadism of the imagery of the first stanza, reminiscent of the ordeal of the slaves during their translocation across the Atlantic, there is an almost redemptive ambivalence in the poet's attitude toward Kepkanly, who had wielded the blade of baptism. The poet talks of

> mystery which I, initiate,
> received newly naked
> upon waters of the genesis
> from Kepkanly.
>
> Elemental, united in vision
> of present and future,
> the pure line, whose innocence
> denies inhibitions.
> (Okigbo 1986, 22)

Thus the alienating missionary ogre Kepkanly would appear to be also responsible for the poet's initiation into prophecy and bardic unity of vision: "Elemental, united in vision / of present and future." The next associated initiation that, placed in close spatial-textual relationship with the one from Kepkanly, is made to contrast sharply with it, is that from John the Baptist, whose message, in the poet's view, is a mere "gambit." In its hypocritical impracticality, impossibility, even denial and negation of life itself, this gospel has been described as "barren orthodoxy, especially in its abstract morality ('life without sin')" (Obiechina 1980, 25). If the sexual union, which is the only enabler and guarantor of a new life, is seen by Western Christian orthodoxy as sinful, then the prescription of life without sex and sin is a proscription of life:

> so comes John the Baptist
> with bowl of salt water
> preaching the gambit:
> life without sin, without
>
> life; *which accepted,*
> way leads downward
> down the orthocenter
> avoiding decisions.
> (Okigbo 1986, 22; italics mine)

This gambit doesn't have to be accepted or imbibed without question, as the poet implies through the use of the conditional phrase "which accepted." This conditionality is thus an expression of the poet's "cynical scepticism about the crux of Christian values" (Anozie 1972, 53). It is this element of skepticism, or honest doubt, that needs to be emphasized as a possible legacy from Kepkanly, and not, as Fraser sees it, an "induction with the safe port of Christian commitment, where the agonizing complexity of moral responsibility disappears in a reassuring 'confluence of planes' corresponding to the 'orthocentre' [*sic*] of a triangle" (Fraser 1986, 108).

The poet who criticizes the dissemination of the gambit "which accepted / way leads downward / down orthocenter / avoiding decisions" cannot be endorsing, much less delighting in, the abdication of moral responsibility, as the following lines indicate:

> Or forms fourth angle—
> duty obligation:
>
> square yields the moron,
> fanatics and priests and popes
> organizing secretaries and
> party managers; better still,
>
> the rhombus—brothers and deacons,
> liberal politicians,
> selfish selfseekers—all who are good
> doing nothing at all;
>
> the quadrangle, the rest, me and you . . .
> (Okigbo 1986, 23)

The sociopolitical-critical implications of the characterology elaborated here are both acute and interesting. For one thing, the geometric delineation leaves no doubt about the poet-critic's attitude toward the representatives of the different "shapes" and their overriding ideologies: thus the pope, as the beginning and end of all earthly (Roman Catholic) orthodoxy, figures here as an undistinguished member of the same class, the "Square," whose other members include all "fanatics and priests," as well as "organizing secretaries and party managers." Interestingly, Kepkanly, like Leidan, also belongs here. And they are all "morons."

The next group, whose sign is the "rhombus," and whom Fraser rightly calls "social parasites," comprises those elements in society whom I have characterized as gastrocentric, monomaniacally preoccupied with the pursuit of "things" to tuck away either in the unsafe and decomposing recesses of their guts, or in the safe and criminally anonymous vaults of the Swiss banks. They are also reminiscent of that group whose trait Thomas Carlyle had long ago identified as "do nothingism."

In the single last line dealing with geometric categories, Okigbo does a most important thing as poet of destiny. That single line, which not only proclaims his identity but also declares his affinities, affiliation, and politics, is the triumphant display of his credentials: I am of the people; I am one of the people; I am for the people: "the quadrangle, the rest, me and you . . . " (Okigbo 1986, 23).

I believe it is possible to read and interpret Okigbo's poetry, complexly intertextual as it is, without losing our critical bearing in our search for trails and scents of influence. Thus although it is possible that "Rockland" echoes, and might well have been taken from Allen Ginsberg's poem *Howl,* as

Anozie thinks, the accuracy of the geography of Jadum's Rockland leaves no one in doubt that there is nothing exotic or even borrowed about it (Anozie 1972, 54–55). Jadum's Rockland is Agba-enu, a term used to designate the semiarid, partly rocky, partly grassy terrain of the uplands, including the Aguata Province, of Igboland. Okigbo's father was once a schoolteacher and headmaster in Ekwulobia in Aguata Province, and Okigbo's poetic sensibility recaptures and remembers not only the geography but also the sociocultural landscape and history of this place of his growing up. The metaphoric landscape of this poem is indeed homespun. The poem also contains Okigbo's critical attitude toward "theoretical Christianity, the dogmas which all manner of charlatans push and behind which they perpetuate atrocities against their neighbours and Mankind" (Obiechina 1980, 35), but thematically it is concerned with an important phase in the chain of *initiations* on which the poet has embarked.

The next and closely related initiation is that which the poet receives from Upandru, "A village explainer" (Okigbo 1986, 25 n. 1). But Upandru is not merely a villager who has acquired linguistic competence or who is "steeped in the use of words," much like the famous masters and "eaters" of words in Achebe's *Things Fall Apart* (Anozie 1972, 56). Upandru belongs to a long line of explicators whose calling connects them to the very core of language as such, to the *logos* itself. It is for that reason that their role is, properly speaking, *divination,* which, on a deeper level, attempts to explicate human destiny. An important item in the diviner's paraphernalia is the shell of the tortoise. This reference to the ubiquitous and sagacious character, the trickster par excellence in Igbo folklore, the Tortoise (Mbekwu, the child of Aniga), underlines the relationship between the explainer-diviner and the trickster, whose duplicitous indeterminacy and liminality enable it to act as a link between transcendence and mundanity, discourse and destiny.

Upandru's explication/divination, *Igba Afa,* is the same thing as the more widely known Yoruba *Ifa.* In both instances, *Fa* and *Afa* refer to Fate, and its divination or explication is the function of the explainer, who is thus "the sole agent of interpretation and hence mediation between man, on one hand, and the Book of Fate *(Fa)* on the other" (Gates 1988, 24). Henry Louis Gates's discussion of Legba, the trickster and linguist, is thus important for our understanding of Upandru. In his discussion, the linguistic function of Legba as divine linguist is elaborated thus:

> To Legba was assigned the role of linguist between the kingdoms of gods and gods, and gods and men. Whereupon, in addition to the knowledge of the "language" of Mawu—Lisa [the primal god], he was given the knowledge of all the "languages" spoken by the other gods in their separate domains. (Melville J. Herskovits, *Dahomey,* quoted in Gates 1988, 23–24)

Gates goes on to say that

Legba, then, stands as the discursive, or textual, principle itself; . . . Legba "is a creator of discourse, for his every movement is . . . a 'raid on the inarticulate,' a foray into the formless, which simultaneously gives shape to the dark and fear-some and new life to structure always in danger of becoming a skeleton." Legba is discourse and . . . discourse upon a text.

   Legba . . . is the divine reader, whose interpretation of the Book of Fate determines precisely what the book says. The interpreter governs meaning. (24)

   Villagers would go to Legba/Upandru the explainer, for he alone can read the divine text of Fate "because of the several stages of mediation and translation that occur in rapid succession in *Fa* divination. A supplicant's query is answered by a cryptogram" (24).

   Appropriately, then, immediately after the introduction of Upandru as the mysterious and enigmatic embodiment of hidden, "screened" texts and their meanings, we have a staging of a linguistic *agon,* or *stychomythia,* between the poet and the explainer, whose resolution yields the definition of poetry as "logistics," involving " 'roads,' or 'pathways,' or 'courses' . . . which lead the supplicant through the maze of figuration," out of the "jungle of ambiguity that is the language of" divination, of poetry itself (24):

> And this from Upandru:
>
> Screen your bedchamber thoughts
> with sun-glasses,
> who could jump your eye,
> your mind-window,
>
> And I said:
> The prophet only the poet.
> And he said: Logistics.
> (Which is what poetry is) . . .
> (Okigbo 1986, 25)

   The excited arrival at this definition of poetry, after the cryptogrammatic test, or *agon,* with Upandru, is not a facile achievement. Okigbo's "logistics" implies not simple mechanical movement but a whole complex of hermeneuti-cal procedures with which no simpleton, only the madman-prophet-poet, can deal. It is a ratiocinative and affective, as well as an imaginative and intellec-tual, exercise, whose almost hyperbolic implication is captured in the image of "jumping the mind-window." Thus, in the stanza that reads,

> And he said to the ram: Disarm.
> And I said:
> Except by rooting,
> who could pluck yam tubers from their base?
> (25)

there is no suggestion of diffidence at all. The poet, having already arrived at the brink of initiation into, and at a definition of, poetry, is defiant and unafraid and challenges Upandru to disarm him, the ram. In the Igbo folk-loric doxa, the ram is asked to "remove" that thing hanging pendulous between his hind legs, to which he replies that one cannot simply or easily "remove" a yam tuber. Only by "rooting," by painstaking and patient and expert "digging," can one "pluck" yam tubers from their "base," their deep anchor in the soil. In other words, far from exhibiting "oestrus pain and heat," the audacious poet is satisfied with his progress so far, even though his initiations are far from over.

Taken together, then, the poet's initiations from Jadum and Upandru represent his solid "identification with the community, especially with its folk outlook that leads to the recognition of the importance of individuals, be they ever so demented, grotesque or waggish" (Obiechina 1980, 28). Depending as heavily on visual as on other senses for its total effect, the poem begins with the following lines:

> Eye open on the sea
> eyes open, of the prodigal;
> upward to heaven shoot
> where stars will fall from
> (Okigbo 1986, 26)

It goes on to evoke the "beachsand," breaking "salt-white surf on the stones," "lobsters and shells," "sunbeaten beach," "man with woman," "armpit-dazzle of a lioness," "white light," "moonlight," "match-flare," "mirrors," and "gold crop sinking ungathered." This close concatenation of concentrated visual imagery describes the poet's "encounter with the watermaid . . . a private experience with wider implications" (Obiechina 1980, 29). One of such implications is epiphanous, for in the poem, the poet, for the first time, reveals the secret of his close connection with the mysteries, his long-standing relationship, as *ogbanje* or changeling, with the spirit world, whose actual or mythological manifestation is the Watermaid or Mammy Water, the "white queen":

> Secret I have told into no ear
> save into a dughole, to hold, not to drown with—
> Secret I have planted into beachsand
>
> now breaks
> salt-white surf on the stones and me,
> and lobsters and shells
> in iodine smell—
>
> whose secret I have covered up with beachsand . . .
> (Okigbo 1986, 26)

In the phenomenon of *ogbanje* (in Yoruba, *abiku*), a child with strong mystical ties to beings of the spirit world enacts a repetitive cycle of coming and going, of premature birth and sudden death. It also has two variants. The terrestrial variant, simply called *ogbanje,* has the child's secret-of-life oath *(iyi-uwa)* buried in the earth. The process of retrieving this secret, usually in the form of smooth stones or pebbles, alone or in combination with other items, is accomplished through the intervention and mediation of an experienced diviner, and with the cooperation of the changeling. The maritime or lacustrine variant is a more intractable case, if only because retrieving the secret from a lake or river is a more tricky exercise and therefore involves series of complex and often futile rituals and sacrifices to placate the Watermaid.

But whether terrestrial or maritime, the *ogbanje* are the enigmatic beings who live as if in a hurry to make their exit from this world. Another remarkable trait of *ogbanje* is their brooding withdrawal and reclusion, which the uninitiated see as shyness or aloofness, arrogance or disconnection. But such solitude is indispensable to them who must commune with, or await the visitation of, the spirit queen. Characteristically such visitations are painfully brief but illuminating:

> So brief her presence—
> match-flare in wind's breath—
> so brief with mirrors around me
> (27)

This poem is full of pain and regret because the ecstatic visit is too brief and tantalizing to be satisfying. Almost onanistic, the visit falls just short of delivering the full gift of poetic inspiration; the "gold crop" comes teasingly within reach but sinks "ungathered." Even then, all is not lost, for the poetic recapitulation of the rare experience results in "some of the most splendid poetic evocations of the collection" (Obiechina 1980, 29). Hence the poet does not descend into unrelieved dejection:

> And I who am here abandoned,
> count the sand by wavelash abandoned,
> count her blessing, my white queen.
>
> But the spent sea reflects
> from his mirrored visage
> not my queen, a broken shadow.
>
> So I who count in my island the moments,
> count the hour which will bring
>
> my lost queen with angel's ash in the wind.
> (Okigbo 1986, 28)

Even though the queen appears to have been "lost," such loss is only momentary, and the poet has been able to learn, through his initiations so far, that the crucial thing is the ability "to clutch at this hour," however evanescent it may be. Moreover, the poet who has cultivated solitude all his life knows that it constitutes part of the strength of the pathfinder. Okigbo recognizes the critical importance of capturing opportunely the precious but transient coruscations of vision and inspiration, even if all that means is "fulfilling each moment in a / broken monody" (29).

It is because the poet is fully aware of his "limitations," aware also of the incompleteness of his initiations without a ritual cleansing, that he undertakes the purification of the next phase in *Lustra:*

> So would I to the hills again
> so would I
> to where springs the fountain
> there to draw from
>
> . . . . . . . . . . . . . .
>
> Here is a new laid egg
> here a white hen at midterm.
> (30)

In this state of achieved purity and clarity, the poet is ready to make an acceptable sacrifice, which in all religious experience is the culminating reestablishment of the cosmic ties between man and God (Douglas 1966). The items of sacrifice here are suitable for the occasion, the egg representing freshness, purity, and the mysterious possibility of life, the "white hen at midterm" symbolizing purity because she has not yet been "known" by a cock. These items of sacrifice fulfill the condition of acceptance and reconnection of the severed bond between the higher powers and humanity, for they contain that most essential element: *blood.* The paradox of sacrifice is that in shedding blood (that is, through the taking of life), life is given or made possible. The supplicant or community "offers" the blood of an animal or sometimes one of its members to mollify the Powers, who in turn revitalize the community, restore social harmony, and reestablish the broken cosmic bond. Usually, the more dire the occasion, the bigger (and therefore higher) the animal is in the evolutionary hierarchy, and the more efficacious the sacrifice. But for the purification and empowerment of an individual, a virgin hen and an egg suffice. Even in these "modern" and "civilized" times, the religions of the world have not abandoned this practice; they have only, in symbolic substitution, replaced humans with animals, and in some cases replaced blood and flesh with red wine and unleavened bread.

Because Okigbo seeks an integrated vision, his sacrifice cannot be complete without the "vegetable" component, which is not necessarily indigenous. So he adds:

> vegetable offering with five
> fingers of chalk . . .
> (Okigbo 1986, 31)

The chalk here is *nzu,* a white or off-white clay that is quarried, molded, and baked into "fingers." Above all else, it is an Igbo religious symbol of purity and cleanliness. Okigbo's "vegetable offering" thus makes his sacrifice complete, but it does not necessarily replace Christian or other forms of sacrifice. As far as Okigbo is concerned—and this is a lesson from deep mystical vision and awareness—all gods, Christian, indigenous, and otherwise, are the same, are only different manifestations and nominations of the same higher power. So his ascent to the hilltop is for unified, not "divided," vision. And even though he continues to be critical of Christianity as distorted and misrepresented by fanatics and morons, there is nothing here to suggest that he privileges one type of vision over another. If anything, in spite of the mockery of the drunken priests and celebrants, the affinity between Christ and Chris is not repudiated in the present remembrance of Christ, who "was silenced":

> The flower weeps, unbruised,
> for him who was silenced
> whose advent dumb-bells celebrate
> in dim light with wine song:
>
> Messiah will come again
> After the argument in heaven
> Messiah will come again . . .
> (31)

The acceptance of his sacrifice, which marks the end of this phase of the poet's life journey, is appropriately heralded by "thundering drums and cannons" and the release, in ecstasy, of spirit. In this instance, which combines the overpowering ecstasy of Pentecostal release with the wonder of ascension, the invocation of the long drums and cannons is significant. Usually deployed only when important people make their exit from this to the other world, the drums and cannons invoke not death as a finality but death as both release of spirit and the passage and acceptance of spirit into the higher, ancestral realm. Thus Okigbo's sacrifice has been accepted:

> Thundering drums and cannons
> in palm grove:
> the Spirit is in ascent.
> (32)

No longer a prodigal, the finally accepted, reintegrated, and empowered poet is careful to memorialize the occasion with his own indelible "signature," the print of his palm with its five digits: "my pentagon." This is also significant for the other reason that the number five, the pentagon, unlike the constraining and inhibiting square or rhombus, represents liberation, of self and vision:

> I have visited;
> on palm beam imprinted
> my pentagon—
> I have visited, the prodigal . . .
>
> (32)

This admission into the limited circle of the called and empowered is a rare achievement, and the moment calls for festivity. But it carries with it grave responsibilities, and the poet-priest, fully aware of this, begins seriously in *Newcomer* with a worship that includes a premier officiation, as in a first mass said by a newly ordained priest, in which the poet-priest is free for the first time to don his "own mask," and to pray directly to Anna—ancestral Mother as "guardian angel"—to protect the poet "from them fucking angels." There is no confusion of theologies here: in Igbo religion, the ancestors are a living and potent reality, and part of their duty is the protection of those still living on earth. The excitation of the present moment collocates the symbols of his alienation: "bells of exile," the "angelus," and "guardian angel" connect "remembrance of calvary" with a past "age of innocence"; but above all, the mature, responsible, and humble poet-priest knows that it is first

> Time for worship—
> softly sing the bells of exile,
> the angelus,
> softly sings my guardian angel.
>
> Mask over my face—
>
> My own mask, not ancestral—I sign:
>
> (33)

But the festivity and hilarity and celebration that are appropriate to this occasion are tempered by a certain premonition, perhaps of the realized dangers inherent in the new status and crusade. Hence *Newcomer II,* which deals with "birth," is also a synthetic structure that deals with arrivals and integration: the arrival of the poet at the state of grace, poetic illumination, purity, and acceptance; the gestation and birth of a new poem, and of a new daughter, the poet's niece, herself a synthesis of "white" and "black" cultures and genes (her mother being Belgian). But the arrivals are given "such synthetic welcome" as the diction, which is deliberately ambivalent and paradoxical, indicates. Hence the arrival takes place in May, the second month in the loveliest season of the year, but in the early morning when it is not simply cold but bitingly so. At this time when everyone and everything in nature is newly and freshly and colorfully attired and bedecked, the smile that is seen is a painted, false one. Finally, the arrival is "at the cock's third siren," which, together with "behind the bulrushes" suggests betrayal and treachery (Izevbaye 1984, 321). Interestingly enough, Okigbo's death would turn out to be a result of treachery and betrayal, and his poetry, especially *Limits,* echoes betrayal, treachery, and martyrdom. But the presence here, in a poem of jubilation, of the motif of betrayal, makes it a cautionary tale and prophecy of the fate of the poet-messiah:

> In the chill breath of the day's waking,
> comes the newcomer,
>
> when the draper of May
> has sold out fine green garments,
>
> and the hillsides have made up their faces
> and the gardens, on their faces a painted smile:
>
> Such synthetic welcome at the cock's third siren;
> when from behind the bulrushes
>
> waking, in the teeth of the chill May morn,
> comes the newcomer.
> (Okigbo 1986, 34)

In the same way that Christ is not deterred from his betrayal by his own disciples, this premonition of danger or betrayal—"synthetic welcome at the cock's third siren"—does not deter Chris. His jubilation is given full rein in *Newcomer III,* which also contains one of the most arrogant synesthesias in Okigbo's poetry: "Listening to incense":

> I am standing above the noontide,
> Above the bridgehead;
>
> Listening to the laughter of waters
> that do not know why:
> Listening to incense—
>
> I am standing above the noontide
> with my head above it;
>
> Under my feet float the waters
> Tide blows them under . . .
> (Okigbo 1986, 35)

Okigbo is now poised, ready, even eager to begin his mission, his preparation finally completed. Because this mission is cultural and political, it is public duty that is motivated by a bardic, even prophetic, impulse. Having overcome his deracination and alienation from his cultural moorings, which the conjuncture of colonialism, colonial education, and cultural imperialism had produced, and having, after a protracted retracing of the exilic route through a series of penitential and purificatory ordeals, achieved acceptance, reintegration, and empowerment, the poet launches his cultural crusade. And sustained by those same forces—reason, truth seeking, patriotism, pity—that were said to have been the firing genius of Samuel Taylor Coleridge (Woodring 1961, 45), whom Okigbo admired, the poet exclaims:

> Suddenly becoming talkative
>     like weaverbird
> Summoned at offside of
>     dream remembered
>
> Between sleep and waking,
> I hang up my egg-shell
> To you of palm grove,
> Upon whose bamboo towers
>
> Hang, dripping with yesterupwine,
> A tiger mask and a nude spear . . .
>
> Queen of the damp half light,
> I have had my cleansing,
> Emigrant with air-borne nose,
> The he-goat-on-heat.
>                   (Okigbo 1986, 39)

The excitement of this passage is unmistakable. So too is the declaration of the poet's readiness. In an almost surreptitious deployment of that beautiful imagery from soccer, "offside," the poet is both called to order and reminded of the urgency of the task at hand; but it is obvious, too, that in his excitement, he had not had an uninterrupted sleep. The references to "yesterupwine," "tiger mask," and "nude spear" are appropriate, for they symbolize energization, bravery, and readiness, as in an unsheathed and drawn spear, respectively. And as if to dispel any doubt about this qualification for participation, he declares to the goddess of intrigue and calculation, of that gray dawn hour when most effective military (especially guerrilla) incursions are launched, when apparently, in a prophetic or proleptic canniness, Okigbo would also later, during the Nigeria-Biafra war, launch his most devastating blows on the forces of genocidal carnage: "I have had my cleansing . . . / The he-goat-on-heat." Confident and bold and eager, the poet is almost arrogant in his new state of readiness: like "the he-goat-on-heat" he is not only ready and willing but anxious to begin. The sexual, even copulatory, imagery here is quite evident, as in many other places in Okigbo's poetry. However, because in the poet's sensibility, sexuality is not a distinct domain but an integral part of his whole being, the important thing becomes the nature of the poetic service to which the sexual symbolism is put. In the present instance, that service is cultural and political.

But the poet's excitement, as well as the urgency of the situation, does not result in unrealistic expectations and overestimation of the poet's ability. He recognizes that his reintegration and empowerment notwithstanding, as one newly called, he still needs, like a seedling, both more time and more nourishment, "to grow to sunlight." Appropriately, then, in an extended botanical metaphor, the poet thirsts for the sunlight without which the sustaining photosynthesis cannot take place:

> For he was a shrub among the poplars,
> Needing more roots
> More sap to grow to sunlight,
> Thirsting for sunlight,
>
> A low growth among the forest.
>
> (10)

But this recognition of his limitations is only a sign of the poet's present maturity. His continuing preparation includes serious and deep introspection and "feeling for [his] audience":

> Into the soul
> The selves extended their branches,
> Into the moments of each living hour,
> Feeling for audience . . .
>
> And out of the solitude
> Voice and soul with selves unite,
> Riding the echoes,
>
> Horsemen of the apocalypse;
> And crowned with one self
> The name displays its foliage,
> Hanging low
>
> A green cloud above the forest.
>
> (40)

The poem, which started as an articulation of the poet's diffidence and tentativeness, here ends with an apocalyptic optimism. A combination of the extirpation of ponderous foreign influences—"Straining thing among the echoes"—sincere and deep introspection, and a committed concern for his audience results in the poet's present sense of purpose, unity or integration of the "selves," and achievement. Neither the fact that he has not quite found his audience, nor that he recognizes the near insurmountability of the obstacles confronting the acolyte, constitutes sufficient deterrence against the inauguration of the campaign. The only thing needed is great caution, deliberateness, and prudence, because, as the poet realizes, he is hedged in by

> Banks of reed.
> Mountains of broken bottle.
>
> *& the mortar is not yet dry* . . .
>
> Silent the footfall,
> Soft as cat's paw,
> Sandalled in velvet in fur,
>
> So we must go, eve-mist on shoulders
> Sun's dust of combat,
> With brand burning out at hand-end
>
> *& the mortar is not yet dry* . . .
>
> Then we must sing, tongue-tied,
> Without name or audience
> Making harmony among the branches.
>
> (41)

The repetition here of imagery from military campaign, which nearly accurately depicts the poet's future guerrilla and commando raids, underlines the kind of urgency with which the poet views his crusade. The "eve-mist on shoulders" recalls the earlier quoted "damp half light," and "dust of combat" reconnects with the "he-goat-on-heat" and "a tiger mask and a nude spear" motifs: again, they are all sadly proleptic. But for now, what matters is the present "crisis point" where it is important to note the subtle coalescence of the military and cultural urgencies, as well as their resolution in *Limits IV* in terms of poetry. Thus the poet tells us:

> And this is the crisis point,
> The twilight moment between
>     sleep and waking;
>
> And the voice that is reborn transpires,
> Not thro' pores in the flesh,
>     but the soul's back-bone.
>
> Hurry on down—
>     Thro' the high-arched gate—

> Hurry on down
> little stream to the lake;
>
> (41)

The tempo of the acceleration here, of the hurrying to the point of climactic resolution, cannot be checked; it is, in fact, almost precipitous, for the poet must rush to the insistent call of the creator/destroyer who, like the mythological Spider of initiation rites, must stitch up the bodies of initiates after they had just been dismembered. It is therefore significant that *Limits IV,* which is said to have been composed after the poet's experience of surgery under general anesthesia, refers not to a hospital bed but to "near the altar" where the poem as sacrifice will be finished and presented:

> An image insists
> From flag pole of the heart;
> Her image distracts
> With the cruelty of the rose . . .
>
> Oblong-headed lioness—
> No shield is proof against her—
> Wound me, O sea-weed
> Face, blinded like strong-room
>
> Distances of her armpit-fragrance
> Turn chloroform enough for my patience—
>
> When you have finished
> & done up my stitches,
> Wake me near the altar,
> & this poem will be finished . . .
>
> (43)

On "waking up," then, not only will the poet have become finally and completely reconstituted, but the mortar will also have become dry. The period of tentativeness and protracted preparation is over. If one may appropriate an ingenious metaphor from General Yakubu Gowon, which he contrived during the Nigeria-Biafra War, Okigbo's cultural "police action" is now on the verge of transformation into full-scale "military campaign."

Interestingly, this campaign begins with the poet's delineation of the terrain of combat. This terrain is characteristically ambitious in its scope and extends beyond Igboland, Nigeria, and Africa to encompass even the Asian victims of imperial avarice, rapacity, and despoliation. The common denominator in all these cases is that the ravage had been deliberate, calculated, and total. But in all these cases, too, Okigbo's optimism envisages a recovery, even regeneration or rebirth, which to him "is no new thing either":

> Smoke of ultramarine and amber
> Floats above the fields after
> Moonlit rains, from tree unto tree
> Distills the radiance of a king . . .
>
> You might as well see the new branch of Enkidu;
> And that is no new thing either . . .
>
> (44)

The identification of the poet with Gilgamesh, the "legendary King of Uruk in Mesopotamia, and first human hero in literature," as well as the incorporation of Mesopotamian and Egyptian mythologies, at this crucial stage of the crusade is Okigbo's strategic postcolonial device of demarcating his field of "combat" by locating in history the source of the cultural and eventually political and economic disaster that has been the lot of Africa and the entire Third World.[2] The ravaging and plunder, the appropriation and despoliation, which left even the sarcophaguses empty; the devastation of the nonwhite, non-Western world by the West, which in turn accuses the non-Western world of having contributed nothing to World civilization, did not begin with latter-day (circa-nineteenth-century) Western adventures into the so-called darker regions of the world. The loot and plunder of the quoted poem had, in fact, built the Hellenic or Greek civilization, which has only recently (actually from about the Renaissance on) been appropriated as the foundation of European civilization (Bernal 1987).

As Samir Amin (1989) has shown, " 'Hellenomania' and the construction of the myth of Greece as the ancestor of the West" laid the foundation for Eurocentrism, which, he claims, is "a recent mythological reconstruction of the history of Europe and the world" (viii–ix). This Eurocentric project succeeded not only in establishing "a nonexistent historical continuity" between Greece and Europe (xi) but also in so widely disseminating that historical "knowledge" that it passes today as common knowledge, even among the highly educated. If the corollary project of the Orientalization and inferiorization of the rest of the world, the white Europeans' *other*, has been at the root of the plight of "the rest of us" (Chinweizu 1975), it is only proper that Okigbo's crusade begins by pointing to the source of the contamination of the stream. With that diagnosis accurately achieved, it is hoped that half the "curative" job will have been done.

In performing that thankless task, Okigbo is not unaware of obstacles and stumbling blocks placed in his way even by the supposed beneficiaries of his mission. These do not just keep looking away, like the patients in Michael Thorpe's earlier famous poem; they do not stop at merely piling "banks of reed / Mountains of broken bottles" in the poet's path; like many oppressed peoples in history who have yearned and prayed for the messiah, they not only will not recognize him when he walks among them but will publicly disgrace him. Thus:

He stood in the midst of them all
   and appeared in true form,
He found them drunken,
   he found none thirsty among them.

*Who would add to your stature,*
*Or in your village accept you?*
          (Okigbo 1986, 45)

The happy thing is that in spite of the suicidal inclination of the people, the prophet, like Christ, like Enkidu, rises again from the dead reenergized for the task in hand:

And from frame of iron,
And mould of iron . . .

For he ate the dead lion,
& was within the corpse—
       (46)

And that is the point. The poet needs this revitalization to be able to confront the "fleet of eagles," the despoilers who now troop into the land, devastating and plundering it, while all the time distracting the people with the cross and the promises of heavenly utopia. In the words of Isaac Delano, a pioneer Christian nationalist, "The word 'Christ' has always been identified here with the British Empire . . . [and] the general feelings are that the Missionaries have been the front troops of the Government to soften the hearts of the people and while people look at the Cross white men gather the riches of the land" (Coleman 1958, 108). It is this "missionary-government conspiracy" (108) that made it possible for the missionaries to embark on the total destruction of the indigenous people's culture and religion without fear of reprisal; the long hand of the imperial military was never far behind the "indignant" and "righteous" cleansers of the pagan world:

And to the cross in the void came pilgrims;
Came, floating with burnt-out tapers;

Past the village orchard where
Flannagan
Preached the Pope's message,
To where drowning nuns suspired,
Asking the key-word from stone;
& he said:

To sow the fireseed among grasses,
& lo, to keep it till it burns out . . .
       (Okigbo 1986, 46)

It is hardly surprising that this fire of both "faith" and cultural destruction would continue and spread unchecked until it burned out. It is also hardly surprising that with the devastating might of the imperial military behind it, the "fleet of eagles," the Christian agents of imperialism led by Reverend Fr. Flannagan and his ilk, would regale themselves in their deleterious achievement. So as in the earlier scene ("Fragments V"), where the despoliation was also systematic, deliberate, and thorough ("nothing suggests accident"),

> where the beast
> Is finishing her rest . . .
>
> Smoke of ultramarine and amber
> Floats above the fields after
> Moonlit rains, from tree unto tree
> (44),

here the eagles rampage and ravage, unchecked and resplendent, holding "the square / under curse of their breath." The poet/sunbird who has already assumed the full bardic role as foreseer and voice of warning "repeats" to his people:

> "A fleet of eagles,
>     over the oil bean shadows,
> Holds the square
>     under curse of their breath.
> . . . . . . . . . . . . . . . . . . . .
> The eagles ride low,
> Resplendent . . . resplendent;
> And small birds sing in shadows,
> Wobbling under their bones . . . "
> (47)

In imagery reminiscent of the "banks of reed" and "mountains of broken bottles," those obstacles that the poet-prophet had to overcome, this poem re-creates a hyperbolic scene of devastation. After a protracted warning, the poet-sunbird-prophet–blind dog is exhausted and squats to catch his breath. But the urgency of the situation hardly allows him that luxury. The imperialist enemy is unrelenting and must be given no quarter. The germ, once planted, germinates, spreads, and becomes part of history. In the case being discussed here, however, it would appear that in spite of the warning

> Give him no chair, they say,
> The dawn's charioteer,
> Riding with the angry stars
> Toward the great sunshine
> (48),

the "visitation" came to be, and the "visitors" did not really care for anyone's hospitality or welcome. They came with malevolence in their hearts and thus deserve the full working out on them of the curse of the poet-prophet: *"Malisons, malisons, mair than ten."*

It is significant that this poem *(Fragments X)* ends in the same way that *Fragments V* began, by creating a close link, an identity, indeed, between "the twin-gods of the forest," the tortoise and the python, totems of Idoto, and "the twin gods of Irkalla," the Sumerian queen of the underworld. The same abomination and despoliation that included even the theft of mummified corpses (of the pharaohs) in *Fragments V* will be reenacted in *Fragments X* with the same systematic thoroughness and rapacity:

> And to us they came—
> *Malisons, malisons, mair than ten—*
> And climbed the bombax
> And killed the Sunbird.
> . . . . . . . . . . . . . . . . .
>
> Their talons they drew out of their scabbard,
> Upon the tree trunks, as if on fire-clay,
> Their beaks they sharpened;
> And spread like eagles their felt-wings,
> And descended upon the twin-gods of Irkalla
>
> And the ornaments of him
> And the beads about his tail
> And the carapace of her
> And her shell they divided.
> (Okigbo 1986, 49)

That Western interest in its *other*, which included the plunder of Mesopotamia and Northern Africa, has run full circle by extending the beaks and talons of imperialism to the rest of Africa. It is my conviction that in spite of the anguish, agony, and the lament of Okigbo's poetry, the real driving force of this poet and his poetry is divine optimism. Hence the total devastation of *Fragments X*, in which the Sunbird was an early casualty notwithstanding, what we have in *Fragments XI* is a lament, not over the desecration and despoliation of the gods as such, but over the neglect by the people of their funerary duties to their slaughtered gods:

> And the gods lie in state
> And the gods lie in state
> Without the long-drum
>
> And the gods lie unsung,
> Veiled only with mould,
> Behind the shrinehouse.
> (50)

But in spite of such culpable cultural neglect, and in spite of the attempted obliteration of indigenous cultures by imperialism and colonialism, the gods, together with their cultures, reassert themselves:

> Gods grow out,
> Abandoned;
> And so do they . . .
>
> (50)

The apocalyptic climax of this resurgence and the archetypal ritual of death and rebirth is the excited reappearance of the Sunbird, who cannot remain "dead," with its duties still undone:

> But at the window, outside, a shadow:
>
> The Sunbird sings again
> From the limits of the dream;
> The Sunbird sings again
> Where the caress does not reach,
>
> (51)

The resurrected Sunbird sings now beyond reach of the talons of the beasts, and it is significant that his song is *"Of Guernica."* If the song of the Sunbird now celebrates the artistic achievement of Picasso (Anozie 1972, 96), it does so because unlike his ancestors who refused to acknowledge the plundered roots of their civilization, Picasso not only acknowledged the African sources of his greatness but also embodied the same serious social conscience that Okigbo exemplifies. Thus it seems that more importantly, the poet invokes *Guernica* here because like *Fragments,* it also deals with senselessness and barbarity, and with the same anguish visited by power and dominance upon its victims:

> *Of Guernica*
> On whose canvas of blood,
> The slits of his tongue
> cling to glue . . .
> (Okigbo 1986, 51)

This close reading enables me to identify the beasts, the proper subject of the verbs—"broke," "grumbled," and "fanned"—as the perpetrators of the despoliation, whereas the folk are the ones who break into the malediction:

> And the beasts broke—
> *Malisons, malisons, mair than ten—*
> And dawn-gust grumbled
> Fanning the grove . . .
>
> (49)

Technically, it is the poet as Sunbird who, on behalf of the folk, pronounces the efficacious malediction on the despoilers. Finally, this invocation of *Guernica* is appropriate because it prepares us for the "jubilee dance above the carrion" with which *Silences* will begin. It prepares us for *Path of Thunder,* that apogee of Okigbo's poetic trajectory, that climacteric summation and capsulization of his poetic prophetic statement. It prepares us also for *Distances,* the poet's Songs of Sorrow, a sequence full of tears and warning, whose dismal and lachrymose atmosphere provides a most logical transition into thunder, eclipse, and the prophecy of repetition.

*Distances* is replete with images of returning and homecoming and even talks about "consummation." But it is clear that the solitary homecoming is not a happy one, not an occasion for rejoicing, because to achieve this homecoming, a transformation "from flesh into phantom" has first to take place "on the horizontal stone," which here not only suggests "the operating table" but also recalls the "marble slab," the "grave stone," or the tombstone. This homecoming is indeed a regress to the primordial womb, to "the birthday of earth," not through illuminated pathways but "through some dark labyrinth" (Okigbo 1986, 69).

This kind of "home" and "homecoming" resonates with the general atmosphere of gloom and disaster that will quickly build up from a simple "ambush" by death, to real carnage where Death, personified as "chief celebrant" "bathed her knees in the blood of attendants; / her smock in entrails of ministrants" (71). This atmosphere is such that even "the wind," ordinarily welcome and soothing in normal evenings, is, on this abnormal evening, an ominous dealer in "bandages," material that we normally associate with wounds, sores, surgery, blood, and death:

> It was an evening without flesh or skeleton;
> an evening with no silver bells to its tale;
> without lanterns, an evening without buntings;
> and it was an evening without age or memory—
>
> for we are talking of such commonplaces,
> and on the brink of such great events . . .
>
> (70)

"Such great events" have already been clearly indicated by the cold and freezing and deathly images. Even though Okigbo's poetic journey had earlier been associated with solitude and anguish, here the cry emitted by the poet is not only "scattered" but also smothered by "anguish and solitude," the same agency that will "smother" the dancers "lost among their own snares." The occasion is totally different. If earlier, in "Elegy for Slit-Drum," the poet had figured as mythmaker and rattle leading his people in a celebratory procession, here "the interstices" are "reddening with blood," the chief celebrant is "Death herself" "in smock of white cotton." The picture evoked here by "smock of white cotton" is neither that of priestly purity nor even ghostliness; the atmosphere suggested by "cotton wool" is that of the emergency ward of a hospital.

In such a situation of chaos and unreason, "the line of pilgrims / bound for Shibboleth" is understandably scattered and in total disarray. It is true that the poet-as-priest bears "the crucifix / the torn branch the censer," but the pilgrimage that stretches "from Dan to Beersheeba" directs us to a particular reference point in time and place. This spatiotemporal reference is important not only because it evokes aridity, sterility, devastation, and futility (for we are talking about the Middle East, whose only reliable sources of water are the River Jordan and the Lake of Galilee, which are uncomfortably close to the Dead Sea) but also because the catastrophe that was Sodom and Gomorrah took place there. It is thus in order that the poet should be talking of "camphor," pest repellent and air seasoner; "iodine," antiseptic used in dressing wounds; and "chloroform," a gas that induces general anesthesia during radical surgery.

Dan is described "as the most northerly point in [this] country" (76). And Beersheeba is said to be so arid that only a particularly sturdy and adapted species, the tamarisk, could grow there. Exposed to extremely inhospitable, almost inhuman elements, the routed pilgrims, desperate for a "cure," still undertook this journey between Dan and Beersheeba! Only the poet-seer-prophet can redirect such a misdirected, almost disoriented, society. For such an undertaking, the poet needs to become one, to be consummated, with the creative essence itself, here imaged as the goddess, "O Maid." But that consummation involves a mental, physical, and spiritual anguish of indescribable excruciation. It is the poet's apprehension of the enormity of this ordeal, as well as his impending sacrifice, that accounts for the sober and somber mood of *Distances V,* which opens dramatically with metaphors of anguish and burden:

> Sweat over hoof in ascending gestures
> each step is the step of the mule in the abyss—
> (74)

The mule is the burdened beast whose labors are hardly appreciated. On account of its thick hairiness, it is not generally recognized that it also sweats, very much like the long-suffering ram that, even before the flashing sword, emits only a muted shriek, a silent prayer to the scabbard. That, too, is the poet-elect's destiny. But most ominously, because it suggests the cosmic impossibility of the question "How does one say NO in thunder?", the first stanza of *Distances V* ends with a terrible hyperbole:

> the question in the inkwell the answer on the monocle
> the unanswerable question in the tabernacle's silence
> (74)

Even the tabernacle, usually the most dependable source of answers to the poet-prophet, is silent. This silence rapidly spreads and envelopes Time itself, envelopes even humanity, and transforms that sign and expression of human affection and bonding, kissing, into a vampiric act that only leaves a "scar" and is associated with "two swords." The apparent excitement of *Distances VI* is therefore appropriate, in this "season" whose atmosphere is suggestive of mating, for the weary acolyte to respond, with hope and expectation, to the invitation of the goddess:

> Come into my cavern,
> Shake the mildew from your hair;
> Let your ear listen:
> My mouth calls from a cavern . . .
> (75)

But although the invitation "into my cavern" and the admonition "Lo, it is the same blood that flows" may indeed suggest consanguinity, they do not fail to reverberate with vampiric implications. In fact, we are yet to recover from the recent blood-chilling and macabre performance of "Death herself / the chief celebrant." Moreover, the whole atmosphere in the cavern is redolent with the smell of death, violence, blood, fear, and predation.

Thus even when the "consummation" is achieved, there is nothing "orgasmic" (Anozie 1972, 151) or ecstatic about it. Instead, the mood of gloom and disappointment, accentuated by the concatenation of images that build up to onanism and anticlimax, prevails in "this chaste instant of delineated anguish," "unquenchable, yellow," "darkening homeward," "cry of wolf above crumbling houses," "bar[ing] the entrails," "feverish, solitary shores," "variegated teeth," and "putrescent laughter." The result is that the "climactic" homecoming—"darkening homeward"—becomes a somber and solitary affair, unaccompanied by buntings and festive reception:

> I am the sole witness to my homecoming.
> (Okigbo 1986, 76)

The consummation has indeed taken place—"I have entered your bridal / chamber" (76)—and with it has come final illumination. But it is the anguished realization that all the poet had dreamed, wished, prayed, and sung for has come to naught; that all he had foreseen, agonized over, and warned against is coming, inexorably, to pass, and only "the glimpse of a dream [now] lies smouldering in a cave, / together with the mortally wounded birds" (79).

The poet's disappointment is total, almost cosmic, and he who in his optimism had earlier prayed Mother Earth to "bind me fast" (89), and had rejoiced that "our dividing airs are gathered home" (89), now laments the insistence "of our dissonant airs" and "our crumbling towers" (99) and prays:

> O mother mother Earth, unbind me; let this be
> my last testament; let this be
> The ram's hidden wish to the sword the sword's
> secret prayer to the scabbard— . . .
>
> Earth, unbind me; let me be the prodigal; let this be
> the ram's ultimate prayer to the tether . . .
>
> (99)

In his departure was contained the crumbling and dissipation of a post-colonial dream. And in the prophecy of his own exit was contained the sad foreshadowing not only of the impossibility of attaining the dream and utopia of Nigerian unity and nationhood but also of the doomed cycle of repetition, for the misleaders of that polity, having learned nothing from its history, were bound to repeat it; they would not only return the country to its precarious condition status quo ante bellum but also set in motion the repetitive cycle of forces, the dance above the carrion, the dance of fireflies, which led the country to the impasse in the first place. Thus:

> An old star departs, leaves us here on the shore
> Gazing heavenward for a new star approaching;
> The new star appears, foreshadows its going
> Before a going and coming that goes on forever . . .
>
> (99)

Between 1966 and the present, Nigeria has repeated, in minute detail, and with great precision, all the stupidities for which nations refuse to be. There is no reason to believe that, suddenly, illumination and sanity will reign and force the rulers to listen to the oracle of doomed repetition.

## Notes

1. See also Moore 1965.
2. See note in Okigbo 1986, 44.

## Works Cited

Achebe, Chinua. 1978. Preface to *Don't Let Him Die,* ed. Chinua Achebe and Dubem Okafor. Enugu: Fourth Dimension Publishers.

Amin, Samir. 1989. *Eurocentrism.* Trans. Russell Moore. New York: Monthly Review Press.

Anozie, Sunday O. 1972. *Christopher Okigbo: Creative Rhetoric.* New York: Africana Publishing Corporation.

Balakian, Anna. 1977. *The Symbolist Movement: A Critical Appraisal.* New York: New York University Press.

Bernal, Martin. 1987. *Black Athena: The Afroasiatic Roots of Classical Civilization. Vol. 1, The Fabrication of Ancient Greece, 1785–1965.* New Brunswick, N.J.: Rutgers University Press.

Chinweizu, Onwuchekwa. 1975. *The West and the Rest of Us.* New York: Random House.

Coleman, James S. 1958. *Nigeria: Background to Nationalism.* Berkeley and Los Angeles: University of California Press.

Douglas, Mary. 1966. *Purity and Danger.* New York: Frederick A. Praeger.

Duerden, Dennis. 1977. *The Invisible Present.* London: Heinemann.

Duerden, Dennis, and Cosmo Pieterse, eds. 1972. *African Writers Talking: A Collection of Interviews.* London: Heinemann.

Fraser, Robert. 1986. *West African Poetry: A Critical History.* Cambridge: Cambridge University Press.

Gates, Henry Louis, Jr. 1988. *The Signifying Monkey: A Theory of African-American Literary Criticism.* New York: Oxford University Press.

Izevbaye, Dan S. 1984. "From Reality to Dream: The Poetry of Christopher Okigbo." In *Critical Perspectives on Christopher Okigbo,* ed. Donatus I. Nwoga, 300–327. Washington, D.C.: Three Continents.

Moore, Gerald H. 1965. "Surrealism and the Congo." In *African Literature and the Universities,* ed. Gerald Moore. Ibadan: Ibadan University Press.

———. 1984. "Vision and Fulfillment." In *Critical Perspectives on Christopher Okigbo,* ed. Donatus I. Nwoga, 274–87. Washington, D.C.: Three Continents Press.

*The New Princeton Encyclopedia of Poetry and Poetics.* Ed. T. V. F. Brogan and Alex Preminger. Princeton, N.J.: Princeton University Press.

Nwoga, Donatus I., ed. 1984. *Critical Perspectives on Christopher Okigbo.* Washington, D.C.: Three Continents.

Obiechina, Emmanuel N. 1980. *Christopher Okigbo: The Poet of Destiny.* Enugu, Nigeria: Fourth Dimension Publishers.

Okigbo, Christopher. 1986. *Collected Poems.* With an introduction by Adewale Maja-Pearce. London: Heinemann.

Said, Edward W. 1993. *Culture and Imperialism.* New York: Alfred A. Knopf.

Udechukwu, Obiora. 1984. "Aesthetics and the Mythic Imagination: Notes on Christopher Okigbo's *Heavensgate* and Uche Okeke's *Drawings.*" In *Critical Perspectives on Christopher Okigbo,* ed. Donatus I. Nwoga, 196–200. Washington, D.C.: Three Continents.

Woodring, Carl. 1961. *Politics in the Poetry of Coleridge.* Madison: University of Wisconsin Press.

# Christopher Okigbo, or The Eclectic Poet as Prodigal and Priest in *Labyrinths*

JONATHAN NGATÉ

Long before his death during the Nigerian civil war in the late 1960s, Christopher Okigbo, through the difficulty of many of his poems as well as the testiness of some of his pronouncements about his craft and the predicament of the Africa of his days, as well as the critical responses they elicited, had already done much to help establish his reputation as a controversial poet. My purpose here is not to stoke, belatedly, the fire of that controversy but rather to focus on what I consider to have been the poet's ability to crisscross cultural boundaries in his work, which can therefore be read as a full and straightforward assertion of his *métissage,* his hybridity.

To that end, I start with quotations from three contributions to *Critical Perspectives on Christopher Okigbo,* the 1984 volume edited by Donatus Ibe Nwoga. Guyanese O. R. Dathorne opens his article by stating that "Okigbo is a very rewarding poet. All his poetry is in fact one long, elaborate poem. He transmutes all experience into ceremony."[1] American Paul Theroux, for his part, concludes his brief article on the poet by stressing that

> we [readers] have to follow his progress from pain to perception and back to pain. Okigbo can be considered from the point of view of all theologies, mythologies—each yields an interpretation. But better we too suffer the ordeal, ending on the edge of new agonies.[2]

From the preceding, it is easy for me to accept Nigerian Chinweizu's view that "if and when, like Okigbo, [African prodigals] return home, we shall gladly celebrate their homecoming. For we cannot reject our prodigals if they come home."[3] But at the risk of restating the obvious, I should like to emphasize that prodigals do not, and in fact cannot, come home unmarked by the experience of their literal or metaphorical wanderings.[4]

This essay has been adapted specifically for this volume and is published for the first time by permission of the author.

"Elegy for Alto," the last poem of *Path of Thunder,* concludes with the following two stanzas:

> THE GLIMPSE of a dream lies smouldering in a cave,
>     together with the mortally wounded birds.
> Earth, unbind me; let me be the prodigal; let this be
>     the ram's ultimate prayer to the tether . . .
>
> AN OLD STAR departs, leaves us here on the shore
> Gazing heavenward for a new star approaching;
> The new star appears, foreshadows its going
> Before a going and coming that goes on forever . . .[5]

If thematically these stanzas take us back to the beginning of *Labyrinths* and its development of the theme of the prodigal, stylistically they also reconnect with the poems of *Labyrinths,* which generally lack the directness and the transparency that characterize the poems of *Path of Thunder.* Having presented events in their linear progression up to this point, through topical allusions to the Nigeria of the first half of 1966, the speaker proceeds to reveal the results of all these events, "a dream [that] lies smouldering in a cave" and the undeniable presence of "mortally wounded birds." Because birds in general, and the weaverbird in particular, had been equated with the creative mind throughout *Labyrinths,* one can see that the speaker is now involved in fitting everything into a recognizable pattern. *Plus ça change, plus c'est la même chose.*

If "An old star departs," it is only to be replaced by a new one, which appears merely to foreshadow "its going / Before a going and coming that goes on forever." What we have here is a mythical pattern, clearly beyond history but understandable only through familiarity with telling historical facts. We are being confronted with a tragic situation, born of that which not only is negative but also is repeating itself endlessly. And though surprising at first, it is in this very pattern that the speaker sees the only possibility for an understanding of what has been happening both around him and to him. The discovery of this pattern and the importance attached to it take us back to *Labyrinths* and also disclose, along the way, the identity of the single most important non-African who had a great influence on the Okigbo of *Labyrinths:* T. S. Eliot.

The importance of T. S. Eliot to the development of Okigbo's early poetry is underlined by some of those who knew him almost from the beginning of his literary career. Aside from Sunday Anozie's recognition of "T. S. Eliot as a major poetic influence on Okigbo,"[6] there is also the following passage from an answer by J. P. Clark (another Nigerian writer of Okigbo's generation) to an inquiry by Anozie about the relationship between Okigbo and *The Horn,* a poetic magazine edited by undergraduate students in English at Ibadan University in the 1950s:

Chris was not part of *Horn* except while he was at Fiditi and shunting to Ibadan to and from me in 1959–60. I introduced him to the paper as he spouted the Old Classics to me and I the New Greats to him. That's how he met Pound, Eliot, and Yeats—he could not stand or swallow the last of that trinity, Eliot he took to immediately *vide Debtor's Lane*, his first sally into writing poetry, which though heavily smelling of *The Hollow Men*, I had published in *Horn*.[7]

Eliot's influence is clearly detectable in *Labyrinths* and in the last verses of "Elegy for Alto." If we consider the last two verses of "Elegy for Alto" as a suitable conclusion to all the poems of *Labyrinths with Path of Thunder*, then they should remind us of the unceasing task of striving to find that which will help give meaning to life:

> There is only the fight to recover what has been lost
> And found and lost again and again.
> (Eliot, "East Coker," 189)

If, on the other hand, we value those verses for what they reveal about the poet-protagonist's attitude in the poems of *Labyrinths* alone, it becomes obvious that they are another version of Eliot's statement in "Burnt Norton, Part 1":

> Time present and time past
> Are both perhaps present in time future,
> And time future contained in time past.[8]

This is an article of faith, and this ability to believe strongly is essentially what makes possible the poet-protagonist's quest, under the guise of a prodigal in *Labyrinths*. If he proclaims his availability in the opening passage of *Heavensgate* ("Under your power wait I / on barefoot / watchman for the watchword / at *Heavensgate*" [19]) and thus starts his quest, it is because of a deep-seated belief that he will be able to regain his position as priest of Idoto, the female deity of his home village stream. Serving Idoto, of course, would be his way of showing that he has found the place that is properly his in a traditional Igbo context.

What this all means is that Okigbo, like Eliot, has chosen to ground the poetry of *Labyrinths* in faith and tradition. The only difference is that the faith and the tradition are primarily West African (Igbo, to be precise) here, and this points to the specificity of his mythical vision:

> BEFORE YOU, mother Idoto,
>     naked I stand;
> before your watery presence,
>     a prodigal
>
> leaning on an oilbean,
> lost in your legend.
> (19)

Along with this focus on Idoto, the goddess, the prodigal also shows, by the way he relates his experiences during the quest, that he is concerned both with the affirmation of a faith and with the creative process: to become a priest of Idoto will also be to become an articulate spokesman, a poet. The mythical (see the reference to Idoto's "legend") and religious vision is so important here that the following words, which describe Eliot and his poetry, also apply to the Okigbo of *Labyrinths*: "the central experience which informs most of the poetry of [Okigbo] is this same age-old pattern of symbolic death and birth, lived through as an intensive personal experience and accepted as a central truth of a religious faith."9

In due course, the prodigal does die to his older self so that he can be reborn in a new state that makes him acceptable to Idoto. Religious faith and its concomitant traditions provide the poet as prodigal with a pattern that helps him "save" himself. Everything in his quest, which is punctuated with severe tests (such as the brief appearance of the goddess as a watermaid and her later reappearance as Death) and the observance of certain rituals (as in "Lustra") as well as the symbolic death in the early parts of *Distances*, leads to the final union with Idoto: "I have entered your [Idoto's] bridal / chamber" ("Distances VI," 76).

The quest has been a long, sustained *individual* effort, but because it enables the prodigal to "lose himself" in Idoto and her legend, it shows, in retrospect, that like many a speaker of Eliot's poems, the prodigal had had a clear sense of his being involved in a mythical and religious drama with a significance extending beyond himself.10 He knows for sure that his quest and its results will have a bearing on the sorry state of traditional gods following colonial conquest of the African continent,

> AND THE gods lie in state
> And the gods lie in state
> Without the long drum.
>
> And the gods lie unsung,
>     Veiled only with mould,
> Behind the shrinehouse.
>
> Gods grow out,
> Abandoned;
> And so do they . . .
>             ("Limits XI," 50)

and especially on Idoto, whose priest he is to become, thus turning himself into an intermediary between the goddess and her worshipers. Consequently, his language in *Labyrinths* becomes a language of religious faith and ritual, a fact that contributes to the obscurity of many of the poems that make up the volume.

The religious vision that informs the prodigal poet's quest is made explicit in a few poems. The opening page of "The Passage" states clearly that the prodigal is "lost" in Idoto's legend, and "Siren Limits III" dwells on the spiritual and atemporal dimensions of the quest,

> And this is the crisis point,
> The twilight moment between
> sleep and waking;
>
> And voice that is reborn transpires
> Not thro' pores in the flesh,
> but the soul's back-bone
>
> (41)

in a way that is repeated, with a slightly different emphasis, in "Distances II":

> It was an evening without flesh or skeleton;
> an evening with no silver bells to its tale;
> without lanterns, an evening without buntings;
> and it was *an evening without age or memory.*
>
> (70; italics mine)

The prodigal finds himself now in a position to reveal that he is fast approaching a moment of great significance:

> for we are talking of such commonplaces,
> and on the brink of such great events.
>
> ("Distances II," 70)

The "great events," we now become aware, started with his descent into an underworld he is not exactly familiar with,

> . . . a voice, from very far away,
> chanted, and the chamber descanted, the birthday of earth,
> paddled me home through some dark
> labyrinth, from laughter to the dream
>
> ("Distances I," 69)

a descent that leads to his meeting with Idoto in the form of Death involved in a religious service in which she appears in the guise of the chief celebrant: "and behind them [the dancers] all, / in smock of white cotton, / Death herself, / the chief celebrant, / in a cloud of incense, / paring her fingernails . . . " ("Distances II," 71). Later on, and while insisting on the hardship marking his quest, the prodigal succeeds in locating Idoto's sanctuary:

> SWEAT OVER hoof in ascending gestures—
> each step is the step of the mule in the abyss—
> the archway the oval the panel oblong
> to that sanctuary at the earth's molten bowel.
>                    ("Distances V," 74)

Aside from the "legend" associated with Idoto that gives meaning to his quest, the prodigal also talks about rituals that make progress possible in the quest. The invocation in "The Passage" proclaims the prodigal's availability to his goddess. And when the latter makes the briefest of appearances in the form of a watermaid who disappears quickly into the sea, the prodigal is dejected at first,

> AND I WHO am here abandoned,
> count the sand by wavelash abandoned,
> count her blessing, my white queen.
>
> But the spent sea reflects
> from his mirrored visage
>
> not my queen, a broken shadow
>                    ("Watermaid," 28)

but slowly starts looking forward again to the goddess' next appearance:

> So I who count in my island the moments,
> count the hour which will bring
> my lost queen with angels' ash in the wind.
>                    ("Watermaid" 28)

Aware, as Anozie notes,[11] that he may not be worthy of meeting Idoto in his present condition, the prodigal goes for a (traditional Igbo) cleansing, with an appropriate set of offerings:

> SO WOULD I to the hills again
> so would I
> to where springs the fountain
> there to draw from
>
> . . . . . . . . . . . . . . . . . . . . .
>
> So would I from my eye the mist
> so would I
> thro' moonmist to hilltop
> there for the cleansing
>
> Here is a new laid egg
> here a white hen at midterm.
>                    ("Lustra," 30)

> Fingers of penitence bring
> to a palm grove
> vegetable offering with five
> fingers of chalk . . .
>
> ("Lustra," 31)

Purified by the cleansing, he now feels that it is "Time for worship" ("New-comer"). It is this new state of grace that enables him to continue his quest, which leads ultimately to Idoto's "bridal chamber" in the last poem of *Distances*.

The great influence of Eliot on Okigbo in *Labyrinths* shows again in the way the Nigerian poet defines his poetry in this dialogue between Upandru, the village explainer ("he"), and the prodigal ("I") in "Initiations":

> And I said:
> The prophet only the poet.
> And he said: Logistics.
> (Which is what poetry is) . . .
>
> (25)

By defining poetry as "logistics" here (let us not forget that it is Upandru who teaches the prodigal how to use words), he is equating his poetry with sure-footed technique and strongly hinting that a great deal of imaginative and intellectual effort would be required of the reader to understand and appreciate it. This is a poetry of verbal dexterity, although from time to time the prodigal poet admits to being unable to express himself exactly the way he would like to: "And there are here / the errors of the rendering . . ." ("Initiations," 25).

The poetry of *Labyrinths* bears an apparent resemblance to that of *Path of Thunder* in that it also relies on repetitive thematic, syntactical, and rhythmic patterns. Unlike *Path of Thunder,* however, *Labyrinths* has a denser texture through which Okigbo's prodigal shows that like his biblical counterpart, he has been out in a wider world that has left its traces on him. He might now know what he wants (to return to the fold), but in cultural and literary terms, he now is a man full of "Ideas, old gossip, oddments of all things / Strange spars of knowledge and dimmed wares of price":[12] he is very much like the woman of Ezra Pound's "Portrait d'une femme":

> You are a person of some interest, one comes to you
> And takes strange gain away:
> Trophies fished up; some curious suggestion;
> Fact that leads nowhere; and a tale or two,
> Pregnant with mandrakes, or with something else
> That might prove useful and yet never proves,
> That never fits a corner or shows use,

Or finds its hour upon the loom of days:
The tarnished, gaudy, wonderful old work;
Idols and ambergris and rare inlays,
These are your riches, your great store; and yet
For all this sea-hoard of deciduous things,
Strange woods half sodden, and new brighter stuff:
In the slow float of differing light and deep,
No! there is nothing! In the whole and all,
Nothing that's quite your own.
Yet this is you.[13]

Long though this passage is, it is worth quoting in full because it helps lay bare the paradoxical situation in which the prodigal finds himself. He can define himself only in negative terms: he is not exactly a Westerner (although his formal education brings him close to Westerners), and he is not a traditional Igbo, as evidenced by his attaching too much importance to individualism (he reminds us in "Newcomer" that the mask over his face at the "time for worship" is "my own mask, not ancestral"), but he still remembers and values the culture he grew up in. In short, he is a cultural mulatto, as Léopold S. Senghor would say, and when, looking for a sense of purpose, the prodigal starts his religious quest (which is also a poetic quest), it comes as no surprise that he chooses to write in a non-African language, English.

Thematically, what we have here is the poetry of a man groping around in an attempt at reaching a goal he never loses sight of. This fact is also discernible at the linguistic level, for in *Labyrinths,* the prodigal poet, laboring under the weight of his dual cultural heritages, is still looking for his own voice: that being the case, one can understand why his poetry at this stage is based on a series of balancing acts between different and often conflicting elements of his cultural and literary backgrounds. He is a man in search of an equilibrium that eludes him until the end of *Distances.*

The intricacy of the syntactical constructions the prodigal uses and his attempt at giving the poetry of *Labyrinths* an organic unity (in spite of its diversity) help us understand that he was right in referring to this poetry as "logistics." Everything in it has been calculated to produce a particular effect on the reader. The kinds of syntactical constructions he uses vary. They include the regular, straightforward syntax that says something without calling attention to itself:

THE STARS have departed,
the sky in monocle
surveys the worldunder

The stars have departed,
and I—where am I?
      ("Watermaid," 29)

There are also the hardy inversions of "Under your power wait I / on barefoot" and "Me to the orangery / solitude invites" in "The Passage," and a syntax of juxtaposition as in the following example,

> Smothered, my scattered
> cry, the dancers,
> lost among their own
> snares; the faces,
> the hands held captive;
> the interspaces
> reddening with blood
> ("Distances II," 71)

or in the even more striking and imagistic "BANKS of reed. / Mountains of
broken bottles" ("Limits III," 41), in which the syntax is divested of all but its
essential elements.

In examples such as "I sign: / remembrance of calvary, / and of age of
innocence, which is of . . . " and the following,

> ON AN empty sarcophagus
> hewn out of alabaster,
> A branch of fennel on an
> empty sarcophagus . . . ,
> (44)

which comes close to being redundant because of the repetition of the opening verse, the syntax takes us to the brink of revelation but always stops short
of it, thus providing us only with an opportunity to appreciate the suggestive
power of key terms or expressions such as "sarcophagus" and "age of innocence." Finally, in "Limits," the poet delights in starting several poems with
the connective "and" in a way that makes little sense in each individual poem
but can be appreciated only in the larger context of all the poems of "Limits":

> AND FROM frame of iron,
> And in mould of iron
> ("Limits VII," 46)

> AND, squatting,
> A blind dog howls at his godmother
> ("Limits IX," 48)

> AND TO US they came—
> *Malisons, malisons, mair than ten—*
> And climbed the bombax
> And killed the Sunbird.
> ("Limits X," 49)

> AND THE gods lie in state.
> ("Limits XI," 50)

Because "Limits" deals with the connection between the prodigal poet's personal experience and some of the negative effects of the colonization of Africa, it would seem that syntax is being used in these poems to highlight continuity in thematic development.

Aside from syntax, Okigbo's poetry fuses disparate and often contradictory elements in other areas as well. There is friction, for instance, between the prodigal's Christian and his indigenous religious heritages, but a careful reading of some of the poems of *Heavensgate* shows that although he tends to prefer his indigenous past, he sometimes presents both heritages as complementary parts of his life experience. Thus, while making an invocation to Anna as his guardian spirit and while talking about his enjoyment of music produced by nature in cornfields (in the last segment of "The Passage"), he seems intent on letting us know that he is also familiar with church music as well as the Book behind it:

> O Anna at the knobs of the panel oblong,
> hear us at crossroads at the great hinges
>
> where the players of loft pipe organs
> rehearse old lovely fragments, alone —
>
> strains of pressed orange leaves on pages,
> bleach of the light of years held in leather:
>
> For we are listening in cornfields
>     among the windplayers,
> listening to the wind leaning over
>     its loveliest fragment . . .
> ("The Passage," 21)

In "Lustra," the penitent prodigal makes a quick allusion to Christ's suffering on earth and then proceeds to draw a parallel between himself and the Son of God by presenting the Second Coming and the offering he (the prodigal) is making in the same way, matter-of-factly:

> THE FLOWER weeps, unbruised,
> for him who was silenced
> whose advent dumb-bells celebrate
> in dim light with wine song:
>
> *Messiah will come again*
> *After the argument in heaven*
> *Messiah will come again . . .*

> Fingers of penitence bring
> to a palm grove
> vegetable offerings with five
> fingers of chalk . . .
>> ("Lustra," 31)

When comes the "Time for worship" in "Newcomer," the prodigal fills the poem with references to Christian elements ("the angelus," "guardian angel," and "calvary") as well as non-Christian ones ("bells of exile" in this context, a "mask" and "Anna," the guardian spirit). The kind of initial tension between the various elements, which is ultimately superseded by the fusion of those same elements, is also to be found in the many registers the prodigal delights in using.

The prodigal poet can adopt a conversational tone when he wants to,

> Then we must sing, tongue-tied
> Without name or audience,
> Making harmony among the branches
>> ("Limits III," 41)

but he also has a love for more formal ways of expressing himself, as in a direct address to Idoto that contains two formulaic expressions at the end:

> Queen of the damp half light,
> I have had my cleansing,
> Emigrants with air-borne nose,
> The he-goat-on-heat.
>> ("Limits I," 39)

Another example is a series of statements of fact in which the speaker's emotional reaction to the predicament of traditional African gods after the colonial conquest of the continent is revealed through the repetition of the opening verse:

> AND THE gods lie in state
> And the gods lie in state
> Without the long drum.
>
> And the gods lie unsung,
> Veiled only with mould,
> Behind the shrinehouse.
>> ("Limits XI," 50)

Equally interesting is his way of moving from the colloquial to the pedantic. Having settled for the colloquial

> When you have finished
> & done up my stitches,

> Wake me near the altar,
> & this poem will be finished . . .
>
> (43)

in "Limits IV," and the unmistakably vulgar

> *Anna of the panel oblongs,*
> *Protect me*
> *from them fucking angels*
>
> (33)

in "Newcomer," he more than compensates for them with a barrage of pedantic forms of expression that seem designed to reveal his erudition as well as his command of the English language. First there are learned allusions to several characters from ancient myths: Enkidu ("Limits V"), Irkalla ("Limits X"), Moloch ("Lament of the Silent Sisters II"), Palinurus ("Lament of the Drums III"), Ishthar and Tammuz ("Lament of the Drums IV") and a reference to the biblical "Babylonian capture" in "Lament of the Drums II." Next comes borrowing of key words, because of their resonance, from Shakespeare (*Heavens-gate* in "The Passage") and from Allen Ginsberg ("Rockland" in "Initiations"). The title of the last collection of poems, *Path of Thunder,* is an almost literal repetition of "The Path of Thunder," which is the title of a novel published in 1948 by the South African writer Peter Abrahams; the subtitle of the same collection, "Poems Prophesying War" is an echo of this passage from Coleridge's "Kubla Khan": "And 'mid this tumult Kubla heard from far / Ancestral voices prophesying war!"[14] And as if to make sure that we don't miss the fact that he is also familiar with Modern Poetry in English, he gives us echoes of Ginsberg (and his polysyllabic qualifiers),

> *the only way to go*
> *through the marble archway*
> *to the catatonic pingpong*
> *of the evanescent halo . . .*
>
> (73)

and Eliot (with his use of polyptoton),

> *after we had formed*
> *then only the forms were formed*
> *and all the forms*
> *were formed after our forming . . .*
>
> (73)

in the same poem, "Distances IV."

Finally, in what seems to be a calculated effort to show that the English language holds no secret for him, the prodigal poet uses archaisms from time to time:

> give ear and hearken
> ("The Passage," 19)

> Say if thou knowest
> from smell of the incense
> a village where liveth
> in heart of the grassland
> a minstrel who singeth
> ("Initiations," 24)

> *To sow the fireseed among grasses,*
> *& lo, to keep it till it burns out . . .*
> ("Limits VII," 46)

As the use of the word "fireseed" in the last quotation indicates, he also likes to use neologisms, or rather, nonce-formations, to be precise. Thus he increases his vocabulary with such words as "salt-emptiness," "sophisticreamy," and "worldunder" in "Watermaid" and "yesterupwine" in "Limits I."

Compared with the poetry of *Path of Thunder* then, *Labyrinths,* with its "stylistic cocktail,"[15] marks the triumph of technique over explicit political engagement and a greater sense of certainty; it is a poetry of experimentation by a young poet still trying to assimilate and make use of several influences on him. Given the difficulties inherent in writing this kind of poetry, it is also a fitting reflection of the many obstacles the poet-prodigal had to overcome in his successful quest for the priesthood of Idoto.

## Notes

1.   O. R. Dathorne, "African Literature IV: Ritual and Ceremony in Okigbo's Poetry," in *Critical Perspectives on Christopher Okigbo,* ed. Donatus I. Nwoga (Washington, D.C.: Three Continents Press, 1984), 261.

2.   Paul Theroux, "Christopher Okigbo," in Nwoga, *Critical Perspectives on Christopher Okigbo,* 260.

3.   Chinweizu, "Prodigals, Come Home!" in Nwoga, *Critical Perspectives on Christopher Okigbo,* 183.

4.   This article is based, for the most part, on a rewriting of a chapter from my "Two African Prodigals: Senghor and Okigbo" (Ph.D. diss., University of Washington, 1979).

5.   Christopher Okigbo, *Collected Poems,* with a preface by Paul Theroux and an introduction by Adewale Maja-Pearce (London: Heinemann, 1986), 99.

6.   Sunday O. Anozie, *Christopher Okigbo: Creative Rhetoric* (London: Evans Brothers, 1972), 28.

7.   Ibid., 12.

8.   T. S. Eliot, "Burnt Norton," in *Collected Poems, 1909–1962: The Centenary Edition* (New York: Harcourt Brace Jovanovich, 1984), 175. For the preceding quotation, see Eliot, "East Coker," in *Collected Poems, 1909–1962,* 189.

9.   Elizabeth Drew, *T. S. Eliot: The Design of His Poetry* (New York: Charles Scribner's Sons, 1950), 14.

10. Ibid., 3.

11. Anozie, *Christopher Okigbo,* 59–60.

12. G. D. Sanders, J. H. Nelson, and M. L. Rosenthal, eds., *Chief Modern Poets of Britain and America,* vol. 2 (New York: Macmillan, 1970), 184.

13. Ezra Pound, "Portrait d'une femme," in *Collected Shorter Poems* (London: Faber and Faber, 1971), 61.

14. Samuel Taylor Coleridge, "Kubla Khan," in *Coleridge's Poems,* ed. J. B. Beer (London: Dent, 1963), 167.

15. I borrow the expression from Donald Burness, who uses it to describe the style of Thomas Mofolo's *Chaka.* See Burness, ed., *Shaka, King of the Zulus, in African Literature* (Washington, D.C.: Three Continents Press, 1976).

# Divided in the Brain: Okigbo as Trickster

KWAME DAWES

1

Christopher Okigbo is a difficult poet. He knew this and was happy with the idea of his difficulty. Like T. S. Eliot, a too haunting influence, Okigbo felt that his verse was better precisely for its intellectual complexity, its difficulty. For Okigbo, as for modernists like Eliot, a poet's difficulty represents a fitting challenge for the reader. A diligent reader will ultimately discover some useful meaning after grasping the intelligence of the poet. There is, therefore, a "truth" or "meaning" underlying the poem's complexity. The reader's task is to gradually arrive at this essential truth that has been elegantly protected by the poet. If there is obscurity, it is because we do not know enough. As we know more, the obscurity will retreat. Okigbo wrote poetry of complexity, density, and intense allusiveness. Even if we grant that Okigbo's fundamental mythic base is Africa or Nigeria, we must concede that the aesthetics and the politics of his verse are wholly modernist in the Western sense of the term.

I introduce this troubling dichotomy so that I can be rid of it quickly. But I did not bring it up; really, Okigbo did. Okigbo never actually denied his Africanness; he merely sought to complicate it by admitting that his imaginative world was inextricably linked to the modernist canon. Moreover, Okigbo read the classics (not brilliantly, one might add) and embraced the contradictory instincts of a poet who was divided in the brain.

I have, at various times, had rather varied responses to his work. I have sometimes declared Okigbo's work to be void of conventional notions of meaning, celebrating instead its musicality, its moment-by-moment beauty of language. But I am always aware that when I have argued thus, I have done so because I fear I have missed allusions in the work or simply not understood the poem. At other times, I have constructed rather convincing mythic readings that are attractive because they make so much sense and

This essay was written specifically for this volume and is published for the first time by permission of the author.

grant me a profound sense of intellectual might. But these readings of mine, I admit, do not work when I seek to accomplish a detailed line-by-line explication of Okigbo's verse, for fear of the dangers of such readings—the potholes and land mines of inconsistency and obscurity. Then there are occasions when I feel better served to read Okigbo's oeuvre as a journey from obscurity to clarity—a journey from Western obscurity to Africa-committed clarity. This approach allows for deeply ideological readings of the early material. This kind of reading fits comfortably into postcolonial paradigms that constantly posit an aesthetic movement from Western influence to more nativist African influences. Here Okigbo's work is shown to follow an easily discernible pattern. The problem, of course, is that Okigbo does not always adhere to such an aesthetic pattern. Too often, the paradigm is undermined by Okigbo's writing, forcing me to try to rationalize the poor fit in quite unreasonable ways. But in all of these approaches, I am trying to crack the enigma of Okigbo's verse—its difficulty. And the enigma is particularly annoying because of Okigbo's untimely death. I am constantly preoccupied with what might have been.

But Okigbo is not a stranger to me. He reminds me a lot of other poets from his generation. Okigbo is important because he, as a Nigerian, wanted to understand poetics, wanted to explore form, wanted to be in dialogue with modernism, and wanted to be a part of the tribe of poets the world over. And in this, he shares a great deal with postcolonial poets all over the world. There is much in Okigbo that reminds us of poets such as Walcott, Brathwaite, Robert Hayden, Rita Dove, and Dennis Brutus—all poets struggling with the tension between tradition and the quest for a new nationalist voice. These are writers grappling with the concept of aesthetics. Okigbo's poetry is important in the discussion of postcolonial poetics, for he carries in his rather slim oeuvre many of the fundamental debates about literary practice in postcolonial society.

Reading Okigbo is as much about attempting to discern the "intention" of the poet as it is about trying to understand how the poet positions himself in relation to the instability of a world not yet tamed by language. In other words, it would appear that Okigbo is fully inscribed in the postcolonial project of giving names to those cultural experiences that have not been inscribed in literary discourse. At the heart of this practice is the desire to regard the written word as the authenticating vehicle of human experience. Okigbo's Nigerian experience, in the colonial epoch, is negated unless it is realized in the colonizing discourse of written language. This is part of the complexity of the colonized mind, and in many ways, Okigbo's writing represents an act of "naming" his reality through the business of writing in the language of the colonizer. It is inevitable that Okigbo be seen in this light, for it is something that we have observed in all poets from the generation of writers who began to construct a postcolonial canon—a body of work that emerged out of the complicated world of preindependent societies.

There is a basic complication here. These writers regarded themselves as pioneers, as artists working within a void. Derek Walcott would make epic this conception by referring to himself and his fellow artists as "New World Adams."[1] Okigbo himself is not immune to this taste of egotism, this sense of newness, this effort of trying to construct something out of nothing. And therein lies the problem; it is a partially false construct because this new work is not emerging out of a void. Yet the poets of that generation (and perhaps all poets) began with a sense of naming, of mastering the chaos of nothingness and the absence of order. Okigbo's quest for voice is unquestionably about filling a void (whether personal, public, intimate, or political) of meaning. He would look for familiar ways to speak to this quest. The enigma of his riddles, his allusions, and his literary conventions are centrally about finding order and some sense of stability. This is why Okigbo is a modernist. He assumes an order, an end that amounts to meaning; and the pressure to name the unnamed in the language of his education, of his passion for the classics, his love of books, words, and tradition that such words represent, leads ultimately to a careful dance with the complicated schizophrenia of divided loyalties.

There is, in the organization of Okigbo's final collection, *Labyrinths,* an explicit articulation of progression. Okigbo organized the book to include five movements that at some point represented separate articulations. In *Labyrinths,* an organizing intelligence argues a progression through a poetic odyssey that is intentionally convoluted and complex even though it remains ordered. There is substantial ordering to *Labyrinths,* for beneath the twisted logic of its many dead ends, lies (as with labyrinths) a correct path. This is the basic language and intelligence of Okigbo's text—a march from mystery to revelation. It is not that the book ends with clarity; it is more that the journey entails a meta-textual "correct path," and the reader is asked to find that path.

According to the poet Kofi Awoonor, there is a dialectic present in Okigbo's work, a movement from thesis—which would constitute his African or Nigerian/Igbo essential innocence—to the antithetical shaping influence of a colonial education characterized by his study of the classics and the modernists, particularly Pound and Eliot. This antithesis consists also of Okigbo's cultured engagement with European music and religion. This third of the triad represents the antithetical world of mimicry and apprenticeship. Okigbo's synthesis, or unifying, of these elements, constitutes a clarification of his original voice and, importantly, a return to his role as priest-prophet. But Awoonor wants Okigbo to have found his "Africanness." He wants Okigbo's final articulations to be grounded in the recognition of his role as a traditional priest of Idoto, a poet inscribed in the oral tradition. Awoonor offers, at least, a working list of those African poetic elements that must be apparent for Okigbo's poetry to effectively represent his return to an original sense of identity. Writing about the poem "Elegy for Slit-Drums," Awoonor claims that Okigbo has come back full circle. His language implies a movement back to a formal essentialism:

> In "Elegy for Slit-Drums," Okigbo deliberately returns to the traditional dirge form, weeping and mourning the death that surrounds him at the onset of the Nigerian civil war. It is a poem that owes its impact almost entirely to the use of repetition, proverbs, allusions, and extensive animal imagery borrowed entirely from the Igbo world. After each poetic segment, consisting of parabolic and proverbial listings, is interpolated a choral voice which follows the voice of the lead as in some types of traditional oral poetic forms.[2]

The theme of return is sounded again at the end of Awoonor's analysis concerning Okigbo's achievement:

> An apprentice poet whose path to poetry began with a fascination with the masters of English and American verse and with myths other than his own, he quickly became his own master, gaining power as a poet who returns in his ideas and techniques to the oral sources, and combining the function of the poet and the priest, he grew into a clear-voiced diviner whose role as a poet in old Africa has always been taken for granted. (225)

In the final paragraph, Awoonor reasserts that although Okigbo began as an "imitative poet," he "returned to a spectacular Igbo voice for his later work" (225).

Awoonor's thesis is compelling, and it can only fairly be defended as a largely ideological position. Okigbo's complexity stems, of course, from the manner in which he positions himself in relation to the art he produces. Is the Okigbo he writes of in the introduction to *Labyrinths*—the critic and path-guide—the same Okigbo who has written the poems? Is his audience the same, and are his tasks the same? There is much in Okigbo's introduction that suggests that he is seeking to guide the European reader to understand the poetry in his (the European's) language and discourse. That is one available construction: Okigbo is translating, offering frames of reference, that would be familiar to the European. But Okigbo is also quite clearly attempting to outline influences that he thinks are important, and in the introduction, a literary text not unlike the kind of cryptic notes in Eliot's *The Wasteland*, Okigbo is posturing in complex ways. Is his dependence on European or Western forms (Rabindranath Tagore, though Indian, arrives in Okigbo through the endorsement of the European literary establishment) purely a reflection of the limitations inherent in trying to *write* about a nonliterary tradition such as his Igbo traditions? If so, Okigbo is not trying hard enough. He offers his explanations as highly sophisticated dialogues with the Western tradition. And our basic challenge here is how to reconcile Okigbo's relative silence about the defining force of his works' traditional African forms with Awoonor's argument that Okigbo has ultimately *returned* to an original self. If we argue that Okigbo, in his introduction, is speaking to a Nigerian or African audience, what then is the message? And must we accept that what he offers in the introduction is something quite different from what happens in the poetry?

Awoonor appears to provide a most useful way of reading Okigbo that, while suggesting a progression, speaks not of a progression inherent in the design of *Labyrinths* but of a progression in Okigbo's quest for a distinctive voice. Awoonor argues that Okigbo, even in some earlier pieces, actually finds a stylistic mastery that is not grossly derivative but uniquely his own. If there is a mythic journey, it is not one of the acolyte poet-prodigal moving along a fully conceived narrative path, but one of the artist, Okigbo, adopting a voice that is most comfortable for him. But we know Awoonor's bias, and echoes of Eliot, Pound, and Hopkins do not, necessarily, constitute poetic achievement for Awoonor.

Okigbo's introduction must not be taken lightly because although it does not do enough to illuminate the poetry per se, it does effectively argue that his audience for the poetry is Eurocentric:

> *Heavensgate* was originally conceived as an Easter sequence. It later grew into a ceremony of innocence, something like a mass, an offering to Idols, the village stream of which I drank, in which I washed as a child; the celebrant, a person-age like Orpheus, is about to begin a journey. . . . The various sections of the poem therefore present this celebrant at various stations of his cross.[3]

But closer readings of passages like this reveal not necessarily a privileging of European traditions but an implication that Eurocentric listeners need to have the work *translated* for them. The use of similes and metaphors in the piece points to a political arrangement that posits the Igbo tradition as the norm, the deeper meaning, and the Western myths as a way to "translate" this norm. Consequently phrases such as "like a mass," "a personage like Orpheus," or "at various stations of his cross" stand in curious contrast to the grounding of the tangible sentence "an offering to Idols, the village stream of which I drank, in which I washed as a child." Okigbo continues as an anthropologist of sorts, seeking to show that African myth is "universal": "cleansing involves total nakedness, a complete self-surrender to the water spirit that nurtures all creation." Seen in this light, Okigbo's work can be read as a grand metaphor, an elaborate translation of one culture for another that holds as its central and defining theme the idea of universality. He is almost explicit about this in the introduction:

> "Between *Limits* and *Distances* an interval, *Silences,* is provided, in which two groups of mourners explore the possibilities of poetic metaphor in an attempt to elicit the music to which all imperishable cries must aspire." (xii)

He then goes on to offer the "true" source, or inspiration, for this movement. It is again concrete history; it is not personal like the Idoto river, but it is still equally compelling. The Western Nigeria Crisis of 1962 and the death of Patrice Lumumba, Okigbo says, inspired the piece. *Lament of the Drums* is inspired by two other African tangibles: the imprisonment of Nigeria's first parliamentary leader of the opposition, Chief Obafemi Awolowo, and the "tragic death of his eldest son" (xii).

Okigbo then reverts to simile to explain and interpret what he is doing. The structure is the same; he uses examples familiar to Western society to explain Africa. It is worth quoting this passage in full, for what we are looking at here may not be mimicry in the classic sense but a curious effort at communication:

> The "Silent Sisters" are, however, sometimes like the drowning Franciscan nuns in Hopkins' *The Wreck of the Deutschland,* sometimes like the "Sirenes" of Debussy's *Nocturne*—two dissonant dreams associated in the dominant motif "NO in thunder" (from one of Melville's letters to Hawthorne). This motif is developed by a series of related airs from sources as diverse as Malcolm Cowley, Raja Ratnam, Stephan E. Mallarmé, Rabindranath Tagore, Garcia Lorca and the yet unpublished Peter Thomas—airs which enable the "Silent Sisters" to evoke, quite often by calling wolf, consonant terms in life and letters. (xii)

The final phrase is enigmatic and riddlelike in its vagueness. Someone is "crying wolf" by these evocations, and one cannot help but wonder at Okigbo's own game of wolf, for that impressive list of influences, or "sources," cannot in themselves illuminate the verse. Instead, the verse is *like* them. We know now, as he wants us to, that Okigbo is "cultured" and "well-read"; he wants to be understood "universally." Tellingly, he lists no African poets here—no traditional griots and diviners. Is Okigbo here echoing Derek Walcott, who, when asked why he never listed black poets as influences, replied that none existed who impressed him? Walcott's understanding was that he would be apprenticed only to the "best," the "masters," and these "masters" were all white. In this sense, Walcott wore the Naipaulian label of a "mimic man" and imitator with some pride. It was all he had.

In contrast to Walcott, Okigbo, it would seem, suggests that his faithfulness to his entrapment within a coherent tradition directly relates to the content of his audience. Needless to say, Okigbo cannot get away with this so lightly, because there is, in the entire tone of his introduction, his poetry, and his articulations, a dependence on the discourse of Western modernism. He has embraced this discourse, and even as he speaks in a language that seems to assert the validity of a black African writing poetry about an Africa that can stand up to poetry anywhere, he betrays, in his poetry, something more disturbing and uncertain: he is torn between these cultural divides. The more

Okigbo relies on allusions as poetic interpreters of his experience, the more he stands in danger of being consumed by the allusion. It is when he abandons such a project that his verse seems most assured. This assurance of voice does not occur *only* at the end of his brief life but also throughout his entire career as a poet.

There is, in all of this, something that must not go unnoticed—the idea of Okigbo as the trickster poet. In "Okigbo as Jock" Bernth Lindfors offers a direct reference to Okigbo as trickster. In doing so, Lindfors turns to Okigbo's athletic prowess for a model of his poetic stance:

> He was, in other words, a quick and elusive trickster-athlete bent on avoiding capture and scoring goals. . . . As a writer, Okigbo remained agile, tricky, unpredictable, evasive, hard to pin down—in short, a stubborn challenge to anyone venturing to confront him.[4]

His summation of Okigbo's poetics at the opening of his essay expands on this trickster image:

> Clarity, transparence and intelligibility were not what he sought when working with words. He preferred operating in an idiom of evocative obscurity, creating rich semantic fogs shot through with lightning bolts of oblique illumination. His images and symbols were ambiguous enough to defy exact explication yet suggestive enough to excite imaginative attempts at coherent interpretation. One might call him an inventor of complex verbal riddles, a puzzler-poet more interested in fascinating than in communicating. Perspicacious perhaps, but certainly not perspicuous.[5]

Of course, Lindfors has fallen into the exact trap that he has seen ensnare other critics of Okigbo; he blames Okigbo for his—that is, the critic's—failure to understand.

Okigbo was deeply interested in communicating. The question is, What did he want to communicate? Language functioned as a complex tool for Okigbo in his quest to negotiate the varied worlds of his literary imagination. As a result, it is his capacity to use allusions and metaphors as means of illumination that fascinates us here.

2

In an Okigbo poem, what we may not know is not always an allusion to Western mythology or to some Western poet. There is undoubtedly much of that, but there is also Okigbo's tendency to include "trick" references to personal moments, clues, really, that might be accessible to only those people who know Okigbo's world and his (auto) biography:

> mystery which I, initiate,
> received newly naked
> upon waters of the genesis
> from Kepkanly.[6]
>
> (22)

His note in the text is only barely helpful: "A half-serious, half-comical primary school teacher of the late thirties." Bernth Lindfors discovers that the
coinage "Kepkanly" sounds (to put it crudely) like the command "left-right,
left-right" in Igbo. Interesting information though this is, it is not enough to
explain the emotional weight that seems to be granted this figure in the
poem. Kepkanly is a representation of Okigbo's primary realization of the
world. It is a divided world of cultural complexity, for while Okigbo stands as
an initiate priest of Idoto, he is also the Western-educated boy who attends a
mission primary school wherein Kepkanly rules. But if this is all, is it enough?
No, and Okigbo is actually doing more. In the same movement of "Initiations" that includes Kepkanly, Okigbo produces several other symbolic figures of his youthful imagination:

> At the confluence of planes, the angle:
> man loses man, loses vision;
>
> So comes John the Baptist
> with bowl of salt water
> preaching the gambit:
> life without sin, without
> life;
>
> (22)

Like Kepkanly, John the Baptist becomes a symbolic figure, a missionary
archetype carrying a message that is read with engaged skepticism by the
poet, the initiate. There is a sense in which Okigbo is embedding in his text a
"Western" explication of Kepkanly, who becomes that peculiar prophetic,
maverick Christian figure John the Baptist. What we have here is a broad
metaphor or simile where the window into its meaning is the word "so."

Sometimes Okigbo is less helpful even with his notes. In this same
movement, Haragin is mentioned:

> and the hand fell with Haragin,
> Kepkanly that wielded the blade;
>
> with Haragin with God's light between them:
>
> but the solitude within me resembles Kepkanly . . .
>
> (23)

And the note on Haragin is a total cipher: "Kepkanly was reported to have died from excess of joy when he received news of salary awarded by the Haragin Commission of 1945." At best, this becomes a "broken monody" to Kepkanly—one that laments his death. But without the note, this movement would be extremely closed, a kind of secret code of meaning locked in Okigbo's experience and in his manner of creating unique and enigmatic symbols. Okigbo leaves us with a mood, a quality of sentiment that is real enough, accessible enough, but his use of symbol and allusion complicates the ideas such that our quest for meaning becomes an exercise in "logistics"—the building of multiple clues into a convincing image.

However, in Okigbo's editorial patterns, the allusions that typically receive notes are invariably those that refer to Africa, allusions from Nigerian culture. Quite clearly, the implication here is that the audience Okigbo is addressing is one that would neither grasp these allusions nor have access to them. This is true until we come to his most involved allusions in the sequence, "Fragments Out of the Deluge," where Egyptian myth (still technically African, but for our purposes "Western") and the myths of Gilgamesh are explicated with footnotes.[7] But Okigbo at least alters the pattern once. In "Fragments Out of the Deluge" XII, he offers a brief note for *Guernica:* "A Work by Picasso." But as we progress further into Okigbo's oeuvre, we note an absence of such notes. What has changed is the poet's allusive style. He continues with his allusions, but the quality of superficial complexity contained in the enigmatic use of private allusions is replaced by an unwillingness to explain too much or to cater to the audience that may not be familiar with non-Western myths. In "Lament of the Drum," for instance, the invocation of spirit and God that is likely from the Igbo culture is established without language that demands notes. Yet Okigbo, in this movement and in later movements, continues to toss out Western allusions with the comfort of one speaking shared ideas and images. We have allusions such as "Babylonian capture" (62), "the feast-of-seven-souls" (61), "Celaeno and her harpy crew" (63), "Palinurus" (63), and "Ishtar's lament for Tammuz" (65).

The dramatic and striking aspect of Okigbo's final sequence of poems is the remarkable absence of Western allusions. Here the poet has clearly made certain decisions about the language and imagery that will undergird the work. If lines that echo those of Western poets do in fact exist, they are not offered in the same self-conscious manner as they are in his earlier work. This, then, represents not simply an ideological shift but an important formal shift. In *Path of Thunder,* Okigbo is not, as some have argued, presenting a poetic that is a thematic and stylistic progression from the earlier work. A kind of rupture takes place, and the poet finds a directness and earnestness in tone and style that constitutes an important shift in his writing:

Fanfare of drums, wooden bells: iron chapter;
And our dividing airs are gathered home.

This day belongs to a miracle of thunder:
Iron has carried the forum
With token gestures. Thunder has spoken,
Left no signatures: broken

Barbicans alone tell one tale the winds scatter.

Mountain or tower in sight, lo, your hostages—
Iron has made, alas, masterpieces—
Statuettes of legendary heroes—iron birds
Held—fount of flight—tight:

For barricaded in iron handiwork a miracle caged
                                                    (89)

Here iron becomes a deeply integrated image of creativity and destruction: the elemental force of the god Ogun. Okigbo uses his inimitable capacity to shape multiple images out of constant and coherent ones. The metamorphoses of iron into jets, statues of death and cages locking-in the possibility of hope, is Okigbo at his allusive best. But here, the central image is that of iron as creative and destructive force; iron, then, functioning in the way it does in Nigerian mythology. It is also found in the way thunder, which will become fire, functions in the piece. The thunder of bombs is clearly the thunder of celestial destruction. The poet, bound to the Earth, appeals to it for protection; this act illustrates his desire for a self-assured arrogance that will later be threatened.

It may be that what we are drawn to in this sequence is a certain desperation, if not despair, that invariably makes trivial the playful allusiveness of some of Okigbo's earlier poems. It is not that Okigbo has forgotten how to laugh but that he laughs now with a strange and serious resignation. One senses a world imposing its chaos on the poet and forcing the poet to search for words to order this chaos. Where the earlier verse reflects a poet in repose, retrieving memory and controlling this memory, the later poetry is caught in the action, and involved in the creation, of the moment. The proverbs tumble out seeking wisdom for the moment:

But already the hunters are talking about pumpkins:
If they share the meat let them remember thunder.

The eye that looks down will surely see the nose;
The finger that fits should be used to pick the nose.

Today—for tomorrow, today becomes yesterday:
How many million promises can ever fill a basket.

If I don't learn to shut my mouth I'll soon go to hell,
I, Okigbo, town-crier, together with my iron bell
(94)

Okigbo remains allusive and elusive, but at this point, it is clear that metaphor becomes a way to obscure language that could be regarded as seditious. Okigbo realizes that language has significant political consequences, and he exploits riddles, similes, metaphors, and proverbs to describe the troubling political world around him. It is little wonder that these pieces by Okigbo are celebrated most by African critics, for in them, the political realities of Africa would seem to have ambushed Okigbo and forced him to discard the decorative use of art in exchange for the pragmatism of art.

If there is calm at the end of Okigbo's poem, it is a calm that harkens back to what he seems to have lost—the hope of poetry of repose and reflection. The last movement of Okigbo's oeuvre represents his final appeal to the efficacy of a poetry of repose and beauty. He recognizes that the tyranny of "logistics" makes this dream something of a myth—something beyond chaos. In Derek Walcott, the dream is found in the quintessential moment of cosmic balance, the twilight; for Lorna Goodison, it is the dream place of a more innocent rural existence, "Heartease"; for T. S. Eliot, it is the "still point" or the "rose garden"; and for Okigbo, it is something of a dream of sacrifice, of completely giving:

THE GLIMPSE of a dream lies smouldering in a cave
together with the mortally wounded birds.
Earth, unbind me; let me be the prodigal; let this be
the ram's ultimate prayer to the tether . . .

AN OLD STAR departs, leaves us here on the shore
Gazing heavenward for a new star approaching;
The new star appears, foreshadows its going
Before a going and coming that goes forever . . .
(99)

This profound vulnerability that underlies Okigbo's final poems defines his voice. It is a voice that no longer explores the self-conscious posturings of a poet seeking to explain Igbo/Nigerian society to a Western reader. It is also now more clearly a poetics that reveal the more sustained groundedness of Okigbo's imagination, his metaphorical reliance on the myths and images that emerge from the Nigerian psyche.

## Notes

1. Derek Walcott, "What the Twilight Says," in *Dream on Monkey Mountain and Other Plays,* by Derek Walcott (New York: Noonday Press, 1970), 7.

2. Kofi Awoonor, *The Breast of the Earth: A Survey of the History, Culture, and Literature of Africa South of the Sahara* (New York and Enugu: Nok Publishers International, 1975), 223.

3. Christopher Okigbo, introduction to *Labyrinths,* in *Collected Poems,* with a preface by Paul Theroux and an introduction by Adewale Maja-Pearce (London: Heinemann, 1986), xxiii.

4. Bernth Lindfors, "Okigbo as Jock," in *When the Drum Beats,* ed. Caroline A. Parker and Stephen H. Arnold (Washington, D.C.: Three Continents Press, 1981), 211.

5. Ibid., 199.

6. Okigbo, *Collected Poems,* 22.

7. Egyptian mythology has long been appropriated as part of Western classical mythologies, a practice that establishes a chronology of "civilizations" stretching from the Egyptian through the Roman to the Greek. Herein, the architects of this chronology believe, lies the foundation of Western thought.

## Bibliography

Awoonor, Kofi. *The Breast of the Earth: A Survey of the History, Culture, and Literature of Africa South of the Sahara.* New York and Enugu: Nok Publishers International, 1975.

Dathorne, O. R. "Rev. of *LIMITS,* by Christopher Okigbo." *Black Orpheus* 15 (1964): 59–60.

Hindmarsh, Roland. "Three Mbari Poets." Review of *Heavensgate,* by Christopher Okigbo. *Black Orpheus* 12 (1961): 46–51.

Jones, Le Roi. "A Dark Bag." Review of *Heavensgate,* by Christopher Okigbo. *Poetry* 103 (1964): 394–401.

Nwoga, Donatus Ibe. "Christopher Okigbo." *DLB* 125 (n.d.): 200–224.

Thomas, Peter. "Shadows of Prophecy." Review of *Labyrinths,* by Christopher Okigbo. *Journal of Modern African Studies* 11 (1973): 339–45.

# CONCLUSION

◆

# Christopher Okigbo: A Toast

PIUS OKIGBO

## ENTRY

He arrived in 1932 wearing a bullet scar on his throat; his grandfather had died of a bullet wound in a war on behalf of his town, Ojoto. The legend of Christopher was that he was a reincarnation of his grandfather, Ikejiofor, and well Christopher might be, for he was small and wiry like his grandfather, had a shrill voice like him, was as stubborn and obstinate and almost as invariably right as he and as undaunted by challenges. His parents named him Ifekandu, "greater than life"; they baptized him Christopher, the name he wore to his grave.

He showed his guts early by learning to cry unremittingly even without provocation, to cry (or better still to shriek) even more so when provoked, to master the alphabet on his own before he was taught to read and write, to drive a five-ton school lorry (of course, without permission) before he had any driving lessons and for which, of course, he was appropriately punished by the school headmaster, to play the trumpet, saxophone, and clarinet without any musical training, to play the piano without being able to read a word of music, to read for a university degree in the classics without any previous foundation whatever in Latin or Greek at school, to write better verses in Greek than in English, to be engaged in a university as assistant librarian without any training in librarianship. These and more marked Christopher as a boy of many gifts and talents and someone to be watched and guided to greater heights to find his mettle in the appropriate calling.

## INITIATION

After graduating from university, he had done all manner of jobs as occasion demanded and as his temperament changed: sometime cigarette salesman for the Nigerian Tobacco Company, sometime tutor in English and Latin in a sec-

This essay is being reprinted by special permission of the author.

ondary school at Fiditi (in Oyo state), political activist on the near anarchist side of the divide, civil servant, failed businessman, resident representative of a major publishing house (for which this very building was hired as his official residence), librarian, publisher in his own right, and soldier. In his free time he was a chess enthusiast, an outstanding cricketer, a prolific and recondite raconteur, a part-time jazz musician, and, most uniquely of all, a poet. No job was beneath him, no task too daunting, no challenge too intimidating for a soul that was free of cant or humbug and for a mind that could only be described as humble almost to the point of acute intellectual arrogance.

More at home in Latin and Greek than in English literature, he read all that came his way, rejected much of what he read and built his own aesthetics and poetic grammar by his own effort. He was immersed in the current philosophic rave of the time: he devoured the existentialism of Martin Heidegger and Jean Paul Sartre but rejected its nihilism and inaction. He was fascinated by the dadaist movement of the twenties but rejected as infantile its manifesto as presented by Crosby except for the precept that the artist should strive for what the movement called pure poetry, namely, that he should write not necessarily to communicate but to express himself. The poetry of Allen Ginsberg, Lawrence Ferlinghetti, Duncan, Brother Antoninus, and the crowd of the Beat Generation was just coming onto the scene in America. For Christopher, the poet's task was to present his thoughts in significant form, to address reason through sense. He therefore wrote a poetry that read better accompanied by the music of either Debussy or Duke Ellington as the mood dictated. Yet he demanded of himself and his peers the highest rigor of thought and language. A purist, he would refine and refine and refine his poems until the final product showed the highest economy of words and phrase often embedded in a private vocabulary of his own and almost unintelligible to the reader. It did not matter that the reader would mistake his local idiom for some abstruse mythological reference taken from his vast arsenal of Greek or Latin literature.

## ANOINTMENT

Christopher plunged into the creative page of his life, a page less than 10 years long, and wrote as if he knew he had no tomorrow. In that time, he created a work marked not by volume but only by the highest rank and quality for outstanding excellence. Almost prophetic, his vision and his sounds were certainly rooted in the social culture of the time; and since the malaise of which he wrote and against which he warned has now come home to roost, his poems ring today with astonishing freshness.

Although he had abounding zest for life, Christopher could, at any time, withdraw from life to concentrate his mind and thought singularly on the work before him. He could, and often did, as occasion demanded, retreat into himself for two or three days with little food. Armed only with a pen and paper, he would scribble all day and all night long until the last drop of verse in him had oozed out onto the pages of the notepaper.

He had the most abiding respect for two contemporaries with whom he thought he formed a trinity: Chinua Achebe in the novel, Wole Soyinka in drama, and himself in poetry. Their galaxy also had distinguished satellites close by: John Pepper Clark and Gabriel Okara in the literary arts, and Demas Nwoko and others in the visual arts. He had, however, placed himself above competition in his chosen field. How else can one explain his refusal to be nominated for the Langston Hughes award for African poetry, for which, in spite of himself, he won the first prize? Or account for his paradoxical behavior in agreeing to travel to Kampala, Uganda, for a conference of writers at the expense of the organizers, only to mount the rostrum and refuse to read his poetry to nonpoets?

Chris rejected the label of "African" writer. He declared that he was neither a "Nigerian" nor an "African" poet. Rather, he believed that he was simply a poet whose tastes and sensibilities would make him a poet in any color or climate or vegetation. That 27 years after his death, with no new work coming or likely to come from him, he is still read avidly more abroad than at home and revered everywhere is, perhaps, the greatest tribute that can be paid any artist of note this side of eternity. It is this permanent luster that makes Christopher Okigbo the poet's poet.

Chris was, in his lifetime and in his death, the greatest friend I ever had. But we were not friends just because we were brothers. Between us there was a total communion of souls and of mind. We shared the same joys and laughter in reading and rereading the Greek and Latin classics in the original: Virgil, Tacitus, Cicero, Homer, and others. We derived great pleasure from other masters translated into, or writing in, English—Mallarmé, Joyce, Eliot, Pound, small-letter cummings, Rimbaud, not to talk of the standard university English classroom classics of the middle and later period. For I, too, had read Latin and Greek in my own earlier training, adventured toward a degree in English literature only to give it up two-thirds of the way to finally take a degree in modern history. Is it any wonder, then, that I should have had the rare privilege to be the one to have introduced him to the literature of the American exiles: Hemingway, Dos Passos, Eliot, Pound, Crosby, and Cowley, among the better known.

## ABLUTION

Endowed with a curious charm built on a frail physique and penetrating wit and intellect that often transfixed his friends, Christopher soon learned that to get on with his work, he had to forget their faces and their names soon after the momentary pleasure or thrill was over. He could, therefore, at once or in cycles as his moods took him, be both exceedingly warm and exceedingly cold. His friends stood by him to the last; his foes denounced him as emotionally a grasshopper.

He successfully wooed and, after a whirlwind courtship that would have racked the nerves of any young woman, married Sefi Judith Attah, the devoted mother of our adorable daughter, Obiageli. For Sefi was perhaps the only girl he met and knew who understood his quixotic personality. And in return, he showered her with the most passionate and enduring love.

## DEPARTURE

Ali Mazrui has tried Christopher for exhibiting and revealing a personal commitment to eradicating the social evils of his times. So be it. Some of us are nothing if not snobs writing for snobs; some of us are merely aesthetes who would step over the murk around us and live as if nothing was wrong. Chris lived intensely, felt intensely, and expressed himself intensely. Only someone versed in the most abstruse form of taxidermy could have lived through the Eastern Nigeria of 1966 to 1970 and pretended that the psychopathology and trauma of the society could not touch him and that his life would ever remain the same or that he could just go about writing inanities while the life experience around him betrayed the most desperate craving. Let no one dare to condemn him, for we, the members of his immediate family, know what it is to lose a revered one, having in the same war lost one favorite uncle, two adorable undergraduate nephews, and a favorite brother in Chris. Chris was immersed in the life of his time—for more than any other artist of his generation, he communed with the so-called common man of his time: the market trader, the street hawker, the buka restaurateur, the foot soldier, the taxi driver. He did not look down on them, and he did not treat them as his inferiors. They were men like him. For he was as easily at home with the nobles and the governors as he was with the taxi drivers with whom he could go to eat and drink as coequals without condescension.

The battered Nigerian psyche of today, the anomie and the catalepsy we see, hear, and smell all around us, the lingering living death that casts its pall over us, the anguish and the torment of body and soul that cry out all the time from the wizened faces of infants—these are today's sources of Christopher Okigbo's poetic vision of 30 years ago. Of such stuff was this extraordinary genius made that his fame far outshone that of any one of the members of his vastly distinguished family that had at one time a world-class forest pathologist, an economist, several lawyers and accountants, an agronomist, as well as the poet laureate himself. He was indeed a meteor, and like a meteor he flashed through the sky for a short speck of 35 years, which is indeed merely a dot in infinite time, and dug a hole in the ground for himself.

## PASSAGE

He was born wearing the mark of war; he died of bullet wounds sustained in a war he fought on behalf of his new country, Biafra. He died at the hands of his so-called countrymen, at Opi Junction, at the outskirts of the university he had helped to build and nurture. He died at the tender age of 35, in the defense of his most cherished values: honor, valor, truth, justice, equity, integrity, and, most of all, freedom. We have a duty, in his honor, to keep these values alive in our younger ones, for that is the true testament to his greatness. Toward this goal, I am authorized to announce that the Okigbo family is creating a trust to establish and administer, with effect from the coming anniversary of his death in October, scholarships and prizes in classics and poetry in the University of Ibadan and the University of Nigeria, the two universities that gave Christopher Okigbo his foundation and his freedom. Even in this we have been anticipated, first by Wole Soyinka, one of the most loyal of his friends, and now by Chief Berkhout. To both of them, I offer my salutations.

I now give you the toast of Christopher Okigbo the poet, born 1932, died 1967, lived at Cambridge House, UAC Crescent, Onireke, Ibadan.

8 July 1994

# Selected Bibliography

◆

J. M. Purcell's "Christopher Okigbo (1932–1967): Preliminary Checklist of His Books," *Studies in Black Literature* 4, no. 2 (1973): 8–10 was the first bibliography of Okigbo criticism. In 1978 Joseph C. Anafulu published "Christopher Okigbo, 1932–1967: A Bio-Bibliography," *Research in African Literatures* 9 (Spring 1978): 65–78, the first annotated bibliography of Okigbo criticism. Other bibliographies published subsequently include Dubem Okafor, "Select Bibliography of Works by and about Christopher Okigbo," in *Nationalism in Okigbo's Poetry* (Enugu: Fourth Dimension Publishers, 1980); Claudia Baldwin, "Christopher Okigbo," in *Nigerian Literature: A Bibliography of Criticism, 1952–1976* (Boston: G. K. Hall, 1980); and Bernth Lindfors, "Addenda to Okigbo Bibliography," in *Critical Perspectives on Christopher Okigbo,* ed. Donatus I. Nwoga (Washington, D.C.: Three Continents Press, 1984). The selected, annotated bibliography that follows updates and complements these. In compiling it, the editor has limited himself to more recent critical studies and a few older but important essays and book chapters.

Azuonye, Chukwuma. " 'I, Okigbo, Town-Crier': The Transition from Mythopoeic Symbolism to a Revolutionary Aesthetic in *Path of Thunder.*" In *The Gong and the Flute: African Literary Development and Celebration,* ed. Kalu Ogbaa, 19–36. Westport, Conn.: Greenwood Press, 1994. In *Path of Thunder,* Okigbo shifts from "mythopoeic symbolism" to "a largely unfulfilled revolutionary aesthetic." The sequence is comparable with the " 'responsibilities' poems" of Blake, Eliot, and Yeats in which the poets abandon "earlier obscure symbolism for mere direct statement of faith and ideology."

Bodunle, Charles A. "Oral Traditions and Modern Poetry: Okot p'Bitek's *Song of Lawino* and Okigbo's *Labyrinths.*" *African Literature Today* 18 (1992): 24–34. The purpose of African oral discourse is to recall the past. In *Labyrinths,* Okigbo uses a variety of African oral genres, including "symbols, images, proverbs, myths," repetition, and "invocational and incantatory devices" to direct attention to traditional religion, "suit" his "socio-political vision," convey his tone, emphasize points, and render his verse musical.

Bouyssou, Roland. "*Labyrinths,* or the Initiation Quest of Christopher Okigbo." Trans. Judith McDowell. In *Critical Perspectives on Christopher Okigbo,* ed. Donatus I. Nwoga. Washington, D.C.: Three Continents Press, 1984. Okigbo's protagonist in *Labyrinths* may be seen as a figure who explores the "origins" of his self or who undertakes "a pilgrimage towards a spiritual and transcendent source" in search of "a primal mystery of a psychic or mystical nature." *Heavensgate, Limits,* and *Distances* are, respectively, poems of "hope and fulfillment," "violence and limited prospect," and a regressive desire for "a return to the maternal womb."

Cooke, Michael G. "Christopher Okigbo and Robert Hayden: From Mould to Stars." *World Literatures Written in English* 30, no. 2 (1990): 131–44. Why did Hayden and Okigbo, both of whom achieved international renown in the sixties and were widely recognized as brilliant and accomplished poets, not place their craft at the service of their communities? To answer this question, one must distinguish between what is proper to poetry and what is "property" to a community. Just as one may eat any food on condition that one can digest it, so poets may consume any literary fare if they can successfully assimilate it into "the workings" of their imagination. Okigbo and Hayden were realist poets. Both saw the poetic craft as a "cleansing" process and use similar images to depict beings existing, paradoxically, in "objective description" and "subjective, solitary trance." They interject prayer, music, and "intimations of love" into their work, perceive the world as being simultaneously positive and negative, and use "modernist, phrasally intense" idiom to explore and articulate the "traditional sense of mystery and ecstasy." Their differences notwithstanding, Hayden and Okigbo saw poetry as "a revolution of consciousness" rather than an escape from revolution.

Dathorne, O. R. "African Literature IV: Ritual and Ceremony in Okigbo's Poetry." *Journal of Commonwealth Literature* 5 (1968): 79–91. Okigbo is indebted to Anglo-American modernist poetry. However, he owes his success to his development of a "distinctive private voice." Poetic utterances made in this voice possess a choric quality and insist on the "infallibility of the statement and its divine nature." Okigbo is a writer who constantly alludes "to a private mythological world" in his poetry, and his poetry envisions humanity's transformation from mere mortal to supernatural "deity." The intensely "private" and subjective quality of Okigbo's verse allows it to transcend its "personal" and "local references" and render a "universal message."

Goodwin, K. L. "Christopher Okigbo." In *Understanding African Poetry: A Study of Ten Poets.* London: Heinemann, 1982. Although Okigbo occasionally draws on African "praise-songs or Ashanti drum invocations," his "poetic milieu is basically European." The "tone and texture" of Okigbo's verse derive from "Debussy, Malarmé and other French Symbolists, the poets of the 1890s and their twentieth-century heirs such as Eliot and Ezra Pound." Still, *Labyrinths* is unsatisfactory because Okigbo tries unsuccessfully to reconcile the individualist "vision" of his art with the political project of nation formation espoused by his critics. On the other hand, individualist "vision" and the project of nation formation cohere in *Path of Thunder;* yet the sequence is equally unsuccessful. Okigbo uses "the musical motif" as his primary poetic technique, thus depriving the poems of "emotional or intellectual shape," and he does not revise them to eliminate "naive applause-winning slogans" that cause arbitrary shifts in "tone and mood."

Ikiddeh, Ime. "Iron, Thunder, and Elephants: A Study of Okigbo's *Path of Thunder.*" *New Horn* 1, no. 2 (1974): 46–67. *Path of Thunder* is Okigbo's "great triumph." In *Labyrinth,* Okigbo explores the "esoteric experience" of the individual subject. In *Path of Thunder,* where his protagonist abandons his futile and narcissistic wandering in the wilderness of symbolism and aestheticism and returns "home" to find his audience and preserve "his soul," Okigbo assumes the "role of the poet in traditional society, at once creator, chronicler, teacher and prophet." Characteristic of *Path of Thunder,* in which Okigbo speaks in "his new-found voice," is his transformation from myth user to mythmaker. Here he has become as proficient in transfusing new meanings into existing local myths and rituals (circumcision) as he is in creating new mythic symbols (iron, thunder, and elephants).

Izevbaye, Dan. "From Reality to Dream: The Poetry of Christopher Okigbo." In *The Critical Evaluation of African Literature,* ed. Edgar Wright, 120–48. London: Heinemann, 1973. Okigbo's poetry should be understood in the context of the "type of poetry written by Eliot to the Symbolists." It is "the accumulation of meaning that gives an essential unity" to Okigbo's work. Although his primary model was Eliot, Okigbo relied more and more on African oral tradition in later sequences such as *Path of Thunder.*

Knipp, Thomas R. "Okigbo and *Labyrinths:* The Death of a Poet and the Life of a Poem." *Research in African Literatures* 25, no. 4 (Winter 1995): 197–205. Judging by how they used *Labyrinths* in the eighties, it is possible to distinguish between three kinds of Okigbo critics: Eurocentrists, Afro-Marxists, and traditionalists. Eurocentrists (Ken Goodman and Robert Fraser) tended to strip *Labyrinths* of its proper historical and cultural contexts and thus to deracinate and de-Africanize Okigbo. Afro-Marxists (Emmanuel Ngara) tended to be prescriptive and to oversimplify "text and context." Traditionalists came in two varieties. Doctrinaire traditionalists (Chinweizu, Jemie, and Madubuike) polemically denounced Okigbo for his supposed mimicry of Anglo-American modernism and espoused a broadly formalist approach based on African oral poetics. Wishing to canonize Okigbo, conventional traditionalists (Emmanuel Obiechina) were adept at evaluating the poet's "sources and echoes" but violated his text by obscuring "the transformation of the prodigal into the town-crier" in *Path of Thunder.* All three groups failed to place Okigbo's poetry in the context of the "paradigmatic experience" of Westernized Africans. This experience takes the form of a "cyclical journey" from Africa to the West and, following a period of cultural alienation, culminates in a "not always successful" return home.

Luvai, Peter. "The Poetry of Wole Soyinka and Christopher Okigbo." In *Standpoints on African Literature: A Critical Anthology,* ed. Chris L. Wanjala. Nairobi: East African Literature Bureau, 1973. Soyinka and Okigbo consider poetry to be "personal." However, Soyinka is a neotraditionalist, and Okigbo is a modernist. Both poets explore the creative process in such poems as "I Think It Rains" (Soyinka) and *Distances* and *Limits* (Okigbo), but Okigbo's poetry, which is inspired by local and foreign, ancient and contemporary sources, is more musical. Drawing on Yoruba oral poetic sources, Soyinka, who is more concerned about the essence of creation and humanity's relationship with it, constructs "highly contrived" poems that, as *Idanre* demonstrates, depict divinity as a force or being exterior to humans but capable of evolving new attributes. Okigbo equates poetic expression with "religious insight" and himself with divinity. For both poets, hope or salvation (both of which follow the secularization of myth and "metaphysical systems") lies in every individual's capacity to "consecrate new activities."

Maduakor, Obi. "Creative Process as Ritual: Okigbo's *Heavensgate.*" *Kiabara: Journal of the Humanities* 3, no. 2 (1980): 159–69. *Heavensgate* may be viewed in two ways: as a dramatic rendering in ritual language of the processes by which creativity manifests itself in artistic form, and as "a poetic statement" of the conflict between Christianity and African "traditional" religions. For Okigbo, writing poetry is a form of "religious worship" precisely because, like worship, poetry is a "holy office."

Ogundele, Wole. "From the Labyrinth to the Temple: The Structure of Okigbo's Religious Experience." *Okike: An African Journal of New Writing* 24 (June 1983): 57–69. For Okigbo, poetry is ritual. Okigbo's work is "a long exploration and casting off" of inimical "intellectual, emotional, and spiritual" contrarieties. It is also "a search for personal belief" that demonstrates that all religions "have a common structure of experience," that religious and aesthetic experiences may be identical, and that religious language may also serve as poetic language. Like G. M. Hopkins, Okigbo reworks "transitive events into the structure of myth" to reach past their temporality to their permanence.

Olaogun, Modupe. "Graphology and Meaning in the Poetry of Christopher Okigbo." *African Literature Today* 17 (1991): 108–30. What and how Okigbo's poetry means depends, at least in part, on graphology; that is, to the visual presence of poetic language. Working in the shadows cast by T. S. Eliot, Ezra Pound, and Dylan Thomas, all of whom were noted for their technical virtuosity, Okigbo uses a variety of graphological devices, including tonality, laconism, ambiguity, and symbolism, to sculpt his poems. In "Song of the Forest," for example, he capitalizes "YOU LOAF," the first two words, to impress their typographic and rhetorical significance as "nominative of address" on readers. Similarly, he uses ellipsis in "Lament of the Flutes" to indicate that the protagonist's memory is vague and fragmentary, and in *Path of Thunder,* a sequence that relies less on obscure graphological devices than earlier sequences, to register the protagonist's perception of the inability of words to adequately express meaning. Contrary to critics who identify Okigbo the poet with his protagonist "I," this pronominal is a "mythical construct" whose function is to enforce a conceptual relation between poet and protagonist rather than establish actual correspondence between them. Recognition of the self-reflexive and intertextual character of Okigbo's poetry should encourage critics to abandon their "monistic" searches for the "sources" and "influences" to which the poems are filiated.

Theroux, Paul. "Christopher Okigbo." *Transition* 22 (1965): 18–20. Contrary to Dathorne's views, Okigbo's poetry is not "the evolution of a personal religion" in which the poet narrates "the 'progress towards *nirvana.*' " To understand the poems, one must trace Okigbo's words to their sources in other poets and listen "to his music"—that is, the "music of youth," "the clamour of passage," and "the sounds of thunder." Okigbo seeks to sublimate religion in himself, not trace its evolution. "Okigbo's art is in moving, movement, being moved, a lived-through victimisation full of symbol and logic and accident and the poet's own plot."

Udechukwu, Obiora. "Aesthetics and the Mythic Imagination: Notes on Christopher Okigbo's *Heavensgate* and Uche Okeke's *Drawings.*" In *Critical Perspectives on Christopher Okigbo,* ed. Donatus I. Nwoga. Washington, D.C.: Three Continents Press, 1984. Okigbo and Okeke are mythmakers. Thus myth, which may be defined as "the innermost recesses" of Igbo and Nigerian culture, makes their work both authentic and relevant.

# Index

# The Volume Editor

♦

Uzoma Esonwanne is associate professor of English at Saint Mary's University, Halifax, Canada. He came to Saint Mary's University after completing his Ph.D. and postdoctoral research at the University of New Brunswick, Fredericton, and the Michigan Society of Fellows (University of Michigan), respectively. Professor Esonwanne has published several essays in literary criticism and theory, including "The Madness of Africa(ns): Or, Anthropology's Reason" (1990), " 'Race' and Hermeneutics" (1992), "Feminist Theory and the Discourse of Colonialism" (1993), and "Enlightenment Epistemology and 'Aesthetic Cognition': Mariama Bâ's *So Long a Letter*" (1997).

# The General Editor

♦

Robert Lecker is professor of English at McGill University in Montreal. He received his Ph.D. from York University. Professor Lecker is the author of numerous critical studies, including *On the Line* (1982), *Robert Kroetch* (1986), *An Other I* (1988), and *Making It Real: The Canonization of English-Canadian Literature* (1995). He is the editor of the critical journal *Essays on Canadian Writing* and of many collections of critical essays, the most recent of which is *Canadian Canons: Essays in Literary Value* (1991). He is the founding and current general editor of Twayne's Masterwork Studies and the editor of the Twayne World Authors Series on Canadian writers. He is also the general editor of G. K. Hall's Critical Essays on World Literature series.